THE JEWISH SOCIAL CONTRACT

NEW FORUM BOOKS

Robert P. George, Series Editor

A list of titles in the series appears at the back of the book

THE JEWISH SOCIAL CONTRACT

AN ESSAY IN POLITICAL THEOLOGY

David Novak

PRINCETON UNIVERSITY PRESS   PRINCETON AND OXFORD

Copyright © 2005 by Princeton University Press
Published by Princeton University Press, 41 William Street,
Princeton, New Jersey 08540
In the United Kingdom: Princeton University Press,
3 Market Place, Woodstock, Oxfordshire OX20 1SY
All Rights Reserved

Library of Congress Cataloging-in-Publication Data

Novak, David, 1941–
The Jewish social contract: an essay in political theology /
David Novak.
p.   cm.—(New forum books)
Includes bibliographical references and index.
Contents: Formulating the Jewish social contract—The covenant—
The covenant reaffirmed—The law of the state—Kingship and secularity—Modern secularity—The social contract and Jewish-Christian
relations—The Jewish social contract in secular public policy.
ISBN-13: 978-0-691-12210-6 (cl : alk. paper)
ISBN-10: 0-691-12210-5 (cl : alk. paper)
1. Judaism and state. 2. Social contract—Religious aspects—Judaism.
3. Judaism and politics. 4. Democracy—Religious aspects—Judaism.
5. Covenants—Religious aspects—Judaism. 6. Secularism—Political
aspects. I. Title II. Series.

BM538.S7.N68 2005
296.3′82—dc22   2005048695

British Library Cataloging-in-Publication Data is available

This book has been composed in Sabon

Printed on acid-free paper.∞

pup.princeton.edu

Printed in the United States of America

10 9 8 7 6 5 4 3 2 1

To
S. E., J. D., E. F., A. F., and A. T.
"From my friends I have learned more . . . "
—*Babylonian Talmud*: Taanit 7a

———————————————————————————

Contents _____

Abbreviations

B.   *Babylonian Talmud* (Bavli)

M.   *Mishnah*

MT   *Mishneh Torah* (Maimonides)

R.   Rabbi or Rav

T.   *Tosefta*

Tos. *Tosafot*

Y.   *Palestinian Talmud* (Yerushalmi)

Preface

This book has been written as a particular reply to a more general question. The more general question is: How can anyone participate actively and intelligently in a democratic polity in good faith? But none of us is merely "anyone." Each of us comes to actively and intelligently participate in his or her democratic polity out of some prior particular identity. To paraphrase the title of Thomas Nagel's well-known 1986 book, there is no view from nowhere. So the question is more accurately formulated as: How can *I* participate in *my* democratic polity in good faith? This question is more likely to be asked by citizens in democratic polities like the United States and Canada that can literally date their founding in an agreement among immigrants coming from somewhere else, both historically and ontologically (that is, one's identity in the cosmos itself). And each citizen, either at the time of his or her naturalization or at the time he or she reaches adulthood, explicitly or implicitly returns to the founding of the polity itself, an event to which no one comes as a blank slate. All of us are immigrants with much cultural baggage.

A major assumption of this book is that this founding and refounding of a democratic polity is best conceptualized through the idea of the social contract. But surely, a contract of any kind cannot be cogently initiated and maintained except by persons who know wherefrom they originally come to the contract and for what purpose beyond the contract itself they have come to it and remain within it. In this book I argue that a democratic polity is neither one's original nor ultimate destination in the world, and that those who think it is, originally or ultimately, inevitably come to deprive their democratic polity of the very limitations that essentially make it the democracy it is meant to be. The fallacy of originality is what "nativists" or racists usually entertain in their democratic politics; the fallacy of ultimacy is what utopians or "idealists" (in the pejorative sense of the term) usually entertain in their democratic politics. Hence no one is merely an "American" or a "Canadian," even members of aboriginal peoples who have to discover their identity in a historical and ontological reality prior to the polity set up by those who have conquered them. So aboriginal peoples, too, have to regard themselves as immigrants in the political if not the geographic sense (although archaeological investigation is showing more and more that even they were once immigrants from elsewhere). In that sense we are all not only immigrants but minorities as well.

It is important to note that the question with which this book deals is not one that a democratic polity itself normally asks or should ask of its citizens. Normally all the polity asks is that its citizens freely subject themselves to the authority of its laws. As such, any violation of these laws is taken to be a violation of an authoritative system of government every citizen has taken upon him- or herself autonomously. A democracy, as Plato noted, does not hold its citizens prisoners (*Crito*, 51D). Only when it is suspected that a person's prior religious or cultural commitments might conflict with the laws of the polity is a more specific commitment to the legal system of the polity called for (think of the more scrupulous investigation of would-be citizens who come from cultures that practice polygamy, for example). So instead, the particular question is not one that is officially asked by the government, but one that is asked by citizens in the broader arena known as civil society, where citizens ought to be continually debating just what the character of their polity is to be. Here the question is both personal and political. It is personal in the sense of being a question of: Why am I here? It is political in the sense of being a question of: What should we be doing as a society? If there is too much disparity between the answers to these questions, then the individual has to be concerned with whether he or she truly belongs here, and one's fellow citizens have to be concerned whether he or she is only using the society for special interests that are inimical to the common good of their society.

Books that deal with the normative quest for ideas make greater claims upon their readers than do books that only offer information about facts. Therefore, it seems, an author of a book like this one ought to identify himself, not in the sense of providing an autobiography (though there is a bit of that in chapter 8), but simply to state the basic question of the book in the first person. Claims by anonymous persons can be ignored in a way that claims of situated questioners cannot in truly public discourse. (Even God had to identify himself to the Israelites before Moses could cogently make God's claims upon them, as we see in Exodus 3:13–15.) In this way his readers can either identify with the questioner, or they can see close analogies (understood as more than one's partisan or professional affiliations within any polity) that they can appropriate in dealing with their own personal-political situation, or they can even see the author's situation as one that threatens their own. For this last group of readers, this book presents a point of view they need to know more about if only to intelligently oppose it. As such, along the lines of this demarcation, I am writing for Jewish readers who might identify with my question, for Christian (and perhaps Muslim) readers who might see themselves asking a similar question, and for atheistic readers who might regard the question itself as too threatening to be ignored. This book, then, addresses diverse readers who are members of democratic polities, and even readers who do not live in a democratic polity but would like to.

In my own case, the question is: How can *I as a traditional Jew* actively and intelligently participate in *my* democratic polity? Actually, in my own case, being a citizen of both the United States and Canada, "my democratic *polities*" is the more accurate way to put it. In fact, another point in this book is that a person can only be part of one primal community in a way a Jew can have only one God, but that a person can be a participant in more than one secular society, which is what a modern democracy is meant to be.

This question can only be avoided by Jews who think their moral commitment to a democratic society trumps all other commitments (like a famous Jewish historian who recently declared that she recognizes no higher authority than the United States of America), or by Jews who think a moral commitment to a democratic polity (especially one where Jews are not the majority) is inimical to Judaism (like a famous rabbi, himself American born, raised, and supported, who awhile back dismissed a commitment to democracy as being the delusion of self-hating American Jews). However, to the former I argue that making their commitment to a democratic polity a matter of primary concern is not only inimical to Judaism, it is also inimical to democracy itself, which, if properly understood, is truest to its essence when the deepest commitments of the vast majority of its citizens lie both behind and ahead of it. And, to the latter, I argue that people living in a democratic polity in such bad faith prevents them from exercising true moral influence in it, and thus makes them far more subject to the moral agendas of the enemies of Judaism (and, indeed, of all religions of revelation) than need be the case. To answer these questions is an ongoing process yielding only tentative results in which I employ theological retrieval, philosophical imagination, and political prudence.

Theological retrieval always comes first because a Jew must always look to the Torah to continually find answers or for data to formulate answers to all questions that involve his or her personal commitment anywhere anytime. Torah, both Scripture (Written Torah) and the normative Jewish tradition (Oral Torah), is what I mean here by Jewish theology. Theology, in the Greek philosophical tradition means talk about God, but in the Jewish tradition, as a synonym for Torah, it means God's talk, that is, God's revealed word and its historical transmission and development. God's word always makes claims upon its hearers, even when those claims require considerable human judgment in order to be intelligible and applicable. At the most basic level a Jew needs to know whether he or she is doing God's will or at least not violating it. It also greatly helps the discernment of God's will if we can get some notion of what ends it is wisely intending in its commandments. The Torah is theology inasmuch as it is the prime place to discover what God wants Jews to do or not do. Much of this book is theological retrieval, which searches the classical Jewish literary sources for guidance, and in which historical description is always part of an essentially normative thrust. That is why the book is subtitled *An Essay in Political Theology*.

Nevertheless, anytime Jews are required to speak and act in a world beyond what the Talmud calls "the four cubits of the Law" (B. Berakhot 8a), philosophical imagination must be employed since here speech and action need to be justified according to more universal criteria. At best, these universal criteria are imagined philosophically. Since the political life of Jews (even in the State of Israel) is conducted more and more among the peoples of the world—what some now call "globalization"—that political life requires political philosophy for its intelligent formulation. Since the world of democratic polities is the only world in which Jews, both individually and collectively, have much of a chance to justify their very presence, the formulation of a democratic political philosophy seems to be a desideratum for Jewish philosophers. That is especially so for Jewish philosophical theologians. We need to find enough evidence for democracy in the classical Jewish literary sources in order to make this kind of political philosophy consistent with the thrust of the Jewish tradition and not just a form of superficial apologetics for some current ethnic agenda.

Yet some philosophers have erred by assuming that things like human nature and human society are universal data immediately given to experience in general, thus only requiring direct analysis in order to be intelligible. Such philosophers have assumed that because of this universal immediacy, one need not begin from a particular historical origin, or one must overcome any such origin in a subsequent universal perspective. But, in fact, things like human nature and human society can only be imagined abstractly since experience is of particular phenomena that are themselves only experienced by persons having a partial perspective. Neither the partiality of the subject nor that of the object can ever be permanently overcome. No one phenomenon ever shows itself to everyone at the same time in the same way—that is, short of universal redemption. Accordingly, universal categories like human nature and human society are imagined or constructed in order to explain how the particular phenomena show themselves as they do. But these categories are not derived or induced from what could only be a sampling of the phenomena themselves any more than the particular phenomena simply illustrate the categories devised to explain them. Thus philosophers can only propose a theory of human nature or a theory of human society to explain what any being needs to show in order to be treated with the respect human nature requires, and what any society needs to show in order to have moral authority over any human being. In other words, the proposal of general theories of human phenomena like human persons and human societies, unlike the proposal of theories of nonhuman phenomena like minerals, plants, and animals, has a clearly normative intent. These theories are meant to guide our speech and actions within our relationships with other humans and societies. They deal with universal norms, not just generalities.

Whereas nondemocratic societies see themselves as having simply emerged at some indefinite point in history or as having been founded by divine revelation, democratic societies see themselves as having been founded by specific human agreement. Such agreement is usually codified in a founding constitution. As such, these democracies represent themselves to themselves and the world as rational human constructs. Here the categories are more than explanatory devices in that they are the blueprint for the creation of a society made to conform to the minimal requirements of universal human social nature. This is why such modern political ideologies as communism and fascism, which also claim to be human constructs, need to be proven irrational. Even if they are chosen by the people—the *dēmos* in "democracy"—they are not constituted in a way that can possibly respect prior human sociality, which is meant to operate rationally. Hence they are inevitably self-destructive. And when such ideologies claim to be rooted in historical revelation, it needs to be shown that their revelation is that of a false god.

At best, when democracies are rationally represented, these democratic societies take their deliberate construction to be the result of philosophical imagination. In other words, they do not see themselves as being without a deliberate human beginning or as the result of God's deliberate election. That is why philosophy is more central to democratic self-understanding than it is to its political alternatives. Philosophy is thought in universal categories, especially when it is constructive. (One sees this best in the American *Federalist Papers*, written by the most philosophically perspicacious of the American founders.) Thus every democratic polity needs to continually and intelligently reinvent itself in a way that is consistent with, but not necessarily deduced from, its original founding. Nevertheless, the task for religious philosophers like myself is to show that the philosophical construction of democratic polity is not the work of persons who have invented themselves; indeed, to assume anything like this is the basic confusion of God and man that characterizes idolatry. This is why this book engages in philosophical as well as theological argument.

Finally, a proper answer to the question of how I can actively and intelligently participate in my democratic polity requires political prudence. This is because the question is inevitably asked in the context of a debate over some specific public policy proposed for one's own society. Just as philosophy requires less than theology requires, so does politics require less than philosophy requires. Thus, for example, theology requires one to worship God in the prescribed way, whereas the most philosophy can do is to show that persons have the right to worship God in any way they want to worship—or not worship—God. Clearly, a duty to worship one God in one way involves more than a right to worship or not worship God in any way. Similarly, philosophy might well require me to continually search for truth, whereas it would be politically imprudent to make such a requirement enforceable by society and its law. The most political prudence could require is that society enable persons who want to search for truth and are capable of doing so to have the educational opportunities to exercise that right. Here again, the exercise of a right involves less than the fulfillment of a duty.

Without an element of political prudence in the presentation of a theory like the one developed in this book, the theory risks being seen as having no connection to the real world of politics, as being an imaginative exercise that has no relevance to anything political here and now. On the other hand, if the theory admits of a political application too easily, it then risks being taken as nothing more than a rationalization for the author's partisan commitments, especially his commitments in what are now called the "culture wars." Since I want to avoid as much as possible either of these dismissals of the book's theory, I have tried to suggest some political applications of the theory, but have chosen relatively modest issues so that there is a better chance readers will want to see how the theory develops than think they can jump from the introduction straight to the conclusion without any need to work through the material that lies between. Moreover, the footnotes, especially in chapters 1–6, where the theory is carefully developed, are at times extensive enough to constitute a subtext. Indeed, some readers might be primarily interested in that subtext.

One last word about what some readers might consider a great lacuna in a work of *Jewish* political theology: Why is there at least no chapter about the question of democracy in the State of Israel; indeed, why is there hardly any mention of the State of Israel in the text (although the land of Israel is quite often discussed)? My answer to this query is that the whole topic of democracy in an explicitly *Jewish* state is one that minimally requires a book of its own. There is also the question of whether a Jew like myself, who is not an Israeli citizen and who lives in the Diaspora, is the proper person to write such a book. Nevertheless, since I consider myself a religious Zionist (in the theological if not the current partisan sense), one who sees religious reasons for a democratic Jewish state in the land of Israel, I might yet write such a book, God willing. In the meantime, this book's argument rejects the assumption of some Zionists that Jewish communal life in the Diaspora is inherently illegitimate when there is a Jewish state in the land of Israel, and that the Diaspora will and should disappear (*shelilat ha-golah*). To my mind and the mind of many Jews (even in the State of Israel), this will not and should not happen until the final redemption.

———————

A brief rundown of the chapters is now in order.

Chapter 1: Formulating the Jewish Social Contract.

This chapter is the introduction to the book. It argues for the value of using the idea of a social contract to justify one's participation in a democratic polity. But it differs from most other social contract theories by arguing that one enters a social contract not from a minimal position of isolation into a greater sociality but, rather, one enters a social contract from a "thicker" communal background and agrees to accept its "thinner" terms in order to be able to live at peace with persons coming from other communal backgrounds and develop some common projects. As such, it sees the idea of a social contract as a blueprint for a truly multicultural society rather than a society that assimilates all differences into a new totality. The chapter also argues that traditional Jews committed to revelation and the authority of the normative tradition built upon it are in a better position to argue politically for cultural autonomy in a democracy than Jews of a more liberal theology or ideology, with their resultant less transcendently grounded point of view, can do.

An earlier version of part of this chapter was a lecture delivered at McGill University in Montreal in October 2002, and that earlier version is scheduled to be published by McGill–Queens University Press as a chapter in a volume, *Recognizing Religion in a Secular Society*, edited by Douglas Farrow.

Chapter 2: The Covenant.

This chapter deals with biblical covenant as the foundation of any Jewish political theology. It distinguishes between a covenant and a contract by showing how a covenant is unconditional and interminable whereas a contract is conditional and terminable. It then delineates the various kinds of covenants found in Scripture, the two basic ones being the Noahide Covenant and the Sinai Covenant. It shows how a covenant, although much more than a contract, nonetheless makes the emergence of contracts possible in Judaism, and illustrates this point with some biblical and rabbinic examples.

Chapter 3: The Covenant Reaffirmed.

This chapter deals with the development of the covenant after the return of the Jews to the land of Israel following the Babylonian exile in the fifth century B.C.E. Whereas Jewish tradition largely sees the original covenant at Sinai as having been forced upon the people of Israel by God, we see from the post-exilic books of Ezra and Nehemiah that the Jewish people in exile voluntarily renewed the covenant while returning to their land. Since a contract is the voluntary coming together of equal parties, the introduction of a more voluntary aspect into the biblical covenant explains why certain social-contract-like phenomena began to appear in Judaism during the Second Temple period into the pharisaic-rabbinic period. It then shows some examples of this historical development.

Chapter 4: The Law of the State.

This chapter views how Jews began to negotiate social contracts with gentile regimes in the Diaspora under whom they lived voluntarily. It shows that because of the subjugated condition of the Jewish people in the land of Israel in Palestine, especially after the destruction of the Second Temple in 70 C.E. and the defeat of the Bar Kokhba revolt two generations thereafter, and because the Jews in Palestine were not living under a regime that practiced the due process of law, they could not develop anything like a contractual relationship with this regime. But in Babylonia, where the Jews voluntarily lived under a regime that did practice the due process of law, they could engage in a type of social contract. This engagement is captured in the principle of the Babylonian theologian and jurist Samuel of Nehardea: *the law of the state is law*, a principle that had a profound effect on Jewish-gentile relations thereafter. The chapter concludes with the great difference between classical Jewish recognition of what could be termed "secularity," but without basing it on anything like modern secularism.

Chapter 5: Kingship and Secularity.

Since Samuel's principle literally speaks about "the law of the kingdom" (*dina de-malkhuta*), medieval Jewish speculation about social contracts were usually centered on the institution of kingship, both the contemporary manifestations of gentile kingship and the vision of Jewish kingship presented in Scripture and rabbinic literature. The chapter deals with the political theories of such medieval Jewish thinkers as R. Samuel ben Meir

(Rashbam), R. Solomon ibn Adret (Rashba), R. Nissim Gerondi (Ran), and R. Isaac Abravanel. All of these thinkers in one way or another saw the political need to supplement the covenant and its law with various forms of social contract. To a certain extent, their theories of social contract reflected the contractual relations Jewish communities had worked out with Christian polities, especially in northern Spain in the late Middle Ages. Nonetheless, it set out important theoretical potential for a time when Jews would be more politically active in the world.

Chapter 6: Modern Secularity.

This chapter deals with the emergence of the Jews from the medieval system of ecclesiastical-royal government where they were at best resident aliens in Christian societies in Europe. The idea of a basically secular state first proposed by a Jewish thinker was that of Baruch Spinoza. Whatever Spinoza's subsequent relationship with the Jewish people and Judaism is taken to be, he largely set the agenda for subsequent Jewish political thought in the West, especially as it dealt with the status of Jews in the new secular nation-states. Spinoza's agenda was most prominently taken up by the unambiguously Jewish philosopher Moses Mendelssohn. The rest of this chapter deals with Mendelssohn's views on social contract and Judaism in his important book *Jerusalem*. The chapter presents a theological and philosophical critique of Mendelssohn for ceding too much to the secular state for its own good and for the good of Judaism. It also attempts to show how Mendelssohn's agenda adversely affected the theological-political dilemma of modern liberal Judaisms.

Part of the section on Mendelssohn will be published by the University of Wisconsin Press in a volume, *The Place of Theology in the Liberal and Globalized World*, edited by Leonard V. Kaplan and Charles Cohen.

Chapter 7: The Social Contract and Jewish-Christian Relations.

This chapter argues that despite earlier Christian opposition to full Jewish participation in secular society, which made modern Jewish-Christian relations suspicious and adversarial because Jews are no longer as politically subordinate to Christians as they were in the Middle Ages and modernity until fairly recently, Jews and Christians are now on a much more even playing field than has been the case heretofore. This new situation has led to a new commonality on three levels: theological, political, and theological-political. I argue here that Jews and Christians have a unique opportunity now to develop parallel political theologies that move beyond the usual political distinctions between "liberals" and "conservatives." It shows how already in the Middle Ages it was recognized that relationships of trust are possible between Jews and Christians because of their worship of the same God and their being rooted in the Hebrew Bible/Old Testament. It concludes with some suggestion of how Jews and Christians can deal with the presence and power of atheistic secularists in societies where we all live together.

Part of this chapter was the Erasmus Lecture delivered at the Institute on Religion and Public Life in New York City on November 2001, and subsequently published in its journal, *First Things*, in February 2002.

Chapter 8: The Jewish Social Contract in Secular Public Policy.

This chapter is my attempt to show the relevance of the theory of the Jewish social contract to the political situation of Jews in Diaspora societies like the United States and Canada. It first criticizes the liberal and sectarian approaches to Jewish public policy: the former that makes the practice of Judaism at best an entitlement from a secular regime, and the latter that regards the Jews as resident aliens in a society that actually regards them as full participants. It then sets forth three practical criteria for determining any Jewish political policies in these secular democracies: (1) the normative Jewish tradition, (2) the common good of the society in which Jews fully participate, and (3) Jewish self-interest. As an example of application of the theory of the Jewish social contract and taking these three criteria, it argues why Jews should support efforts to enable parents to receive state support for the type of schools (in the case of Jews, Jewish day schools) in which they want their children to be educated.

Parts of this chapter were published as chapters in two books, *Jews and the American Public Square*, published in 2002 by Rowman and Littlefield, and edited by Alan Mittleman, Jonathan D. Sarna, and Robert Licht; and *Religion as a Public Good*, published by Rowman and Littlefield in 2003, edited by Alan Mittleman. Both books were published through major grants from the Pew Charitable Trusts.

Many of the points presented in this book were worked out during the course of lectures and colloquium presentations at the Institute of Traditional Judaism (Teaneck, New Jersey), Trinity Western University, Georgetown University, University of Chicago Law School, the Institute on Religion and Public Life (New York City), the University of Wisconsin–Madison, McGill University, McMaster University, and Northwestern University. I thank the good people who came to hear these lectures and presentations for their excellent queries and criticisms, a number of which have led to ongoing revision of my thoughts on the subject of this book.

I also thank various colleagues and friends with whom I have discussed a number of points of my theory and who offered sound counsel about them, among whom are Jean Bethke Elshtain, Hillel Fradkin, Barry Freundel, William Galston, Robert Gibbs, Mary Ann Glendon, Lenn Goodman, David Weiss Halivni, Stanley Hauerwas, Russell Hittinger, Leonard Kaplan, Joshua Mitchell, Richard John Neuhaus, Martha Nussbaum, Edward Oakes, S.J., Peter Ochs, Kenneth Seeskin, Cass Sunstein, Shmuel Trigano, David Weisstub, Leon Wieseltier, Robert Louis Wilken, John Witte.

My thanks are also due to the Research Fund of the University of Toronto, which has generously supported the research and other expenses involved in writing this book and two earlier books. I am also grateful to my University of Toronto doctoral student Matthew LaGrone for his efforts in preparing the index.

I am indebted to Fred Appel, my editor at Princeton University Press, for his true commitment to the improvement of the manuscript, including soliciting important criticisms and suggestions from three anonymous readers, and for shepherding it through the publication process. Marsha Kunin's sensitive copyediting is very much appreciated. Thanks too to my friend, Robert George, McCormick Professor of Jurisprudence at Princeton University, for once again including this book in his New Forum Series, as he included my earlier book, *Covenantal Rights*, among the distinguished works in that series. My involvement in the James Madison Program in American Ideals and Institutions at Princeton, which Professor George founded and still directs, has been a great stimulus to my scholarship and reflection.

Toronto, which has been my home for almost eight years, has provided me with a vibrant traditional Jewish community in which to live and learn, especially in the company of some serious Jewish scholars and students. Many of the points in this book have been first discussed with the Tuesday night Talmud class I lead in the home of Sholom Eisenstat, where we have been learning the tractate *Sanhedrin* in the Babylonian Talmud for the past seven years. This tractate contains more material for the development of a Jewish political theology than any other classical source. Also, many of the points in this book have been tested in the company of James Diamond, Eugene Feiger, Albert Friedberg, and Rabbi Arnold Turin, with whom I regularly study medieval responsa. It is to these five special friends that I dedicate this book.

Toronto, Ontario
Av 5764
July 2004

THE JEWISH SOCIAL CONTRACT

Chapter One

Formulating the Jewish Social Contract

The Democratic Contract

To argue intelligently for the idea of the Jewish social contract today, one must situate the argument within current discussion of social contract theory in general. One must then take a stand on what an authentic social contract is and how sources for it can be activated from out of the Jewish tradition.

The original justification of a society as an agreement between its equal members has long been known as the idea of the social contract. It is a highly attractive idea as evidenced by the amount of discussion it has evoked for at least the past four hundred years, and especially during the past thirty years or so.[1] Many contemporary political thinkers in democratic societies, who are loyal to their societies in principle, believe that this idea best explains how a democracy—especially *their* democracy—can cogently respect and defend the human rights of each of its citizens. These rights are the claims persons are justified in making *before* these societies can subsequently make their own claims on these persons as citizens. Moreover, even these subsequent claims are all essentially redistributive, that is, they are justified by being given an instrumental status. As such, the claims democratic society makes upon its members, to which they are to dutifully respond, are ultimately for the sake of the respect and defense of the prior human rights of the citizens of that society.[2] Therefore, posterior social claims cannot contradict or overcome these prior human claims on society without losing their own derivative justification.

---

[1] The point of departure for all social contract theory today is John Rawls's *A Theory of Justice* (Cambridge, Mass.: Harvard University Press, 1971). There (p. 11) Rawls writes: "[W]e are not to think of the original contract as one to enter a particular society or to set up a particular government. Rather, the guiding idea is that principles of justice for the basic structure of society are the object of the original agreement . . . the principles which are to assign basic rights and duties." For Rawls and his followers, then, the social contract *assigns* rights and duties, but it does not *presuppose* that these rights and duties are what the parties to the social contract bring to it themselves. In effect, then, the parties come to the social contract normatively naked. See M. J. Sandel, *Liberalism and the Limits of Justice* (Cambridge: Cambridge University Press, 1982), 143–46.

[2] In liberal social contract societies, there are no original communal rights/claims on the individual members of the society. The society only has what the members give to it originally. Cf. D. Novak, *Covenantal Rights* (Princeton, N.J.: Princeton University Press, 2000), 153–58.

Respect and protection of human rights are considered the hallmark of a modern democracy. Respect and protection of these rights are what differentiates a modern constitutional democracy from democracy per se, for without the recognition of the prior rights of its citizens, a democracy could easily become nothing more than the dictatorship of the majority, whether that dictatorship be more spontaneously exercised by a mob (*demōs*) or more systematically exercised by some authority (*archē*) acting in the name of a mob. Such majority dictatorship is always conducted at the expense of the minorities who have no rights against it, no prior claims to make upon it.[3]

As the basis of a democracy, a social contract presupposes that its parties come to it with rights that are theirs *already*.[4] The contract itself is specifically designed to respect, defend, and even enhance these prior rights. Any attempt to rescind these rights puts the society in violation of its founding mandate, even if only a small minority might actually object to such rescission. Conversely, in any secular society not based on the idea of a social contract, even where human rights are acknowledged, these rights are at best conceived to be entitlements *from* the society rather than claims made *to* the society. In such societies, human rights are a matter of social largesse or tolerance rather than the duty of a society to ever respect and defend. This is why in societies that do not recognize anything prior to themselves, whatever human rights they do recognize are only entitlements granted *by* the society at will. As such, these rights can just as easily be rescinded from the citizens as they were granted to them by the society; and that can be done without the society contradicting its founding mandate. This type of a society can just as easily decide that these rights are useless for its projects as it can decide that they are useful, whenever any such perceived need arises. For this reason, it is inadequate to the human need for inalienable rights to argue, as one prominent liberal legal theorist has, that "the assumption of natural rights" is not "a metaphysically ambitious one," that it is no more than a "hypothesis," or a

---

[3] Hence the apt insight of Ronald Dworkin, *Taking Rights Seriously* (Cambridge, Mass.: Harvard University Press, 1978), 205: "The institution of rights is therefore crucial, because it represents the majority's promise to the minorities that their dignity and equality will be respected. . . . rights are . . . the one feature that distinguishes law from ordered brutality."

[4] Even though he had an aversion to Enlightenment notions of rights, Edmund Burke still understood how basic moral obligations are precontractual. In his *Appeal from the New to the Old Whigs*, ed. J. M. Robson (Indianapolis: Bobbs-Merrill, 1962), he writes (p. 96): "We have obligations to mankind at large which are not in consequence of any special voluntary pact. They arise from the relations of man to man, and the relations of man to God, which relations are not a matter of choice. On the contrary, the force of all the pacts which we enter into with any particular person or number of persons amongst mankind depends upon those prior obligations."

"programmatic decision."[5] It would seem that if human rights in a democracy are to "have teeth," and not be vague, hypothetical claims made by rootless persons, then a real and sufficient foundation for these rights should be found and explicated. And, this requires substantial historical research and ontological reflection in order to be rationally persuasive.[6]

Because the social contract stems from the rights of persons even prior to their becoming citizens of a democracy, a society based on a social contract can also respect and defend the human rights of all human beings everywhere or anywhere. By virtue of simply being human, those other persons who are not *now* democratic citizens *could* in principle become citizens of this or any democracy *later*. Rights-based democracy, then, affirms an idea of human nature, and it is potentially global therefore. The social contract presupposes that humans are by nature rational beings capable of making contracts and keeping them. That view of human nature has huge political consequences everywhere. The question remaining, nonetheless, is whether we need to see human nature as more than the mere capacity of humans to make and keep contracts between themselves.

This emphasis on human rights is what makes modern constitutional democracy so attractive in theory, especially to Jews, who have greatly benefited from it in practice. Thus very few Jews today would want to live in anything but such a democracy. The other modern political alternatives

[5] Ronald Dworkin, "The Original Position" in *Reading Rawls*, ed. N. Daniels (Oxford: Blackwell, 1975), 46.

[6] In his last work, *The Law of Peoples* (Cambridge, Mass.: Harvard University Press, 1999), Rawls claims to have made a significant departure from *A Theory of Justice*. He no longer requires someone who accepts his "reasonable conception of justice" (*The Law of Peoples*, 79) politically to also accept as its philosophical presupposition liberalism's "comprehensive doctrine" (ibid.), which seems to be liberalism's basic concept of human nature. As such, a citizen of a democracy who publicly affirms his or her prepolitical commitments need not be ruled out of political discourse by Rawlsian liberals. Nonetheless, Rawls reiterates in the end what he asserted in the beginning (*A Theory of Justice*, 11), viz., that the social contract itself "specify the basic rights . . . of citizens" (*The Law of Peoples*, 180). But how is this subsequent "specification" any different from the "assignation" of rights in *A Theory of Justice*? In both cases, citizens can make no prior rights claims on society. Politically, they are still quite "naked." It is still as if they came from "nowhere"—culturally speaking (see *A Theory of Justice*, 137). So the "overlapping consensuses" of *Political Liberalism* (New York: Columbia University Press, 1993), esp. sec. 3.2, only seem to designate the "values" liberalism is willing to tolerate in what citizens from nonliberal cultures bring to civil society. This tolerance turns out to be only for what has always been consistent with liberalism's values in the first place. But our current "culture wars" show how little liberalism is willing to tolerate in those coming from preliberal cultures, and how little those coming from these cultures are willing to be tolerated by liberals, even by liberals as generous as John Rawls. See Will Kymlicka, *Multicultural Citizenship* (Oxford: Clarendon Press, 1995), 163–72.

(namely fascism, communism, and clerical oligarchy) have proven disastrous for any society that has adopted them, and especially disastrous for Jews (and many other minorities), who, unfortunately, have found themselves having to live in such societies. For this reason alone, Jews first need to think out a democratic theory by themselves for themselves, especially a democratic social contract theory, inasmuch as social contract theory seems to be the best explanation of a rights-based democratic order. Only in this way can Jews be participants in a contractually based democratic social order in good faith, and not regard the benefits that have accrued for them from such a social order as some sort of historical accident. But that must first be done in traditional Jewish terms, and only thereafter in terms that could appeal to rational persons who are taken to be actual or potential citizens of a democracy.

The Jewish social contract is the means by which a Jew can actively and honestly—as a Jew—engage the democratic society in which he or she lives. This engagement is what is "Jewish," not the social contract itself, which operates among Jews and non-Jews and must, therefore, function in neutral secular space. This engagement is not located in a singular event like that of Exodus-Sinai, which for Jews has cosmic significance and is regularly celebrated whenever Jews faithfully practice the commandments of the Torah. Rather, that engagement is an ongoing process of negotiation and renegotiation among human beings coming from different cultural backgrounds. It is not a real covenant, as we shall see in the next chapter. Nevertheless, the social contract is more than the hypothetical construct of some philosophers. It is marked by such real events as voting in an election according to Jewish criteria (which does not necessarily require voting for Jewish candidates), and proposing public policies according to Jewish criteria (which need not always involve issues of special Jewish self-interest).[7]

The two tasks for Jewish political theorists—the theological and the philosophical justification of democracy—are not at odds with each other. In fact, they can be correlated. Accordingly, this book should be taken as an implicit polemic against those who theologically reject democracy due to their view of Judaism. It should also be taken as an implicit polemic against those who philosophically reject Judaism due to their view of democracy. Nevertheless, Judaism and democracy are by no means placed on an equal footing here. Instead, the historical and theological priority of Judaism over democracy, for Jews, shall be affirmed. Then it will be shown how Jews can be parties to a democratic social contract in good

[7] See D. Novak, "Toward a Jewish Public Philosophy in America," *Jews and the American Public Square*, eds. A. Mittleman, J. D. Sarna, R. Licht (Lanham, Md.: Rowman and Littlefield, 2002), 331–56.

faith because of their Judaism, not in spite of it. Indeed, this book attempts to show how Jews can cogently formulate an idea of the social contract out of their own traditional sources. Thereafter members of other cultural traditions can appropriate by and for themselves whatever intersections with these representations of Judaism they find at home. This can be done when these representations of Judaism are philosophically attractive and can be argued for in a secular, democratic society.

Unfortunately, though, most modern arguments for democracy have been based on basically secularist, liberal ideologies, whether formulated by Jews or adopted by Jews from non-Jewish thinkers. As such, they have not been formulated with much perspicacity, either theological or philosophical. Theologically, they have not shown how the Jewish tradition can allow Jews to participate in a social contract as Jews. Philosophically, these modern arguments have been dependent on views of human nature that do not give a reason why any rational person should enter into a relationship of trust, like a contract, with any other rational person, even though these arguments have frequently recognized the social benefits of relations of trust among the members of a society.[8] Nevertheless, secularist admiration for interhuman trust has been more phenomenological than ethical, that is, most secularists only describe *how* trust benefits society rather than *why* anyone ought to trust anyone else or be trusted by anyone else.

In fact, most of these modern secularist arguments for democracy have called for mistrust by their claims, both implicit and explicit, that persons coming from traditional cultures like Judaism need to break faith—that is, mistrust and thus overcome—their cultural origins in order to fully participate in civil society. Accordingly, most of these modern arguments for democracy have been, in fact, recipes for the public disappearance of Judaism and the traditional Jewish community. But without a defense of Judaism's *public* participation in civil society, which is theologically and philosophically cogent, individual Jews do not have enough cultural capital to maintain their Jewish identity even in private. For these privatized Jews, a democratic commitment turns out to be the sale of their very souls as Jews. This is why this book shall argue for a Jewish religious justification of a secular democratic order. It is an argument for a finite *secularity*, but it is against any secularist ideology that claims to be a sufficient foundation of that secularity. Because of this, this book shall not engage in the type of apologetics (with its hidden secularist premises) that looks to a secular democratic order to justify the Judaism lived by Jews who participate in that order.

[8] See 205–12 below.

This prior affirmation of Judaism does not mean, though, that one should argue that Judaism is the sufficient foundation for a democratic order. That would very much imply that one ought to convert to Judaism for the sake of having the best reason to be a citizen of a democracy. But were that argument to be made, as some Christian social theorists have tried to do for Christianity from time to time, the very secularity of the democratic social order would be threatened and one's theological commitments would become ultimately mundane.[9] Indeed, when such political theology is applied, the secular social order for which this occurs inevitably takes on messianic pretensions. One should not argue that Judaism (or any religious tradition) is either the one necessary source or the one desired end (*telos*) of democracy. The fact that Judaism can enable Jews to participate in a democratic social order does not necessarily mean that Judaism entails democracy or that democracy should be regarded as the ultimate fulfillment Judaism anticipates. Democracy does not emerge directly from Jewish (or any other) revelation nor does it preview the kingdom of God. So the most this book can do is to attempt to show that Judaism can *authorize* a democratic commitment from faithful Jews *for* Judaism's own sake. Therefore, I shall only argue why Jews *can be* active participants in this social order in good faith, not that Jews *must be* such participants, or that all such participants in this social order *ought to be* Jews at all.

However, a Jew's commitment to Judaism is far more profound than any commitment to democracy can or should be. A Jew's commitment to Judaism must be lived as one elected by God to be part of the Jewish people covenanted with God. That election is either by birth or conversion.[10] One chooses to participate in a democratic social contract; one is chosen to be part of the covenant. One initially affirms the social contract; one only chooses to reconfirm the covenant initiated by God. Hence a Jew needs to live by Judaism, whereas he or she opts for a democratic society. Although one's democratic commitment should be consistent with his or her prior Jewish commitment, it neither can nor should be identical with it. Accordingly, a Jew should evaluate democracy by Jewish criteria rather than evaluate Judaism by democratic criteria. Whereas one can say that democracy is the best political option available to Jews, one must say that Judaism is the only religion Jews can live by with Jewish authenticity.

[9] For a still powerful critique of that Christian tendency, see Reinhold Niebuhr, *An Interpretation of Christian Ethics* (New York: Harper and Bros., 1935), 103–22.
[10] See B. Yevamot 47a—b; B. Kiddushin 68b re Deut. 7:4.

The Political Value of the Social Contract

What, then, is the current political value of the idea of a social contract for Jews as a people and then as individuals that would inspire Jewish thinkers to search for its positive theological and philosophical justification in the Jewish tradition? It would seem that the value of the idea of a social contract is that it is better able to justify a multicultural society than any other idea of political authority. As we shall see, Judaism can function most successfully in a modern multicultural or pluralistic society. The plurality built into the idea of multiculturalism or pluralism is also built into the idea of the social contract. Furthermore, in the idea of the social contract presented here, in which the parties to the contract retain their original rights, these parties are not required to become *parts* of the whole that the contract itself creates. Instead, the parties are *participants* in a multiplicity they themselves create out of their own prior commitments. These prior social commitments are not overcome or meant to be overcome in the social contract.[11] These earlier communal commitments will survive intact as they have survived other types of subsequent social arrangements in which Jews have had to participate in the past. Indeed, this covenant will transcend this world and all its mundane social arrangements.[12]

Persons enter into a social contract not only *because* of their prior commitments, but just as much *for the sake of* them. As I shall argue in this book, if what people bring to the social contract are their prepolitical, cultural rights, which are their rights to be rooted in their original communities, then the social contract can be seen as an ongoing agreement as to what is necessary for different cultures to justly and peacefully transact with one another in common social space. This should by no means require the members of any of these cultures to surrender their communal identity to some sort of "melting pot." Furthermore, what people obtain in their original communities is not only the way they are to justly interact with their own kind, but also the way they are to justly interact with all

[11] Conversely, for the view that all original rights with which one entered the social contract are turned over to the state, see Thomas Hobbes, *Leviathan*, chap. 21, ed. M. Oakshott (New York: Collier Books, 1962), 161; Baruch Spinoza, *Tractatus Theologico-Politicus*, chap. 16, trans. S. Shirley (Leiden: E. J. Brill, 1989), 247; Jean-Jacques Rousseau, *The Social Contract*, 1.6, trans. W. Kendall (Chicago: Henry Regnery, 1954), 19.

[12] The redemption of Israel promised to be God's "peaceful covenant" (*brit shlomi*) in Isa. 54:10 is interpreted by the fifteenth-century Jewish political theologian R. Isaac Abravanel to be the salvation of the Jews intact, and the whole world along with them, who will then be free from all human rule and subject only to the direct rule of God. See his *Commentary on the Latter Prophets*: Isa. 54:5.

others—including all others in civil society. As we shall see, this interaction with others in a democratic society enables Jews to develop certain more general tendencies in their own tradition. It is where Jews need to constitute the idea of natural law, that is, the idea of a universal law binding on both the Jews and the gentiles.[13]

Because of Jewish interest in a multicultural society, a more communitarian idea of social contract should be more attractive to Jews. Surely, Jews should want civil society to respect Jewish communality and not foster the assimilation of Jews, whether as individuals in the Diaspora or even collectively in the land of Israel, into some amorphous "democratic culture." Accordingly, I shall argue that civil society ought not and, indeed, cannot construct its own culture.[14] Instead, civil society ought to depend on the plurality of cultures that in truth precede and transcend the construction of civil society through the social contract.

The very creation of a secular realm by humans is the result of an *intercultural* agreement to create a space distinct from the sacred space of any primal community, an invented realm in which many cultures can participate. But even the suggestion that this should lead to the creation of some new secular culture to replace the older cultures of the contracting parties is to be firmly rejected. The very secularity of this *new* space—as distinct from the *older* sacred spaces of traditional cultures like Judaism—requires that it be both participated in and limited by the members of the cultures who need such space for their own communal survival and flourishing. Thus a social contract is both useful and desirable for the members of any historical culture, certainly for Jews. By means of such a social contract, a historical culture can claim from civil society its prior right to continue to function as a primal community for its own members. In return, a historical culture like Judaism allows civil society to claim its loyalty and support in that society's political, economic, and even its intellectual efforts on behalf of all the citizens of that society. Furthermore, an intercultural social contract makes the political life of civil society far more exalted—even more inspiring—than a social contract fundamentally conceived in terms of economic rights. A society dedicated to the protection and enhancement of its participating cultures surely commands more respect and more devotion than a society merely established to protect and enhance private or corporate property.

[13] See D. Novak, *Natural Law in Judaism* (Cambridge: Cambridge University Press, 1998), 1–12.
[14] Cf. Richard Rorty, "Rationality and Cultural Difference," *Truth and Progress* (Cambridge: Cambridge University Press, 1998), 195–201, for the contrary view.

When, however, a civil society no longer respects that communal priority, it inevitably attempts to replace the sacred realm by becoming a sacred realm itself. That is, such a society attempts to become the moral authority over which there is no greater authority in the lives of its citizens. Thus by becoming "civil religion," civil society usurps the role of historic faith traditions and becomes what it was never originally intended to be: unlimited authority.[15] But the hallmark of a democratic social order is the continuing limitation of its governing range. Without such limitation, any society tends to expand its government indefinitely. But such limitation cannot come from within; it can only come from what is both outside it and above it.[16] Today that external and transcendent limitation can be found in the freedom of citizens of a democracy to find their primal identity by being and remaining parts of their traditional communities. This is what has come to be known in democracies as "religious liberty."

Membership in these traditional communities is outside the range of civil society because of their historical precedence, and it is above the range of civil society because of the ontological status the relationship of these communities with God gives them. For Jews, this means that their historical and ontological identity in God's covenant with the people of Israel is what both limits secularity and entitles its limited range to be beneficial for them. Judaism is both older and deeper than any civil society. Without historical priority, the assertion of ontological priority tends to become hypothetical rather than real, abtsract rather than concrete; it becomes formal rather than substantial, tentative rather than permanent. And without ontological priority, the invocation of historical priority can easily be overcome by the present-day secular world; it can become a mere precedent rather than an ever present foundation, a matter of nostalgia rather than an active normative force.[17]

---

[15] The term "civil religion" first appears, as far as I can see, in Rousseau, *The Social Contract*, 4.8, p. 221. The notion that true religion (i.e., inner conviction) is a purely private, individual matter was first enunciated in modernity by Spinoza, who saw public religion (i.e., morals and ritual) as a department of a secular state. See *Tractatus Theologico-Politicus*, 19; *Tractatus Politicus*, 3.10. In this matter as in many others, Spinoza is followed by Hegel. See *Philosophy of Right*, sec. 270, trans. T. M. Knox (Oxford: Clarendon Press, 1952), 165–69. Contemporary secularists, going beyond Rousseau's, Spinoza's, and Hegel's role for civil religion, deny any public role for any religion at all. Instead, they sacralize the state itself in more subtle ways. See Richard John Neuhaus, *The Naked Public Square* (Grand Rapids, Mich.: Eerdmans, 1984), 80–82, 152, for a critique of this type of secularism.

[16] For the idea that all limitation is external, see Ludwig Wittgenstein, *Tractatus Logico-Philosophicus*, 5.61. Cf. Immanuel Kant, *Critique of Pure Reason*, B295.

[17] Accordingly, Jewish identity must be more than simple loyalty to one's Jewish past, as Leo Strauss suggested in his 1962 lecture "Why We Remain Jews" (*Jewish Philosophy and*

A Contract between Minorities

Multiculturalism, in my understanding, assumes that all the bearers of the various cultures participating in the social contract are minorities. Any notion of a majority rule, except for purposes of election to public office, legislation, or judicial decision, requires the type of singular or monoculture that is inimical to the cultural rights of any and all minorities. Surely, multiculturalism is for the sake of minority groups.[18] Only when that logic is carried further does it also function for the sake of the individual person and his or her rights. An individual person is the smallest minority possible, but he or she is not the only minority possible. As such, that individual minority only functions as a rights bearer in cases involving certain political, legal, or economic claims on society. But in cases involving larger social claims, such as religious liberty or domestic sanctity, cultural rights—which are the claims of persons to be able to exercise their cultural identity both in their primal communities and in the secular realm—much more is at issue.[19] And, more often than not, the minorities by themselves and between themselves can come to a common consensus with good reason, and that can be without having to formally designate a majority conclusion. Certainly that is the case with a social contract as distinct from a formal political pact. The social contract is not adjudicated in a court or argued in a legislature, even though its negotiation in the larger civil society often has judicial and legislative effects.

Jews have experienced minority status probably longer than any other people on earth. Indeed, at the very beginnings of their history as a people, Moses tells them, "you are the smallest [ha-me'at] of all the peoples" (Deuteronomy 7:7), which turned out to be as much a prediction of their future as it was a description of their original condition. And, several of the later prophets referred to "the remnant" [she'erit] of Israel, which was immediately intelligible to the Jews (that is, the "Judeans" of the tribe of Judah), who knew that the majority of the whole people of Israel (the Northern Kingdom, also known as the Lost Ten Tribes) had gone into exile at the hands of the Assyrians in 721 B.C.E., and that it was most unlikely that those lost tribes would ever return.[20]

---

the Crisis of Modernity, ed. K. H. Green [Albany: State University of New York Press, 1997], 320–29). Jewish identity, in order to have present validity, must affirm the truth *of* Judaism and not just what has been true *about* Judaism.

[18] See D. Novak, "The Jewish Ethical Tradition and the Modern University," *Journal of Education* 180 (1998), 22–38.

[19] See Charles Taylor, *Multiculturalism* (Princeton, N.J.: Princeton University Press, 1994), 61.

[20] See e.g., Jer. 42:2; Ezra 9:8.

Most Jews today, even in the Jewish State of Israel, live in multicultural societies where they thrive as minorities. Even religious Jews in the State of Israel are a cultural minority and must, therefore, play by multicultural rules in order to survive in that secular society. The establishment of a specifically religious state in Israel, that is, a state governed by Jewish law, both ritual and civil-criminal, would no doubt require a coup d'état that would very likely destroy the already besieged Jewish state by bringing about a civil war. This would be a far greater threat to the survival of Israel than any of the considerable foreign threats it has successfully resisted to date. For this reason of realpolitik alone, many religious Israelis would rather be a powerful minority (indeed, in Israel today there is no cultural majority in any real sense) in a multicultural society than a hated oligarchy. And even if Israel were to become a monocultural society, and even were that to happen through a peaceful transfer of power to a religious establishment, Israel would become more and more of an outcast in an increasingly multicultural, globalized world. It would not even be a minority society among the multicultural democracies of the world, especially the Western world in which almost all Jews want to be included. If that is true even in the State of Israel, all the more so is it true in the Diaspora.

As we shall see in the course of this book, any contract between persons, be it a private contract between some individual parties or a public contract between all parties to the society and for the sake of the society, any such contract is not the most original or even the most persistent social bond, certainly not for Jews. Truly, without the presupposition of more original social or communal bonds, the idea of the social contract becomes incoherent since there are no real persons to come to it. Only full persons and not abstractions can contract with one another in any substantial way. Persons are social beings by nature, not by mutual agreement.[21] There cannot be contracting persons, as distinct from hu-

---

[21] The term "social beings by nature" is borrowed from Aristotle, but my use of it differs from his, as my idea of human sociality differs from his idea of human sociality, which he uses this term to express. In *Politics*, 1.1/1251b1ff., Aristotle distinguishes truly human *political* nature from the *domestic-communal* nature humans share with other animals who also live in groups (cf. *Nicomachean Ethics*, 1.7/1097b10–15). In the domestic-communal sphere, biological dependence and its inherent inequality characterize the personal relationships conducted there. In the political sphere, however, intelligent freedom and its inherent equality characterize the personal relationships conducted there (*Politics.*, 3.6/1279a8ff.; also, *Nicomachean Ethics*, 8.6/1158b1; 9.6/1167a21ff.; 9.9/1171b32ff.). Unlike Plato, who wanted to sunder domesticity from politics altogether (*Republic*, 458Eff.), Aristotle recognized everyone's need for it, even those engaged in politics (*Politics*, 2.1/1261a5ff.; also, *Nicomachean Ethics*, 8.12/1162a15–20). Nevertheless, the household (*oikos*) and its extension, the village (*komē*, what we would call a "community") is clearly subordinate to the *polis* (see *Nicomachean Ethics*, 8.9/1159b25ff.). The familial-tribal community cannot

manoid phantoms, who are not *already* socialized. And that socialization takes place in the family as the basic component of a primal community.[22] Thus no contract between persons can create a primal community because a primal community, one's original society, hovers *around* persons before there are any real agreements *between* persons within it, much less agreements between persons crossing over original borders and coming together from their different communities into a civil society. However, this precontractual, natural priority does not preclude a subsequent social contract. In fact, it can encourage the formulation of subsequent social contracts, as we shall see. Furthermore, one can derive a very positive evaluation of the democratic social contract from the sources of Judaism and then through reasoning about human sociality per se. And that positive yet critical evaluation can be done with theological and philosophical perspicacity. This requires the presentation of the most cogent justification of the idea of a social contract, one whose very cogency claims neither too much nor too little for it.

Community and Society

The difference between an *original* human association and a *contractual* one is the difference between a *community* and a *society*, something modern social theorists have often discussed. It has been best described when designating an original, organic, human association by the German term *Gemeinschaft*, and a contractual, procedural, human association by the German term *Gesellschaft*.[23] The difference between a society and a community can be most powerfully located in the family's role in a community in contrast to its role in a society.

The fact is that for all of us, our original human association, our primal community, is our family. That is why our greatest childhood fear is or-

---

make any original claims on the *polis*-society. It would seem Hegel saw the political subordination of the family much the same way as Aristotle did. See *Phenomenology of Spirit*, trans. A. V. Miller (Oxford: Oxford University Press, 1977), 268–73; *Philosophy of Right*, secs. 256 and 261, pp. 154–55, 161–62. Both Aristotle and Hegel underestimate the amount of political justice (including many equal rights) in communal life, and they both overestimate the ability of any secular polity to meet the basic human need for community.

[22] Arguments for the moral need to transcend the family have been made most strongly by Lawrence Kohlberg, "The Claim to Moral Adequacy of a Highest Stage of Moral Development," *Journal of Philosophy* 70 (1975), 631–47, and with more hesitation by John Rawls, *A Theory of Justice*, 74, 301, 511. Cf. Michael Walzer, *Spheres of Justice* (Oxford: Blackwell, 1983), 229–32.

[23] This terminological distinction was originally made by the German sociologist Ferdinand Tönnies, *Community and Society*, trans. C. P. Loomis (East Lansing: Michigan State University Press, 1957).

phanhood, and even less radical familial breakup (as in the divorce of one's parents), which usually means the loss of our primal community in its most original manifestation. And this is why a community is looked upon not as a negotiated amalgamation of separate families into some new social entity but, rather, as an *extended* family itself.[24] To be sure, as we shall soon see, one can look upon this original condition as something to be developed or overcome. It can be affirmed or denied in a variety of ways. But much social contract theory, whether explicitly or implicitly, has avoided consideration of the family as the most immediate and persistent locus of one's primal community altogether. It assumes that there is nothing that mediates the relation of an individual and civil society. Accordingly, this type of social theory cannot recognize that even those who believe they have overcome their communal origins most often find another community in which to be reborn. Frequently this is done through marriage, remarriage, or religious conversion, which are the most basic ways one can alter one's communal status. Even persons making this momentous existential decision rarely choose to become noncommunal beings in any full sense. Usually, they exchange one primal community for another. This is why it is important for the authorities of the community to impress upon the newcomer the gravity of his or her existential transition, and that it is irrevocable.

Conversely, much social contract theory has looked upon the parties to the social contract as lone individuals who are the bearers of rights. The familial status of these lone individuals is at most a matter of privacy; indeed, for them the right to privacy becomes the greatest of all rights. But, following this logic, "privacy" itself is that which is abstracted (*privatio*) from the public realm (*res publica*); hence public considerations ultimately trump the interests of the family on every front as they easily trump privacy itself. In fact, when the priority of traditional familial existence is denied, some democratic theorists want to redefine the family altogether. Yet this flies in the face of the remarkable consensus among traditional cultures as to what the family is, namely, a procreative, conjugal union of a woman and a man for the sake of bearing and raising the children that union intends to bring into the world and usually does bring into the world. This traditional consensus is no doubt under heavy attack in current democratic discourse.[25] The question is whether civil society can radi-

---

[24] Cf. Aristotle, *Politics*, 1.1/1252b15–20, where the village (*komē*) grows up *from* the gradual association among several families (*apoikia*), unlike the *polis* that moves *out of* communal life to become a truly new and perfected (*teleios*) human entity (ibid., 1.1/ 1252b29–35).

[25] See, e.g., Andrew Koppelman, "Sexual and Religious Pluralism" in *Sexual Orientation and Human Rights in American Religious Discourse*, eds. S. M. Olyan and M. C. Nussbaum (New York: Oxford University Press, 1998), 215–33.

cally redefine the family as its own institution when in fact the family is an institution civil society received from—that is, was given by—historical cultures like Judaism. It is not something civil society creates by itself de novo, let alone ex nihilo. To be sure, there are contractual elements involved in family structure, even in traditional Judaism.[26] Nevertheless, to reduce familial existence to a series of contractual agreements is to belittle the richness and depth of familial existence, certainly as it has been lived by Jews traditionally. That is why almost all Jewish cultural claims on civil society inevitably involve family issues in one way or another. For Jews to abandon these claims is theologically unjustifiable, philosophically shallow, and politically self-defeating.

If the family is no more than a unit of a contractual society, then why should it not be looked upon as one more private contract within a larger, public contractual realm? If, however, this notion were made known to most traditional Jews living in democratic societies, for whom their extended families are both their necessary and desirable primal communities, they would find much contemporary social contract theory to be morally repugnant. Very few traditional Jews would really want their children to be, de facto if not yet de jure, wards of the state, which is *the* institution emerging out of the social contract. Yet that is the most obvious result of looking at the liberty of the family as an entitlement from civil society through the state. As we shall see later in this book, familial liberty, as something prior to the founding of civil (or contractual) society and its expression in the state, is intimately linked to religious liberty. Most traditional Jews regard their familial bonds, like their religious bonds, as having a sanctity beyond the reach of civil society and the state. This includes the recognition that the so-called nuclear family, which is a family adrift in civil society without a communal anchor, is exceptionally vulnerable to disintegration. The high rate of intermarriage and the low birthrate among nontraditional Jews in the Diaspora are clear demonstrations of that vulnerability.

The respect and protection of the sanctity of the traditional family, which its survival in civil society requires, is surely not something anyone could cogently claim for his or her property, whose very value is made by the state in terms of its currency, and which is wholly taxable by the state. That is why any movement for communal rights is quite different from movements for economic rights. The movement for communal rights,

---

[26] Thus the traditional Jewish marriage document (*ketubah*) contains stipulations mandated for and conditions contracted *between* the marrying parties. See, e.g., B. Kiddushin 19b; M. Ketubot 5.1. Nevertheless, the non-negotiable stipulations mandated by Scripture and rabbinic legislation take precedence over any private contract negotiated between the husband and the wife. See M. Ketubot 4.7–11; B. Ketubot 47b re Exod. 21:10.

often seen as cultural conservatism, need not entail a specific stand on economic rights. Contrary to the views of many neoconservatives, cultural conservatism (or traditionalism) does not require one to simultaneously endorse economic conservatism—nor does it preclude it. They are separate issues.

Indeed, most traditional Jews regard their familial bonds as part of their religious bonds without, however, making those familial bonds into a self-sufficient community.[27] For Jews, in one way or another, the covenanted Jewish people is made up of "all the families [*mishpehot*] of Israel" (Jeremiah 31:1).[28] This is why Jewish devotion to family has become proverbial in the modern world, even though too much nostalgic kitsch (which is an attempt to select from tradition without an affirmation of its founding and coordinating revelation) has made Jewish familial devotion a vulgar, sentimental parody.

As we shall also see, the only cultural minorities who can resist the inner tendency of the secular state to turn all alternative societies into private corporations (the modern German word for "corporation" is *Gesellschaft*) within its own purview are religious minorities. In fact, it is the distinction between culture as religiously founded, as opposed to culture as racially founded, that enables a minority religion-culture to resist the totalizing expansion of civil society by its very participation in that society. Cultures that are racially defined, by contrast, either claim some special privileges within civil society, usually as the result of a claim for compensation for past persecution against their members, or they attempt to totally dominate civil society by absorbing it into themselves. That is inevitably done with the simultaneous exclusion of those whom they perceive to be inferior races. Unlike religious cultures who define themselves by their founding, sustaining, and fulfilling relationship with the universal creator God, racial cultures inevitably define themselves in relation to their persecutors or to their victims.[29] Racial identity always in-

---

[27] Thus, e.g., duties to one's teacher (*rav*) take precedence over duties to one's father (see M. Baba Metsia 2.11; Maimonides, MT: Talmud Torah, 5.1), since one's teacher is a leader of a community in which one's family, led by one's father, is a part. Nevertheless, one's teacher should not require one to neglect one's parents (see B. Kiddushin 31b re R. Assi). Even the community is an extension of one's family, not a substitute for it. There is also a rabbinic debate as to whether one's familial obligation to marry or one's communal obligation to study Torah in a yeshivah takes precedence. See T. Bekhorot 6.10; B. Kiddushin 29b. As for permanent neglect of marriage for the sake of full-time Torah study, note the differing views of Maimonides (MT: Ishut, 15.3) and R. Asher (*Tur*: Even Ha'Ezer, 1) re B. Yevamot 63b concerning Gen. 9:7.

[28] See B. Kiddushin 70b.

[29] This is the most basic thesis of Jean-Paul Sartre's 1946 book, *Anti-Semite and Jew*, trans. G. J. Becker (New York: Schocken, 1972), viz., "Thus the authentic Jew . . . thinks of himself as a Jew because the anti-Semite puts him in the situation of a Jew" (150). In other

volves some kind of biological or historical determinism, even fatalism. Also, there is nothing voluntary about it. As such, anyone can convert to Judaism (or to Christianity or to Islam), but no one can convert to a race or adopt a new one.[30]

I can think of no better expression of the political and cultural inadequacies of both economically based liberal (*and* socialist) ideologies and racist mythologies than this magnificent insight of the French Catholic philosopher, Jacques Maritain.[31] Writing in 1942, when the racist culture of Nazism could have destroyed the Jewish people and Western, multicultural civilization along with us, Maritain noted:

> In the bourgeois individualist type of society there is no . . . form of communion. Each one asks only that the State protect his individual freedom of profit. . . . Nor in the racial type of community . . . Nothing is more dangerous than such a community: deprived of a determining objective, political communion will carry its demands to the infinite, will absorb and regiment people, swallow up in itself the religious energies of the human being. Because it is not defined by a work to be done, it will only be able to define itself by its opposition to other human groups. Therefore, it will have essential need for an *enemy against whom* it will build itself; it is by recognizing and hating its enemies that the political body will find its common consciousness.[32]

Even though religiously based cultures (and here I can only speak directly of Judaism, even though there are analogies in other religions to be sure) also have the tendency to either withdraw from or dominate others, unlike racially based cultures they also have within themselves the resources

---

words, racial definitions of Jews are made by their persecutors, who frequently become their murderers. Jews who are alienated from Jewish tradition accept these self-definitions. Assimilated Jews even accept the pejorative value the anti-Semites build into these racial definitions of Jews and try to escape their Jewish identity. Nationalistic Jews invert this pejorative value, taking what was meant by the anti-Semites to be a badge of shame and turning it into a badge of pride. But neither the assimilationists nor the nationalists know how to access the classical Jewish definition of "Jewishness," which is the doctrine of God's election of the Jewish people, collectively and individually. Only this definition enables Jews to transcend dependence on the world's opinions of them. Only God's opinion of the Jews should matter to them. This divine judgment is far more generous than any Jewish self-esteem and far more merciful than any Jewish self-hate.

[30] For the elimination of racial barriers to full conversion to Judaism, see M. Yadayim 4.4; Maimonides, MT: Isurei Biah, 12.22, 25.

[31] For Maritain's great appreciation of Judaism and his concern for the Jewish people as the prime victims of European racism, see his "The Mystery of Israel," Eng. trans. in J. Evans and L. R. Ward, *The Social and Political Philosophy of Jacques Maritain* (New York: Charles Scribner's Sons, 1955), 195–216; also, *Jacques Maritain and the Jews*, ed. R. Royal (Notre Dame, Ind.: University of Notre Dame Press, 1994).

[32] *The Rights of Man and Natural Law*, trans. D. C. Anson (San Francisco: Ignatius Press, 1986), 122–23.

of critical self-judgment. These resources enable Jews to live in good faith in a multicultural society, where no one culture is civilly privileged over another. That is because Judaism (and, at least, Christianity as well) has an idea of universal human personhood as the "image of God." Mainstream biblical-rabbinic theology sees the image of God (*tselem elohim*) to encompass all humankind and not to be the exclusive and essential designation of the Jews.[33] All humans are capable of a relationship with the same God we Jews believe ourselves to be serving most fully. The image of God does not designate a substance or attribute conveyed by God to humans. Instead, it is a relational capacity for what pertains *between* God and all humans.[34] Thus the image of God is not a peculiarly Jewish domain. Jews can accept the fact that other cultures enable their members to function as the image of God. So, in the end, our human differences with other people about God are often more differences of degree than of kind. Everyone outside of Israel is neither an atheist nor a pagan. Indeed, it is only those religious cultures who claim a totally exclusive relationship with God who tend to become racistlike in their attempts to withdraw from or dominate others even in civil society. Truth be told, Judaism too has such tendencies, but they can be resisted with the full force of much of Jewish revelation and tradition behind such resistance.[35]

One might very well see the beginnings of the multicultural pluralism required for civil society's social contract to be located in interreligious respect. And that respect can only be genuine, and not merely a rhetorical instrument, when it is the result of each religious community being able to constitute a universal horizon looking out from its own traditional sources. On that universal horizon Jews can discover, with theological authenticity, other cultures in their own moral integrity, and without Jews presuming to judge the truth or falsity of the singular revelations the members of these other cultures affirm among themselves. But this means Jews can only discover the moral integrity of those other cultures who themselves constitute a similar universal horizon, and for much the same reason Jews do.[36] Racially based cultures, conversely, have no such transcendent orientation or universalizing ability and cannot, therefore, demand or extend any such respect from others. For racially constituted cultures, all foreign relations are adversarial, and frequently belligerent as well.

---

[33] See Novak, *Natural Law in Judaism*, 167–73.

[34] The same relationality is denoted by the scriptural term "holy spirit" (*ruah ha-qodesh*), e.g., Ps. 51:13. See Hermann Cohen, *Religion of Reason out of the Sources of Judaism*, trans. S. Kaplan (New York: Frederick Ungar, 1972), 104–105.

[35] See Novak, *Jewish Social Ethics*, 187–205.

[36] See D. Novak, *Jewish-Christian Dialogue* (New York: Oxford University Press, 1989), 138–42.

Following this ethical analysis of cultures, one can see why cultures based on class or gender have even less of a prior claim on civil society than do racial cultures. Being ideological constructs, they are without either the historical or ontological roots of religious cultures, and they are without even the historical roots of racial cultures. They can only function as special interest groups within civil society. As such, they are most dependent on civil tolerance and most vulnerable to civil intolerance, all according to what is currently perceived to be useful, useless, or troublesome for civil society itself. Tolerance is most definitely a vague entitlement *from* civil society, not a prior rights claim like that of respect for one's communal roots made *on* civil society. The type of cultural agenda determined by class or gender is usually advocated by secularist intellectuals who, despite their lack of historical and ontological roots, nevertheless believe themselves capable of creating a new culture in their own image and likeness. But without any such roots, these new cultures turn out to have little more content than the ephemeral practices of opinion groups or elitist subcultures. It is no surprise, then, why the advocates of these new cultures frequently oppose the public presence and influence of the older cultures, who can present themselves with historical and ontological backing, with impressive logical consistency, and with the capacity for intellectual development that can adequately deal with new historical situations. In relation to these older cultures, it is remarkable how the advocates of the newer "cultures," despite all their talk about "inclusiveness," become intolerant, even bigoted.

When one begins with civil society as the primary locus of human sociality, there is no real place for community. But when one begins with community as the primary locus of human sociality, there is the potential to make a real place for society. When one makes civil society socially foundational, it is then impossible to recognize community as being anything more than a matter of privacy, which itself is a transient entitlement from society. The moral priority of community becomes vigorously denied accordingly. But, of course, no historical community could possibly accept this role for itself in good faith. A historical, religiously constituted community asks for more than tolerance from civil society; it asks for respect of its historical and ontological priority.[37] And these communities are able to respect the secondary importance of society, which, indeed, is the way many civil societies have been seen by most of their citizens. This is expressed in the value many citizens of a democracy see in the notion of limited government.

Furthermore, affirming the primacy of civil society inevitably requires the creation of a hypothetical—that is, a fictitious, even mythical—"state

[37] See Taylor, *Multiculturalism*, 63–64.

of nature" or "original [individual] position" as its starting point.[38] The primacy of community, on the other hand, which does lead to civil society, can be really located in history—especially in Jewish history, as will be shown later in this book. Furthermore, that historical origin cannot be regarded as part of a dead past because it is the point of reference from which Jews anticipate a transcendent future, lying after the end of history, and including the resurrection of the dead.[39] Compared to this type of historical and ontological priority, which is very much alive in the traditional Jewish community, modern social contract theory with its hypothetical starting point pales. It lacks any real history and ontology; it has no past to sustain continuing memory and no future to sustain continuing hope. Indeed, this theory seems to be little more than the imaginative, utopian projection of some secularized, liberal intellectuals in the West. This is why it is blind to the true social significance of a historical culture like Judaism.

I contend that civil society as truly *secular* space can only emerge out of intercultural agreement, precisely because cultures have a *religious* need for that space. These communities are rarely if ever politically, economically, or intellectually, self-sufficient. In one way or another, they need to make alliances with others outside their own cultural domain, alliances in which no one party dominates the others, or one in which all the parties merge and create a new identity for themselves. Communities need to engage in foreign relations if they do not want to be vulnerable to political, economic, or intellectual conquest, or to stagnating isolation. All of this, in one way or another, is continually done through negotiation. Negotiation, of course, is the stuff of any contract, including the social contract. But no community should ever be required to negotiate away its communal identity as the price for the admission of its members to the social contract.

Secular space, especially for the Jews, came in the wake of the French Revolution of 1789, which ended the social, cultural, and political isolation of the Jews and our subordination to essentially Christian societies. Jews became individual citizens of societies that were becoming more and more secular, that is, neither Christian nor Jewish. The political identity of such "emancipated" Jews was no longer determined by their membership in the semi-autonomous Jewish communities (*qehillot*), which functioned for the most past as their own civil society.[40] Nevertheless, despite

---

[38] See Rawls, *A Theory of Justice*, 13–22. Cf. Novak, *Natural Law in Judaism*, 22–23. For some critiques of this overly formal approach, see, e.g., Robert C. Solomon, *A Passion for Justice* (Reading, Mass.: Addison-Wesley, 1990), 56–57; Ron Replogle, *Recovering the Social Contract* (Totowa, N.J.: Rowman and Littlefield, 1989), 67.

[39] See B. Sanhedrin 90b re Exod. 6:4.

[40] See Jacob Katz, *Tradition and Crisis* (New York: Schocken, 1971).

the continuing suspicion of some Jewish traditionalists that Jewish communal integrity requires such a semi-autonomous ghetto polity, this new
situation gave a radically improved function to the Jewish social contract
with civil society. Whereas in the medieval past the social contract meant
Jewish acceptance of a communal life *under* Christian civil authority, in
modernity the social contract was now *between* Jews and gentiles in a
society where no historical community could claim the civil order to be
its own domain. Jews were no longer aliens in someone else's society, no
longer foreigners dependent on the largesse of a host society that at best
tolerated us, and at worst exploited us, persecuted us, and even killed us.
Jews could now engage in communal negotiations on a more level social
and political playing field. Unfortunately, though, too many modern Jews
became convinced—consciously or unconsciously (largely by anti-Semites)—that they could only enter the social contract as anonymous, deculturated, individuals. As such, they deprived themselves—and frequently
their less deculturated brethren as well—of much of their rich culture.
They brought a rootless cosmopolitanism to civil society instead of the
riches of their ancestral heritage, riches that would have more greatly
empowered their status in a civil society, which is made up of other people
having similar cultural riches in their background.

However, to be able to make such strong claims on civil society requires
the creation of neutral or secular space in order to conduct social negotiations and achieve some positive social benefits. Yet what is lost on most
social contract theorists is the fact that political, economic, and intellectual interests are all for the sake of cultural survival and development.
Ultimately, any community's will to live depends on the desire of its members to preserve and advance their traditional way of life as a cosmic
desideratum. For Jews, this means looking to revelation—Torah—as the
foundation for which the created world (including the social world) is the
context.[41] From this historical foundation Jews are able to consistently
look toward messianic redemption (*ge'ulah*) as the final culmination of
their history and that of all others in the world together with them. Here
is where history and ontology meet: History is more than a dead past;
ontology is not about a timeless, disembodied eternity.

Jews need to believe themselves in the vanguard of those who wait for
this end of all history, even though they are not the only ones who wait
for this end (*eschaton*).[42] All political, economic, and intellectual pursuits
are for the sake of this end, which must be hoped for, even though its

---

[41] See B. Pesahim 68b re Jer. 33:25.
[42] See Franz Rosenzweig, *The Star of Redemption*, trans. W. W. Hallo (New York: Holt,
Rinehart, and Winston, 1970), 415–16.

content is beyond all human ken.[43] Without this orientation, Jews can only be seen as one more special interest group within the mundane world. Thus participation in a civil society (or a larger civilization of civil societies) is useful for the human flourishing of Jews in Judaism and its traditional community. Moreover, this participation can also be seen as a means to a greater (if not yet final) end. In today's world that participation might well be politically necessary. This, surely, is quite consistent with the limited aims of a democratic society, which ought never regard its programs, no matter how serious, of ultimate importance in the lives of its citizens. This is why Jews (or the members of any other minority culture) should not ask for their rights as a matter of public entitlement but as their just desert. The social contract is a matter of ongoing negotiation and renegotiation: asking for the protection and enhancement of prior *communal rights* and accepting subsequent *social duties* in return. But the social contract loses its limiting power whenever a secular society founded upon it assumes a messianic role for itself in and for the world. This inevitably calls for the elevation of one religion/culture within the social contract to the level of a state religion of one kind or another.

Claims for Cultural Autonomy

The cogency of the claims Jews can make in the ongoing negotiation of their engagement in the social contract are largely determined by the cogency of their commitment to the Jewish tradition. The more cogent that commitment, the more cogent is their claim on secular society for their cultural autonomy. The less cogent that commitment, the less cogent is their cultural claim on that society. Minimally, that claim is to be free *from* social interference in their cultural life. Maximally, it is a claim *for* social recognition, even at times support, of that cultural autonomy because of its positive contribution to the common good of that society as a whole.

The human environment or community in which we live has been determined for us by others, yet it is also something we are free to determine for ourselves. Initially, our worldly locale is determined for us since we could not have chosen our birth or our birthplace for ourselves. Our communal origins, like our biological origins, are there for us without our prior consent. Nevertheless, whenever we do become aware of our freedom to choose among multiple possibilities in the world, we eventually learn that the most important possibility is the option of *whether or not*

---

[43] See Novak, *Jewish-Christian Dialogue*, 155–56.

we want to be situated in our original community at all. It is the momentous discovery that the initial social status given to us as children is not
necessarily the only one available to us as adults. At this point, we have
two fundamental choices: We can either identify with our community or
we can repudiate it. The choice is to be there or not as a free person. And
the modern world has made that choice a more real opportunity for more
people than was ever the case in the past, primarily because of the real
opportunity for geographic dislocation and relocation.[44]

There are three ways one can freely engage one's cultural community,
and three ways to freely disengage. We now need to see exactly how one's
relation to the Jewish tradition determines the type of cultural claim a
Jew can make on a democratic society.

Regarding cultural engagement, the first and most usual positive option
is to confirm that one's birth locale or native community is *now* the place
where one would have chosen to be born and grow up had the choice
been available *back then*. The choice is retroactive. As such, one can regard one's present communal status as too good to be considered a mere
accident.[45] This person sees his or her community as even more desirable
than is necessary and thus becomes a willing and active member of this
community. Most people make this kind of social confirmation a continual process throughout their active lives. In fact, no community (let alone
any society) could survive if the vast number of its members were not able
to confirm their continued and continuing existence in the community by
living freely and actively in it and for it of their own volition.

For most people, though, this choice is largely implicit; it is a matter of
tacit consent to remain in the community where they have always been.
This usually means taking their community and its practices for granted:
an acceptance of the status quo.[46] This conformity declares that their community and its practices are essentially good for them. All of this indicates
the force of custom (*minhag*), which is the habitual continuity of the cultural life of the community.[47]

[44] Cf. David Hume, *A Treatise of Human Nature*, 2.3.8, ed. L. A. Selby-Bigge (Oxford: Clarendon Press, 1888), 548.

[45] Thus one is to thank God early each morning for "not having made me [*she-lo asani*] a gentile" (T. Berakhot 6.18 re Isa. 40:17; also, B. Menahot 43b).

[46] This is like the assumption in the Talmud (B. Yevamot 87a) that silence (*shetiqah*), i.e., lack of protest, is tantamount to agreement (*hoda'ah*). Also, one need not make an explicit commitment to practice any particular commandment, or even all the commandments, since this commitment has already been made by the Jewish people's oath at Mt. Sinai to keep the commandments. But anyone who wishes to make such a commitment to keep a specific commandment does so as an act of personal volition greater than the simple choice to keep or violate that specific commandment (see B. Nedarim 7b–8a re Ps. 119:106).

[47] See Y. Pesahim 4.1/30a–b.

But, as regards cultural claims made on civil society, such conformists (and the term is not being used here pejoratively) are rarely if ever capable of making them, or even wanting to make them. It would seem that the ability to make a cogent Jewish claim on external society in the name of the community requires that one be able to articulate *why* one has remained faithful to the tradition. This requires greater knowledge of the tradition and a greater desire to intelligently explicate it and transmit it to other members of the community.

This second option regarding positive cultural engagement can only be taken by those few members of the community who can articulate their commitment in and for the community. Their commitment to the tradition needs to be much more conscious and conscientious than the largely tacit consent most of the other members of the community give to the tradition. As true leaders, they need to develop a vision of how the community is to operate by itself and then how it is to operate in the world. There is little that they can or should simply take for granted.[48] They should thus agree with Goethe, who said: "What you have inherited from your fathers, acquire it in order to possess it. What one does not make use of is a heavy burden."[49]

Authentic Jewish leaders, who are knowledgeable and purposeful, are well equipped to cogently make the cultural claims of the community on civil society, to be the spokespersons of the community.[50] Unfortunately, though, too many traditional Jewish leaders in modern times have lacked the self-confidence to come forth and speak for the community to the outside world and, especially, to civil society. Accordingly, they have been willing to leave the tasks of Jewish diplomacy to Jews far less knowledgeable of and committed to the Jewish tradition. These modern Jewish diplomats have, to be sure, usually been far more sophisticated than traditional Jewish leaders have been. Nevertheless, their lack of authentic cultural engagement with Judaism has prevented them from making authentic Jewish cultural claims on civil society.

The third way a Jew can engage his or her cultural community is by the conversion to Judaism of someone who was previously part of a gentile community. Although Jews have long avoided active proselytism, they have never ceased to accept converts. But if being Jewish is a matter of birth, then how can one who is born a gentile *become* a Jew? The answer worked out in the tradition is that a convert to Judaism (*ger*) is, through

---

[48] See, e.g., Y. Baba Batra 8.2/16a re Deut. 33:4 and R. Moses Margolis, *Pnei Mosheh* thereon.

[49] *Faust*, 682–84 (Hamburg: Wegner Verlag, 1949), 29 (my translation).

[50] See, e.g., B. Yoma 69a.

the event of conversion, "born again."[51] As such, even though a person may not be converted to Judaism against his or her will, freedom of choice is a necessary but not sufficient condition of becoming a Jew.[52] A former gentile becomes a Jew by virtue of a proper Jewish tribunal accepting that person into the people of Israel and conducting the appropriate rites of initiation.[53] Nevertheless, the fact that the candidate for conversion was not compelled in any way does not automatically require a Jewish tribunal to accept him or her as a convert.[54] In other words, the tribunal acts like God, *in loco Dei* as it were, by electing a former group of gentiles to be his people at Mount Sinai.[55] Just as the people's free acceptance of election was a necessary condition for the covenant to be humanly effective in the world, so it is with the individual gentile who is converted to Judaism now.[56] And, just as the people's free acceptance of election confirmed rather than initiated the covenantal relationship, so it is with the gentile who is converted now. Moreover, just as a native-born Jew who does not exercise his or her Jewish duties forfeits many covenantal privileges, so it is with a convert who, in effect, does not develop the normative status he or she obtained at the event of conversion.[57] Therefore, aside from a few details involving marital status, a convert is as much a child of Abraham, Isaac, and Jacob, Sarah, Rebekah, Rachel, and Leah, as is a native-born Jew.[58]

In terms of the cultural claims that can be made on civil society, it would seem that a convert to Judaism can make the very same claims a native-born Jew can make. Nevertheless, a convert has one additional cultural claim to make on civil society, namely, the democratic claim to be able to convert to a religion of his or her choice. The fact is that in most premodern societies, dominated as they were by Christianity or Islam, Jews were only a tolerated foreign entity. Often one of the conditions of that civil toleration by gentile authorities was that Jews would not accept converts, let alone actively proselytize gentiles in those host societies, gentiles who were almost always Christians or Muslims. One of the innovations of modern secular democratic society was that a Jew could leave the traditional Jewish community without having to become a Christian or a Muslim as had been the case in the past. Another similar innovation was that Jews could accept converts from anywhere, even though they have been

[51] B. Yevamot 22a and parallels.

[52] See B. Ketubot 11a.

[53] B. Yevamot 47a–b.

[54] See ibid., 24b.

[55] B. Keritot 9a.

[56] See esp. B. Shabbat 88a re Est. 9:27.

[57] B. Yevamot 47b. See, also, B. Sanhedrin 27a re Exod. 23:1 for the status of a person who willfully and publicly violates commandments, but is still taken to be a Jew.

[58] Cf. M. Yevamot 6.5 re Lev. 21:7.

reluctant to do so.[59] Both innovations were the result of the official recognition of religious liberty for the citizens of a democracy. Therefore, a convert to Judaism can make the claim of religious liberty with even greater force than a native-born Jew.[60] So, converts (and returnees to traditional Judaism) have reminded native-born Jews that Judaism itself cannot be effective when simply taken for granted.[61] And these converts and quasi converts have reminded civil societies that religious liberty entails the right of religious conversion for anyone in those societies.

There are three ways a Jew can disengage from his or her primal Jewish community. Here too there are implications for the type of cultural claims such a disengaged Jew can make on civil society.

The most radical form of disengagement from Judaism is conversion to another religion, what is called apostasy (*shmad*).[62] And the fact that apostasy very often results from intermarriage indicates how closely familial and religious bonds operate, especially for Jews.[63]

Most Jewish apostates have coupled their attraction to their new religion and its adherents with an aversion to Judaism and the Jewish people. Since they usually do not want to hear the claims the Jewish people make on them to return to the fold, they can hardly be expected to make Jewish cultural claims in a society where they no longer identify themselves as Jews.[64] Thus the attitude of most Jews toward apostates has been to pray for their later return, but to recognize that in fact they and their descendants are probably lost forever.[65] And, furthermore, concerning the apos-

[59] See *Encyclopedia Judaica*, 13:1187–91.

[60] This is because a convert to Judaism must explicitly accept the authority of all the commandments of the Torah and Jewish tradition as a prerequisite of his or her conversion. See T. Demai 2.5; B. Bekhorot 30b. For a native-born Jew, however, such acceptance is implicit because of ancestral acceptance of the entire Torah at Mt. Sinai. See, e.g., M. Shevuot 3.6.

[61] See B. Kiddushin 70b and Tos., s.v. "qashim gerim" (the opinion of R. Abraham the Proselyte on 71a). Cf. B. Pesahim 91b and Tos., s.v. "shema."

[62] B. Sanhedrin 74a (following Ms. Munich). The Greek term *apostasia* (lit. "standing away"), which is termed "apostasy" in English, denotes the specifically religious abandonment of one's faith as distinct from merely political rebellion, which was its earlier meaning in pre-Hellenistic Greek texts (see Liddell and Scott, *A Greek-English Lexicon* [Oxford: Clarendon Press, 1925], 218–19). It seems to have been coined by Hellenistic Jewish authors in regard to their contemporaries, whose abandonment of Judaism was more a religious than a political rebellion. See, e.g., Septuagint on Num. 14:9 (for Heb. *marad*, lit. "rebel"; cf. Vulgate thereon: *Nolite rebelles*). Cf. I Macc. 1:10–16. In Christian sources, *apostasia* had much the same meaning as *shmad* had in contemporary Jewish sources. See G.W.H. Lampe, *A Patristic Greek Lexicon* (Oxford: Clarendon Press, 1961), 208.

[63] See B. Kiddushin 68b re Deut. 7:3–4 and Tos., s.v. "binkha;" B. Sukkah 56b; Y. Sukkah 5.8/55d.

[64] For continuing Jewish claims even on apostates, see Novak, *The Election of Israel*, 189–99.

[65] See B. Yevamot 16b–17a.

tates themselves, there seems to be a feeling among many Jews that the community might actually be better off without such unwilling members at present. Although the community must care *about* apostates in the ultimate sense, it need not care *for* them in the more immediate sense.

The second way Jews can disengage from the traditional Jewish community is through avowed secularism. In the most radical form of secularism, like that of Spinoza, a Jew leaves the traditional Jewish community, indeed the Jewish people totally, without, however, converting to another religion.[66] In less radical forms of Jewish secularism, a Jew leaves the Jewish tradition but remains part of the Jewish people in some nonreligious, or even antireligious, way. Here we find the assertion that the Jewish people is a nationality or an ethnic group whose identity can remain intact without faith in the God who elects the Jewish people, who reveals the Torah to them, who authorizes their tradition, and who will redeem them in the end. Unlike some the old-time Jewish Marxists, though, who made the Communist Party their primal community and who thus left the Jewish people for all intents and purposes, most contemporary Jewish secularists fall back on a racial definition of the Jewish people and Jewish culture in their desire to remain identifiably Jewish. Since racial definitions of Judaism and the Jewish people have proved so convenient for the ideologies of the worst and most dangerous enemies of the Jewish people, especially in recent times, it is rather shocking that so many Jewish secularists would be so oblivious to the paradox of presenting definitions of Jews and Jewish culture that seem racial, if not actually racist.

Most Jewish secularists today are atheists of one sort or another. But the question is whether atheistic Jewish secularism can be considered Judaism in any way that makes sense either historically or ontologically. For this reason, then, it is easy to see why such avowed secularists cannot make any cultural claims on civil society that are not merely those of a human opinion group employing special pleading. Accordingly, they can only ask for entitlements from civil society, entitlements that civil society can take away *from* them as easily as it can give these entitlements *to* them. Denying historical and ontological priority, secularists must rely on social largesse inasmuch as they have no transcendent point of reference from which to truly demand human *rights* as prior claims. This is as much a problem for Jewish secularists in the State of Israel, who want to define the Jewish people and its culture in modern nationalistic terms, as it is for Jewish secularists in the Diaspora, who want to define the Jewish people in ethnic terms.[67] These secularist ideologies ignore too much Jewish tradi-

---

[66] For the now definitive biography of Spinoza, see S. M. Nadler, *Spinoza* (Cambridge: Cambridge University Press, 1999), esp. 153–54.

[67] Cf. Martin Buber, *Israel and Palestine*, trans. S. Godman (London: East and West Library, 1952), chap. 1.

tion to maintain any real Jewish continuity. That is why their adherents inevitably turn out to be poor advocates of Jewish cultural claims on civil society or Jewish national claims on the world. Jewish culture (including Jewish nationality and ethnicity) cannot be separated from Jewish religion. Nonreligious Jews who define themselves as "cultural Jews" have as little understanding of culture as they do of religion.[68] Perceptive Jews and non-Jews usually see that sooner or later.

The third way Jews can disengage from the traditional Jewish community is through what must be called "antinominianism." The disengagement of antinomians is far less radical than that of apostates, and even less radical than that of avowed secularists. Antinomianism might be defined as self-chosen religious doctrines that are contrary to the dogmas of traditional Judaism. Although traditional Judaism has very few dogmas, at least three can be discerned, especially when seen in the light of their modern denials. One, the Written Torah (minimally the Pentateuch), is the direct revelation of God (*torah min ha-shamayim*), even though there is much that can be said about the human transmission of the revealed text.[69] Two, the Jewish legal tradition (*halakhah*), often called the Oral Torah, is the normative interpretation, application, and supplement of the precepts of the Written Torah, even though there is much flexibility in that interpretation, application, and supplementation.[70] Three, the destiny of the Jewish people (and most likely all humankind with them) will not be fulfilled until the final redemption, including the bodily resurrection of the dead by God, even though that can hardly be described by any human mind short of it actually happening.[71]

Truth be told, modern liberal Judaisms have, in one way or another, rejected all three of these dogmas.[72] That is why it is not unjust to term

---

[68] See Neuhaus, *The Naked Public Square*, 27, 132; Novak, *Natural Law in Judaism*, 14–15.

[69] M. Sanhedrin 10.1. For traditionalist flexibility in understanding the human transmission of the Torah text, see David Weiss Halivni, *Revelation Restored* (Boulder, Colo.: Westview Press, 1997); B. Barry Levy, *Fixing God's Torah* (New York: Oxford University Press, 2001).

[70] B. Berakhot 5a re Exod. 24:12; Maimonides, MT: intro., and Mamrim, 1.1–2. For traditionalist understanding of halakhic flexibility, see Eliezer Berkovits, *Not in Heaven* (New York: KTAV, 1983).

[71] M. Sanhedrin 10.1; B. Berakhot 34b re Isa. 64:3. For the flexibility of Jewish eschatological speculation, see Novak, *The Election of Israel*, 152–62.

[72] This can be seen by looking at the official Torah translation and commentary published by even the most "conservative" of the nontraditionalist Judaisms, the largely American Conservative Movement: *Etz Hayyim* (New York: The Rabbinical Assembly and the United Synagogue of Conservative Judaism, 2001). Concerning the denial of Mosaic revelation of the Pentateuch, see 1406, 1477; cf. M. A. Meyer, *Response to Modernity: A History of the Reform Movement in Judaism* (New York: Oxford University Press, 1988), 273. Concerning the presumption of a right to change Jewish law at will, which, of course, denies the

them antinomian. Revelation has been denied when it is asserted that the Written Torah is a work *by* human beings, even "inspired" human beings, which means much less theologically than saying that the text of the Torah has been transmitted *through* human beings. The authority of the normative tradition has been denied when changes in the law have been made by fiat rather than by reasoned judicial interpretation and its inevitably conservative restraint. And the transcendent character of the final redemption has been denied when a "Messianic Age" of one sort or another has been proposed, which seems more like an idealistic human projection, a utopia, than an apocalyptic event. Nevertheless, all this is not apostasy inasmuch as these liberal Judaisms have not been presented by their proponents as entrances into the tradition of some other community. (In fact, I think liberal Judaisms have saved many modern Jews, who are not yet ready to fully retrieve the Jewish tradition, from apostasy or total assimilation into the secular world.) This is why those traditionalists who proclaim these liberal Judaisms are "not Judaism" are mistaken. Instead, it would be more accurate (and probably more effective) for Jewish traditionalists to try to persuade the followers of liberal Judaisms that their Judaisms are inadequate in the light of the full Jewish tradition, both in terms of their selective correspondence to the classical sources of Judaism, and in terms of what turns out to be their incoherent alternatives to the tradition. It is a needless insult to compare liberal Jews to apostates, and it is a needless compliment to apostates to see them as no different from liberal Jews.

Despite the fact that religiously liberal Jews do not espouse the atheism that has been espoused by so many secularist Jews, because of their inadequate notions of revelation, tradition, and redemption, the claims they make on civil society for Judaism are rarely any different from those made by secularist or "cultural" Jews. Lacking a truly transcendent source from which to make their religious-cultural claims, they are left with the immanent option of presenting themselves as a merely human opinion group, whose religion is an essentially private matter. In other words, they do not have enough of a consistent connection to the historical Jewish tradition, nor do they have a truly ontological point of reference beyond that

---

authoritative veto of the law for any innovation, no matter how attractive it might be to Jews in the present, see *Etz Hayyim*, 1478; cf. Meyer, *Response to Modernity*, 324. Concerning the designation of traditional Jewish eschatology as "mythic" rather than intending what is true, see *Etz Hayyim*, 388; cf. Meyer, *Response to Modernity*, 388. Thus one can see that whatever theological differences exist between the various liberal Judaisms today, they are matters of degree not of kind. On most social and political issues that are debated in civil society, they seem to speak in a voice rarely distinguishable from that of secularism per se.

of mere human projection from which to argue a fully Jewish case with conviction, even passion. In terms of political effect, therefore, liberal Jews cannot make claims on civil society that are as powerful or as consistent as the claims made by those traditional Jews who speak with more historical and ontological weight, and who know how to enter civil discourse intact, and also exit it intact.[73]

[73] Cf. T. Hagigah 2.4 and parallels.

Chapter Two

The Covenant

Covenant and Social Contract

It is quite easy to surmise that covenant (*berit*), which plays such a central role in scriptural revelation, is a form of the social contract so frequently discussed by modern thinkers. When first glancing at biblical covenants from a modern perspective, one could very well take the institution of covenant to be a precursor of modern ideas of social contract formulated in the political theories of philosophers from Hobbes to Rawls (and, perhaps, even earlier). Even now there are those who still use the two terms "contract" and "covenant" interchangeably.[1] But this is a serious mistake if one takes the English term "covenant," in its usual modern sense, to be a translation of the Hebrew term *berit* as it is used in Scripture.[2] A covenant in its original Hebrew sense is much more than a merely primitive contract, and a contract is much less than a more highly developed covenant. Neither term can be reduced to the other without great conceptual confusion.

Contract and covenant designate two different types of social, political, and legal relationships. The confusion of covenant and contract arose in early modernity, and it has found its way into some Jewish political theory as well.[3] Those who mistake a covenant for a contract inevitably overestimate the role of a social contract while simultaneously underestimating the role of the covenant, at least as far as Judaism is concerned. Here, though, we shall examine the original idea of covenant and see how it is

[1] See *Oxford English Dictionary*, 2nd ed. (Oxford: Clarendon Press, 1993), 3:1070b. Even the great medieval commentator R. Abraham ibn Ezra in his *Commentary on the Torah*: Gen. 6:18, ed. Weiser, p. 38, defines *berit* as a general "agreement" (*haskamah*), basing this etymology on the word *barah* as in 1 Sam. 17:8. Nevertheless, one could interpret his definition of *berit* to mean that in Scripture, anyway, all agreements are covenantal, which is different than saying all covenants are mere agreements.

[2] Some have questioned whether the term "covenant" itself is adequate to the Hebrew *berit*. See Roland de Vaux, *The Early History of Israel*, trans. D. Smith (Philadelphia: Westminster, 1978), 450–51. Nonetheless, I shall use the more religious connotation of "covenant," carefully distinguishing it from the more secular connotation of "contract."

[3] The confusion of covenant and contract is even made by some traditionalist Jewish thinkers, who erroneously assume that one can contract with God as one can contract with a human equal. For a critique, see D. Novak, *Jewish Social Ethics* (New York: Oxford University Press, 1992), 33–36.

prior to the idea of contract, especially prior to the idea of a social contract. Nevertheless, covenant and contract are not totally disparate since contracts can be seen as emerging from covenants. The very priority of covenant to contract within classical Jewish sources, beginning with Scripture, indicates that there is a relation between the two, not one of equality or identity but, rather, a hierarchal relation. Once these classical sources are examined and analyzed, the suspicion that the idea of a social contract is something imposed on Judaism from foreign sources might well be dispelled. Jews could not engage in social contracts with outsiders in good faith if they had no experience of social contracts among themselves.

The priority of covenant to contract in Judaism is historical, ontological, and teleological. Historically, any contract presupposes that there is a covenant already in place. Ontologically, the covenant already in place is always more foundational than the contract related to it. Teleologically, a contract is ultimately for the sake of the very covenant that made it possible. The covenant is, therefore, the past, present, and future of any contract. The covenant is the background, the ground, and the foreground of any contract.

To guide our examination and analysis of the phenomenon of *berit* or "covenant" in Scripture and the rabbinic tradition, let us begin with an ostensive definition of "covenant." The definition is fivefold: (1) A covenant is a perpetual relationship of mutual trust between two persons, who are either individual, collective, or both. (2) The terms of the covenant are stipulated by the initiating party for the party who accepts them; they are not negotiated between the parties. (3) Violation of covenantal stipulations does not terminate the covenant either automatically or by decree from a third person; it only entitles the offended person to demand rectification from the offending person, or from a third party. (4) The covenant cannot be terminated even by subsequent mutual agreement of the covenanting persons. (5) The covenant cannot be terminated by any subsequent event that might happen to the covenanting persons, short of the permanent disappearance of one or both persons.

A covenant begins with an initial promise and a promise in response, a mutual pledge, taken as an oath (*shevuʿah*) by each side.[4] Yet it cannot be terminated by breach of promise on either side. Even though conditions are stipulated within a covenant—"if you do this, I shall do that"—there is no condition of the covenant that could terminate the covenant itself if breached. Only rectification is possible, which often requires adjudication. Yet there is no possibility of a judgment whose conclusion warrants secession from the covenant, with or without penalties. In plain language, the personal parties to a covenant are stuck with each other. There is no

---

[4] See R. David Kimhi (Radaq), *Commenatary on the Latter Prophets*: Isa. 54:9–10.

chance for divorce. All problems have to be worked out within the norms of the covenant itself. There are no exit or termination clauses. The covenant itself can only be wounded; it cannot be destroyed from without or self-destruct from within. And even its deepest wounds can be healed now or in the future.

Thus when the people of Israel in exile in Babylonia after the destruction of the First Temple in 586 B.C.E. claim that "we shall become like the nations [ke-goyim] like the families of the other lands serving idols of wood and stone" (Ezekiel 20:32), the prophet Ezekiel brings them the following message from God: "As I live . . . I shall rule [emlokh] over you. . . . As I contended [nishpateti] with your ancestors in the Wilderness of the land of Egypt, so shall I contend with you" (20:33, 36). Here it is assumed that the sin of worshiping the Golden Calf was Israel's archetypal attempt to release itself from its covenantal obligations to God. But, just as it could not do this in the time of Moses in the wilderness of the desert, so it cannot do it in the time of Ezekiel in the wilderness of the exile.[5] But in the Exodus account of what transpired between God and Israel in the incident of the Golden Calf, the emphasis is more on Moses' threat to God of what will happen to God's authority in the world if God destroys Israel for its sin, thus releasing God from his covenantal obligation. "Why should Egypt be able to say that it was for ill [be-raʿah] that He brought them [Israel] out to kill them in the mountains and to wipe them off the face of the earth?" (Exodus 32:2). Indeed, Israel wants to die in the Wilderness if God will not lead them in their journey in the world. "If Your Presence [panekha] does not go with us, do not bring us up out of this place" (33:15). So, from both sides of the covenant, termination of the relationship is a moral impossibility either by God or by humans.

The moral impossibility of any Jew releasing himself or herself from covenantal obligation is emphasized in the medieval interpretation of the talmudic statement: "Even [afʿal-pi] when Israel sins, he is still Israel."[6] Though this statement might well have originally been meant to counter Christian supersessionist claims that because of their sins God had rejected Israel in favor of the Church, since the eleventh century it came to mean: No matter what any Jew does, even converting to another religion, one cannot nullify his or her covenantal identity.[7] And as for the moral

---

[5] This is what is called "being bound by the covenant" [masoret ha-berit] in Ezek. 20:37. See R. David Kimhi (Radaq), *Commentary on the Latter Prophets* thereon.

[6] B. Sanhedrin 44a re Josh. 7:11. For further discussion of the historical career of this statement, see D. Novak, *The Election of Israel* (Cambridge: Cambridge University Press, 1995), 189–99.

[7] This new meaning was the result of the responsum of Rashi, *Teshuvot Rashi*, ed. I. Elfenbein (New York: n.p., 1943), no. 171. See, also, *Midrash Agagdah*: Mattot re Num. 31:19, ed. Buber, p. 162; R. Isaac Abravanel, *Commentary on the Torah*: Deut. 29:9–14.

impossibility of God releasing himself from his own covenantal obligation, it is pointed out in the Talmud that because God took his covenantal
oath in his own name (Exodus 32:13), there is no possible dispensation
from the oath.[8] In the case of oaths taken by humans, there is always the
possibility of dispensation from an oath from a higher court.[9] In God's
case, of course, there is no such higher court.

Generically, a contract is like a covenant in that it is a relationship of
trust between two parties, either individual or collective. Specifically,
though, a contract differs from a covenant in the following five ways: (1)
A contract is not perpetual; it can be negotiated for a finite period of time.
It has both a *terminus a quo* and a *terminus ad quem*.[10] (2) A contract has
conditions negotiated by the parties themselves that, if violated, automatically terminate the contract.[11] (3) A contract can be terminated by subsequent agreement between the parties, even without violation of prior conditions by either party.[12] (4) A contract can be terminated by subsequent
accidents beyond the control of either party.[13] (5) The parties to a contract
function as equals, at least as far as the contract is concerned.[14]

The term *berit* is used in Scripture to designate five kinds of interpersonal relationships: (1) a relationship between God and humans; (2) a
relationship between humans themselves; (3) a relationship between God
and Israel or the Jewish people; (4) a relationship between Jews themselves; (5) a relationship between Jews and gentiles. Whether or not all of
these agreements (*britot*) comply with the pure definition of a covenant
remains to be seen.

Despite the fact that the term *berit* is used to designate all five of the
relationships mentioned above, there are only two such covenants that

[8] B. Berakhot 32a. See *Tanhuma*: Nitsavim, ed. Buber, 25a re Cant. 7:6; also, D. Novak,
Halakhah in a Theological Dimension (Chico, Calif.: Scholars Press, 1985), 124–30.

[9] See B. Nedarim 22b and 28a; Maimonides, MT: Nedarim, 4.5–6.

[10] See T. Ketubot 9.3; Maimonides, MT: Sheluhim ve-Shuttfin, 4.4 and R. Joseph Karo,
Kesef Mishneh thereon.

[11] See B. Nedarim 27a–b; Maimonides, MT: Mekhirah, 11.1–7 for acceptable and unacceptable contractual conditions.

[12] See B. Baba Metsia 105a.

[13] See Maimonides, MT: Sanhedrin, 7.10 and R. Joseph Karo, *Kesef Mishneh* thereon re
Y. Kiddushin 3.2/63d. It is only when a contract's retroactive effectiveness is negotiated by
the parties in advance to be contingent on accidental circumstances (called *asmakhta*, lit.
"contingency") that the contract is invalid. See B. Baba Metsia 66a and parallels.

[14] So, e.g., instead of A lending money to B, where there is always the possibility of violating the prohibition of giving and taking interest (Lev. 25:36; Deut. 23:20; B. Baba Metsia
75b), it is better for A to enter a contractual partnership with B (called *eseq*, lit. "involvement"). This contract has the effect of equalizing the roles of the two partners (A being the
"capital partner" and B the "working partner"), which is a sharp contrast with the essentially hierarchal relation of lender and borrower. See M. Baba Metsia 5.5; Maimonides, MT:
Sheluhin ve-Shuttfin, 6.1.

could be termed "*the* covenant" (*ha-berit*) in the pure sense of that term. First, there is the *Noahide covenant*, which is God's perpetual relationship with humankind after its near destruction in the Flood, from which only Noah and his family survived as the progenitors of humankind restored. That relationship is consummated by the perpetual human acceptance of what can be seen as God's universal law (and what some have called "natural law").[15] Then there is the *Sinaitic covenant*, which is God's relationship with Israel, consummated by the revelation of the Torah at Mount Sinai. Conversely, the other three covenants—those between humans, between Jews, and between Jews and non-Jews—all require one of these *master covenants* as their past or background, their foundation or ground, and their future or foreground. Both of these master covenants are seen as being perpetual (*berit olam*), so that the Noahide covenant is called "everlasting" (Genesis 9:6) and the Sinaitic covenant is called "everlasting" (I Chronicles 16:17). Furthermore, an essential difference between the two master covenants and the three derivative covenants is that the persons who are parties to the master covenants cannot be equal, but must be different in kind since one is divine and the other human. But in the three derivative covenants, because both parties are human, they are both usually equal, at least for the life of the covenant between them. And when they are unequal, their inequality is one of degree rather than of kind.

As for the relation of the two master covenants themselves, the Noahide covenant and the Sinaitic covenant, one could arguably assert that the Sinatic covenant presupposes the Noahide covenant, not as its ground but as a necessary precondition for its acceptance by humans. That is, if Israel had not considered itself bound by the universal law of God perpetuated by the Noahide covenant with humankind on earth, it would have been in no position to conscientiously accept the more singular law of God revealed at Sinai to it and for it.

Let us now examine and analyze the first of the two master covenants: the Noahide covenant.

The Noahide Covenant

We know that in the ancient Near Eastern milieu in which Scripture was written, a covenant itself was usually initiated and sustained by an oath or sacred promise (*shevuʿah*) made in the name of a god.[16] Although we know that among themselves gentiles took oaths in the names of various gods, it seems that in any one mutual covenant the parties had to be able

[15] See D. Novak, *Natural Law in Judaism* (Cambridge: Cambridge University Press, 1998), esp. 36–39.

[16] See D. J. McCarthy, *Treaty and Covenant* (Rome: Pontifical Biblical Institute, 1963), 169.

to acknowledge the same god in order for their respective oaths to be cogent.[17] Without that common godly invocation, their bilateral pact could be initiated at cross purposes by the separate parties, thus lacking the type of unconditional commitment a covenant requires. Worshipers of one god had no good reason to believe that worshipers of another god would be trustworthy, indeed, whether they could be trustworthy. Perhaps their different gods were at war with one another, a war in which treachery rather than fidelity and fairness to another was the norm. Moreover, perhaps the "other" god did not require trustworthiness, especially if that god himself or herself did not appear to be an exemplar of trustworthy justice.

This is why Abraham had to be assured that the God who had just initiated a singular covenant with him was indeed "the judge of all the earth" (Genesis 18:25), namely, the One who practices consistent "justice" (*mishpat*) and who is, therefore, the paradigm of trust to be trusted, obeyed, and imitated in his trustworthiness (*emunah*) by humans created in his image.[18] Indeed, it seems that only the creator God could be this paradigm of trust because only the creator God has the power to keep his promise under all circumstances. Any lesser "god" would be subject to forces beyond his or her control, forces that could prevent the covenantal promise from being fulfilled. The Noahide paradigm of God as maker of covenantal promises is emphasized by Isaiah. "As I swore [*nishba'ti*] that the waters of Noah would never flood the earth again, so do I swear . . . my loyalty [*hasdi*] shall not depart and my covenant of peace [*u-vrit shlomi*] will not be shaken" (Isaiah 54:9–10).

Only the God who is the creator of the world could have promised humankind at the time of Noah that he would sustain the earth for human habitation by not letting humankind ever become as thoroughly corrupt

---

[17] Many commentators (e.g., R. Abraham ibn Ezra, R. Joseph Bekhor Shor, R. Isaac Abravanel, Moses Mendelssohn) interpret Gen. 31:55 ("May the God [*elohei*] of Abraham and the [*elohei*] God of Nahor judge between us") to mean that Jacob and Laban were invoking different gods in their respective covenantal oaths (see Josh. 24:2). But from a rabbinic perspective, how could Jacob be seen as participating in a covenantal oath involving another god (see B. Sanhedrin 63b re Exod. 23:13)? Yet the rabbinic source upon which these interpretations are based (*Beresheet Rabbah* 74.16; *Soferim* 4.5) simply indicates that "God of Nahor" is "secular" usage (*hol*) whereas "God of Abraham" is "sacred" usage (*qodesh*). What is the difference? *Elohim* either directly refers to God or indirectly refers to God as mediated by a human judge (see B. Sanhedrin 66a re Exod. 22:27; also, ibid., 7a re Ps. 82:1; B. Shabbat 10a re Exod. 18:13). Hence two different gods are not being invoked here. Rather, the same God is being invoked differently by Jacob in the name of his grandfather Abraham, and by Laban in the name of his grandfather Nahor (see Gen. 22:20–23; 24:23, 29). Laban might well have worshiped other gods (see Gen. 31:19; 35:2). Nonetheless, one can also assume that he also worshiped the same God as did Jacob, hence they both could take covenantal oaths together in good faith. Jacob's relationship with this same God is simply more direct than Laban's. For a later treatment of the problem of whose God is being invoked, see 206–9.

[18] See Novak, *The Election of Israel*, 120–28.

as the generation of the Flood had indeed become (Genesis 8:21–22). Only this God demonstrated such power and faithful concern for his creation. The fact of cosmic order is taken to be the demonstration of God's powerful fidelity. God is "the maker of heaven and earth, the sea and all that is in it, keeping faith [*ha-shomer emet*] forever" (Psalms 146:6). That faithful concern is most explicitly demonstrated in the natural law God provides for the cosmos. It is what other creatures do instinctively, but what human creatures are to do consciously and freely. "Behold God is exalted in power; who can make law [*moreh*] like him? Who can prescribe the way for him; who can say 'you have done wrong [*avlah*]'? Remember to exalt his work . . . which humans see but from afar" (Job 36:22–24).

Divine Interest in the Covenant

The question that needs to be asked now is: Why does a covenant between human parties require an oath in the name of the creator God in order to be valid?

The usual explanation is that a covenant is accompanied by an oath because the God invoked functions as both witness and enforcer of the covenantal obligations in situations beyond human ken or control. God functions, then, as the one witness who is able to discern the sincerity of the covenantal partners, and as the one enforcer who is able to discern their covenantal transgressions however much they are hidden from human view. As witness and enforcer God is able to prevent or rectify violations of the covenant however and wherever they might occur. To be sure, all of this is true, but it is incomplete nonetheless.[19] Recalling these divine interventions is not a sufficient explanation of why an oath is an essential component, indeed the primary component, of a covenant. Left at this level, such an explanation inevitably allows some theologically dubious inferences to be made.

If God were only the witness and enforcer of the covenant, we would then have the theologically dubious inference that God becomes, in effect, the agent of the relationship created by the human parties to the covenant. A witness functions as the agent of the community who enables the community in the person of an enforcer to rectify breaches of the common good. The common good of a covenanted community is covenantal peace (*shalom*).[20] As enforcer of the covenant, so understood—the cosmic po-

---

[19] Any false oath is a denial of God as omniscient witness. See *Sifra*: Vayiqra, ed. Weiss, 27d re Lev. 5:21–22 and commentary of R. Abraham ben David (Ravad) thereon. God's faithfulness (*emunato*) is not only the guarantor of a human transaction but, even more important, it is the model for the faithfulness that transaction is supposed to emulate.

[20] See B. Sanhedrin 6b re Zech. 8:16.

liceman as it were—God would be carrying out the rectifying orders of the community itself. Obviously, this turns God into the servant of the community, servant rather than the Lord (*adon*) Abraham declared him to be in the world.[21] In this role, God is not even "the judge [*ha-shofet*] of all the earth" (Genesis 18:25) in its deepest sense. In this role God is, in effect, a civil servant.

Confining God to the role of witness and enforcer avoids the most basic theological questions: Why would God be interested in a covenant between two human parties, anyway? Why would God allow his name to be invoked in the oath that gives an interhuman covenant its authority? Would God allow his name to be *used* as one would use any other disposable human instrument?[22]

What needs to be emphasized here is that God does not enforce essentially human agreements promised in his name. Rather, human promises are to be modeled on God's covenantal promise to humankind. Human care in promising one to another presupposes God's care in what must be seen as the cosmic promise. This original covenant, rooted in the promise of God, is not a postulate of an essentially interhuman agreement.[23] It cannot be stipulated by humans; they can only invoke it.

The covenant is what God gives *to* creation. It is not something negotiated *with* creation.[24] Thus in the first translation of Scripture into a non-Jewish language, the Greek Septuagint, the Hebrew *berit* is consistently translated as *diathēkē*, literally "what has been set down in-between," not as *synthēkē*, literally "what has been set down together."[25] A *diathēkē* is a "testament" as when a father turns over his estate to his son.[26] This transmission is not negotiated with the son; the son simply takes what has been given to him, indeed what might very well be forced upon him.

What was the purpose of God's covenantal promise never again to flood or destroy the earth as God almost did during the generation of the Flood, a flood that wiped out all of humankind, with the exception of

[21] See B. Berakhot 7b re Gen. 15:8; *Sifre: Devarim*, no. 313 re Gen. 24:2.

[22] Although "taking the name of the Lord in vain" (Exod. 20:7) is seen by the Rabbis to essentially mean one who swears falsely about something in the past (B. Shevuot 20b), it is also given a secondary meaning, viz., anyone who invokes the name of God needlessly or carelessly (see B. Berakhot 33a; Maimonides, MT: Shevuot, 12.11).

[23] This was the logic of Hermann Cohen's very Jewish critique of Kant's notion of God as a postulate of pure practical reason, viz., a postulated God cannot be the Absolute in any true sense. See Novak, *The Election of Israel*, 54–55, 59–60.

[24] See E. Jenni and C. Westermann, *Theological Lexicon of the Old Testament*, trans. M. E. Biddle (Peabody, Mass.: Hendrickson Publishers, 1997), 1:258–59, 262–64.

[25] See W. F. Arndt and F. W. Gingrich, A Greek-English Lexicon of the New Testament (Chicago: University of Chicago Press, 1957), 183; also, G.W.H. Lampe, *A Patristic Greek Lexicon* (Oxford: Clarendon Press, 1961), 348.

[26] See M. Baba Batra 8.6; B. Baba Batra 135b.

Noah and his family, and that made the earth, at that time, uninhabitable? And this question leads us to recall why God almost did destroy all humankind—namely, all humankind had violated elementary norms designed for inner-human justice, both communal-political and familial-sexual. It is assumed that humankind, in any society, cannot violate these basic norms without disastrous social consequences. The generation of the Flood are the children of Cain, this time as the collective heirs of his individual, paradigmatic character. So, "the earth became full of violence [*hamas*] . . . all flesh had destroyed [*hish'heet*] its way on earth" (Genesis 6:11), just as Cain shed his brother's blood, which cried up from the ground to God for justice (4:10).[27] Clearly, humankind already knew what its way or nature on earth was to be, and they perverted it nonetheless.[28] This had worldly consequences. As such, humankind no longer deserved the earth for their habitation, which, as Isaiah put it, God had "made to be a dwelling [*la-shevet*] not a wasteland [*tohu*]" (Isaiah 45:18).[29]

Due to the earlier human violation of the cosmic order by their violent perversity (Genesis 6:12–13), Noah and his family, as the few humans who had survived the Flood in the Ark, and who were therefore the progenitors of humankind renewed and restored to their earthly habitation, had to be reassured that "the seasons of the earth . . . would not cease [*lo yishbotu*]" (Genesis 8:22). In other words, they had to see moral law as their inclusion in the law by which God governs the cosmos, and that divine law itself would prevail in heaven and on earth no matter how much some humans might ever violate it again. After the Flood, God promises better enforcement of his own law. God is thus interested in his name being used in interhuman covenantal promises because that will enhance human imitation of God as world builder. The image of God will better reflect God's creative activity in and for the world.

This is why, it seems, the Noahide covenant, when initiated immediately upon humankind's return to its earthly habitation, actually begins with the reiteration of God's concern for the violent shedding of human blood, a concern that emphasizes that God will not allow injustice to prevail. "Of man, too, I shall require a reckoning [*edrosh*] for human life [*nefesh ha'adam*], of every man for that of his fellow man" (Genesis 9:5).[30] The prohibition of human bloodshed is here assumed as it was in the case of Cain, the first human to shed the blood of a fellow human.

[27] See B. Sanhedrin 108a.

[28] See ibid., 58a re Gen. 2:24.

[29] This verse is taken to be a general commandment to procreate in a familial way. See M. Gittin 4.5.

[30] See Maimonides, MT: Rotseah, 2.3, where it is emphasized that the scope of divinely effected justice is far greater than the human punishment of violent criminals.

Here too God presents himself as the prime lawgiver, and the ultimate judge of whether his law of antiviolence has been kept or not. "Where is Abel your brother?" (Genesis 4:9) is the question of a judge asking a defendant in a trial to plead innocent or guilty.[31]

Divine justice is total; human justice at best is partial, the latter an inclusion in God's effecting of justice in the cosmos. This is why human courts only function as God's agents in punishing bloodshed committed before human witnesses (Genesis 9:6).[32] Even though God can certainly effect justice wherever and whenever, it would seem that just as the human victim must be avenged because he or she is in the image of God, so must a human community, through its courts of justice, function in the image of God effecting justice on God's behalf. Without that participation in the administration of cosmic justice on earth, such human inaction could only suggest communal indifference to the plight of the victims of human violence. "Silence is tantamount to agreement," in the language of the Talmud.[33] Thus in the story of Noah and his family, who have returned intact from the ravages of the universal Flood, the reason for both the prohibition of bloodshed of the innocent and the punishment of those guilty of such bloodshed is given: "[I]n the image of God are humans made" (Genesis 9:6). Since humans are the only creatures capable of a conscious and free relationship with God, they alone can be directly protected by God and by one another.[34] Those who harm them are to be punished through the due process of law as Cain was punished in a trial conducted by God.[35]

Law is primarily administered by God who gave it, sometimes with the assistance of humans to whom it has been given. Nevertheless, the final and complete justice belongs to God not to humans. "Justice per se [ha-mishpat] belongs to God" (Deuteronomy 1:17). Whenever human adjudication is appropriate and thus required, the judges are to remember that "it is not for humans that you judge but for the Lord, who is with you in matters of justice" (2 Chronicles 19:6).[36] As the one who is "the first" and the one who is "the last" (Isaiah 44:6), God is both the primary subject of the verb "to do justice" (asot mishpat—Micah 6:8) and the ultimate object of that justice. All justice is first done by God; all human justice is finally done for God; all human injustice is finally done against God. Thus when the people of Israel want to renew their covenant with God through the prophet Jeremiah, they say "[L]et the Lord be a true

[31] See Rashi, Commentary on the Torah thereon.
[32] See Novak, Jewish Social Ethics, 163–64.
[33] B. Yevamot 87b.
[34] See Novak, Natural Law in Judaism, 167–73.
[35] See M. Sanhedrin 4.5 re Gen. 4:10.
[36] See B. Sanhedrin 6b.

and faithful witness [*l ͨed emet ve-ne'eman*] against us if we do not do everything the Lord your God has sent us" (Jeremiah 42:5). By that pledge, the people are asking God to enforce his law for them, not that God should be invoked to enforce somebody else's law. Like the Noahide law, the law of Sinai did not originate in a human promise made before God; it originated in a promise God made to humans, in this case the promise God made to Israel. Any oath humans take to obey the law of God and implement it is only a confirmation of what God had already promised to them.[37]

It would seem, then, that the purpose of God's initial covenant is to assure humankind that they can dwell on earth justly, thereby deserving God's earth as their dwelling by furthering God's creation with the enhancement of life rather than the retarding of it by the pursuit of death. The covenantal promise means that God will not let things get so out of hand universally as he did during the generation of the Flood. Only localities like Sodom can forfeit their right to earthly habitation. But like Noah during the Flood, Lot and his family are enabled by God to escape before the deluge (Genesis 19:13–26).[38]

Interhuman Covenants

Let us now look at a covenant between humans that Scripture treats as an ordinary occurrence in ancient times. From this example we can see how serious covenant making was taken in the cultural and political climate in which Judaism first emerged historically. And this interhuman covenant is grounded in the Noahide covenant between God and humankind.

At the beginnings of Israelite history, when the people start out as a bedouin clan, Abraham, the first patriarch, concludes an agreement, called a *berit*, with Abimelech, a local chieftain in Canaan, someone with whom Abraham and his clan have had some serious misunderstandings in the immediate past over familial and territorial matters. The agreement is proposed to Abraham by Abimelech. Although, in principle, this agreement could have been proposed by Abraham to Abimelech, in fact it probably had to be initiated by Abimelech since he was the older settler

---

[37] See B. Nedarim 7b–8a re Ps. 119:106.

[38] According to one rabbinic comment (*Beresheet Rabbah* 51.8 re Gen. 19:31), the daughters of Lot committed incest with their father, which was one of the sins that brought the Flood as punishment (see B. Sanhedrin 57a re Gen. 6:11 and Rashi, s.v. "ki hish'heet"), because they were convinced the world was coming to an end as it had during the Flood. In other words, disbelief in God's promise to maintain the world, no matter what humans might do, can lead to the justification of any human action done in desperation. See R. David Kimhi (Radaq), *Commentary on the Latter Prophets*: Isa. 23:13.

in Canaan. It is the first example given in Scripture as to how an interhuman covenant is made.

Abimelech says to Abraham: "God [*elohim*] is with you in everything you do. Therefore swear to me here by God that you will not deceive [*im tishqor*] me or my kith and kin, but will deal with me and with the land in which you have sojourned as loyally [*ka-hesed*] as I have dealt with you" (Genesis 21:22–23).[39] This narrative concludes by reporting that "the two of them made a covenant" (Genesis 21:27), literally "cut [*va-yikhretu berit*] a covenant," which probably refers to the preparation of a sacrificial animal for a joint cultic act consummating the covenant between the two parties before God.

Despite the fact that Abraham had entered into a special covenant made directly with God, one for which the distinguishing sign of circumcision had already been prescribed, in this interhuman covenant with Abimelech he does not claim any special status because of that special covenant. He does not invoke God's direct election of him and his descendants. Furthermore, he does not invoke God's promise of the entire land of Canaan to his own descendants (Genesis 17:1–14). Abraham and Abimelech basically function as two human equals. Their agreement is very much a bilateral pact. It is an agreement between equals inasmuch as Abraham does not make any claims on Abimelech that the head of any other clan at that time could not have made as well. This type of covenant, then, seems to be one generally in practice at the time. It is an agreement of trust, a fidelity pact that anyone in a situation similar to that of Abraham and Abimelech could enter for their own interests. So, even though Abimelech recognizes Abraham's greater closeness to God, the name of God Abimelech uses here is not the name used in scripture to denote God's unique covenant with Israel (YHWH). This type of special recognition does not come until Moses makes the claim on Pharaoh in the name of God as the redeemer of Israel: "Let my people go!" (Exodus 5:1). Instead, Abimelech invokes the universal name of God (*elohim*). This name designates God to be the universally acknowledged creator, lawgiver, and judge. "Surely there is a judging God on earth" (Psalms 58:12).

Abimelech's recognition of Abraham's superiority is a recognition only of his religious superiority. Nevertheless, this does not lead Abraham to claim any special political privileges for himself from Abimelech. Their political status is equal. Accepting Abraham's status as "a prophet" (Genesis 20:7) means that Abraham has a personal relationship with God that makes his prayers more effective. It might even mean that Abraham is an

---

[39] Note D. J. Elazar, *Covenant and Polity in Biblical Israel* (New Brunswick, N.J.: Transaction Publishers, 1995), 71: "*Hesed* is the operative term in a covenant relationship, which translates the bare fact of covenant into a dynamic relationship."

especially enlightened teacher of God's moral law.[40] Yet that moral law
of God is not one to which Abraham has to introduce Abimelech. He only
has to remind him of it. This is also why Abraham can admonish Abimelech about a robbery committed by Abimelech's servants. Abimelech protests that this is something of which he had been unaware until Abraham
had so informed him. "I did not know who did this thing; moreover,
neither did you tell me nor did I hear about it any time except today"
(Genesis 21:26). Like Abraham, though, it is assumed Abimelech recognizes that robbery is a moral offense rectified by law. He had not yet been
told the facts by Abraham and he has not heard them from somebody
else. Nevertheless, he knows the law and is ready to adjudicate the case
based on that universal law.[41] He knows and acknowledges that justice
must be done, and is aware of what that justice is in this particular case.

Just before the conclusion of the covenant between them, Abimelech
had protested Abraham's assumption that the abduction and rape of mar-
ried women is tolerated, even approved of, in Abimelech's society, the
society he rules. Abraham's willingness to pray for Abimelech (Genesis
20:17), and his willingness to covenant with him (Genesis 21:32), indicate
that both of them occupy a common moral universe, and, as such, they
can live together in an ongoing political relationship. Each member of
this covenant is able to morally admonish the other. This is why, earlier,
Abimelech could protest Abraham's assumption that "surely there is no
fear of God [yir'at elohim] in this place" (Genesis 20:11). "Fear of God"
denotes a proper moral climate in any society.[42] Thus Abraham's willingness to forgive the unwitting offense against Sarah, when Abimelech took
her away from her husband and placed her in his harem (Genesis 20:2–
3, 16), constitutes his admission that he was wrong to condemn the moral
climate in Abimelech's society. There is "fear of God in this place" after
all, hence Abraham is now able to authentically enter a covenant with the
leader of such a place. Their common moral universe makes a permanent,

[40] See B. Baba Kama 92a re Gen. 20:7. Cf. B. Makkot 9b.

[41] In *Midrash ha-Gadol: Beresheet*, ed. Margulies, p. 343, "the seven lambs" mentioned
in Gen. 21:30, which Abimelech offered to Abraham, are seen as representative of "the
seven commandments the Noahides were commanded, which were in force [nohagot] in
that generation." Even though the number seven was not determined as the number of the
Noahide commandments until the late 2nd century C.E. (see D. Novak, *The Image of the
Non-Jew in Judaism* [New York and Toronto: Edwin Mellen Press, 1983], 28–35), this
midrash assumes from the interaction of Abraham and Abimelech that some universal law
was in place then. It is understandable why some Rabbis saw the number later assumed to
be the number of these universal laws here in this early scriptural text.

[42] See, e.g., Exod. 1:15–21; LXX on 1:15; Josephus, *Antiquities of the Jews*, 2.206;
R. Isaac Abravanel, *Commentary on the Torah* thereon; R. Samuel David Luzzatto (Shadal),
Commentary on the Torah thereon; Deut. 25:18 and, also, Rashi, *Commentary on the
Torah* thereon.

unconditional inter-national treaty between them possible. This seems to be the reason that Abraham's son Isaac could renew that covenant with Abimelech or his successor (Genesis 26:27–30).

Whether this covenant between Abraham's clan and Abimelech's could be violated with impunity by the Israelites was the subject of some considerable rabbinic discussion. The question hinges on whether or not Abimelech is representative of all the Philistine clans in the land of Israel. If he is taken to represent them all, then how can one justify subsequent wars of conquest conducted with the Philistines by the Israelites?[43] Some Rabbis, though, did not consider Abimelech a representative of all the Philistines, hence the covenant with his clan was not violated by subsequent wars with the other Philistine clans.[44] This covenant was permanent and inviolable. Some other Rabbis saw the covenant with Abimelech as terminable, having been initially intended to last for only three generations.[45] As such, it seems to have been more like a contract than a covenant in the strict sense of the term and as it has been used in this book. Furthermore, as regards at least one Philistine clan, the Avvim, it was argued by those who assumed the covenant with Abimelech included all the Philistine clans in the land of Israel, that the Israelites could conquer their land because the Avvim had already been displaced from it by a Canaanite nation, a nation with whom there was no covenant nor could there be one (Exodus 34:12; Deuteronomy 7:2).[46] Thus neither this Philistine clan nor the Israelites violated the covenant between them. Rather, the covenant was already terminated for them by the elimination of one of the parties by a third nation (enabled to do so by divine providence), one who could replace the Avvim in their former land, but who could not replace them in their inviolable covenant with Israel.

One can perhaps see those Rabbis who were uncomfortable with the idea of the inviolability of the covenant with Abimelech as also uncomfortable with the idea of there being any unconditional relationship between Jews and gentiles. On the other hand, those Rabbis who were able to explain the difference between the covenantal status of Abimelech's

---

[43] One view (B. Sotah 9b–10a re Judg. 13:5 and Rashi s.v. "huhal shevu'ato") is that this covenant had been violated by the Philistines during the time of Samson, hence the Israelites were justified in releasing themselves from any further prohibition of aggression against the Philistines.

[44] *Sifre*: Devarim, no. 72; *Pirqei de-Rabbi Eliezer*, chap. 36; R. Samson of Sens's comment on B. Sotah 10a re Rashi, *Commentary on the Former Prophets*: 2 Sam. 5:6, also: Josh. 15:63.

[45] *Beresheet Rabbah* 54.2 re Gen. 21:23 (alluding to Y. Baba Batra 9.3/17a); *Mekhilta*: Be-shalah, ed. Horovitz-Rabin, p. 76 re Exod. 13:17; Nahmanides, *Commentary on the Torah*: Deut. 2:23.

[46] B. Hullin 60b re Deut. 2:23 and Rashi, *Commentary on the Torah*: Deut. 2:23.

clan and the non-covenantal status of the other Philistine clans were closer to the explicit use of the term *berit* used by Scripture in this case, and they were perhaps more comfortable with the idea of an authentic covenant between Jews and gentiles as something that could occur again.

In contrast to the covenant with Abimelech, especially when considered authentic, we can see why Abraham refuses to covenant with the king of Sodom (Genesis 14:21–24), Sodom being a city "whose sin is very excessive" (Genesis 18:20). That sin is accepted as moral in Sodom is evidenced by the way the Sodomites abuse strangers in their midst (Genesis 19:4–5). With societies like this, any dealings Abraham has to have with them are conducted on a purely commercial basis. In a commercial transaction, unlike in a covenant, after the exchange is concluded and the money and object of purchase change hands, there is no further relationship between the parties. This explains why Abraham insists on paying the Hittites for a cave in which he wants to bury his wife Sarah (Genesis 23:16), even though the Hittites seem to have been interested in a more covenant-like relationship with him (23:6).

From the scriptural evidence, we see that Abraham could enter a covenant with some people but not with others. This means that at least some people in his world were worshipers of this one universal God, too. Accordingly, the criterion for whether to enter a covenant or not was determined by whether the covenantal oath could be taken in the name of the God commonly acknowledged to be "creator [*qoneh*] of heaven and earth" (Genesis 14:19), as was the case with Melchizedek, priest-king of Salem, whose blessing Abraham readily accepted.[47] Therefore, Abraham's differences with his fellow monotheists were of degree not kind—his greater closeness to God did not mean they had no God at all. Accordingly, Abraham and his fellow monotheists could make covenants with one another in good faith.

Being a "fearer of God" meant that others could assume that one would not lie when taking an oath, when making a covenantal promise. Even before Sinai, it could be assumed that God-fearing persons would "not swear by My name deceitfully" (Leviticus 19:12) and that those who swore deceitfully were not, therefore, God-fearing persons.[48] This is why Abraham can make his servant Eliezer his fiduciary agent to obtain a wife for Abraham's son Isaac among his old clan in Padan Aram. He can assume that Eliezer will be faithful to the promise he has been asked to make in the name of "the God of heaven, the God of the earth" (Genesis 24:3), and that Abraham's old clan will appreciate how much this mission

[47] See *Bemidbar Rabbah* 4.6 re Gen. 14:18.
[48] See *Tanhuma*: Mattot, no. 1 re Exod. 20:7, ed. Buber, p. 79a.

is authorized by the one who is their God too (Genesis 24:48–50). But one could not assume this about the Canaanites or Amorites, who are seen as incorrigibly sinful (Genesis 15:16; Leviticus 18:27–28). So, it seems the only acceptable covenantal partner is one with whom the covenantal oath could be jointly taken in the name of the God both partners could acknowledge as "the transcendent God [*el elyon*], creator [*qoneh*] of heaven and earth" (Genesis 14:22). This is why Abraham invokes this God when he tells the king of Sodom why he cannot, in effect, enter into a long-term, covenant-like relationship with him similar to the one he has just confirmed with Melchizedek.

That also explains why Jacob was so upset when his sons Simeon and Levi avenged the abduction and rape of their sister Dinah by the prince of Shechem: "You have made trouble for me by making me odious [*le-hav'eesheni*] among the inhabitants of the land" (Genesis 34:30). As far as the public was concerned, his sons had broken the agreement between his people and the people of Shechem; they had broken what was meant to be a "brotherly covenant [*berit ahim*]" (Amos 1:9). That agreement was ratified by both parties in spite of the abduction and rape of Dinah. Moreover, it seems to have been proposed as a sacred or covenantal agreement since its prerequisite was circumcision (Genesis 34:14–15), which was the sign of the covenant between Abraham and God (17:10–11). Nevertheless, when the brothers justify violating what was never meant to be an agreement at all (Genesis 34:13) by the retort, "[S]hould our sister be treated as a whore?!" (34:31), they seem to be saying that people who would let their prince abduct and rape a woman with impunity could not have been a party to any such covenantal agreement in good faith. The moral prerequisites for making a covenant are absent in their case, and it can be assumed that these moral prerequisites are known universally. Simeon and Levi seem to be arguing with their father that a covenant with the people of Shechem is no more valid than a covenant with the people of Sodom. In both cases, there could be no mutual acknowledgment of the Noahide covenant and the law it perpetually establishes.[49]

As for Abraham and Abimelech, what they are doing in their covenant is extending God's universal justice into their own particular political situation. They are negotiating the conditions that will enable their clans to live in peace with one another. This is taken to be a creative transaction; indeed, one of the etymologies suggested for the Hebrew word *berit*, that of the great thirteenth-century theologian and exegete Nahmanides, is

---

[49] See Maimonides, MT: Melakhim, 9.14.

that it comes from the verb *bar'o*: "to create."[50] As such, it is very much a relationship of *imitatio Dei*, an emulation of God's creativity in making the earth fit, both physically and socially, for peaceful human habitation. Abraham and Abimelech can trust each other's promises because each of them trusts God's universal promise, thus confirming the law the promised covenant brings with it.

The conditions of the covenant, which Abraham and Abimelech did make for themselves, have moral authority because they are modeled on the original Noahide covenant Abraham and Abimelech did not make for themselves, and which could not have been made by anyone other than God. This original covenant was made by God for humankind, not by humankind for itself—or by humankind for God. Just as God does not break his word to those with whom he has covenanted, so Abraham and Abimlech may not break their covenantal promises. Their mutual promises are rooted in what they did not make, hence they may not be broken by any autonomous reinvention of themselves. The most either of them can ever be is a covenanted, junior partner of God. Only then can they become equal partners with each other. Of course, each of them could break the covenant; but due to the covenantal oath, they could not do so with impunity—anywhere in all of creation. "The eyes of the Lord range over the entire earth, to strengthen those who are wholeheartedly with him" (2 Chronicles 16:9). Once all of this is made publicly explicit, Abraham and Abimelech have good reason to believe each other and proceed with mutual trust.

When one takes Genesis to be one coherent narrative, one can then see how all that is described earlier in the book forms the foundation of the covenant between Abraham and Abimelech. This covenant, which we have just analyzed, is very much a universal paradigm for every covenant that does not stem from the special covenant between God and Israel, his elect people: the covenant grounded in the revelation or theophany at Sinai. The implications for all of this for social contract theory are striking, even at this early stage. Nevertheless, the Noahide covenant can only be appreciated for purposes of social contract theory when first seen as the precondition for the covenant between God and Israel, primarily located at Sinai. Israel's acceptance of the universal Noahide covenant made it possible for them to accept the special covenant from a God of whose general faithfulness to his creation, especially to humankind, they already had some inkling from the inescapable claims made by universal moral law.[51]

---

[50] *Commentary on the Torah*: intro., ed. Chavel, p. 4 based on *Shir ha-Shirim Rabbah* 1.29 re Deut. 4:13. Cf. ibid.: Gen. 9:12.

[51] See Novak, *The Image of the Non-Jew in Judaism*, 257–73.

The Covenant between God and Israel

Even though common monotheism was sufficient for multicultural or inter-national relations, without a common historical revelation, any truly unified community was not to be pursued. There could only be inner-communal unity, not intercommunal unity. All intercommunal relations had to be transactions over borders, with more left behind the borders than inside their overlapping. But there should not be one cultural border enclosing all humankind within itself, at least not yet in history. There is no real universal history short of the messianic centered in Zion and extending throughout the world. That will be God's accomplishment, not the successful conclusion of any human project no matter how exalted. Only then will there be one full language for all humans as the only creatures capable of speaking to God, which means responding to God with what they have heard from him. Only then will God "make the peoples pure of speech [*safah berurah*] so they may all call upon the Lord by name" (Zephaniah 3:9).[52] A universal language could only be rooted in a direct universal revelation and the liturgy enacted as an answer to it. But there is no universal liturgy, no worshiping-together humanity as yet. There is only a universal covenant that makes lawful human relations possible, but there is no real universal community at present or in the humanly foreseeable future.

Full inner-communal unity, with its own concrete culture, requires a univocal language. But that was deemed impossible for a universal culture brought about by human means after the fiasco of the Tower of Babel, which resulted in "the Lord confusing [*balal*] the speech of all the earth" (Genesis 11:9). Human attempts at a universal monoculture, like those of the generation dispersed after Babel, could only result in the self-divinization of the people leading such attempts insofar as they attempted to replace God's real omnipotence with their own idealized omnipotence.[53] Such humans are inevitably at war with God and with one another. Moreover, a monoculture for all humankind inevitably requires a process of elimination: the enslavement or extermination of all those who do not quickly fit the mold of the dominant, universalizing, or totalizing culture. After Babel, Abraham and Isaac and Jacob well understood the possibilities and limitations of transnational covenants initiated by the children of Adam and Eve. They were attempting to survive in the world, not redeem it by themselves. Their presence in the world would be a

[52] Maimonides based much of his messianic universalism on this verse. See MT: Melakhim, 11.4, ed. Frankel, 12:289.

[53] See B. Hullin 94a re Gen. 11:4.

blessing (Genesis 12:3), but they themselves were not commanded to bless the world directly.[54]

This did not mean that members, even leaders, of different peoples could not talk *to* one another. Yet, in the deepest sense, they could not speak *with* each other, especially with each other together *with* God. They could only make covenants with each other in promises spoken *before* God. This is why even covenantal language across cultural-national borders is abstracted from the real languages spoken within the borders. It is like today's "legalese": a language everyone needs from time to time, but whose depth of expression pales in comparison to real, culturally developed languages. "Babel" was the name for the ancient attempt to develop a neutral international language like Esperanto, that is, a language rooted in no culture and, therefore, a language with no real speakers.

The possibility or impossibility of this transcultural covenantal language, abstract to be sure, designates an essential difference between the gentiles themselves. The difference is one that enabled Israel to distinguish between gentile monotheists, with whom it had some theological commonality (however abstract), and gentile polytheists with whom Israel had no such commonality (not even an abstract one). It is only with gentile monotheists that Israel could covenant; with the others, only contracts are possible (and they are shaky at best). Thus Abraham would only covenant with some people just as he refused to covenant with others.

Looking at the sequence of events in Genesis, the Noahide covenant appears to be socially necessary, but culturally insufficient. That is, it can still provide the basic structure for just social relations, as we have seen in the covenant between Abraham and Abimelech, but it cannot provide enough concrete content for a direct relationship between God and humans to be sustained in time. The Noahide covenant is too abstract for this. Its very general content only alludes to a distant God. The Noahide covenant assumes *that* humans are related to God, or at least have the capacity to be related to God, but it cannot provide *what* that relationship consists of. The Noahide covenant pertains to the natural order, especially to human nature, but it does not generate a history any human community could celebrate as its cultural content. The Noahide covenant generated no festivals of its own. But history is communal celebration of events that define that community's identity and destiny: its identity from the past toward the present, its destiny from the present toward the future. Celebration is the stuff of the community's life. Thus a faithful Jew really lives his or her week from one Sabbath to the next, and lives his or her year from one festival to the next. There is no universal human commu-

---

[54] See *Midrash ha-Gadol*: Beresheet on Gen. 12:3 re Isa. 61:9, p. 219. Cf. M. M. Kasher, *Torah Shelemah*: Gen. 12:3, no. 84.

nity because there is still no universal history, and there is not any universal history yet because there is not yet any event universally celebrated.[55] There are no such events short of the coming of the Messiah. There is humankind, but there is no concrete humanity. There is human nature, but no human history as yet. Humanity is now an abstract ideal of God, and one that God alone can realize. "Never has anyone heard or noted; no eye has seen but yours O' God what you will do for those who wait for you" (Isaiah 64:3).[56]

Events are not the same as general experiences, whether social or physical, which are regularly accessible to anyone of sound mind and senses, and which can then be universalized for everyone in theories, in the language of science (broadly conceived). Science takes these regular occurrences and represents them in processes that can explain them, predict them, even prescribe them. But these general experiences are not celebrated as such. Theorizing is not a higher form of celebration. Theory is about general nature; celebration is about singular history. Even when natural occurrences are celebrated, as for example when a blessing is said before partaking in a meal, it is not the natural event of eating that is being celebrated. Rather, it is a celebratory anticipation of the messianic event when God will directly feed a redeemed humankind.[57] Such a celebration elevates this simple, natural act into the trajectory of the community's history of salvation (*Heilsgeschichte*); it does not subsume that communal history back into nature.

Most of Scripture assumes that God is only directly present in singular historical events, not in natural occurrences that anyone could experience. At most, God's presence is hinted at from afar in these general experiences, and even that is a question of considerable philosophical debate.[58] (And even if there is some natural knowledge of God, there is no natural worship of God. Worship—as distinct from private contemplation—is a communal matter.) This is why a miracle (*nes*) as a special event in which God is present is "miraculous"—not because of the impressive physical occurrences that take place, occurrences that can be given natural explanations after the fact. The splitting of the Red Sea by the command of Moses (Exodus 14:26–29) is also explained as the result of "a strong east wind" (14:21), that is, it was unusual but not "supernatural." The miracle is miraculous because "the Lord spoke to Moses" (14:15) at that time, a speech that the people can regularly remember every time that portion of

---

[55] See Zech. 14:16–21.

[56] See B. Berakhot 34b thereon; also, R. David Kimhi (Radaq), *Commentary on the Latter Prophets*: Zech. 14:16.

[57] See Y. Berakhot 6.1/10a and B. Ketubot 111b re Ps. 72:16.

[58] See D. Novak, *Law and Theology in Judaism* 2 (New York: KTAV, 1976), 21–22.

the Torah is read in the synagogue. This is what made this occurrence an event, an event that Israel subsequently and perpetually celebrates on the seventh day of Passover.[59] Also, this is why Elijah, who is like a second Moses, does not apprehend God's presence in the wind or in the earthquake or in the fire, but only in the "thin murmuring voice" (1 Kings 19:12). Only from that voice could he have truly "heard" (19:13) what he is to be commanded by God (19:15). Only the imperative voice of God cannot be explained as a natural occurrence.

This is why, it seems, in the rabbinic speculation as to what the actual normative content of the Noahide covenant is, which resulted in the doctrine of the Seven Noahide Commandments (*mitsvot bnei Noah*), there is no positive commandment as such to affirm the existence of God required of humans.[60] Such a commandment would involve a universally experienced event of divine revelation. But there is none. There is only a commandment against idolatry, which would apply even if one were not yet worshiping God himself. One can only "have faith [*va-ya'aminu*] in the Lord" (Exodus 14:31) when seized by the events in which God spoke.[61]

Furthermore, the fiasco of the Tower of Babel proved that a concrete universality among humankind, at least when initiated by humans themselves, could only be negative. It inevitably self-destructs. (This might very well also be true about a specific human community that attempts to create its own culture de novo.) The only concrete universal human project, according to Scripture, was the project of humans to replace God with themselves. Just as that project led to the expulsion of the first humans from the Garden of Eden (Genesis 3:22–23), so did that project lead to the dispersion of all humankind into inter-national misunderstanding and suspicion. And just as the first humans playing God led to interhuman strife and oppression (Genesis 3:9–13), so did the attempt to play God among the builders of the Tower lead to the same result (Genesis 11:6–9).[62]

In the scriptural vision, the abstract universality of the Noahide covenant lies in the background of creation, and the concrete universality of the kingdom of God lies on the eschatological horizon.[63] Hence a positive relationship with the universal God is going to have to be presented to a specific people by a special revelation to them in a covenant in which they can be together with God. Since God seems to want a direct relationship with humans created in his image, which can only mean a relationship with humans as the essentially communal beings they are, it seems the best way to do this is for God to elect one people among the peoples of the

---

[59] Thus the Torah reading for that day in the synagogue liturgy is Exod. 13:17–15:26, which is the story of the miraculous crossing of the Red Sea. See B. Megillah 31a.

[60] See T. Avodah Zarah 8.4 and B. Sanhedrin 56b re Gen. 2:16. Cf. Maimonides, *Guide of the Perplexed*, 2.33.

[61] See M. Pesahim 10.5 re Exod. 13:8.

[62] See *Pirqei de-Rabbi Eliezer*, chap. 24 re Gen. 11:5.

[63] See Novak, *Natural Law in Judaism*, 142–48.

earth for this covenantal relationship. There is no real universal human community with whom to have that relationship here and now. So, if much of the stuff of that relationship is cultic, then the Temple as the center of Israel's cult will not become "a house of prayer for all peoples" (Isaiah 56:7) until the messianic end of Israel's history, which will then become the beginning of a truly universal humanity. Any attempt to construct that universal sanctuary here and now will be an act of confused religious syncretism, or dangerous religious triumphalism involving some sort of pseudomessianism.[64]

Despite the commonality sufficient to initiate and sustain a theological-political relationship between Abraham and his fellow monotheists, various attempts at the time of the patriarchs to turn this commonality into one real community were rejected, or when actually tried, were abortive.[65] A covenant *between* nations, at least between Israel and other nations, was not to become a covenant *of* several nations merging into one all-inclusive nation. To be that all-inclusive nation requires an all-inclusive national covenant, initiated by divine election, not by interhuman agreement. Only at Sinai does Israel become "a singular nation [*goy ehad*] on earth" (1 Chronicles 17:21) . After Sinai, the theological possibility of Israel ever merging with any other people is now out of the question. Indeed, after Sinai that impossibility became *the* great difference between Israel and the other nations of the world (*ummot ha'olam*).[66] Even at the time of the Messiah, the nations will have to come to Israel (Zechariah 14:16–17), but Israel will not extend itself into the nations and thereby lose its true covenantal character. Israel is not "a light to the nations," implying some sort of active universal mission.[67] Instead, Israel is "to be a covenanted people [*le-vrit am*] a light of the nations [*or goyyim*]" (Isaiah 42:6). Perhaps this means Israel *enlightens the nations when God and Israel demonstrate their faithfulness to each other*. This, then, is what "opens [the nations'] blind eyes" (42:7), what enables "[m]y salvation [*yeshu'ati*]" to reach "the ends of the earth" (49:6). It is when "the nations will walk towards your light [*le-orekh*]" (60:3), which will be when Israel will "be enlightened [*ori*]," which is, "when the Lord will shine [*yizrah*]" (60:1–2) on Israel.

[64] See Maimonides, MT: Melakhim, 10.9, 12.4.

[65] Gen. 13:5–13; 31:55–32:1; 34:9–10.

[66] See *Shemot Rabbah* 15.8 re Num. 23:9.

[67] Yet this is how "light of the nations" is understood in the New Testament, viz., "For so has the Lord commanded [*entetlatai*] us: 'I have made you to be [*eis*] a light of the nations.' " (Acts 13:47). The context here is about Christians actively proselytizing pagans. However, as the medieval Jewish exegete R. David Kimhi (Radaq) points out in his *Commentary on the Latter Prophets*: Isa. 42:6; 49:6, the verse is a prediction of what God *will* do later, not what Israel *shall* do now. See Novak, *The Election of Israel*, 159–60. As for the morality about which the gentiles themselves will seek instruction from the redeemed Jews, Kimhi on Isa. 42:6 emphasizes that this will only be instruction in the Noahide laws,

There are, nonetheless, universal implications of this specific covenant with Abraham even at its inception. God tells Abraham that "all the families of the earth will be blessed through you" (Genesis 12:3). Future illustration of this promise can be seen when looking at how Christians, through the text of Scripture and the experience of the Jewish people, and Muslims make their connection to the one God through the historical memory of Abraham.[68] And there is a rabbinic teaching about how mention of "the persons" (*ha-nefesh*) that Abraham and Sarah "made in Haran" (Genesis 12:5) refers to the converts attracted to the monotheistic quest of this new clan even before God's specific command to Abraham to leave Haran as he himself left Ur, his birthplace. Nevertheless, it is doubtful that this refers to active proselytizing, even though some did see it that way.[69]

The covenant that began with Abraham and his clan becomes actualized in the Exodus from Egypt and consummated in the Sinai revelation, which Jews since rabbinic times have named "the giving of the Torah" (*mattan torah*). When Scripture refers to *the* covenant (*ha-berit*), it is almost always referring to the sinaitic covenant. For example: "These are the words of the covenant that the Lord commanded Moses to make with the Israelites in the land of Moab, in addition to the covenant [*millvad ha-berit*] he made at Horeb" (Deuteronomy 28:29). It is the most important cosmic event, even though Israel seems to be the only people to have experienced it.[70] The sinaitic covenant is seen to be the very reason for which the world was created, and for which Israel was chosen. "Were it not for my covenant [*beriti*] by day and by night, I would not have made the laws [*huqqot*] of heaven and earth; I would have rejected [*em'as*] the stock of Jacob and David my servant" (Jeremiah 33:25–26).[71]

In rabbinic tradition, the universal significance of Israel's being given the Torah is that the Jewish people have a fiduciary responsibility to the rest of humankind to also hold the Torah in trust for them.[72] As such, the gentiles can always come to Israel to take as much of the Torah as they can.[73] It is not Israel's task to bring the Torah to them as missionaries. So, full acceptance of the Torah by all of humankind, when constituted into a real humanity, will have to wait for the coming of the Messiah. Then and only then, "at the end of days [*b'aharit ha-yamim*]," the nations of

---

laws that the gentiles are supposed to know from the beginnings of humankind on earth, long before God gave the Torah to Israel at Sinai (see B. Avodah Zarah 2b re Isa. 43:9).

[68] See Maimonides, MT: Melakhim, chap. 11, ed. Frankel, p. 416.

[69] Cf. *Beresheet Rabbah* 39.14.

[70] See B. Shabbat 88a and parallels re Gen. 1:31. Cf. B. Kiddushin 31a re Ps. 138:4.

[71] See B. Pesahim 68b.

[72] See *Mekhilta*: Yitro, ed. Horovitz-Rabin, p. 205 re Exod. 19:2; p. 222 re Exod. 20:2.

[73] See T. Sotah 8.6 and B. Sotah 35b re Deut. 27:8; Saul Lieberman, *Tosefta Kifshuta*: Nashim (New York: Jewish Theological Seminary of America, 1973), 700 (the view of R. Yose).

the world will say, "let us go, let us go up to the mountain of the Lord, to the house of the God of Jacob, and he will instruct us in his ways and we shall walk in his paths" (Micah 4:1–2). But before that time, in its full covenantal reality, Israel is to be "a people dwelling alone, not to be taken seriously [lo yit'hashav] by the nations" (Numbers 23:9), and accepting of the fact that "each one of the nations will walk in the way of its god" (Micah 4:5).[74] Jews need to keep in mind the universal human significance of the Sinaitic covenant so that they not arrogantly assume they are a superhuman species. And Jews need to keep that universal human significance in mind so that they not contemptuously look upon themselves as some sort of peculiar aberration from the rest of humankind, a humanity that has already achieved some sort of higher, more universal, more godly way of life in the world. The universal concretization of the covenant is Israel's radically future, messianic expectation.

The initial normative content of the Sinaitic covenant is the Decalogue, the Ten Words (aseret ha-dibbrot), or what has come to be called the "Ten Commandments." For Jews, the Decalogue is the general structure of the Sinaitic covenant, and the rest of the commandments of the Pentateuch are considered the further specifications of its more general norms.[75] Later rabbinic tradition came to see 613 such commandments in the Written Torah of Moses.[76] This finite number became important when Jewish tradition wanted to make clear distinctions between the law given directly by God and the law devised by human authorities for the sake of the divine law and its conceived purposes.[77] The covenant, to be sure, is more than the law of the Torah. It also includes God's acting upon and with Israel in history. Nevertheless, the covenant is never less than the Torah, so that at times when Jews have not felt God's active presence in present history, they have still been able to experience God's presence in their study of the Torah and their practice of its commandments.

Covenants between Jews

The covenant of Sinai is between God and Israel. Through it, every member of the people is directly related to God. Even though the covenant is communal, this does not mean that any individual Jew can consider him- or herself anonymous. One is not simply a small, dispensable part of a larger whole and, therefore, of no concern to God. No one should think "I will be all right [shalom], though I follow my own willful heart" (Deu-

---

[74] See R. David Kimhi (Radaq), Commentary on the Latter Prophets: Micah 4:1–2, 5.
[75] See Y. Sheqalim 6.1/49d; Y. Sotah 8.3/22d; Shir ha-Shirim Rabbah 5.12 re Cant. 5:14; also, R. Joseph Albo, The Book of Principles, 3.26.
[76] B. Makkot 23b–24a re Deut. 33:3.
[77] See Maimonides, Sefer ha-Mitsvot: intro., no. 1.

teronomy 29:18). Being a community with God makes the covenanted people more than a mere collectivity, more than a crowd. And just as no individual Jew is anonymous to God, so no individual Jew is anonymous to any other Jew. No Jew can claim God's concern unless he or she is concerned with fellow covenant members. Every Jew is equidistant to God in the covenant, and every Jew is equidistant to every other Jew in the covenant. Since God is at the center of the covenant, any offense to another covenant member is offensive to God as well.[78] All intersecting lines have to cross over the center. This is why all covenants between members of God's people have to be made before God.[79] In rabbinic teaching, this idea of covenantal interdependence is expressed in the principle "all Israel are sureties [*arevim*] for one another."[80] This expresses mutual responsibility, especially mutual responsibility for the wrongdoing of others. Accordingly, one Jew should always try to prevent another Jew from sinning, that is, whenever he or she is aware of that other Jew's intended action and could prevent it by calling attention to it.[81]

An example of this inner-covenantal concern is when Jeremiah in the name of God condemns the people who have violated their covenantal agreement to release their fellow Jews from indentured servitude after six years of service. Thereafter, no one is to recapture "his Jewish brother" (Jeremiah 34:10). To be sure, this had already been commanded in the Torah (Exodus 21:2–6; Leviticus 25:47–55). Nevertheless, because many rich Jews were violating the prohibitions of enslaving fellow Jews indefinitely, these property holders had to "conclude a covenant before Me" (Jeremiah 34:15) to release those fellow Jews they had enslaved again. One had to renew the covenant in this matter and not just rely on the old law on the books. So, these people are condemned by the prophet as those "violating [*ha'ovrim*] My covenant by not keeping the words of the covenant they made before Me" (34:18). By this we see that the covenant made *between* Jews can only be a covenant made *before* God. This is the analogue of the covenant made *with* God that is always placed *before* the people. Thus when Moses concludes the covenant of Israel with God, he puts "this Torah before [*lifnei*] the Israelites" (Deuteronomy 4:44).

In rabbinic teaching, among the various ways norms are differentiated is the division of norms pertaining to the God-human relationship and those pertaining to interhuman relationships. One could say the former set of norms are "religious" and the latter "ethical."[82] Yet both are seen

---

[78] See Isa. 1:15 and B. Berakhot 32b thereon.

[79] See D. J. Elazar, *Covenant and Civil Society* (New Brunswick, N.J.: Transaction Publishers, 1998), 265.

[80] B. Shevuot 39b re Lev. 26:37.

[81] See B. Shabbat 54b–55a; B. Sanhedrin 44a; B. Avodah Zarah 18a.

[82] The Rabbis do make a formal distinction between commandments pertaining to what is "between humans and God" and those pertaining to what is "between humans themselves." See M. Yoma 8.9. This distinction was also methodological in that "religious" law

as "being given from One Shepherd" (Ecclesiastes 12:11).[83] Furthermore, there is no religious norm that does not have ethical implications, just as there is no ethical norm without religious implications. This is what happens in a covenanted community with God at the center. So, for example, the Sabbath is a covenant "between Me and the Israelites" (Exodus 31:17); but it is also a covenant between a master and his servants, who are not to be worked on the Sabbath so that the Sabbath not be enjoyed by their master at their expense (Exodus 20:10).[84] Therefore, the division of these two normative categories is more formal than substantial. The communal covenant between God and Israel makes covenants between individual Jews themselves possible. Whether religious or ethical, being made before God, these covenants between Jews must be consistent with the archetypal covenant. Optimally, these subsequent covenants should enhance the master covenant of Sinai.

Another example of interhuman covenantal responsibility is Jewish marriage. Thus the prophet Malachi in the name of God castigates a man who has "betrayed her, she who is your companion, and your covenanted wife [*eshet britekha*]" (Malachi 2:14). Commenting on the whole passage in which this verse appears in Scripture, the Talmud sees divorce as causing "the altar to weep." That is, marital betrayal by either partner is an affront to *the* covenant with God, the covenant that is celebrated in the rites of the Temple.[85]

This also explains why the erotic poetry of Song of Songs was included in Scripture. The Rabbis saw in the text of Scripture a simile between interhuman eros and the eros between God and his people.[86] Usually, it is assumed that divine-human eros is being likened to male-female eros. However, thinking in covenantal terms, it might be better to say that the love between a man and a woman in marriage is likened to the love between God and Israel in the covenant.[87] Accordingly, marital unfaithfulness is an erotic breach, not only of the relationship between husband and wife, but even more so of the covenantal relationship in which this interhuman relationship has been included and into which it has been elevated. Indeed, this is what Joseph told Potiphar's wife when she was trying to seduce him into adultery. "How am I to do this evil thing and

---

(*isura*) is not to be derived from "ethical" law (*mamona*) and vice versa. See B. Berakhot 19b; B. Ketubot 40b; B. Baba Batra 92b; also, Maimonides, MT: Berakhot, 11.2 and R. Joseph Karo, *Kesef Mishneh* thereon; R. Israel Lipschuetz, *Commentary of the Mishnah* (*Tiferet Yisrael*): Baba Batra 10.8, n. 84. Also, there is the distinction made between acts that are meant to harm God (*ra la-shamayim*) and acts that are meant to harm fellow humans (*ra la-beriyot*). See B. Kiddushin 40a re Isa. 3:10–11; B. Sanhedrin 27a.

[83] B. Hagigah 3b. See Maimonides, MT: Melakhim, 8.11.

[84] B. Shabbat 150a and parallels; Maimonides, MT: Shabbat, 6.1.

[85] See B. Gittin 90b re Mal. 2:13; also, Novak, *Law and Theology in Judaism* 1, pp. 6–12.

[86] See e.g. *Shir ha-Shirim Rabbah* 1.3. For other scriptural examples of the relation of the covenant of marriage with *the* covenant, see Ezek. 16:59–62; Hos. 2:21–22; Prov. 2:17.

[87] See Novak, *Jewish Social Ethics*, 94–98.

sin against God?" (Genesis 39:9). By giving into Potiphar's wife, Joseph would not only have been cuckholding his master, and enabling his mistress to betray her husband, he would have been especially offending the universal God to whom both he and Potiphar's wife were beholden by virtue of the Noahide covenant. The Rabbis add that Joseph would also be in violation of the Abrahamic covenant to which his family was bound.[88]

Despite the essentially covenantal character of Jewish marriage, due to rabbinic interpretation and development of this institution, it did assume some secondary features that could be considered contractual. Thus if a man betroths a woman on condition that he will do such and such, and he violates his obligation, then the betrothal (*erusin*) is automatically null and void. No divorce proceedings are required.[89] Nevertheless, even though a conditional betrothal (*erusin*), like a contract, requires no formal dissolution if its conditions are not met by either party, once the couple actually live together as husband and wife (*nisu'in*), the marriage can no longer simply be annulled automatically. Formal divorce proceedings are now required.[90] Also, certain financial matters may be negotiated by the couple themselves on a contractual basis.[91] But here, too, noncompliance with these financial conditions still does not automatically annul the marriage; formal divorce proceedings are required as well.

Covenants between Jews and Gentiles

There are three types of covenants between Jews and gentiles: (1) covenants between Jews and gentiles as equals; (2) covenants between Jews and gentiles where gentiles are subordinate; (3) covenants between Jews and gentiles where Jews are subordinate.

After the full constitution of the people of Israel as a covenanted community in the revelation at Sinai, it seems that covenantal relations with gentiles became more difficult to propose than was the case during the days of the patriarchs. Perhaps this was because the Sinaitic covenant, with its more specific prohibitions of idolatry, made Israel a nation more apart from the world than it had been when it was a mere clan in the days of the patriarchs. Thus any sort of alliance that could lead to theological-political syncretism would be more suspect.[92] And so, if marriage is considered a covenant, one can understand why Scripture sees the beginnings

---

[88] B. Sotah 36b re Prov. 29:3; Y. Horayot 2.5/46d re Gen. 49:24.

[89] M. Kiddushin 3.2.

[90] B. Ketubot 72b–73a; Maimonides, MT: Ishut, 7.23. See, also, B. Yevamot 107a; B. Gittin 81b.

[91] See B. Kiddushin 19b re Exod. 21:10.

[92] See B. Avodah Zarah 20a and Tos., s.v. "d'amar."

of the decline of King Solomon's dynasty in the undoubtedly dynastic marriages he concluded with foreign princesses, first and foremost with the daughter of Pharaoh. The result was that "they turned his heart after other gods" (1 Kings 11:4), which probably means his willingness to tolerate the practice of their polytheistic rites for the sake of his inter-national realpolitik.[93]

The closest we come to a bilateral covenant between Jews and gentiles is the covenant between King Solomon and Hiram, king of Tyre (1 Kings 5:26). Nevertheless, even here it seems clear that Hiram is economically, and possibly militarily as well, subordinate to Solomon.[94] Interestingly enough, in the days of Amos, Tyre (Phoenicia or what is now Lebanon) is castigated for betraying Israel (Amos 1:9), the people of Solomon, whom Hiram called "my brother" (1 Kings 9:13).

Military inferiority, leading to a decision by the weaker party to make a political alliance with the stronger party, seems to be at the heart of the covenant between Ahab, of the Northern Kingdom of Israel, and Ben-hadad king of Aram. Although appearing to be a "covenant of brothers" (Amos 1:9), it is more likely the desperate move of Ben-hadad to make a conditional surrender to Ahab before being totally defeated by his army in battle. Assuming the kings of Israel are "kind kings" (I Kings 20:31), Ben-hadad hopes for the best. "Kindness" (*hesed*) means covenantal consideration or loyalty.[95] So, Ben-hadad might have thought that because of covenantal traditions, he could be Ahab's vassal without being subjected to humiliating defeat and conquest.[96] Perhaps Northern Israel, despite its culture being more idolatrous than that of Judah at the time (especially due to the power and influence of Ahab's Phoenician wife, Jezebel), still had a reputation for covenantal loyalty. This covenant of vassalage is expressed in the words, "he [King Ahab] made a covenant with him [Ben-hadad] and sent him forth [*va-yishallhehu*]" (1 Kings 20:34). Nevertheless, the fact that this event took place in the Northern Kingdom of Israel, which was always more assimilated to pagan ways (and as evidenced by the fact that these "lost tribes" did not, like Judah, return to the land of

[93] For rabbinic speculation on the type of rationalization that led King Solomon to this type of covenantal compromise, see B. Sanhedrin 21b; also, B. Kiddushin 68b re Deut. 7:4.

[94] Scripture recognizes this type of covenant, whereby a weaker nation subordinates itself to and is protected by a stronger nation, as an international reality, even when Israel is neither nation. See Ezek. 30:5–6.

[95] See 44, n.39 above.

[96] This is what a number of modern biblical scholars have called a "suzerainty treaty." See George Mendenhall, *Law and Covenant in the Ancient Near East* (Pittsburgh, Pa.: Presbyterian Board of Western Pennsylvania, 1955). That this type of treaty is not the model for *the* covenant in Scripture, but only a model for the type of covenant between Ahab and Ben-hadad, has been well argued by de Vaux, *The Early History of Israel*, 439–43.

Israel after their expulsion by the Assyrians in 724 B.C.E.), and the fact that this covenant was made with Ahab, the persecutor of Elijah and the rest of the prophets of the Lord, probably removed this event from ever becoming a precedent for Jewish-gentile covenants.

The classic example of gentile covenantal subordination to Jews is the case of the Gibeonites. The latter were a Canaanite people who decided that rather than risking war with the invading Israelites under Joshua, they would disguise themselves as a non-Canaanite people with whom the Israelites could more readily conclude a peace treaty, making the Gibeonites vassals rather than killing them (Deuteronomy 20:10–15). Approaching Joshua, their emissaries request that he and the Israelites "make a covenant for us" (Joshua 9:11). That is done by taking an oath (9:15). Despite their deception, which was soon discovered, the leaders of Israel refused to harm the Gibeonites because of the oath they had taken (9:19). Perhaps they were afraid that word would get out that the Israelites do not honor their covenants, even when they take an oath to God. Perhaps their thinking was due to considerations of what the Rabbis called "profanation of God's name" (*hillul ha-shem*), which means action that is legally valid, but still appears to be morally debased and makes the Jews look morally debased.[97]

Despite the fact that the covenantal oath was honored, however, the Gibeonites are punished for their treachery by being turned into serfs rather than vassals, "hewers of wood and drawers of water" (Joshua 9:23). Indeed, the Gibeonites were the only Canaanite people who "made peace" (Joshua 11:19) with the Israelites.[98] They became the paradigm of the resident-alien (*ger toshav*) of whom the Rabbis spoke, namely, non-Jews who by promising to abide by the Noahide covenant and its few commandments, plus respecting Jewish sovereignty in the land of Israel, were thus entitled to permanent residence there.[99] This relationship with resident-aliens can be called covenantal inasmuch as it has no temporal limit nor does it have conditions for its subsequent annulment. Indeed, it was very much like full conversion to Judaism (*gerut*), which itself is a covenant that also cannot be annulled however much it might be breached.[100] The difference between these two forms of covenantal attachment to the Jewish people seems to be more of degree than of kind.[101]

---

[97] B. Yevamot 78b–79a.

[98] See Y. Sheviit 6.1/36c; *Sifre*: Devarim, no. 204; Maimonides, MT: Melakhim, 6.5.

[99] B. Avodah Zarah 64b; *Sifre*: Devarim, no. 199 re Deut. 20:11; Maimonides, MT: Melakhim, 6.1.

[100] T. Demai 2.4; B. Yevamot 47b.

[101] Thus one can see the 7 Noahide commandments, which the *ger toshav* must accept unconditionally, as the potential for the 613 commandments, which the *ger tsedeq* must

A covenant whereby Jews become subordinate to non-Jews is troublesome since it suggests that a non-Jewish ruler can have covenantal authority over Jews in lieu of God or his messianic regent. Nevertheless, the prophet Ezekiel speaks of the covenant the king of Babylon made with the royal Judean stock (Ezekiel 17:13). The prophet, in the name of God, regards this covenant as binding, even though it was no doubt forced upon the Jews. Indeed, he castigates the Jews for being in "covenantal violation" (17:15) for betraying the king of Babylon by making an alliance with his enemy Egypt.[102] Breaking a covenantal oath seems more important to him than the fact that this oath makes Jews wholly subordinate to a gentile ruler. Nevertheless, according to the commentator R. Isaac Abravanel, the Jews were only able to take such an oath if it was in the name of the Lord.[103] Otherwise, wouldn't the Lord be angry with the people for invoking somebody else's god? Thus Israel was to keep this covenant, that is, as long as Babylon was in power, especially in power over them. But God solved their political problem by letting Cyrus, the Persian king, vanquish the Babylonians and permanently destroy their empire (Isaiah 45:1–3). It was as the prophet Isaiah had predicted: God would "cut off from Babylon name and remnant" (14:22). The Jews would have to live under other kings in their subsequent history, but never again would they be bound to them by a covenantal oath. They would, nonetheless, be able to make contracts with whatever powers-that-be they had to live under in postbiblical times. This will be examined in chapters 3 and 4.

Contracts: Social and Private

If a contract is distinguished from a covenant by its conditionality and negotiability, there is an explicit scriptural example of such a contract. Moreover, as a contract between one collective and another, it could well be a paradigm for a Jewish social contract. The case in point concerns the time when the people of Israel were about to enter the Promised Land after completing their forty years of wandering in the Sinai Desert. The tribes of Reuben and Gad (and one half of the tribe of Manasseh) wanted to retain for themselves land adjacent to Canaan, land that had already been conquered.

---

accept unconditionally (T. Demai 2.5; B. Bekhorot 30b). Along these lines, see Maimonides, MT: Melakhim, 9.1.

[102] See 2 Chron. 36:13.

[103] *Commentary on the Latter Prophets*: Ezek. 17:19.

At first, Moses is angry with their request to retain this land, and he
accuses them of not wanting to participate in the conquest of Canaan
along with the rest of the tribes of Israel. He believes that fulfilling their
request will result in "turning the hearts of the Israelites from crossing
over into the land which the Lord has given them" (Numbers 32:7). To
dispel this suspicion, the two tribes negotiate a conditional agreement with
Moses in his capacity as the leader of Israel. It is no accident that this
agreement is not designated a *berit*. Moses proposes the following conditions of an agreement between Israel and the tribes of Reuben and Gad:

> If you do this, if you will arm yourselves for war . . . and every one of your
> armed soldiers [*haluts*] will cross over the Jordan . . . and the land has been
> conquered . . . and then [*v'ahar*] you will return. You shall be exonerated [*neqi-
> yyim*] by the Lord and by Israel, and this land shall be yours as your holding
> [*l'ahuzah*] before the Lord. But if you don't do this, then you will have sinned
> against the Lord. (Numbers 32:20–23)

The Rabbis consider this case a paradigm for how a contract should be
structured.[104] Thus Maimonides derives four essential points pertaining
to all conditional agreements (*ten'ai*) from the way Moses negotiated with
the two tribes: (1) that both the positive and negative conditions be explicitly stated; (2) that the positive condition be stated before the negative
condition; (3) that the conditions of the agreement be stated before it is
acted upon (*qodem le-ma'aseh*); (4) that it is humanly possible (*efshar*)
to uphold the conditions of the agreement.[105]

Despite the social character of the original agreement between Moses
and the two tribes, though, the points that emerge from the description
of their negotiations were only applied by the Rabbis to contracts between
private parties, specifically certain monetary agreements that could be negotiated between the individuals themselves.[106] The reason for this specific
limitation might well have been that the Rabbis did not want the relationship between Jews and the larger Jewish community to be strictly contractual, but wanted it to retain a more covenantal character. Thus *ten'ai*, the
term the Rabbis used for the "conditions" in Moses' negotiated contract
with the 2½ tribes, can also mean a "prior stipulation" as is the case with
covenantal terms. Along these lines, the Talmud discusses how Joshua

---

[104] M. Kiddushin 3.4; T. Kiddushin 3.2; B. Kiddushin 61b–62a. Nevertheless, in the Mishnah text cited, Rabban Simeon ben Gamliel emphasizes that the portion the two tribes are
allotted in the land of Israel itself was to be given to them unconditionally, irrespective of
whether or not they had fulfilled their contract with Moses over the territory outside the
land. In other words, like all the other tribes, their portion in the land of Israel proper was
to be given to them unconditionally as in any true covenant.

[105] MT: Ishut, 6.1–2, 14. See, also, *Tur*: Even ha'Ezer, 38.

[106] See B. Kiddushin 19b; Maimonides, MT: Ishut, 6.9–10; 12.1–9.

stipulated ten conditions (*tena'in*) in order for the Israelites to inherit their ancestral portions in the land of Israel.[107] Such stipulations are taken to be like those of a court (*ten'ai bet din*).[108] Like all rabbinic enactments, they are not formally negotiated between the Rabbis and the people, even though the former certainly have to take popular acceptance into consideration when making such enactments.[109] Inasmuch as Joshua's stipulations supplement the covenantal allotment of the land of Israel, there is no mention that noncompliance with any of these conditions would retroactively or even subsequently forfeit anyone's covenantal right to dwell in his or her ancestral portion of the land of Israel.[110] Moreover, it is not suggested that these stipulated conditions would ever be repealed.

Only the collective Jewish occupancy of the land of Israel is considered conditional. Thus noncompliance with the Torah's commandments by the people of Israel is sufficient for God to exile them from the land of Israel. This is unlike their relationship with the Torah, from which the people are never even temporarily separated.[111] Nevertheless, the separation of the Jewish people from the land of Israel is not considered permanent. They can return to it anytime they are able, and, at the time of the Messiah, the whole people of Israel will be permanently restored to the land. "I shall take them from among the peoples, and I shall gather them from the countries, and I shall bring them to their own land" (Ezekiel 34:13).[112]

Along the lines of a private contract as distinct from a social contract, let alone a covenant, there is an interesting legal discussion among some important rabbinical authorities in the sixteenth and seventeenth centuries, just before the dawn of Jewish modernity. The question they dealt with is whether or not an oath (*shevu'ah*) employed to unite two persons in an active relationship is still binding when one of the parties does not fulfill his or her sworn obligation. Does the other party need a formal court procedure (*hatarah*) to be released (*patur*) from the obligation, or does the obligation become null and void (*betelah*) retroactively as would be the case in an ordinary contract?[113] If the former, then an agreement

---

[107] B. Baba Kama 80b–81b, 114b. These stipulations also apply anywhere Jews own property and are under the political rule of a Jewish community. See ibid., 81b; Maimonides, MT: Nizqei Mamon, 5.5.

[108] B. Baba Kama 81b. See B. Ketubot 51a.

[109] See Baba Kama 79b.

[110] See n. 104 above.

[111] See *Mekhilta*: Yitro re Deut. 11:17, ed. Horovitz-Rabin, p. 201.

[112] For the messianic meaning of this prophecy, see R. Isaac Abravanel, *Commentary on the Latter Prophets* thereon.

[113] Normally, oaths are taken with utmost seriousness, especially since many of them involve the invocation of God's name (see B. Nedarim 22b and commentary of R. Nissim Gerondi [Ran], s.v. "amar Rava"). The procedure of release (*hatarah*) of oaths is the same procedure as that employed in the release of vows (*nedarim*), even though vows involve less

sealed with an oath partakes of a more covenantal character, as we saw earlier in the case of marriage.[114] But if the latter, then the presence of the oath is little more than a formality and what we have is an essentially contractual relationship.

The scriptural paradigm for this discussion is found in the oath that Joseph required his brothers to take just before his death. "Joseph made his brothers swear [*va-yashba*] saying: 'when God will have attended [*yif-qod*] to you, you shall take my bones from this place'" (Genesis 50:25). Later, Scripture reports that "Moses took the bones of Joseph with him" (Exodus 13:19) in order to fulfill this oath. But what if Moses had been unable to fulfill the oath? Would this have prevented the Exodus? To answer this question, the Rabbis imagine Moses saying to the metal coffin of Joseph, which the Egyptians had supposedly sunk in the Nile to prevent its retrieval, hoping to prevent the Exodus thereby, as follows: "Joseph! The time has arrived when God is to redeem Israel. . . . if you reveal yourself, good; but if not, we are exonerated [*neqiim*] from the oath you had our fathers take."[115] The story concludes with Joseph's compliance with Moses' request.

It would seem from this rabbinic speculation about Moses and Joseph's oath that at least some mutual oaths are contractual rather than covenantal (using our distinction in this chapter) since they are contingent on the continuing compliance of both parties and are nullified retrocatively if there is noncompliance on either side. Nevertheless, two rabbinical authorities, R. Moses Isserles (d. 1572) and R. David Halevi (d. 1667), indicate that this is the case only when the agreement is made to be essentially conditional, dependent on the *willing* compliance or noncompliance (*be-mezid*) of the parties.[116] The example usually used concerns prenuptial agreements (*shidukhin*). The agreement is contractual, even when accompanied by an oath, which in Scripture, is an essential part of a covenant. Only when accidental factors (*me'ones*) prevent compliance with negotiated preconditions by either party does the oath require formal judicial

---

of a personal obligation (see ibid., 2b) and never invoke the name of God (see ibid., 28a; Maimonides, MT: Shevuot, 6.1–8; ibid.: Nedarim, 4.5–6; *Tur*: Yoreh Deah, 228). The procedure consists of the person wishing to be released from his or her oath expressing regret (*haratah*) to a rabbinical tribunal for having ever taken the oath, and stating that had he or she known what would subsequently transpire (in our case, the noncompliance of the partner), he or she would have never taken the oath.

[114] See 55–56 above.

[115] *Tosefta*: Sotah 4.7, ed. Lieberman, p. 172. See B. Sotah 13a; *Mekhilta*: Beshalah, p. 78.

[116] Isserles (Rema), note on *Shulhan Arukh*: Yoreh Deah, 236.6; Halevi (Taz), *Turei Zahav* thereon, n. 13. There Halevi criticizes his teacher and father-in-law, R. Joel Sirkes, *Bayit Hadash* on *Tur*: Yoreh Deah, 236, for not making the basic distinction between willful and accidental noncompliance.

dissolution. Nevertheless, even in this case, the situation under consideration is still only *more covenantal*, but not a covenant per se. In the scriptural covenants, either primary (Noahide and Sinaitic) or derivative (like Abraham and Abimelech), it will be recalled, there is no way the agreement can be nullified, either retroactively or by a court action (*ma'aseh bet din*). This might very well explain why in rabbinic legal discussions of interhuman agreements (as distinct from rabbinic exegesis of Scripture), the term *berit* is no longer used.[117]

So, in conclusion, it seems one cannot find any direct precedent for social contract thinking in Scripture or in the rabbinic exegesis of Scripture. Nevertheless, the fact that conditional interhuman agreements are already recognized in the Torah and developed by the Rabbis indicates that the conditionality common to both private and social contracts is not foreign to Jewish legal theory. And, as we shall see in the next chapter, Jewish legal theory can engender Jewish political theory. Furthermore, the precedence of private contracts to social contracts is historically accurate. It is the best reason a social contract cannot be truly foundational, since only those having experience with private contracts, in a society itself not founded in a social contract, could possibly engage in a social contract. Thus a social contract like a private contract presupposes that the primary social structure is already in place. Like a private contract a social contract is constructed on this foundation, that is, those who so contract must already have a status within this social structure, a status that has been assigned to them not chosen by them. But, whereas a private contract need only refer back to the noncontracted social structure underneath it, a social contract needs to be both constructed *on* and constructed *for* that basic social structure. In Judaism, any social contract ultimately intends *the* covenant of Sinai; it is the basic social structure that is irreducible to any other social structure. Any social contract has to be constructed *because of* and *for the sake of* the basic social structure already in place.

---

[117] The closest to covenantal language one finds in legal discussion of an interhuman agreement is the use of the term *herem* (e.g., by Halevi, see n. 116 above). In Scripture, *herem* has the absolute sense of *berit*; indeed, it could be considered the negative of a *berit*. E.g., "You shall surely destroy [*tahreem*] them; you shall not make a covenant [*berit*] with them" (Deut. 7:2). However, in rabbinic usage, *herem* is often a synonym for *shevu'ah* (oath), see, e.g., M. Arakhin 8.4. And, as we have just seen, unlike a *berit*, a *shevu'ah* can be terminated due to noncompliance by either of the parties who took it, either automatically or by subsequent court action (see R. Isaac bar Sheshet Parfat, *Sheelot u-Teshuvot ha-Rivash*, no. 178). Rabbinic discussion of the literal term *berit* is confined to the covenants between God and humans: either the Torah itself as the content of the covenant (B. Nedarim 32a re Jer. 33:25), or circumcision as the sign of the covenant (ibid., re Gen. 17:2 and Exod. 34:27), or the covenant as the confirmation of the giving of the Torah by God and its reception by the Jewish people (B. Berakhot 48b–49a and Rashi, s.v. "shalosh beritot").

Like all construction, the social contract is made of something uncon-
structed by its makers. In ontological terms, what is conditional or contingent is ultimately dependent on what is unconditioned or absolute.[118] In
the next chapter we shall see how the conditionality of a social contract
emerges from the unconditionality of the covenant.

[118] See Immanuel Kant, *Critique of Pure Reason*, B364–65.

Chapter Three

The Covenant Reaffirmed

Covenantal Necessity

The Torah as the content of God's covenant with Israel appears to have been forced upon the people, at least during the prophetic career of Moses. The very first words of the Decalogue are: "I am the Lord your God who has brought you out [*hots'etikha*] of the land of Egypt" (Exodus 20:2). God chooses Israel in the covenant, and that choice is totally free—from God's side, that is. God no more *had* to choose Israel than God *had* to create the world.[1] But did Israel *have* any real choice in responding to that covenantal election? Could Israel have stayed in Egypt instead? If not, how has Israel experienced the covenantal obligation as spelled out in its acceptance of the Torah in general and in its specific commandments? Did Israel really accept the Torah or was the Torah, in effect, accepted for Israel without its full consent? Were there any real alternatives? Is the Torah merely necessary, that is, when directly enforced, or is it a desideratum that the people would have surely chosen to accept for themselves despite there being real alternatives?

Answers to these questions must be sought if moral claims based on the covenant are to be cogently made, whether to Jews among themselves or to the outside world. It is hard, if not impossible, to persuade others to freely accept what one did not accept freely but only under duress. Of course, these sound like questions modern liberals might ask. Nevertheless, traditionalists cannot dismiss these questions as stemming from modern rejections of the tradition, since they have been asked, even since ancient times, by the most revered, authoritative personalities in the history of Judaism. They have been asked both by the prophets and the Rabbis. Thus they cannot be dismissed as heretical.

The first one to explicitly question whether Israel freely entered the Sinaitic covenant was the prophet Jeremiah. Thus when speaking of a new or renewed covenant (*berit hadashah*—Jeremiah 31:30), Jeremiah says it is "not like the covenant I made with our ancestors on the day I forced them [*heheziqi be-yadam*] to be taken out of the land of Egypt,

---

[1] See Yehezkel Kaufmann, *The Religion of Israel*, trans. M. Greenberg (Chicago: University of Chicago Press, 1960), 298–99.

which they repudiated [*heferu*], and into which I had to compel [*ba'alti*] them" (31:31). It would seem that God's coercion of Israel to leave Egypt is to make them accept the covenant that will be consummated at Sinai.[2]

In the Talmud, one Rabbi dramatically imagines what actually happened at Sinai. Just before the giving of the Torah at Sinai, Scripture says about the people of Israel, "they stood at the foot of the mountain" (Exodus 19:17). The word for "at the foot of" (*be-tahteet*) is almost identical with the word for "under" (*tahat*). As such, the verse is reread to say "they stood up under the mountain." The following scenario is then envisioned: God held Mount Sinai over their heads like a trough and told them: "If you accept [*meqabblim*] the Torah well and good; if not, there will be your grave."[3] This is like saying Israel accepted the Torah "under the gun." Thus on the heels of the scenario of Mount Sinai being held over the heads of Israel, another Rabbi complains: "this is a great moral indictment [*mod'aa rabbah*] of the Torah."[4] The term "moral indictment" is a legal term that indicates how one can claim that the sale of property made under duress should be nullified retroactively by a court.[5] What is lacking in such circumstances is the leeway to deliberate between two viable options.[6] As Nahmanides points out, since this choice was forced upon the people by God their king, it is valid, and there is no one who could nullify it.[7] After all, as for God's kingship over Israel, it is the king who elects *his* people, not the people who elect *their* king.[8] Nevertheless, this choice can hardly be seen as one made *willingly* with sufficient deliberation beforehand. Truly moral deliberation cannot be conducted under such pressure.[9]

This problem is further emphasized in the subsequent discussion in the Talmud when noticing the strange sequence of verbs in the scriptural description of Israel's initial acceptance of the covenant: "All that the Lord has spoken we shall do and we shall hear [*na'aseh ve-nishm'a*]" (Exodus

---

[2] For the idea that the Exodus is for the sake of the revelation at Sinai, i.e., liberation is for the sake of being commanded by the right God, see *Shemot Rabbah* 3.4, ed. Shinan, p. 126; also, M. M. Kasher, *Torah Shelemah*: Exod. 3:12, no. 167; Maimonides, *Guide of the Perplexed*, 3.43 re Lev. 23:15–16.

[3] B. Shabbat 88a.

[4] Ibid.

[5] B. Baba Batra 39b–40a.

[6] See B. Baba Kama 62a; Maimonides, MT: Ishut, 4.1 and note of R. Abraham ben David (Ravad) thereon. Cf. ibid.: Gerushin, 2.20.

[7] See *Hiddushei ha-Ramban*: B. Shabbat 88a.

[8] See D. Novak, *The Election of Israel* (Cambridge: Cambridge University Press, 1995), 22–38.

[9] See S. Federbush, *Mishpat ha-Melukhah be-Yisrael*, 2nd rev. ed. (Jerusalem: Mosad ha-Rav Kook, 1973), 36, n. 28.

24:7).[10] Doesn't one have to hear the commandments before doing them? How else would one know *that* something is to be done? How else would one know *how* it is to be done?[11] However, "hearing" here is taken to mean "understanding," that is, Israel accepts the commandment to be obligatory before understanding *why* the commandment is to be done. Rational decision-making requires knowledge of the end one's action intends. Therefore, the Jews are taken by one scoffer to be "an impetuous people [*ama paziza*] for putting your mouths before your ears."[12] The Jews are here indicted, as it were, for having committed themselves to a set of practices before any real deliberation over *why* they should be doing *what* they are doing. At Sinai the people were overwhelmed by God's power, so they had neither the time for deliberation nor the opportunity to ponder any alternative to the acceptance of God's authority. That might be why the people reverted to idolatry so easily as soon as they no longer experienced the revealed power of God after the Sinai theophany and the departure of Moses to receive more of the Torah. Not having freely internalized what they had experienced under duress, the people did not think they had to assume responsibility for what they had just accepted in the second of the Ten Commandments: "You shall have no other gods before Me" (Exodus 20:3).[13]

In the Talmud, it is also taught that even when the covenant was renewed on the Plains of Moab before Israel was to enter the Promised Land, Moses made the people swear an oath (*hishbiʿa et yisrael*) to obey God's covenantal commandments.[14] According to one talmudic commentator, God himself commanded Moses to make the people swear this oath.[15] But how can one *be made* to swear an oath or make a promise? Indeed, in ordinary oaths, one is only obligated if one does so out of one's own free will.[16] But this means more than simply submitting oneself to someone else's free will as a leap of faith. Simple obedience precludes deliberation. Making a promise, though, requires such deliberation. This is what occurs when an oath is made: One obligates oneself, even if that

[10] On B. Shabbat 88a several Rabbis praise Israel's unquestioning faith at Sinai, when they "put practice before understanding" (*she-hiqdimu naʿaseh le-nishmʿa*).

[11] Thus R. Samuel ben Meir (Rashbam) in his *Commentary on the Torah* thereon, contrary to the usual rabbinic interpretation of this verse, interprets it to mean that Israel pledges to do now what God has commanded, and what God will command thereafter.

[12] B. Shabbat 88a.

[13] According to one Rabbi at least (B. Sanhedrin 63a re Exod. 32:8), Israel did not totally substitute another god for the Lord, but only included another god in their worship of the Lord. As such, their sin is somewhat diminished. See B. Sukkah 45b re Exod. 22:19.

[14] B. Nedarim 25a and B. Shevuot 39a re Deut. 29:13–14.

[15] B. Shevuot 29b, Tos., s.v. "ki."

[16] Ibid. 26a re Lev. 5:22.

self-obligation is a self-motivated response to a law another person is asking one to accept.[17]

Self-obligation in the scriptural sense should not be confused with radical autonomy in the Kantian sense, where the rational will of the human person is the foundation of all moral law. All law is theonomous, either directly or indirectly, certainly for Judaism. The self, whether mine or that of anyone else, has prima facie authority. In fact, I think radical autonomy can be revealed as an incoherent idea.[18] How can one command oneself? *Who* is commanding *whom*? Isn't the verb "command" a transitive verb, thus involving one distinct subject and another distinct object?[19] The question is not whether the law came from someone else; the question is whether one person has the right to make such a claim on another.[20] Nevertheless, one's own free will is still required for any promised acceptance of that law-from-another to be cogent, even if one's own free will is not the ontological origin of law per se. Yet the Talmud indicates that Moses told the people their oath was not according to their will at all (*lo al da'atekhem*); that it was not really their own deliberate response to the law God is giving them.[21] Even the form of their response had to be according to God's will and Moses' will. It would seem that by making the people take a covenantal oath, God and Moses did not trust the people to have enough will to truly pledge themselves to the covenant in good faith. But then, as one talmudic commentator asked: Why should the people's promise be believed at all if God and Moses were convinced that the people were too ambivalent to make their own promise in good faith?[22]

Perhaps this lack of will explains, too, why the people of Israel made Moses their agent to accept the rest of God's law after they themselves had heard the Ten Commandments directly. Their reason for this: "[Y]ou speak with us and we shall be able to hear it, but let not God speak with us lest we die" (Exodus 20:16). According to the Talmud, this means that God himself only imposed the first two, most basic commandments on the people: "I am the Lord your God" (Exodus 20:2) and "You shall have no other gods before Me" (20:3).[23] The rest of the more specific commandments were accepted for the people by Moses, and it was Moses

---

[17] See B. Nedarim 7b–8a re Ps. 119:106; Y. Shevuot 3.9/35a and 5.3/36b.

[18] See D. Novak, *Jewish-Christian Dialogue* (New York: Oxford University Press, 1989), 148–49. Cf. Karl Barth, *Church Dogmatics* 2/2, Eng. trans. (Edinburgh: T. & T. Clark, 1957), 649–51.

[19] See Plato, *Republic*, 431A.

[20] See D. Novak, *Covenantal Rights* (Princeton, N.J.: Princeton University Press, 2000), 12–25.

[21] B. Shevuot 29a and 39a; B. Nedarim 25a.

[22] B. Shevuot 29a, Tos., s.v. "ke-she-hishbi'a."

[23] B. Makkot 24a.

who had the authority, both from God and from the people, to impose these commandments on the people. Just as there was no real alternative when directly confronted by God, so there was no real alternative when directly confronted by Moses (and indirectly by God).

So, when Korah and his colleagues complain to Moses that Moses has taken too much authority upon himself and that "all the assembly, all of them are holy [*qedoshim*] and the Lord is in their midst" (Numbers 16:3), they seem to have forgotten that this is the result of their own general agreement with Moses to rule them specifically. This agreement was, then, confirmed by God, who told Moses: "[T]hey have done well [*heteevu*] by all they have spoken" (Deuteronomy 5:25). Thus their accusation that Moses "has raised himself up [*titnass'u*] over the congregation of the Lord" is not true. Moses' exaltation over them is the result of God's election of him to be God's prophet so as to bring the covenantal revelation to the people (Exodus 4:15–16), but Moses' exaltation is also the result of the people's election of Moses to get that revelation for themselves. The people missed their chance to be addressed directly and specifically by God, a point Moses regretted when he wished that "all the people of the Lord would be prophets, that God would place his spirit upon them" (Numbers 11:29).[24] Nevertheless, even had they been directly addressed by God in all the specific details of the Torah, the people would still have had no real choice since they had no real alternative to choose another god without imminent disaster.

As for the second covenantal confirmation on the Plains of Moab, the scriptural text itself only speaks of the people being made to enter the covenant with God (Deuteronomy 29:11). Yet that could simply mean that they had to accept what God is doing for them and with them in God's act of covenantal initiation. How could they deny that God keeps his promises, since God promised to take Israel out of Egypt and God kept his promise? The text speaks too of a covenantal curse (*ha'alah*), but this could simply mean that God threatens the people with punishment if any of them violates the commandments secretly, thinking this can be done with anonymous impunity (29:17–19). The text speaks of the promise or oath God made before (presumably at Sinai) and to the patriarchs to take Israel as his people (29:11), but there is no positive act of acceptance of this covenant by the patriarchs themselves other than the fact they obeyed God without question. They simply did as they were told by God, for God is to be obeyed without any previous deliberation over why one is to obey him. The question is, though, whether such obedience comprises all of the covenant between God and Israel.

[24] See Nahmanides, *Commentary on the Torah*: Deut. 5:24.

Even Abraham's famous interrogation of God over the fate of the evil cities of Sodom and Gomorrah (Genesis 18:17–33) is still at the invitation of God (18:27); Abraham does not presume to indict God by his own initiative (18:27).[25] Here Abraham obeys God by questioning God, just like he obeys God, without complaint, when bringing his son Isaac to be sacrificed as commanded (Genesis 22:3). When faced with the direct commandment of God, there are no real alternatives. Thus the rabbinic addition of an oath taken by the people on the Plains of Moab seems superfluous inasmuch as the key precondition of an oath, which is informed free will, seems to be missing there as it was forty years earlier with the previous generation at Sinai. The people are only asked to confirm a law they have had no real say in formulating, let alone any understanding as to why it was formulated.

The Voluntary Covenant

If covenantal freedom is only the freedom to obey or disobey commandments of God imposed upon one, then what is the real difference between God's covenant with Israel and God's covenant with the Noahides? Is the only difference that Israel gets more specific commandments than do the Noahides? If so, what is Israel's advantage in being chosen for what is promised to be a singular relationship with God, the relationship of "a kingdom of priests and a holy nation" (Exodus 19:6)? Is the difference between the 7 commandments of the Noahides and the 613 commandments of the Mosaic Torah only numerical? Is the difference one of degree rather than of kind?[26]

We get an inkling of the answer to this overall question when we look at Jeremiah's distinction between the old covenant of coercion and the "new covenant" (*berit hadashah*) he is anticipating prophetically, which we noticed above. In this new—or better, *renewed*—covenant, God says "I shall place my Torah inside them [*be-qirbam*] and I shall write it on their heart . . . for all of them will know me from the small to the great" (Jeremiah 31:32–33).[27] Although the usual interpretation of this text is eschatological, meaning that the people will keep the Torah automatically at the end of history, one could plausibly interpret it to be more mun-

---

[25] See *Beresheet Rabbah* 49.2 re Ps. 25:14 and Prov. 3:32, where it is emphasized that Abraham can reason with God only because God has revealed his will to Abraham.

[26] Cf. Maimonides, MT: Melakhim, 9.1.

[27] For *hadash* meaning "renewal" rather than "innovation," see 1 Sam. 11:14. Cf. Isa. 65:17.

dane.[28] Thus one could say that this prophecy is about a time within history, when the people of Israel will finally accept the Torah not only because they *have* to confirm what God has already decreed, but they *shall* accept it because they will freely affirm what they really *want* for themselves from God.

The difference between having to confirm the Torah and wanting to affirm it for onself is that mere confirmation often means that there is no real alternative to obedience, whereas in affirmation there is a real alternative to voluntary service to the covenant and its maker. Furthermore, affirmation requires some distance between the time the Torah *was* given by God voluntarily and the time it *will be* voluntarily accepted by Israel. In the interim there *is* the deliberation needed in order for the affirmation of the people to be based on careful knowledge from the past for the sake of careful intention into the future.[29] But what was that alternative? When did it present itself to Israel? How did the people say no to that other option and yes to the Torah? In other words, why did the people reaccept the Torah first given at Sinai? What made their reacceptance of the Torah different from their initial acceptance? What made their later affirmation of the covenant freer than their earlier confirmation of it?

As for Jeremiah's prophecy about the "new covenant," which could be speaking of a foreseeable future rather than a more transcendent end-time, we can better appreciate how the Talmud dealt with the question of God's holding Mount Sinai over the heads of the people, thus depriving them of any alternative to immediate compliance and any time for deliberation. The answer to the moral dilemma posed by this theology of revelation is proposed by the fourth-century Babylonian Rabbi, Rava, who said: "Despite all this [af-al-pi-khen], the generation at the time of Ahasuerus did accept it as it is written 'they upheld it and accepted it' (Esther 9:27), namely, they upheld what they had already [kvar] accepted."[30] But the usual word order should have been: "they accepted [qibblu] the Torah and then upheld [kiyyamu] it." Rava plays upon this unusual word order to emphasize that the "acceptance" is retrospective. Hence the word refers to a time before the present "upholding." But, the retrieval of that earlier acceptance in the past requires a renewed acceptance in the present. This reacceptance is more than a mere repetition of the past, more than a mere confirmation of ancient history.

---

[28] See R. David Kimhi (Radaq), *Commentary on the Latter Prophets*: Jer. 31:30, who argues, contrary to Christian claims about the messianic supersession of the Mosaic Torah (see Hebrews 8:7–12), that even in the future the Mosaic Torah will continue to be kept (see Y. Megillah 1.5/70d; cf. T. Berakhot 1.12; B. Niddah 61b). Nevertheless, Kimhi still sees Jeremiah's prophecy as pertaining to the radical messianic future or end-of-history.

[29] See Aristotle, *Nicomachean Ethics*, 3.2/1112a16–17.

[30] B. Shabbat 88a.

What made the difference? The difference was made by the historical circumstances of the time of Ahasuerus as distinct from the time of Moses. At the time of Moses and, indeed, from the time of Moses to the time of the destruction of the First Temple in 586 B.C.E. and the exile of the Jewish people into Babylonia, the Jewish people enjoyed political sovereignty. For almost all that time, they ruled themselves. As such, whatever commandments of the Torah were publicly kept were kept as matters of public policy. Generally, "religious" or cultic matters were handled by the institution of the Temple priesthood (*kehunah*); "moral" or civil and criminal matters were handled by the institution of kingship (*melukhah*).[31] Since the Torah had been given through a prophet, it was the task of the institution of prophecy (*nevu'ah*) to warn both priests and kings—and the people in their cultic and civil-criminal dealings—when they had departed from God's law for the sake of their own autonomy. The moral power of those prophets who refused to be on either the ecclesiastical or the royal payroll (Amos 7:12–15), or who refused to pander to popular prejudice (Jeremiah 28:15), was irresistible because it was incorruptible. Nevertheless, the people had no real alternative to "Judaism," however well or badly formulated, under these political circumstances. They were living under a univocal state religion. There was no theological-political alternative except individual exile. So the young David complained that his being chased out of the land of Israel by the servants of King Saul was tantamount to being "banished from the Lord's possession, being told: 'go worship other gods'" (1 Samuel 26:19). Not to live under Israelite polity was taken to be the equivalent of having to find another—all by onself, elsewhere.[32]

All of this changed when the Jewish people went into exile. In Babylonia there was an alternative, and it was not only the option of individuals to live outside Israel and become assimilated into some other culture. In Babylonia, unlike in the land of Israel, the Jewish people had the communal option of saying together: "[W]e will be like the nations [*nihyeh ka-goyim*], like the families of the lands, serving wood and stone" (Ezekiel 20:32). In Babylonia they had the real option of communal assimilation. And despite the fact that the prophet tells them (in the very same verse) that from God's perspective their proposed theological-political disappearance "will not be," still there was no state or sanctuary to keep them from this radical loss of their covenantal identity. The people now had a real choice of retaining their national character or assimilating into the larger empire to which they lost their sovereignty, never to fully regain their communal identity even after the Babylonian empire gave way to the Persian empire, which became the empire of Ahasuerus.

---

[31] See e.g., Lev. 10:8–11; 2 Sam. 15:2.
[32] See T. Avodah Zarah 4.5; B. Ketubot 110b.

Why did the people change their minds and abandon their assimilation-ist project? Why did they opt for a retrieval, a reacceptance, of their cove-nantal identity? Scripture itself only tells us *that* the people reconstituted themselves as the covenanted community. "Now let us make a covenant [*nikhrot berit*] for our God . . . and let it be done according to the Torah" (Ezra 10:3). Let it be noted that this new covenant is not "from our God," but "for our God (*le'loheinu*)." In other words, unlike the covenant at Sinai and even its renewal on the Plains of Moab, this new covenant is made at the initiation of the people themselves. Even the oath that Ezra "has the priestly, levitical, and popular officials swear [*va-yashb'a*]" (10:5) is an oath for them to do as they themselves had proposed.

The great medieval commentator Rabbenu Jacob Tam, developing the Talmud's answer about the willing acceptance of the Torah during the days of the exile that we saw above, explains that at Sinai the people experienced direct divine revelation. The intensity of that experience was such that the people were "overwhelmed" (*b'al korkham*). But during the days of Ahasuerus, when they were not living under the rule of God and divinely mandated political institutions like the priesthood and kingship, "they accepted [the Torah] by their own will [*mi-da'atam*] because of their love [for God stemming from] the miracle [*ha-nes*]."[33] The miracle was that their ultimate assimilation, the extermination plot of Haman designed to eliminate Jewish distinctiveness altogether (Esther 3:8) was foiled by "relief and deliverance from elsewhere [*mi-maqom aher*]" (Es-ther 4:14), which the Rabbis take to mean what came from the hidden God.[34] (This oblique reference is the only "religious" factor in this other-wise very "secular" book.) According to the Rabbis, this loving accep-tance of the miracle performed on their behalf led the already highly as-similated Jews in the Persian empire to publicly reaffirm their national identity and, also, to reaccept their uniquely Jewish religious practices. The people finally experienced God's desire for them to be his people again. Their response to this divine desire was their own desire for it. They were now willing not coerced.[35]

The decision of the people to initiate the renewal of the covenant with God contains a great theological irony. That is, in order for the people to recover their national singularity as the covenanted people of God, they had to affirm the universality of God in a new and more explicit way. To be sure, as the late Israeli biblical scholar and theorist Yehezkel Kaufmann

[33] B. Shabbat 88a, Tos., s.v. "mod'aa."

[34] *Esther Rabbah* 8.6.

[35] In ordinary matters of law, if one is coerced to sin, he or she is exempt from punishment (B. Baba Kama 28b re Deut. 22:26). On the other hand, there are times when even if one is coerced to perform a commandment, one is taken to have fulfilled the commandment nonetheless (B. Rosh Hashanah 28a; also, B. Ketubot 86a–b).

never tired of emphasizing, monotheism as faith in the one God, creator of heaven and earth, was predominant in ancient Israel from its very beginnings.[36] Even when there were various idolatrous diversions in the days of the First Temple, these diversions were confused, syncretistic attempts to see the worship of minor deities as being compatible with worship of the one God; they were not attempts, though, to replace the one God altogether. Nevertheless, at least de facto, the people of Israel were worshiping a national deity as long as they were confined to their own land. One can assume that they were actually "henotheists," who were worshiping *one* God, yet it could be assumed that *this* God is for them *a* god rather than *the* God who is for everyone everywhere. Their faith in the universality of God had not yet been put to the test.

It was only when the Jews were exiled from their land that they were able to discover three things from their own experience and not just believe them based on what the prophets had been telling them. All three of these things reflected the more universal and the more voluntary character of the covenant that had emerged in the exile.

One, the Jews were not the only worshipers of this God; his influence is indeed universal. Thus a post-exilic prophet (indeed, the last of the prophets), Malachi, tells the people that their worship of God is inferior to that of some other nations. "From the rising of the sun to its setting, My name is magnified [*gadol*] among the nations . . . but you profane Me" (Malachi 1:11–12).[37] This experience might very well have led to the later rabbinic teaching that polytheism (*avodah zarah*) is universally prohibited.[38] After all, if there were no gentile monotheists, how could anyone believe that monotheism was not in fact confined to Israel? Would there be any difference between monotheism and henotheism?

Two, because the Jews now experience the universal God, his bond with Israel is not terminated when Israel is living outside her ancestral borders. Indeed, faith in this universal God is what enables Israel to return to her ancestral borders since only a universal God, a God who can be *everywhere* (Exodus 3:14; 20:21), could possibly enable the people to go from the *nowhere* of exile to the *somewhere* of the Promised Land. "And you, Israel, My servant, Jacob whom I have chosen, seed of Abraham My beloved [*ohavi*]; you whom I drew from the ends of the earth and called from its far corners . . . I will uphold you with My righteous right hand" (Isaiah 41:8–10). This is why the great medieval commentator and theolo-

---

[36] *The Religion of Israel*, 60–63, 122–48.

[37] In relation to this verse, there is a profound rabbinic dispute (B. Menahot 110a) as to whether recognition of the One God is truly universal or only extends as far as those nations who have had contact with the Jews and *their* One God.

[38] T. Avodah Zarah 8.4 and B. Sanhedrin 56a–b.

gian Nahmanides points out that only the universal creator God could be the one to say: "I am the Lord your God, who took you out of the land of Egypt" (Exodus 20:2).[39] Any lesser god would not have this kind of international power and mobility.

This newly emphasized universality also enabled those Jews who chose to remain in exile, for whatever reasons, not to regard themselves as cut off from either God or Israel. One could continue to worship the one God of Israel anywhere as a Jew. Thus Jeremiah tells the exiled community to "seek the welfare [shlom] of the city whereto you have been exiled and pray to God on its behalf, for your welfare is included in its welfare" (Jeremiah 29:7).[40] To be sure, the preferred life for Jews is always in the land of Israel; nevertheless, living in the land of Israel is not a necessary condition of being a Jew or remaining a Jew.[41] It is true that a Jew can practice more of the commandments in the land of Israel; it is not true, however, that one can practice none of the commandments in exile (galut).[42] The difference between Jews in the land of Israel and Jews in the Diaspora, then, is one of degree, not of kind. Israel is centered in the land of Israel, not confined there. As such, Diaspora Jews are "dispersed" (Ezra 10:8), but they are not colonists. And, in fact, Diaspora Jewish communities from time to time declared their political and legal independence from the Jewish community in the land of Israel, but without losing their love and respect for the land of Israel and its religious centrality for the entire Jewish people.[43] So, Judaism is very much a universal religion—that is, it can be practiced *throughout* the whole world, even though it does not claim the whole world for itself. It is universal, not imperial. Thus the place of residence of a Jew is not an entirely obligatory matter, at least in the strict legal sense of obligation.[44]

[39] *Commentary on the Torah* thereon; see, also, ibid.: Gen. 1:1.

[40] In fact, there were times when the presence of a greater center of Torah learning made a Diaspora location preferable to domicile in the land of Israel. See B. Ketubot 110b–111a re Jer. 27:22.

[41] If living in the land of Israel is a positive commandment of the Torah, then whoever can live there but chooses to live elsewhere would be in violation of that commandment. In affirming this view, Nahmanides disagrees with both Rashi (see their respective comments on Num. 33:53) and Maimonides (see his *Notes on Maimonides' Sefer ha-Mitsvot*: Addenda, pos. no. 4). Of course, even for Maimonides, who would not deviate from the rabbinic tradition in matters of practice, it is still preferable for a Jew to live in the land of Israel (see MT: Ishut, 13.19; cf. B. Ketubot 110b, Tos., s.v. "hu").

[42] See M. Kiddushin 1.9.

[43] See B. Gittin 6a and 88a; Y. Gittin 1.2/43c; B. Baba Kama 80a; B. Sanhedrin 5a and Tos., s.v. "de-hakha;" R. Moses Schreiber, *Sheelot u-Teshuvot Hatam Sofer*: Orah Hayyim, no. 84.

[44] Nevertheless, the Rabbis did make decrees that seem to be aimed at discouraging Jewish emigration from the land of Israel. See B. Shabbat 14b; also, T. Parah 3.5. Cf. B. Shabbat

Three, the new more voluntary character of the covenant seems to have enabled a considerable number of gentiles, especially in the Diaspora, to choose to become Jews. Thus late in the book of Isaiah, the prophet speaks of "the foreigners who attach themselves [ha-nilvim] to the Lord to minister to him, loving the name of the Lord to become his servants" (Isaiah 56:6). He even goes so far as to say that they are "better than sons and daughters" (56:5). Although the sufficient condition of their becoming Jews was that the Jewish people in the person of an official tribunal had to accept them, their free choice to become Jews was the necessary condition for their conversion.[45] Nobody could be converted to Judaism against his or her will. In fact, the book of Ruth, which describes the person who became the paradigmatic convert to Judaism, the person who could not be persuaded to not become a Jew (Ruth 1:16–18), in later Jewish tradition was selected to be read on the festival of Shavuot, which celebrates the giving of the Torah (mattan torah) at Mount Sinai and, perhaps even more important, the continual reception of the Torah (qabbalat torah) by the Jewish people.[46] What probably happened during the exile was that the voluntary reacceptance of the Torah by the Jews—their willing reaffirmation of the covenant—inspired many gentiles to do the same on their own initiative. No longer able to take the covenant for granted because of the lack of societal coercion and the presence of real alternatives, the Jews were finally given a real choice. And if the attraction for the Jews was the Torah and its commandments, why couldn't these same commandments have a wider, more universal appeal than merely to those already Jewish? Judaism was now considered too good to be kept from those who by the accident of birth had not been automatically granted covenantal identity. And it would seem that the attraction of gentiles to Judaism also had a reverse effect on the native-born Jews, that is, it made them realize that they could very well be replaced in the covenant unless they actively reaffirmed it and stopped taking it for granted through nostalgia.[47] Furthermore, in this atmosphere of the renewed covenant, gentiles no longer had to wait for generations to be fully integrated into the Jewish people (through gradual intermarriage), which was the case in the days of the First Temple when full communal status depended on ancestral, landed patrimony. And gentiles did not have to wait to become full Jews until the messianic age when "all the nations [kol ha-goyim] . . . will come to worship before you Lord" (Psalms 86:9).[48]

14b and Rashi, s.v. "al erets ha'amim;" M. Ohalot 2.3 and Maimonides, *Commentary on the Mishnah* thereon; MT: Tumat Met, 2.16.

[45] See Maimonides, MT: Melakhim, 8.10.

[46] See *Yalqut Shimoni*: Ruth, no. 596; also, Novak, *The Election of Israel*, 187, n. 87.

[47] See B. Kiddushin 70b–71a and Tos., s.v. "kashim."

[48] Cf. B. Yevamot 24b re Isa. 54:15.

All of this voluntary universalism involves loving deliberation. One can deliberate out of love in a way one cannot deliberate out of fear. One wants to ponder how to love, but not how to fear. There is also a difference between action stemming from fear and action stemming from love. In fear, one is usually inhibited from positive action; in love, one is motivated to positive action.[49] At Sinai the people were largely intimidated; in the exile the people were largely inspired. Furthermore, not yet having had any experience with the commandments of the Torah, the people at Sinai could not very well deliberate about whether to accept them or not. Unlike love, there is no preparation for fear. Like love fear embraces one; unlike love, though, one does not re-embrace fear; one simply endures it. But after centuries of having at least some experience with the commandments of the Torah, the people were in a much better position to make a more deliberate, a more willing, a more loving choice. They knew whom they could love, and they chose to do so in the exile. (Thus even converts are required to have some knowledge, both theoretical and practical, of the commandments before their conversion can actually be consummated. In the interim between presenting themselves for conversion and actually being converted, they have sufficient time for informed deliberation.)[50] As we have just seen, the Jews came to God rather than the reverse, as was the case at Mount Sinai (Exodus 19:4, 20). As the kabbalists would say, "the motivation [*it'aruta*] came from below."[51] This had profound political ramifications.

Covenantal Autonomy

The covenant was renewed as soon as the people who had returned to the land of Israel with Ezra and Nehemiah were ably to safely assemble in Jerusalem. But the decision to return to the land of Israel and renew the covenant there had already been made in Babylonia. Everyone who returned and renewed the covenant on behalf of the whole Jewish people did so voluntarily, because "God had stirred up [*he'ir*] his spirit to go" (Ezra 1:5). This phrase does not mean that God *caused* this kind of person to go. Instead, it means God *inspired* this kind of person to go in the sense of placing this attractive option before him for him to choose.[52] Furthermore, unlike previous covenantal renewals during the days of the First Temple, the people did not accept the covenant as a "leap of faith," only

---

[49] See Y. Berakhot 9.5/14b.
[50] B. Yevamot 47a.
[51] See *Zohar*, 1:164a re Num. 28:22; ibid., 78a.
[52] See Rashi, *Commentary on the Latter Prophets* thereon.

to hear the specific instructions (*torah*) thereafter. Rather, the people first heard the words of the Torah. "They said to Ezra the scribe [*ha-sofer*] to bring the book [*sefer*] of the Mosaic Torah that the Lord commanded Israel . . . and the Levites explained [*mevinim*] the Torah to the people . . . making it intelligible [*ve-som sekhel*] so that they could understand what was being read [*ba-miqr'a*]" (Nehemiah 8:1, 7–8). A few weeks later they assembled again, saying: "In view of all this, we conclude a firm agreement [*amanah*] in writing, signed by our officials, our Levites, and our priests" (Nehemiah 10:1).[53] In the earlier covenantal renewals, the written word came from God. In this covenantal renewal, the written word came from the people (duly represented by their leaders, that is). That might very well be why the new word *amanah* ("firm agreement") is used in lieu of the older word *berit*. From this new covenant, we can see that a number of new rights seem to emerge, what could be called *covenantal entitlements*. Of course, the exercise of rights means that the voluntary range of Israel's part of the covenant has now been considerably expanded.

Before examining these new rights, we need to remember that this new covenant for all its novelty is not a contract. It is perpetual and it has no exit clauses. Like the older covenant it requires a total, unconditional commitment to God's law. Upon signing the faith-covenant, the people "agreed to be cursed [*b'alah*, that is, if they would breach the covenant] and took an oath [*u-bi-shevu'ah*] to follow the Torah of God . . . to carefully observe all the commandments [*kol mitsvot*] of the Lord our master, his ordinances and his statutes" (Nehemiah 10:30). God's absolute authority remains intact; indeed, it is actually enhanced by the uncoerced character of its acceptance by the people. It is human authority that is expanded.[54]

The first right emerging from this new covenant is the right of the people, albeit in the person of Ezra the scribe, to determine the correct text of the Torah by which they will be governed. Ezra seems to be the first person since Moses (Deuteronomy 31:24, 30) to have read the whole Torah (or from the whole Torah) to the people from a text that is undisputed.[55] By contrast, the Torah scroll found during the days of King Josiah, from which the king read in order to make a covenant for the people before God (2 Kings 22:8–23:3), seems to have been only partial.[56] But the scroll Ezra read from seems to have been the full Torah, and it was accepted by virtue of his scribal accuracy. As the great contemporary talmudist and theologian David Weiss Halivni put it so well:

---

[53] See M. W. Duggan, *The Covenant Renewal in Ezra-Nehemiah* (Atlanta, Ga.: Society of Biblical Literature, 2001), 241–42.

[54] Re more voluntary piety, see B. Kiddushin 31a and Nahmanides, *Hiddushei ha-Ramban* and R. Yom Tov ben Abraham Ishbili, *Hiddushei ha-Ritva* thereon.

[55] Cf. B. Baba Kama 82a re Exod. 15:22; Y. Megillah 4.1/75a; Josephus, *Against Apion*, 2.175.

[56] See Gersonides (Ralbag), *Commentary on the Latter Prophets*: 2 Kings 22:11.

After ages of straying from the path of God—after their bitter repentance in exile—the people gathered close; willing and attentive, they were prepared, finally, for revelation. This was the age when idolatry ceased in Israel; it was also the end of prophecy. Once the nation had embraced a book, no need remained for the admonition and the vision of the prophets. Interpretation took the place of revelation.[57]

Thus the Rabbis were perfectly willing to admit scribal editing of the text of the Torah.[58] All of this made "the sage (*hakham*) more important than the prophet," as a later Rabbi is quoted in the Talmud.[59] In other words, the one who can interpret the Torah infinitely is greater than the one who only brought the finite revelation.

The right to determine the correct text of the Torah goes hand in hand with the right to interpret the text of the Torah. Frequently this meant assigning more meaning to the text than what could possibly be derived from the prima facie sense (*peshat*) found *in* the text. The most one has to do is show that the assigned or attributed meaning (*derash*) given *to* the text does not blatantly contradict the text's prima facie sense.[60] (One engages as much in *eisegesis*, "reading-into," as *exegesis*, "reading-out-of," a scriptural passage. In fact, it is usually unclear just how to separate these two procedures in any one *midrash* or "interpretation.") The interpreter "seeks out" (that is, *darosh*, the verbal root of *derash*) the meaning of the text in order to know what to do but, of course, that interpreter does not come to the text empty.

The very act of "seeking-out" appears to be different from the time of Ezra on, in contrast with the pre-exilic period. About Ezra it is said: "he prepared his mind to seek out [*levavo li-drosh*] the Torah of the Lord in order to practice and teach law and justice [*hoq u-mishpat*] in Israel" (Ezra 7:10). But in pre-exilic times, more often than not, one went to a prophet or seer to seek an oral message directly from God (1 Samuel 9:9), never knowing whether or not a message would come (28:6). Or, God himself, through prophets, sought persons to deliver his response to their violations of God's law (Ezekiel 33:6). But now, one had the time and the opportunity to "prepare one's mind to seek out [what] the Torah" commands be done in the particular situation now brought before it.

---

[57] *Revelation Restored* (Boulder, Colo.: Westview Press, 1997), 83.

[58] See B. Sanhedrin 21b–22a. Most of Halivni's theory of the transmission of revelation, with which I wholly agree, is based on this Talmud text.

[59] B. Baba Batra 12a; also, Y. Berakhot 1.4/3b; Y. Avodah Zarah 2.7/41c re Deut. 13:2 and 17:11; R. Judah Loewe (Maharal), *Gevurot ha-Shem*: intro., 2a..

[60] Cf. B. Yevamot 24a; B. Sotah 16a; Y. Kiddushin 1.2/59d. Nevertheless, even when a rabbinic interpretation is admittedly not derived from the scriptural text to which it is attached, it is still considered to be "stretching the text" rather than substituting it with something totally foreign (see B. Yevamot 11b; *Midrash Leqah Tov*: Vayetse, ed. Buber, 72b–73a).

Prophecy, on the other hand, more often than not comes "suddenly" (Numbers 12:4), with no time to prepare for it.[61]

As much as possible, the thrust of the scriptural text is taken to be practical. Description is for the sake of prescription. (One can move back to an "is" from an "ought" in a way one cannot move forward from an "ought" to an "is.")[62] So even in texts dealing with the ways of God, the purpose of the interpretation is to instruct us *how* to talk about God or *how* to imitate God. More often than not, the practical thrust of the text is taken to be a direction for more bodily, communal activities. Thus when the leaders of the people come to Ezra for him "to give meaning [*le-haskeel*] to the words of the Torah" (Nehemiah 8:13), he immediately instructs them how to observe the festival at hand: Sukkot. In other words, Ezra functions like all the Rabbis after him, offering instruction about revelation, not revelation itself.[63]

These two activities: determining the text and seeking its normative meaning, are still wholly covenantal. We do not seem to have arrived at any contractual phenomena as yet. Neither activity involves any conditional agreements and neither has any termination clauses built into it. But the contractual implications are now lying just beneath the surface. Furthermore, just as the new covenant is not meant to supersede the old one but to strengthen and enhance it, so the contractual implications of the new covenant are not meant to supersede it but to strengthen and enhance it. I am not suggesting some sort of progressive trajectory "from covenant to contract," where covenant is overcome by social contracts that outstrip it. Nor am I proposing an evolutionary scheme where a lower species is overtaken by a higher species and thus becomes extinct. The presumption of progress in history (as distinct from historical development or mutability) is intellectually erroneous, religiously triumphalist, and politically dangerous. The tradition changes within history, but that does not mean either progress or regression.[64]

<hr/>

[61] See comments of R. Abraham ibn Ezra and Nahmanides thereon. And even if one isprepared for prophecy, there is no guarantee that prophecy will actually occur when one wants it to occur. See Maimonides, MT: Yesodei ha-Torah, 7.4–5.

[62] See Novak, *Covenantal Rights*, 21–24.

[63] The Rabbis imagine (B. Eruvin 54b) how Moses first functions as prophet receiving God's law for the people, and then functions as rabbi teaching God's law to the people. Whereas in Scripture Moses is *the* prophet (e.g., Deut. 33:10), in the rabbinic sources he is *Mosheh Rabbenu* ("Moses our rabbi").

[64] As far as I know, there is no notion of historical progress in the classical Jewish sources. Indeed, attempts to actually predict the messianic end of history have been discouraged (see B. Sanhedrin 97b re Isa. 30:18), although with only partial success. Although there are opinions that regard the present as regression from the past (e.g., B. Shabbat 112b), they can be countered with opinions that regard such atavism as morally irresponsible (e.g., *Avot de-Rabbi Nathan* A, chap. 12, ed. Schechter, p. 27b re Eccl. 9:4; B. Rosh Hashanah 25b re Eccl. 7:10) see, also, B. Hagigah 3a; Y. Sotah 3.4/18d.

The covenant of Sinai remains predominant for Judaism. Those political phenomena in Judaism we could call "social contracts," and the ideas that propose them, are not meant to supersede the covenant. Contracts are meant to serve the covenant; they are not an essential component in a progressive trajectory away from it. Because of this, I am suggesting that a Jewish political theology as Torah (that is, as normative teaching) should justify these contractual components by its own traditional criteria, showing how they emerge from the covenant within Jewish history and how they function for the sake of the covenant throughout Jewish history. The covenant of Sinai will reach its final, transhistorical conclusion in the messianic covenant of Zion (Isaiah 61:1–8). Any contracts that are made between Sinai and Zion are merely temporary episodes within covenantal history; they are not cumulative efforts to transcend the past for the sake of a better, humanly attainable future. Contracts are postulated for the sake of the covenant, they are not improvements of the covenants. The covenant has operated before any contractual arrangements were proposed and put into effect; the covenant will endure long after any such contractual arrangements are needed.

Some Social Contracts within Judaism

The manifestation of scribal-pharisaic-rabbinic Judaism, beginning in the Babylonian exile, and the subsequent return of the Jewish people to the land of Israel under the religious leadership of Ezra, is also the beginning of recognizable contractual phenomena in Judaism. These phenomena emerge in the interpretation and implementation of the norms of the Written Torah (what I have been calling Scripture), the text of which is now virtually agreed upon by the time Ezra reads it to the people as their constitution, which they willingly accept (Nehemiah 8:1–18). And that willing acceptance, let us recall, required covenantal experience, real cultural alternatives, and deliberation over whether to reaffirm the covenant or walk away from it. All this was lacking, it will be recalled, when the people stood at Sinai. Then they were religiously naive, being without covenantal experience, standing in the middle of a wilderness with nowhere else to go, and under supernatural pressure to immediately accept a covenant and its law about which they knew next to nothing. Nevertheless, at Sinai the people were closer to God than anytime afterward.

To be sure, the earlier imposition of the Torah at Sinai was necessary for the initiation of what truly becomes the covenant *between* God and Israel in the exile and beyond. The Torah had to begin as the Torah *from* the active God *to* passive Israel. We know this from the moral experience of childhood. We had to obey the commandments of our parents and teachers out of fear before we could reflect upon that experience to either

love it—or hate it. Through our reflection on that experience we are able
to discern retrospectively the reasons why we ourselves *would* have chosen these commandments God has given *to* us if we *could* have chosen
them *for* ourselves back then. Deliberate choice of an existential commitment as basic as that of the covenant is always a reaffirmation. As a famous rabbinic doctrine teaches: the covenantal affirmation was made for
us before we were born (or "born again" if one is a convert to Judaism).[65]

I would locate three such contractual phenomena in general that characterize rabbinic Judaism, which is the Judaism that emerged from the new
covenant of Ezra (as distinct from the old covenant of Moses) and that is
the normative Judaism still intact today. They are (1) exegetical proposals
subject to either literary acceptance or refutation; (2) extra-scriptural legislation subject to rational acceptance or repeal; (3) the appointment or
removal of rabbinic officials. Let me briefly represent them here.

By noting these social contracts *among* Jews *within* Judaism, we can
better appreciate how social contracts could be made *between* Jews and
non-Jews *outside* Judaism. We need to deal with the internal Jewish phenomena before we get to the external Jewish-gentile phenomena of social
contracts as foreign relations. Indeed, we need to see how these internal
relations prepare Jews to engage in those foreign, contractual relations
with authenticity and intelligence. Without this "homework," however,
Jewish efforts to formulate foreign policy will be as disingenuous as modern religious apologetics, modern political propaganda, and modern economic "public relations."

Let us look at the question of exegetical proposals and refutations. In
rabbinic texts, whether the issue under discussion is theological or practical, more often than not differences of opinion are presented. The holder
of each opinion, or a later scholar who agrees with that opinion, argues
for his opinion as the correct interpretation of a scriptural source. In this
process, each opinion claims to have properly "sought out" (*midrash*) its
scriptural source, which then functions as the revealed support (*semakh*)
of that opinion.[66] Sometimes the dispute between the Rabbis is over one
scriptural source: A reading it one way and B reading it another. Sometimes, each side of the dispute marshals a source or several sources as a
support for its own opinion. In such cases, especially over practical questions, each side not only marshals its own sources, but it also (or a later
editor in its name) tries to show that the sources marshaled by the other

---

[65] B. Shevuot 39a re Deut. 29:14; *Tanhuma*: Nitsavim, ed. Buber, p. 25b re Deut. 29:11;
also, Y. Peah 2.4/17a re Eccl. 1:10. Re conversion as rebirth, see B. Yevamot 22a and
parallels.

[66] See, e.g., Y. Sheviit 10.2/39c; also, David Weiss Halivni, *Peshat and Derash* (New York:
Oxford University Press, 1991), 155–57.

side do not mean what the other side thinks they mean.[67] Thus, so to speak, the way to win a theological argument is to make sure the scriptural rug upon which you stand will not slip out from under you, and, at the same time, you should try to pull the rug from out from under your opponent.

This is how rabbinic exegetical disputes operate. More often than not, they are simply left at the level of a stalemate.[68] Nevertheless, in practical matters, where communally uniform behavior requires a conclusive legal decision one way or the other, the matter is to be decided by the majority opinion of the contemporary Rabbis, and how well this rabbinical majority influenced or was influenced by a clear consensus among the people (what others would call *consensus fidelium*). "When there is a minority opinion [*yahied*] and a majority opinion [*ve-rabbim*], the law is according to the majority" is a staple of rabbinic jurisprudence.[69]

Sometimes, though, one side is actually able to persuade the other to change its mind and agree with the opinion it had theretofore disagreed with.[70] Thus, despite the fact that the most serious disputes took place between the School of Hillel and the School of Shammai (often going back to their respective founders, the first-century Rabbis Hillel and Shammai), and despite the fact that later generations were convinced that the Hillelites are always to be taken as the majority, there were times when "the Hillelites reversed themselves to rule [*hazru . . . le-horot*] like the Shammaite opinion."[71] In fact, the general political success of the Hillelites is attributed to their intellectual openness, which was their willingness to be persuaded by others as much as their desire to persuade others of the greater plausibility of their own opinion.[72] Along these lines, some of the aspects of communication ethics meant to characterize what democratic discourse ought to be, especially as developed by the contemporary German philosopher Jürgen Habermas, are useful in clarifying the situation of Jewish normative discourse with which we are now dealing.

> Pragmatism and hermeneutics oust the traditional notion of the solitary subject that confronts objects. . . . In its place they put an idea of cognition that is mediated by language and linked to action. Moreover, they emphasize the web of everyday life and communication surrounding "our" cognitive achievements, the latter one intrinsically intersubjective and cooperative.[73]

[67] See, e.g., B. Gittin 90a re Deut. 24:1.

[68] For subsequent procedural rules to determine which opinion in such a stalemate is the law, see B. Eruvin 46b and Rashi, s.v. "le-hanei kellalei."

[69] B. Berakhot 9a and parallels.

[70] M. Eduyot 1.4.

[71] See M. Gittin 4.5; M. Eduyot 1.13.

[72] B. Eruvin 13b. Cf. Y. Shabbat 1.4/3a.

[73] *Moral Consciousness and Communicative Action*, trans. C. Lenhardt and S. W. Nicholsen (Cambridge, Mass.: MIT Press, 1993), 9.

What distinguishes this type of rabbinic discourse from the purely covenantal dicta of the prophets is that in rabbinic discourse one's opinion can
always be *disputed* by one's contemporaries. Usually, one must present
his own *arguments*.[74] If not, or if these arguments have been lost, then
later scholars who agree with this earlier opinion will themselves supply
arguments for it. The prophets, conversely, speak apodictically without
presenting any arguments at all; indeed, without inviting or even allowing
an intellectual challenge from anybody else. After all, how could one argue
with a claim introduced by the words "thus saith the Lord"?[75] As such,
one cannot dispute a prophetic dictum as being false. Instead, one has to
claim that a prophet is willfully lying (*sheqer*), hence engaged in moral
deception (Jeremiah 5:31; 18:18); or one has to claim that a prophet is
deranged (1 Kings 22:22). Of course, how does one prove such a charge
by means of human argumentation? For such a challenge to the personal
authenticity of a prophet to be effective, it seems a new dramatic revelation
from God is required: confirming the true prophet and identifying the false
ones as was the case when the prophetic authority of Moses was either
challenged or denied (Numbers 12:1–10; 16:23–33). And even then, the
effectiveness of such new revelations is itself questioned by Scripture as,
for example, in the story of how disappointed Elijah was in the effectiveness of his prophecy, even after the miraculous confirmation of his prophetic authenticity and the identification of the prophets of Baal as the
charlatans or psychotics they in fact were (1 Kings 18:19–40; 19:1–11).

The most one can do by means of argument is to show that the prophet
is contradicting what the people already know to be the commandment
of God (Jeremiah 23:13–14), accusing him of telling the people what they
want to hear—that they are doing right—rather than telling them what
they need to hear—that they are in fact doing wrong (Ezekiel 13:1–7).
But people already involved in the great lie of idolatry are usually too
remote from the Torah to be able to appreciate such moral arguments.
Indeed, when the Talmud says that by the time of the Second Temple (the
time of Ezra and Nehemiah) the Jews had lost the inclination to engage
in idolatry, it associates this with Ezra's public reading of the Torah,
which, as we have seen, marks the beginning of Pharisaic-Rabbinic Judaism.[76] This time is also the beginning of the end of public prophecy in
Israel. The demise of public idolatry among the Jews seems to be con-

---

[74] "His" arguments can sometimes be "her" arguments. See, e.g., T. Kelim: Baba Metsia
1.6; also, B. Niddah 50a, Tos., s.v. "kol."

[75] Re the personal authority of a prophet, see B. Yevamot 90b and Tos., s.v. "ve-leegmor."

[76] B. Yoma 69b.

nected with the demise of prophecy among the Jews, since the primary function of the prophets was to admonish the people, often with accompanying miracles, about their sins, especially that of idolatry. With this sin no longer the public menace it once was, the people seem to be better prepared to listen to moral arguments about the Torah's specific commandments from the scribes and the Rabbis. These moral arguments are more about what the people ought to be doing and are likely to be persuaded to do, and less about their lack of connection to the Torah altogether by their violation of the Torah's most basic prohibition, "[Y]ou shall have no other gods before Me" (Exodus 20:3), as was the case in pre-exilic times.

This shift from prophetic apodictic authority to rabbinic argumentative persuasion is famously discussed in the Talmud. Even when Rabbi Eliezer ben Hyrcanus, who is frequently called "the great" (*ha-gadol*), invokes a heavenly echo (*bat qol*) on behalf of a legal opinion of his, he is reminded that he has no prophetic authority, that the Torah "is not in heaven [*lo ba-shamayim hi*]" (Deuteronomy 30:12).[77] The authoritative opinion can only be the one the majority of the Rabbis have been persuaded to accept as right.

The more contractual character of rabbinic public discourse becomes more apparent when we recall the characterization of contracts as distinct from covenants presented in the previous chapter. This difference is most apparent when we contrast scriptural commandments with rabbinic ordinances.

When, late in the talmudic period, the difference between scriptural/divine legislation (*d'oraita*) and rabbinic/human legislation (*de-rabbanan*) becomes more pronounced, the distinction between covenant and contract in Judaism becomes more apparent. Distinctly rabbinic legislation is no longer presented as having been literally *derived* from a specific scriptural text.[78] That is primarily due to the growing sense that the number of actual scriptural commandments is finite.[79] Since the literal expansion of scriptural law by the designation of new commandments was waning, legislation needed for new circumstances had to come from reasoning *about* Scripture rather than about what is specifically *within* Scripture. The earlier rabbinic approach, which saw itself able to derive a ruling for any circumstance new or old *from* Scripture, seems to have assumed that the number of such possible interpretations is infinite. Making revela-

---

[77] B. Baba Metsia 59b. Re "R. Eliezer the Great," see, e.g., B. Berakhot 6a re Deut. 28:10.
[78] See B. Shabbat 23a re Deut. 17:11 and 32:7.
[79] See B. Makkot 23b.

tion's norms finite, though, now made the possible range of human legislation infinite.[80]

There are two basic types of rabbinic legislation. Both exhibit contractual characteristics. One, there is a rabbinic "decree" (*gezerah*) designed
to protect a specific scriptural law from possible violation: "a fence [*siy-
yag*] for the Torah."[81] Thus the Rabbis decreed certain positive practices
to enhance the commandment "[R]emember [*zakhor*] the Sabbath day to
sanctify it" (Exodus 20:8), such as requiring the use of wine in the ritual
of Sabbath sanctification (*qiddush*).[82] And the Rabbis also decreed certain
additional Sabbath prohibitions to enhance its sanctity, such as the discussion of business matters on the Sabbath, this being in the spirit of
"[G]uard [*shamor*] the Sabbath day to keep it holy" (Deuteronomy
5:12).[83] Unlike a scriptural commandment, though, there are many more
conditions under which a rabbinic decree may be adjusted or waived.[84]

Two, there is an "enactment" (*taqqanah*), literally "an improvement,"
designed to positively promote the overall purposes of the Torah, such as
requiring that certain interpersonal practices be performed "for the sake
of the ways of peace [*mipnei darkhei shalom*]," since the whole Torah is
considered to have been given as "paths of peace" (Proverbs 3:17).[85] Such
practices are considered to have been enacted "for the sake of the improvement of civilization" (*mipnei tiqqun ha'olam*), which means to promote a well-ordered, benevolent, community.[86] Another prominent example, which we examined earlier, is the festival of Purim. Clearly, as a
rabbinic enactment it conforms to the overall Torah purpose of celebrat-
ing the saving acts of God, here God having saved the Jewish people from
near extermination at the hands of Haman and his genocidal followers.[87]

---

[80] See B. Avodah Zarah 35a. When a scriptural verse is connected to rabbinic legislation,
it is considered a secondary "allusion" (*asmakhta b'alma*). See, e.g., B. Nedarim 49a and
R. Nissim Gerondi (Ran), s.v. "ve'af'al-pi" thereon. Some medieval commentators, though,
did consider the difference between literal exegesis (*derashah gemurah*) and an *asmakhta*
one of degree rather than of kind. In other words, the former is more specific revelation
and the latter more general. See R. Yom Tov ben Abraham Ishbili, *Hiddushei ha-Ritva*:
Rosh Hashanah 16a. Cf. R. Judah Halevi, *Kuzari*, 3.76; B. Menahot 92b and Tos., s.v.
"girsa."

[81] M. Avot 1.1.

[82] B. Pesahim 106a and Tos., s.v. "zokhrehu"; B. Nazir 4a and Tos., s.v. "m'ai."

[83] B. Shabbat 113a–b re Isa. 58:13; Maimonides, MT: Shabbat, 21.1 re Exod. 23:12 and
R. Abraham de Boten, *Lehem Mishneh* thereon.

[84] See, e.g., M. Yoma 8.1 and R. Yom Tov Lippmann Heller, *Tosfot Yom Tov* thereon.

[85] M. Gittin 5.8–9; T. Gittin 3.13–14; B. Gittin 61a; Maimonides, MT: Melakhim, 10.12.

[86] M. Gittin 4.2–9.

[87] See 71–73 above.

There are two aspects of distinctly rabbinic legislation that seem to be contractual in character: (1) its justification; (2) its being subject to repeal.

All rabbinic legislation requires rational justification (*ta῾ama*), namely, it must be argued prior to legislation just *how* a proposed decree or enactment fulfills an agreed-upon purpose. As a means to an end, the proposed means is conditional; it requires a rational argument to persuade others of its theological (in the case of a matter between humans and God) or its ethical (in the case of a matter between humans themselves) value.[88] At the time of the legislation (and perhaps even long after it), one must be convinced *why* it is to be done before one can be asked to do it. The rationality of the proposed new decree or enactment must have been initially accepted by the colleagues of the Rabbi proposing it. It is thus conditional on their reasoned approval. Thereafter, the public must be persuaded that the law being considered by the Rabbis is truly in the public's best interest, that is, what they themselves would want.[89] Thus a basic principle of rabbinic legislation-jurisprudence is that "a decree is not to be decreed [*ein gozrin gezerah*] unless it can be assumed that the majority of the community will be able to live by it."[90] Moreover, popular dissatisfaction with a rabbinic decree could lead to its being radically reinterpreted and reapplied.[91] As such, one can see a kind of social contract here between the Rabbis and the people of their community.

Almost all rabbinic legislation is subject to repeal, irrespective of how well reasoned it was initially or how popular it was initially.[92] Repeal can take place in one of three ways. First, a later Supreme Court (*bet din ha-gadol*) can repeal (*mevatel*) a decree or ruling of an earlier Supreme Court if it considers itself greater in wisdom and if it has a greater range of influence, that is, more disciples.[93] Second, because of the overall conservatism of rabbinic authorities, later generations were reluctant to explicitly repeal any earlier decision. "If earlier generations are angels, we are but humans" is a talmudic statement that expresses this rabbinic conservatism.[94] Nevertheless, there are exceptions to this trend in the form of radical reinterpretations of existing rabbinic norms.[95] Third, Maimonides seems to have argued that even if an earlier generation has accepted a

---

[88] See B. Gittin 14a and Tos., s.v. "ke-hilkhata;" B. Keritot 20a; B. Baba Batra 173b.

[89] See Maimonides, MT: Mamrim, 2.1–2, 5–6.

[90] B. Avodah Zarah 36a and parallels; Y. Shabbat 1.4/3d. See, also, T. Sanhedrin 2.13.

[91] See, e.g., B. Avodah Zarah 35a; Y. Shabbat 1.4/3c.

[92] B. Avodah Zarah 36a and Tos., s.v. "ve-ha-tenan" re Y. Shabbat 1.4/3d.

[93] M. Eduyot 1.5; Maimonides, MT: Mamrim, 2.2.

[94] B. Shabbat 112b; also, B. Eruvin 53a.

[95] See, e.g., Maimonides, MT: Mekhirah, 11.18; ibid.: Malveh ve-Loveh, 11.11.

rabbinic ruling (literally, "it became prevalent [*pashtah*] among most of the Jewish people"), if this was no longer the case in a later generation, then formal repeal was not necessary.[96] All that was needed was for the contemporary authorities to "sit and do nothing" as the Talmud put it about another situation where current practice seemed to be at odds with a past ruling.[97] In essence, then, what can be repealed can only be accepted as tentative, as is the case in any contractual proposal.

The appointment and removal of rabbinic authorities is perhaps where the contractual character of rabbinic Judaism is most apparent. In principle, Rabbis received their authorization to issue rulings in Jewish law— that is, ordination (*semikhah*)—from older Rabbis.[98] This in itself reflects a hierarchal system of judicial authority. Furthermore, the judicial authority of Rabbis in the land of Israel during the talmudic period was broader than that of Rabbis outside the land of Israel, even in Babylonia, the largest and most important Diaspora community.[99] Nevertheless, there are enough examples to indicate that the authority of a Rabbi, whether in the land of Israel or in the Diaspora, was only as effective as the willingness of his community to elect him and reelect him to office (albeit informally).[100] This makes rabbinical authority conditional, hence contractual, whether that contract is actually put in writing or is only a tacit agreement.

The very function of a Rabbi, which is primarily that of judge (*dayyan*) in civil disputes, or respondent (*poseq*) on questions of ritual doubt, has this contractual character. In civil disputes, the parties have the right to pick their own judges, turning what could have been a case before a judge who judges *above* them into a case before judges who judge *between* them.[101] In other words, Rabbis become opposing advocates of the interests of their clients.[102] Furthermore, within the general boundaries of Jewish civil law there is a good deal of leeway for the parties themselves to negotiate, to contract, the rules by which the case will be settled by arbitration (*pesharah*).[103] In ritual matters, where there are no opposing parties, there is still the tension between the theoretical law in the mind of the respondent and the popular custom of his community. Since theoreti-

---

[96] MT: Mamrim, 2.7 and R. Joseph Karo, *Kesef Mishneh* thereon. Cf. B.. Avodah Zarah 36a and Rashi, s.v. "lo pashat." See also, MT: Ishut, 14.14 and 16.7.

[97] See R. Asher, *Teshuvot ha-Rosh*, no. 77. Re "sit and do nothing" (*shev ve'al ta'aseh*), see B. Yevamot 90a and parallels. Cf. B. Baba Batra 60b.

[98] B. Sanhedrin 13b re Num. 27:23.

[99] B. Baba Kama 84b; B. Gittin 88b.

[100] See B. Sanhedrin 26a for a discussion of the extent to which rabbinic tolerance of popular laxity in religious observance is to be tolerated by higher rabbinical authorities.

[101] M. Sanhedrin 3.1.

[102] B. Sanhedrin 23a and Rashi, s.v. "yetse din le'amito;" Y. Sanhedrin 3.1/21a.

[103] B. Sanhedrin 5b–6a.

cal law usually has more than one theoretical option, the deciding factor in favor of one of these options over the other is popular custom (*minhag*). Thus the Talmud tells Rabbis to "go out and see what is the people's custom."[104] It is only when a humanly proposed scheme is in direct conflict with the Torah that we must say: "There is to be no wisdom, there is no understanding, there is no counsel against the Lord" (Proverbs 21:30).[105] The covenant always trumps any contract, but it does not have to do that very often, that is, when the contract is made in good faith by those committed to the covenant.

Lastly, there are cases where Rabbis, even Rabbis with large jurisdictions, have been removed from office. A prophet could only be removed from his or her prophetic office when it could be proved that he or she willingly misrepresented him- or herself, or when he or she willingly advocated a permanent violation of revealed law.[106] But a Rabbi could be removed from office simply because his exercise of authority was considered by his constituents to be tyrannical. The most famous such case in the Talmud involves the removal from office of Rabban Gamliel II in the late first century C.E. because of his abusive treatment of R. Joshua.[107] The fact that Rabban Gamliel was wealthy and came from an aristocratic family, and the fact that he was the leader (*nasi*) of the Jewish community who dealt with the Roman conquerors, may have been the main factor in his shabby treatment of R. Joshua, who was very poor and from humble origins. Nevertheless, the other Rabbis, undoubtedly with popular support, removed Rabban Gamliel from office and replaced him with R. Eleazar ben Azariah. The point here is that even Rabban Gamliel "the Prince" was removed from office because he had, in effect, broken a social contract with his colleagues and their larger constituencies. There is no evidence, though, that his misconduct in any way violated the covenant. Therefore, after his removal from what seemed his exercise of absolute power, a compromise was worked out that restored him to a position of shared power with R. Eleazar ben Azariah.[108] In his case, then, a social contract among Jews had been successfully renegotiated. Yet, of course, this was secondary to the covenant between Jews, a covenant that requires mutual involvement at all levels. "All Jews are responsible [*arevim*] for one another" as the Talmud puts it, and that seems to mean they are

---

[104] B. Berakhot 45a and parallels; Y. Yevamot 7.6/8a; B. M. Lewin, *Otsar ha-Geonim*: Rosh Hashanah 34a, p. 62.

[105] B. Berakhot 19b and parallels; ibid., 31a–31b and Tos., s.v. "davar" re Lev. 19:17. Cf. B. Shabbat 148b and B. Betsah, 30a; R. Yom Tov ben Abraham Ishbili, *Hiddushei ha-Ritva*: B. Makkot 20b.

[106] See Maimonides, MT: Yesodei ha-Torah, 8.3–9.5.

[107] B. Berakhot 27b–28a.

[108] Ibid., 28a.

Chapter Four

The Law of the State

Political Subordination

In chapter 1, we saw how the Jews had to subordinate themselves to their non-Jewish rulers during the Babylonian exile, and that this political arrangement is termed a "covenant" (*berit*).[1] There is an agreement here, some degree of mutuality between the parties to the covenant, yet there is still no equality between the government and the governed; this will have to wait for the emergence of a social contract. Despite this lack of equality, though, this relationship between the Jews and the king of Babylon is also quite different from what obtains in a relationship of domination between master and slave. Thus, in the master-slave relationship in Egypt, at the very beginning of the corporate life of the Jewish people, there was no covenant between Pharaoh and the Israelites. Pharaoh's enslavement of them is morally unjustified—they were not captives taken in war, but only an imagined "fifth column" due to Pharaoh's political paranoia (Exodus 1:10). Nevertheless, Pharaoh was not guilty of any breach of covenant since one cannot breach what never had existed. The very presence of this clan in Egypt to begin with was but an act of largesse on Pharaoh's part due to his respect and affection for Joseph, whom he had made his prime minister, and due to his impression that Joseph's brothers could be useful servants of the state (Genesis 47:6).[2] And the Israelites themselves saw no covenantal permanence in their now being in Egypt. In their words: "We have only come to sojourn [*la-gur*] in the land because [*ki*] there is no pasture for the flocks that belong to your servants" (47:4).[3]

---

[1] See 59 above.

[2] Why Joseph's legacy was not sufficient to save his clan from being enslaved is discussed on B. Eruvin 53a. One view is that "a new king arose over Egypt" (Exod. 1:8) literally means a new pharaoh who did not believe himself bound by his predecessor's commitment to Joseph and his clan. The other view is that this was the same pharaoh who "made new decrees," i.e., broke his personal commitment to Joseph and his clan. But regardless of which pharaoh enslaved the Israelites, the commitment, whether past or present, was noncovenantal. As such, no unconditional agreement could be cited when petitioning Pharaoh for the Israelites' freedom (see Exod. 2:23–25).

[3] A number of rabbinic sources emphasize that the Israelites did not go to Egypt to "permanently settle" (*le-histaqeʿa*) there, but only to stay there as transients until the famine that caused them to leave their land ended. See, e.g., *Midrash ha-Gadol*: Beresheet on Gen.

So, for example, if Pharaoh had expelled them from his country because he felt he had already paid his debt to Joseph for his great service to the Egyptian state, then the Israelites would have had no right to complain about Pharaoh's injustice to them.

However, since Pharaoh had unjustly enslaved the Israelites, Moses had to come to forcibly emancipate them, having already been told by God that Pharaoh would not negotiate with him for their release (Exodus 4:21). That is, Pharaoh would not listen to the moral argument that the Israelites belong to their God, and not to him. Pharaoh regarded the Israelites as his property. The Israelites saw themselves as belonging to the God who would redeem them from slavery. Pharaoh did not recognize this God (Exodus 5:1–2), and this God was quite determined to declare his own sovereignty at Pharaoh's expense (Exodus 7:5). Thus the Exodus is a power struggle with God taking back what is his, and Pharaoh failing to keep what he had previously stolen from the Israelites: their liberty. The Israelites did not live independently in Egypt nor could they leave Egypt with the free consent of Pharaoh and the Egyptians. So, Pharaoah's sin was not his breach of covenant with Israel but his interference in Israel's covenant with the Lord, its God. But the Lord was fulfilling his own covenantal commitment—taken upon himself autonomously, to be sure (Genesis 15:13–14)—to rescue his own people from Egyptian slavery. That slavery was preventing them from responding to God's full covenantal claims on them. "God heard their cry, and God remembered his covenant with Abraham, with Isaac, and with Jacob" (Exodus 2:24).[4]

In the case of the Babylonian exile, conversely, the relationship between the ruler and the ruled is designated by Ezekiel to be a covenant (Ezekiel 17:13), one sealed by an oath. As in any other covenant, it would seem that the oath was taken mutually, and that the covenantal obligations are now owed to God over and above what the parties owe each other. Moreover, since the Jews were already living under the archetypal covenant of Sinai, any subsequent covenant, whether with fellow Jews or even with non-Jews, must be consistent with that covenant, *the* covenant par excellence. So, even in a covenant where the parties to it are not equal, as

---

47:4, ed. Margulies, p. 789; also, the discussion of M. M. Kasher, *Torah Shelemah*: Gen. 47:4, p. 1702, n. 5.

[4] Thus the Jewish communal obligation to rescue fellow Jews—fellow covenant members (*bnai berit*—see, e.g., M. Baba Kama 1.3)—sold as captives into slavery (*pidyon shevuyyim*) is an act of *imitatio Dei*. It is covenantal faithfulness (see Deut. 7:9–12). See Lev. 25:47–55; B. Kiddushin 15b; M. Gittin 4.6; B. Baba Batra 8b re Jer. 15:2; Maimonides, MT: Mattnot Aniyyim, 8.10 and 10.2; also, D. Novak, *Covenantal Rights* (Princeton, N.J.: Princeton University Press, 2000), 163.

THE LAW OF THE STATE

was the case between the Babylonian king and his Jewish subjects, this
interhuman covenant would still be invalid if it contradicted the Sinaitic
covenant. Indeed, if the more dominant human power in the covenant
claimed ultimate sovereignty by replacing God's direct sovereignty over
Israel with his own, the Sinaitic covenant could still not function for the
Jews as their primary and ultimate frame of communal reference.

This is why Daniel and his cohorts could not keep the covenant with the
king of Babylonia after the king had demanded that all his subjects, the
Jews included, worship the statue he had set up (Daniel 3:1–18). It is very
likely that this statue was meant to be an image of the king himself since
the worship of this statue was to be exclusive, as when a later king ruled
that no "request be made from any god or man" but only from himself
(6:8).[5] Whereas Daniel could accept political subordination to the gentile
king, he could not accept such religious subordination. Political subordination can be partial when it is kept separate from the ultimate commitment
of religious subordination. It is only when political subordination replaces
one's covenantal obligation to God that it oversteps its boundaries insofar
as there is nothing left to limit it by transcending it. So despite the king's
ruling, Daniel continued his usual Jewish practice of praying three times
daily, facing Jerusalem, the site of the Temple, whose sanctity still remained
even though the Temple itself had been destroyed (6:11).[6]

The Jews could accept political subordination in good faith as long as
their religious right to serve God above all others was respected. But they
could not accept subordination to a truly absolutist state in the person of
its divinized monarch. And, in fact, such self-divinization seems to have
been anomalous in Babylonia. The book of Daniel describes an unusual
state of theological-political affairs there. But, as for Egyptian pharaohs,
who could say even to God: "The Nile is mine; I made it for myself"
(Ezekiel 29:3), self-divinization was very much the norm. This might be
the reason Jeremiah had earlier warned the Jews about political subordi-

---

[5] The exact intention of this statute and others like it is the subject of much rabbinic and
medieval discussion. Was its erection for political homage or religious worship? See B. Shabbat 72a and Tos., s.v. "Rava;" B. Pesahim 53b and Tos., s.v. "mah;" B. Ketubot 33b and
Tos., s.v. "ilmalei"; B. Sanhedrin 61b–62a and Tos., s.v. "Rava" (esp. re *Esther Rabbah* 7.6
on Est. 3:2; also, re B. Megillah 10b and 19a); B. Avodah Zarah 3a and Tos., s.v. "andrati";
Y. Avodah Zarah 3.1/42b. Nevertheless, even if a statute was originally intended only for
political homage, any subsequently worshipful behavior toward it is deemed idolatrous.
This implies, of course, how easily political megalomania and its symbols inspire a religious
response. See Maimonides, *Commentary on the Mishnah*: Avodah Zarah 4.7; MT: Avodah
Zarah, 1.16.

[6] See M. Megillah 3.3 and Maimonides, MT: Bet ha-Behirah, 6.16 re Lev. 26:31; also,
Entsyqlopedia Talmudit, 3:233–34, s.v. "Bet ha-Miqdash."

nation to Egypt rather than to Babylonia, the latter of which he approved (Jeremiah 43:10–13).

Because of the covenantal status of the political relationship between the exiled Jews and the Babylonian state, personified by its king, Ezekiel castigates the Jews for their disloyalty to the Babylonian king by their treasonous involvements with his enemy, Pharaoh king of Egypt (Ezekiel 17:11–21). Such treason is a covenantal violation, one deserving prophetic rebuke. But since we do not know the actual stipulations of this Babylonian-Jewish covenant, it is impossible for us to extract any guidelines from the passage in Ezekiel as to how Jews ought to be related to the non-Jewish regimes in which they now live.

The only thing we can infer from this type of gentile-Jewish covenant presented in Scripture is that, being a covenant, it is not automatically terminated by noncompliance with its stipulations by either covenanting partner.[7] Like any covenant, noncompliance is only an occasion for the aggrieved party to complain, both to the other offending party and to the God in whose name the covenanting oath has been taken. A covenant does not admit of a divorce between the parties. It only ceases to operate when one of the parties dies, at least as an intact political entity. Accordingly, the Jews no longer had a covenant with the Babylonians once the Babylonian empire was conquered by the Persians and, therefore, permanently ceased to exist as a distinct political entity. This is why the covenant between God and Israel, which both precedes and succeeds all these interhuman covenants, not only presupposes the permanence of God, but also the permanence of Israel. "But My loyalty [ve-hasdi] shall never be moved away from you, and My peaceful covenant [u-vrit shlomi] shall not be shaken" (Isaiah 54:10).[8] Compared to this, all interhuman covenants are ephemeral, even though they cannot be terminated willfully by either or both of the human partners. Nevertheless, their perpetuity is not guaranteed by the God whose name is invoked when they are initiated and renewed. God holds the parties to their mutual commitments only for as long as they both continue to exist intact.

The political subordination of the Jews is, of course, a historical fact. When it has been the result of conquest pure and simple, the only moral significance it has for the Jews is to find the means by which to be freed from such involuntary slavery. Minimally, Jews have done this by secretly subverting the authority of their conquerors while paying lip service to them in public. Maximally, Jews have been able to flee their conquerors in order to settle in places affording them more communal independence and personal freedom. Most radically, Jews have attempted revolution

[7] See 30–32 above.
[8] See Y. Sanhedrin 10.1/27d.

against their conquerors as was the case in 66 C.E. before the destruction of the Second Temple, and again in 135 C.E. about three generations after the destruction of the Second Temple in 70 C.E. Indeed, many Jews saw their situation under the imperial Roman conquerors of the land of Israel as one of subjugation to a foreign power that had no valid moral claims on them.[9] What the Jews needed was redemption, not the type of mutual persuasion involved in the establishment and maintenance of a covenant. Persuasion is only possible when the terms of an agreement are freely proposed and accepted by both parties.

A possible change in Jewish attitudes toward the Roman rulers of the land of Israel, however, can be seen in this rabbinic text:

> R. Yose son of R. Hanina said: Why were there three oaths [*shevu'ot*]? One was that the Jews should not ascend the wall. One was that God made the Jews swear [*hishbi'a*] that they would not rebel against the nations of the world. One was that God made the gentiles swear that they would not subordinate [*yisht'avdu*] Israel more than need be [*yoter mid'ai*].[10]

The usual interpretation of the first clause of the agreement ("not to ascend the wall") is that the Jews promise not to immigrate en masse back to the land of Israel until God sends the Messiah to bring them back. "The wall" here refers to rebuilding the walls of Jerusalem, that is, making it once again the fortified capital of the independent Jewish state. In fact, it is pointed out by one commentator that when the Jews did return to the land of Israel from the Babylonian exile (sometime in the sixth century B.C.E.), their leader, Nehemiah, did so with the express permission of the king of Persia.[11] Nehemiah was already serving as a high official of the king in Persia. Thus his political clout with the king enabled him to put the renewed Jewish settlement in the land of Israel on a solid foundation, both politically and militarily. As such, the Jews were coming back to *their* land to be sure, but they were coming anew as Persian colonists. They had the full authorization of the government under whose rule they were now living voluntarily (Nehemiah 2:18). It could very well be that the idea of an oath between the Jews and the "nations of the world"— meaning the Roman Empire—meant that the Jews saw themselves negoti-

---

[9] Thus all the conquerors of Israel, especially Rome, are compared to Egypt as the paradigmatic persecutor. See, e.g., *Vayiqra Rabbah* 13.5.

[10] B. Ketubot 111a.

[11] See R. Enoch Zundel, *Ets Yosef* on *Shir ha-Shirim Rabbah* 2.18. This text has also been used by modern religious anti-Zionists to argue against the religious legitimacy of any premessianic independent Jewish state. For an argument against such use of this text, however, see R. Isaac Halevi Herzog (the first Ashkenazic Chief Rabbi of the State of Israel), *Sheelot u-Teshuvot be-Dinei Orah Hayyim*, no. 115, ed. S. Shapira (Jerusalem: Mosad ha-Rav Kook, 1989), p. 52.

ating a colonial status for themselves within the Roman Empire as they had done in the Persian Empire centuries earlier, and for which there was scriptural precedent.

The second clause of the agreement is that the Jews promise not to rebel against their gentile rulers. Taken by itself, this commitment does not seem to be anything more than what Ezekiel took to be the covenantal relationship between the Jews and their Babylonian rulers. Yet there are three factors here that are not found in the text from Ezekiel. One, the term *berit* is clearly avoided. By limiting the relationship to mutual promises expressed in an oath, the rabbinic text could be implying that noncompliance with the terms of the agreement, especially on the part of the gentile rulers, constitutes sufficient grounds for its termination. In that sense, the agreement is more contractual than covenantal. Two, in this rabbinic text, we find the reciprocity that was missing from the scriptural text: The gentiles will not subordinate their Jewish subjects unduly. So, one could say that *in return for* being tolerated by their gentile rulers, the Jews promise patriotic loyalty, thus abjuring any rebellion. Rebellion on the part of the Jews would now be treason, not just against their rulers but against God, to whom they have taken this oath. And, *in return for* the political loyalty of their Jewish subjects, these gentiles promise them fair treatment. Three, in the scriptural text, the treason being condemned is a Jewish alliance with a foreign enemy of the Babylonian state, Pharaoh, king of Egypt. A Jewish struggle for self-liberation, though not even considered in the scriptural text, is very much considered in the rabbinic text.

So far, the rabbinic text only deals with the question of political subordination. It certainly could not endorse any religious subordination. By the time of the author of the statement, R. Yosé son of R. Hanina, in the third century C.E., the Jews had bitter memories of how, in the previous century, the Romans had persecuted them by proscribing the public practice of much of their religion in the aftermath of the aborted Bar Kokhba revolution. However, at the theological-political level, there also seems to have been some major rethinking. Being a communal phenomenon, religion—certainly Jewish religion—can never be totally separated from politics. This comes out in the continuation of the Talmud text we have been analyzing.

> R. Levi said: Why are there six oaths?—Three have already been stated [that is, in the name of R. Yose son of R. Hanina]. The other three are—: They should not reveal the end [*ha-qets*]. They should not force [*yidahqu*] the end. They should not reveal the mystery [*ha-sod*] to the gentiles.[12]

---

[12] B. Ketubot 111a.

What we see here is that a much more apocalyptic messianism is being advocated. In other words, the Messianic Age (*yemot ha-mashiah*) is no longer to be seen as something the Jews themselves can or should bring about. Therefore, even if Jewish prophets know when the end will come, they should not reveal it to anyone lest the Jews take this as their cue to begin to exercise political independence now, the independence the Messiah is to finalize later. The Messiah as the regent of God himself will both initiate and finalize his own reign. Premessianic activism is, in effect, taken to be an illegitimate attempt to force the hand of God.[13] And, along these lines, the "mystery" referred to here is the Jewish method for proclaiming an extra month when the need arises. Such a need arises when Passover, whose actual date is determined by a lunar month, will fall too early in the solar year to be the barley harvest festival it was intended to be. Adding the extra month just before the month in which Passover is supposed to occur enables dates set according to the moon to be consistent with seasons of the year determined by the sun.[14] There were both religious and economic reasons for the need to do this. Politically, the procedure was considered the special domain of the Sanhedrin. So if the Sanhedrin was not to reveal its activities to the gentiles, this meant they had to operate in secret, if at all.[15] In other words, the Sanhedrin's secrecy was, in effect, its acceptance of the loss of its own public authority in the life of the Jewish people.

That all of this might very well be a disappointed reaction to Bar Kokhba's failure comes out in a cognate rabbinic text to the one we have been analyzing. This disappointment is because of how the Jewish people had so greatly suffered during and after two aborted revolutions less than a century apart. The first led to the destruction of the Second Temple; the second led to the demise of the Sanhedrin as the supreme legislature of the Jews, and even the outlawing of public Judaism for a while.[16] The Bar Kokhba factor comes out in this cognate text.

R. Helbo said that there were four oaths: God made Israel swear that they would not rebel against the worldly kingdoms [*malkhiyot*]; that they would not force the end; they would not reveal their secret [*mystirin*] to the nations of the world; and that they would not ascend the wall from the Diaspora [*min ha-*

[13] See B. Sanhedrin 97b re Isa. 30:18; also, R. Jacob of Marvege, *Sheelot u-Teshuvot min ha-Shamayim*, no. 72, ed. R. Margaliot, pp. 80–83, and Margaliot's long discussion in n.1 thereon.
[14] See B. Sanhedrin 11b–13b.
[15] See B. Ketubot 111a and Tos., s.v. "she-lo" re B. Shabbat 75a; also, B. Sanhedrin 11b and Tos., s.v. "ein."
[16] See B. Berakhot 61b; B. Kiddushin 39b; B. Sanhedrin 74a–b.

golah]. . . . R. Onia said that God made them swear four oaths because of [what happened] in four generations that forced the end and failed [*ve-nikshalu*]. . . . one of them was in the days of *Koziba*. . . . Why was this? Because they did not have faith [*she-l'o he'eminu*] in the Lord and they did not trust in his salvation . . . and they violated [*she'avru al*] the oath.[17]

Here we see quite clearly that the whole idea of the oaths God supposedly made the Jewish people take (we have no dating or location of this event in the rabbinic sources) concerns the interrelated issues of Jewish political independence and failed messianism. This is epitomized by the failed revolution of Simeon bar Kokhba and the religious persecution of the Jews by the Romans that came in its wake.

Simeon bar Kokhba's revolution originally had at least some support from the Rabbis. R. Akiva ben Joseph, the most prominent second-century Rabbi in the land of Israel, was an avid supporter of Bar Kokhba, taking him to be the Messiah. After Bar Kokhba's defeat, R. Akiva and those like him were castigated by some of their colleagues for their failed messianism. And this explains why Bar Kokhba was subsequently called "Koziba," meaning "deceiver."[18] Conversely, those who had called him "Bar Kokhba" (literally, "a star") did so because of the verse: "What I see for them is not yet; a star [*kokhav*] arises from Jacob . . . Edom becomes a possession . . . and Israel does mightily [*oseh hayil*]" (Numbers 24:17–18). This is taken as a messianic prophecy: The "star" is the Messiah; "Edom" is the rabbinic synonym for Rome; and Israel's "doing mightily" refers to the anticipated military victory over the Roman conquerors that was supposed to verify the messiah-hood of the Jewish leader able to accomplish this extraordinary feat.[19]

The result of the great historical disappointment in Bar Kokhba's defeat might very well have led to a more apocalyptic messianism than that previously promoted by Bar Kokhba's rabbinical sponsors. It also seems to have led to a more modest Jewish realpolitik. The Messiah would not be brought *by* the Jews; rather, he would be directly sent *to* the Jews from God. The Jews would not have to wait for any future verification. The Messiah would come at once totally or not at all. Full redemption would

---

[17] *Shir ha-Shirim Rabbah* 2.18.

[18] See Y. Taanit 4.5/68d; *Eikhah Rabbati* 2.5 re Lam. 2:2; also, Maimonides, MT: Melakhim, 1.3.

[19] Throughout the rabbinic sources, "Edom" is the synonym for "Rome," undoubtedly because King Herod, who was of Idumean-Jewish origin, was the epitome of Jewish collaboration with imperial Roman tyranny. See Josephus, *Jewish Antiquities*, 15.1ff. Jewish troubles with Edom go back to the patriarch Jacob/Israel and his conflict with his brother Esau "the red" (*edomi* in Hebrew). See Gen. 25:22–30; Amos 1:10–11; Obadiah 1:1–21.

be immediate.[20] The kingdom of God would descend from heaven wholly intact and complete. In the meantime, the Jews would have to make what are in essence temporary political arrangements. The very temporality of these arrangements makes a social contract, as distinct from a covenant with its suggestion of atemporal permanence, possible. Thus the messianic restoration of the full covenant would not involve any temporally conditioned negotiations with the gentile nations, because in the end of days, God would be ruling the whole world from Jerusalem through the Messiah as his regent on earth. As such, these nations would be coming to Jerusalem, as the world capital of the messianic kingdom, for moral and religious governance, not for a good political deal from the Jews. "And many peoples shall come and say, 'Let us go and ascend the mountain of the Lord to the house of the God of Jacob that he may instruct us [ve-yorenu] by his ways and we shall walk in his paths" (Isaiah 2:3; Micah 4:2).[21]

This more apocalyptic, and less political or military, messianism is reflected in a further point made by R. Helbo in the second rabbinic text quoted above. He continues his point about the futility of "forcing the end" by asserting that the ingathering of all the Jewish exiles (le-qabbets goliyoteihen) back to the land of Israel *will be* the supernatural task of the Messiah and is, therefore, *not to be* the political task of by now futile, even dangerous, Jewish political activism.[22] A more modest Jewish realpolitik involves resignation to the fact that it is more politically expeditious for Jews to try to work with their gentile rulers, most likely through some kind of negotiation, than to engage in active rebellion against them.

Mention of the reciprocal oaths taken by the gentile rulers to not unduly subordinate the Jews could refer to some actual modus vivendi that emerged after the Hadrianic persecution (in the wake of Bar Kokhba's defeat) began to ease. Even if the idea of the oaths taken by both the Jews and their gentile rulers is only historical speculation about what may have happened to bring about this political reconciliation, however partial and transitory, it still seems to reflect an atmosphere of greater tolerance of the Jews in the land of Israel. The Jews seem to have been able to move beyond the tragic times when Bar Kokhba was killed at Betar (the last Jewish stronghold against the Romans), and when R. Akiva was martyred for having taught the Torah in public, something the Romans no doubt suspected of being a pretense for political organization and incite-

---

[20] In other rabbinic texts (e.g., Y. Berakhot 1.1/2c re Micah 7:8), though, it is emphasized that redemption is a process not a single apocalyptic event. See E. E. Urbach, *Hazal* (Jerusalem: Hebrew University/Magnes Press, 1971), 604–15.

[21] See *Sifre*: Devarim, no. 1, ed. Finkelstein, pp. 7–8; *Pesiqta Rabbati*, no. 41, ed. Friedmann, pp. 173a–b.

[22] *Shir ha-Shirim Rabbah* 2.18.

ment to revolution.[23] One needs to contrast this period of Jewish persecution and political impotence with the more stable Roman-Jewish relationship that seemed to be the case after the death of the Emperor Hadrian in 138 C.E., especially during the political and religious leadership of R. Judah the Prince.[24]

The Law of the Gentiles

Even when the Jews could accept the political rule of the gentiles, the question still remained whether or not they could live under the law of the gentiles as it pertained to civil and criminal matters. The negative answer to this question comes out in the following text:

> R. Tarfon says that wherever you find gentile courts [agoriy'ot], even when their laws are like the Jewish laws, you are not permitted [rash'ai] to become attached to them, for it is written: "And these are the lawsuits [mishpatim] which you shall put before them [lifneihem]" (Exodus 21:1)—"before them," but not before the gentiles.[25]

The scriptural proof text cited is, ostensibly, God's command to Moses, who has just brought the Ten Commandments to the people of Israel, to present them with further, more specific, laws.[26] But in this interpretation, the word for "laws" (mishpatim) can also mean "cases" brought to the law courts for adjudication. Thus the "them" is no longer taken to refer to the people who are the subjects of the law but, rather, to the judges who apply the law to its subjects. As such, the Jews are not allowed to seek justice from the gentiles, even when there is no specific difference between Jewish law and gentile law in the particular case at hand. Why is this so? It is because at Sinai the Jews could have only accepted the law *from* God *through* Moses, who was both God's prophet *for* Israel and Israel's agent *back to* God (Exodus 3:10–12; 20:16). Thereafter, God's law for the people was to come through the rabbinical successors of

[23] See B. Berakhot 61b.

[24] Thus full rabbinical ordination (*semikhah*), which had been interrupted during the Hadrianic persecution, was restored by the time of R. Judah the Prince (see B. Sanhedrin 5a). Also, he restored the rabbinical authority to declare adjustments in the calendar (see Y. Rosh Hashanah 2.1/58a), something R. Akiva, a generation earlier, had to leave Palestine to do (see B. Berakhot 63a). None of this could have been accomplished, though, without the approval, indeed the cooperation, of the Roman government in Palestine. R. Judah the Prince's good relations with high Roman officials no doubt had an influence on improving the the political condition of Palestinian Jewry. See, e.g., Beresheet Rabbah 11.4; also, A. M. Rabello, *The Jews in the Roman Empire* (Aldershot, U.K.: Ashgate, 2000), 301.

[25] B. Gittin 88b.

[26] See *Mekhilta*: Mishpatim re Exod. 21:1, ed. Horovitz-Rabin, p. 246.

Moses, and the people had to bring their cases back to God's law through the successors of Moses they had appointed.[27] Accordingly, both the presentation *of* the law *for* the people and the adjudication of the people's cases *by* the law had to take place within this closed circle. Conversely, to go to the gentiles for any justice would be the equivalent of reverting to the time before the Sinaitic revelation when, at best, both Jews and gentiles were living under a much more general law, what the Rabbis were to call "Noahide commandments" (*mitsvot bnei Noah*).[28] To be sure, this law had been incorporated into the Sinaitic revelation rather than having been repealed by it, so that there would inevitably be great similarities between the two.[29] Hence, if gentiles were living under a system of positive law that reflected the moral laws the Rabbis assumed to have been set down at the dawn of humanity, that system of positive law would have much in common with Jewish civil law especially. Nevertheless, a Jew was not, as the Talmud puts it in another context, to "descend [*moridin*] from a higher to a lower level of sanctity [*ba-qodesh*]."[30]

The most Jewish-gentile contact in legal proceedings, according to those Rabbis who thought like R. Tarfon, is that gentiles may come to Jewish courts for justice, even though Jews may not return the favor. Thus in another version of the passage we have just analyzed, it is suggested that whereas the Jews may not go to the gentiles for justice, the Jews may render justice for those gentiles who request it from a Jewish court. "You may judges theirs [*shelahem*], but they may not judge yours."[31] In such cases, the gentiles could be seen as "ascending [*ma'alin*] to a higher level of sanctity."[32] This legal view seems to be based on the theological idea that the Torah is not only for Israel but for the gentiles as well, that is, whenever any gentiles want to partake of it.[33] That gentile partaking of the Torah would have to be partial if these gentiles are to remain gentiles, since full acceptance of the Torah would entail full conversion to Juda-

[27] See *Beresheet Rabbah* 72.5; Maimonides, MT: Sanhedrin, 1.3 and Mamrim, 1.1. For the distinction between official Mosaic authority and that of ordinary laymen (*hedyotot*), see B. Gittin 88b re Exod. 21:1 (the variant opinion); B. Sanhedrin 23a.

[28] See T. Avodah Zarah 8.4–6; B. Sanhedrin 56b; also, D. Novak, *The Image of the Non-Jew in Judaism* (New York and Toronto: Edwin Mellen Press, 1983).

[29] See D. Novak, *Natural Law in Judaism* (Cambridge: Cambridge University Press, 1998), 76–82.

[30] M. Menahot 11.7; B. Berakhot 28a and parallels. See B. Yevamot 22a.

[31] *Mekhilta*: Mishpatim re Exod. 21:1, p. 246.

[32] See *Sifre*: Devarim, no. 16, p. 26 and n. 9 thereon; B. Baba Kama 113a. See Novak, *The Image of the Non-Jew in Judaism*, 60–73.

[33] See *Mekhilta*: Yitro re Exod. 19:2, p. 205; T. Sotah 8.6–7; Saul Lieberman, *Tosefta Kifshuta*: Nashim (New York: Jewish Theological Seminary of America, 1973), 700; B. Sotah 35b.

ism.[34] So, it would seem that this gentile partaking of the Torah is only
moral not religious (that is, not involving one's positive relationship with
God). Interestingly, that gentile partaking of the Torah now portends the
messianic prophecy that "at the end of days [be'aharit ha-yamim] . . .
for from Zion the law [torah] will go forth, the word of the Lord from
Jerusalem" (Isaiah 2:3; Micah 4:2). In other words, whereas it seems to
have been prophesied that with the coming of the Messiah gentile acceptance of God's law will be corporate and complete, in the meantime, gentile acceptance of God's law will be individual and partial (particular case
rulings rather than specific legislation).[35]

The view of R. Tarfon quoted above seems to be typical inasmuch as
no opposing opinion from another authority is mentioned in the later
texts that cite it.[36] Yet even here, there are at least two exceptions to this
seemingly categorical rejection of any Jewish involvement with non-Jewish jurisprudence.

First, there is this passage in the Mishnah: "All official documents [ha-
shtarot] deposited in the courts [arka'ot] of the gentiles, even if their sig-
natories are gentiles, are valid [kesherim], except bills of divorce and manumission of slaves. R. Simeon says that even these are valid, since what
were mentioned [as invalid] only refer to what were done unofficially [be-
hedyot]."[37] One could, of course, infer from this that permission to use
the gentile courts for the validation of documents is an example of a more
general permission to use the gentile courts for the administration of justice among Jews. However, were that so, it seems likely that subsequent
talmudic discussion of this Mishnah passage would have at least suggested that it seems to contradict R. Tarfon's prohibition of Jews going
to the gentile courts to obtain justice for themselves. Since this seeming
dispute is not mentioned, it is probably better to interpret the permission
to use the gentile courts for the validation of signatures on Jewish legal
documents to be a specific recognition that the gentile courts take better
care of documents deposited with them.[38] In other words, this is a case
where a Jewish court, in effect, can use a gentile court to perform a specific

---

[34] See T. Demai 2.4; B. Bekhorot 30b.

[35] See D. Novak, *The Election of Israel* (Cambridge: Cambridge University Press, 1995),
157–62.

[36] Thus in the 12th century, R. Jacob Tam, the foremost halakhic authority in northern
France and the Rhineland, threatened excommunication (*herem*) for any Jew who went to
the gentile courts for justice. In this he was joined by some of his most distinguished rabbinical colleagues. See *Kol Bo*, no. 117, ed. Naples; also, A. Gulak, *Yesodei ha-Mishpat ha'Ivri*,
4.11 (Tel Aviv: Dvir, 1967), pp. 24–30.

[37] M. Gittin 1.5.

[38] See R. Mordecai ben Hillel Ashkenazi, *Mordecai: Gittin*, no. 324. See, also, B. Moed
Qatan 11a and Rashi, s.v. "u-ma'aleh b'arka'ot."

task on its behalf. In this case, the specified task would be the performance of notarial services. Perhaps documents deposited in the official gentile courts were safer there than in Jewish courts, which had less official status because of their precarious civil authority.

Second, whereas in the case above it seems that the accepted rabbinic view was that gentile courts could only be used for the validation of civil documents, there is also a passage in the Mishnah that allows Jews to use gentile courts in a matter pertaining to Jewish marriage, which is regarded as a Jewish religious matter. "A divorce coerced [*get me˓usseh*] by Jewish authorities is valid [*kasher*]; by gentile authorities is invalid [*pasul*]. But when gentile authorities force [*hovteen*] him by saying to him: 'do what the Jewish authorities tell you,' it is valid."[39] Here we see that the most Jews could ever expect from a gentile court was that it enforce the religious decision of a Jewish court when the Jewish court is incapable of such enforcement due to its lack of police power. In other words, it is recognized that the most significance gentile legal jurisdiction can have for the Jews is the occasional opportunity for a desperate Jewish court to, in effect, deputize it. Nevertheless, this kind of use of the gentile courts is not so much going *to* "them" as it is bringing "them" *to* "us." Thus what we have here is not so much a Jewish court recognizing the authority of a gentile court as it is a gentile court recognizing the authority of a Jewish one.[40]

Palestine and Babylonia

The early rabbinic passages we have been discussing at best authorize some very specific exceptions to the avoidance of gentile justice generally promoted by the Rabbis. It is important to know that they come from the land of Israel. That is, they come from Roman Palestine, from a political milieu where Jews are living under Roman military rule. As such, gentile jurisprudence is to be avoided there not only because going to the gentiles implies the Torah has nothing to say about basic issues of interhuman relations that are the subject matter of civil and criminal law, but also because the gentiles do not have a coherent system of law whereby they can adjudicate such matters consistently, especially for Jews who have no rights of citizenship in their society. Haphazard jurisprudence inevitably leads to unfair adjudication. Moreover, even when Roman-Jewish rela-

---

[39] M. Gittin 9.8.

[40] For the problems of transposing this notion of the formal recognition of the jurisdiction of a Jewish court in a secular democracy, see D. Novak, "Jewish Marriage and Civil Law: A Two Way Street?," *George Washington Law Review* 68 (2000), 1059–78.

tions seemed less volatile, the Romans had surely not forgotten the Bar Kokhba revolution, when Jews became explicit enemies of imperial Roman rule. Because of this, Jews were quite wary of getting any real justice from the Romans and their more favored pagan subjects in Palestine. The most that could be hoped for from the Romans, especially once things had settled down after the Bar Kokhba defeat, was for the Romans to leave the Jews alone with some degree of communal autonomy.[41]

As far as we know, Roman rule in Palestine in the second and third centuries C.E. was not conducted according to codified Roman law as was mostly the case elsewhere in the Empire. In Rome itself, and for those in the Empire who were privileged to be able to declare "I am a Roman citizen" (*civus Romanus sum*), there was the impressive system of Roman civil law (*ius civile*). For those communities outside of Rome that had long been under Roman rule, there was "the law of nations" (*ius gentium*). This was a more general system of law, expressing what could be considered more internationally accepted rules and procedures, but was, nonetheless, administered by a Roman official for what might be called "foreign affairs" (*praetor peregrinos*).[42] But one must remember that Palestine was essentially a troublesome Roman-occupied territory. It seems that it was to be administered by a Roman military governor whose job it was to collect taxes, to build up military defenses to hold back the often menacing Parthian Empire to the east, and to keep civil order—by whatever means seemed best at the time.[43] The non-Roman residents of this military district had no rights, especially the Jews, many of whom no doubt desired the restoration of their long lost national independence. Accordingly, few Jews could look with any confidence to this imperial regime under which they had to live in their own land in such degrading circumstances. Jews were best advised, then, to "be careful in dealing with the ruling powers [*ha-reshut*] since they only draw one near for their needs."[44]

To be sure, some Rabbis thought even this kind of Roman "law and order" was preferable to anarchy, since without it everyone would "swallow his neighbor alive" in the words of one early Rabbi.[45] But most others regarded Roman rule as totally self-serving, being, in effect, nothing more than a criminal regime.[46] Thus R. Simeon bar Yohai, who had been a fugi-

---

[41] See *Megillat Taanit*, chap. 12, ed. Amsterdam (reprint/Jerusalem, 1997), pp. 488–89.

[42] See D. Daube, "The Peregrine Praetor," *Journal of Roman Studies* 41 (1951), 66–70.

[43] See A. N. Sherwin-White, *Roman Society and Roman Law in the New Testament* (Oxford: Oxford University Press, 1963), 1–23.

[44] M. Avot 2.3.

[45] Ibid. 3.2; B. Avodah Zarah 4a; Beresheet Rabbah 9.13 re Gen. 1:31.

[46] This is why, it seems, the principle "the law of the state is law" is not found in the Palestinian Talmud, indeed in any Palestinian sources. See Samuel Atlas, "Ha-ratson ha-Tsibburi be-Tehuqah ha-Talmudit," *Hebrew Union College Annual* 26 (1955), 35 (Heb. Sec.).

tive from the Romans during the Hadrianic persecution, summarized a prevalent Jewish attitude when he stated: "Everything they have instituted, they have only instituted [*taqqnu*] for their own needs. They have established marketplaces in which to install prostitutes; bathhouses for their own pleasure; bridges in order to collect taxes [*mekes*] from their use."[47]

In Babylonia almost all of this was different, at least as far as we know from the third, fourth, and fifth centuries C.E. This great difference between Palestine and Babylonia is rooted in one basic historical fact: In Palestine, Jews were living as a conquered people in their own land, and political power had been stolen from them. In Babylonia, conversely, the Jews were voluntarily living in another land (even though many of them had originally gone there as captives from Judea), with political power and under a legal system that was consistent and in which there were definite civil rights that, as far as we know, Jews shared with other members of the realm.

If Jews were to avail themselves of the jurisprudence of their gentile rulers, yet still maintain their own communal identity, they would have to employ that jurisprudence on their own turf in good faith. This meant that Jews would have to be able to administer non-Jewish law for themselves. Indeed, they might even make a Jewish contribution to the development of that non-Jewish law. But in order to do that, they would have to become officials of the non-Jewish regime. Furthermore, this administration of non-Jewish law for Jews did not mean simply replacing Jewish civil and criminal law with non-Jewish law. Rather, it more often meant making the Jewish law of interhuman relations more consistent with what one Rabbi had called the "fittest (*ke-metuqqanim*) of them," that is, the most rationally compelling of the gentile laws.[48]

In terms of the ability of Jews to function as officials of a non-Jewish regime under which they themselves lived, it is illuminating to contrast the Babylonian situation with the Palestinian one. The story is told that R. Eleazar son of R. Simeon, a Palestinian Rabbi, suggested to a certain Roman official (*parhagavna*), who seems to have been a Jew, that his method of detecting thieves was inaccurate. As such, this official might very well be indicting innocent people and releasing guilty ones. The official protests: "This is the royal appointment [*harmana de-malka*]!"[49] In other words, this is my job; this is what I have been authorized to do. But when R. Eleazar's suggestion is made known to the royal authorities, they are so impressed with its wisdom that they send for R. Eleazar to implement it, which he does quite effectively. Yet R. Joshua ben Korhah sends

---

[47] B. Shabbat 33b.
[48] B. Sanhedrin 39b re Ezek. 5:7 and 11:2.
[49] B. Baba Metsia 83b.

a message to R. Eleazar: "How long will you turn over [*moser*] the people of our God for execution?!" R. Eleazar says that he is only "weeding [*mekhaleh*] the vineyard of thorns," namely, he is removing undesirable persons from society. R. Joshua's retort is: "Let the Master of the vineyard weed His own thorns."[50] In a similar incident cited in this text, another Jewish official of the Roman government also says that he is only doing his job. The response here comes from Elijah the Prophet, the heavenly arbiter of right and wrong. He tells this official, R. Ishmael the son of R. Yosé, that he should flee Palestine rather than continue working there as an official of this regime.[51]

The upshot of both of these stories is that, even when a Jewish contribution to non-Jewish jurisprudence is just, Jews should not participate in a political and legal system that is fundamentally unjust, especially in its overall treatment of Jews. We may contrast these stories, though, with the following Babylonian incident. "A certain Bar Hama killed someone. The Exilarch [*reish galuta*] told R. Aha bar Jacob: 'Go look into the matter. If he really killed, then dim his eye [*leekh'heiyuhu l'eineih*].'"[52]

Although some post-talmudic commentators take the term "dim his eye" to literally mean physical mutilation, considering the fact that the elimination of punitive physical mutilation and the payment of monetary damages in its stead was a hallmark of the pharisaic-rabbinic tradition from its earliest manifestation, it is understandable why this literal interpretation was not widely accepted.[53] Moreover, since it is presumed Jews did not have the power of capital punishment at that time, either in the land of Israel or in Babylonia, it is even more unlikely that it meant "a life for a life" (Exodus 21:23; Leviticus 24:18).[54] According to most commentators, it meant the imposition of some sort of fine on the convicted culprit.[55] (Whether these punishments were usual Persian law in such cases, or whether they were procedures devised by the Jews themselves in cases where they could not execute a criminal deserving of death according to original Jewish law, is difficult to ascertain.) But, for our purposes here, the important thing to note is that R. Aha is being commissioned by the Exilarch, not a rabbinical authority, to deal with a criminal

[50] Ibid.

[51] Ibid. 84a. See, also, B. Gittin 7a re Ps. 39:2; B. Baba Kama 117a for Jewish concerns about gentile justice for Jews who were to be punished under their law; Maimonides, MT: Hovel u-Maziq, 8.9.

[52] B. Sanhedrin 27a.

[53] See H. Z. Taubes, *Otsar ha-Geonim*: B. Sanhedrin 27a, pp. 220–21. Cf. B. Baba Kama 83b–84a.

[54] See B. Sanhedrin 41a; Y. Sanhedrin 1.1/18a and 7.2/24b; also, B. Berakhot 58a. Cf. John 18:31.

[55] See B. Sanhedrin 27a and Rabbenu Hananel and Rashi, s.v. "leekh'heiyuhu" thereon.

matter. Yet he conducts the deposition of the witnesses according to Jewish criminal law. As such, what we see here is an interaction between Jewish law and Persian law. Here we begin to see something like a social contract with give and take between the government and the governed in the way the Jewish community in Babylonia both took from and gave to the Persian government under whose essentially just rule they lived voluntarily. But that voluntary interaction would not have been possible without a distinction having been made, however imprecisely, between religious and secular realms, between the sacred and the profane.

This distinction is also reflected in the principle enunciated by the editors of the Babylonian Talmud: "Ritual matters [isura] are not inferred from civil matters [mamona]," and "civil matters are not inferred from ritual matters."[56] Ritual matters involve all those actions that pertain to the positive relationship between God and humans—specifically, between God and the Jews. Civil matters involve all those actions that pertain to the relationship between humans themselves—and this includes not only inter-Jewish relationships, but Jewish-gentile relationships as well.[57]

Regarding civil matters, as we shall see, involvement with non-Jewish law is inevitable since the actions dealt with there are not uniquely Jewish phenomena. In ritual matters, though, since the actions dealt with are uniquely Jewish, it stands to reason that their adjudication should always be a strictly Jewish affair. It is also important to note how the editors of the Babylonian Talmud settled the many differences of legal opinion between the two most important Jewish legal authorities in third century c.e. Babylonia: Rav of Sura and Samuel of Nehardea. The law in ritual matters is to be according to Rav, who came to Babylonia from the land of Israel with the authorization of the Palestinian rabbinate.[58] This is despite the fact that Rav had numerous opinions on civil matters, and there were many who followed his civil rulings during his lifetime and afterward.

Moreover, deciding to follow the opinions of Rav in ritual matters is significant since despite the tendency of the Babylonian Rabbis to regard

[56] B. Berakhot 19b and B. Ketubot 40b and parallels. Cf. B. Sanhedrin 34b re Deut. 21:5.

[57] Thus Jewish law is to be reinterpreted—even radically so—when it seems to treat gentiles unfairly compared to the way Jews (or anyone else for that matter) would be treated under their law. See B. Baba Kama 38a and 113a–b; also, Novak, *Natural Law in Judaism*, 76–82.

[58] B. Bekhorot 49b; also, B. Kiddushin 79b and Tos., s.v. "ve-hilkhata." Cf. B. Betsah 29a–b and Tos., s.v. "Shmuel"; B. Menahot 41b and Tos., s.v. "kol." This might explain why in the Passover narrative (*haggadah*) Rav emphasizes the religious degradation of the Jewish people that called for redemption, whereas Samuel emphasized their political subservience that called for redemption (B. Pesahim 116a). For Rav's emigration to Babylonia and its legal and religious impact, see B. Sanhedrin 5a; B. Hullin 110a.

themselves as independent of the civil authority of the Palestinian rabbinate, they were much more deferential to them on religious questions.[59] Conversely, in civil matters, the law is to be according to Samuel.[60] Here it is significant to note that Samuel, unlike Rav, was born, bred, and educated in Babylonia, and that he had close relations with the highest levels of the Persian government.[61] Samuel also derived his own political power from and through the clearly secular head of the Babylonian Jewish community: the Exilarch (*Reish Galuta*).[62]

The Exilarch functioned, in effect, as the Jewish prime minister in the Persian Empire (Babylonia—contemporary Iraq—being the place where the largest Jewish community in the Diaspora was located). Being appointed by the Persian authorities, probably by the king himself, his political authority over his fellow Jews was that of an imperial official.[63] Part of his power was the appointment of judges.[64] Indeed, the power of Jewish judges to effect civil and criminal law depended on how close they were to the Exilarch and his office.[65] Even Rav, who, as we have just seen, came to Babylonia under a religious warrant from the Palestinian rabbinate, still, nonetheless, had to acknowledge the civil authority of the Exilarch.[66]

---

[59] See B. Pesahim 51a and Tos., s.v. "keivan" re B. Baba Batra 158b and B. Sanhedrin 5a and Tos., s.v. "de-hakha."

[60] B. Bekhorot 49b. See, also, B. Ketubot 43b; Y. Ketubot 4.2/28b. Samuel's "royal" status was widely recognized by post-talmudic commentators. See, e.g., B. Shabbat 53b and Rashi, s.v. "Shmuel"; B. Hullin 76b and Rashi, s.v. "Aryokh."

[61] See B. Baba Batra 115b and Rashbam, s.v. "amar Rabbah." Samuel's Persian patriotism extended to his refusal to mourn a large number of Diaspora Jews who were killed because of their rebellion against the Persians (B. Moed Qatan 26a). Nevertheless, one wonders if he would have taken the same attitude had the Jewish victims been members of a Jewish state in the land of Israel. Cf. Y. Sotah 9.15/24b–c, where he berates a colleague for not properly mourning those Jews who died in the unsuccessful Jewish rebellion against the Romans of 66–70 C.E. (see M. Sotah 9.14; also, B. Baba Batra 60b). For Samuel's view of the essentially political character of the messianic era, i.e., that it would remove the "rule of the kingdoms" (*sh'ibud malkhiyot*) over the Jews, obviously even including the rule of Persia, see B. Berakhot 34b re Deut. 15:11; also, Maimonides, MT: Melakhim, 12.2.

[62] His title as one of the two "judges of the exile" (*dayyanei golah*)—B. Sanhedrin 17b according to Rashbam on B. Baba Batra 100a, s.v. "hakhi garsinan"—suggests a close connection to the *Reish Galuta*.

[63] See Y. Shevuot 1.1/32d; B. Shevuot 6b for the rank of the *Reish Galuta* in the Persian government hierarchy. Also, see B. Horayot 11b (and B. Sanhedrin 5a) re Gen. 49:10 for recognition of the greater political power of the *Reish Galuta* over his counterparts in Palestine. As for recognition of the lack of Jewish sovereignty in Babylonia, however, see B. Arakhin 10b re Ps. 113:1.

[64] B. Sanhedrin 5a.

[65] See B. Baba Batra 65a. In fact, it is noted that some Rabbis were known as "house Rabbis" of the *Reish Galuta* and that they wore special insignia designating them as such (B. Shabbat 58a).

[66] See B. Sanhedrin 5a. For certain tensions between Rav and the *Reish Galuta*, see Y. Baba Batra 5.5/15a–b.

Moreover, as we have seen, the Exilarch often submitted civil and even criminal cases to Rabbis for actual adjudication, even though when he himself adjudicated cases, it was according to Persian law.[67] In cases of ritual law, though, the Exilarch did not seem to have had any interest in getting involved at all. In these matters, he most often turned to the Rabbis for direction.[68] The Rabbis in turn were often quite lenient in ritual questions affecting the Exilarch and his official household.[69] All of this demonstrates a growing distinction between secular and religious authority in the Babylonian Jewish community.

What we see in the development of Jewish law in Babylonia is the growing sense of independence in that Jewish community from the authority of the Jewish community in the land of Israel. This comes out quite clearly in the differences between civil and criminal procedures in Palestine and Babylonia emphasized by R. Nahman, who was considered the leading Jewish authority in civil and criminal matters in Babylonia.[70] He is recorded in the Talmud as defining the area of Jewish jurisprudence in Babylonia (and, by implication, anywhere else in the Diaspora) as follows: "We exercise proper agency from Palestinian authorities [shelihuteihu] in usual cases [be-milta de-shekhiha] where there is recompense for actual monetary loss [hisaron kees]. But in usual cases where there is no recompense for actual monetary loss, or in unusual cases where there is recompense for actual monetary loss, we do not exercise such agency."[71] Thus R. Nahman is formulating the secularization of Jewish law in the Diaspora inasmuch as he is declaring all the civil punishments stipulated in the Torah that do not conform to equal reciprocity (quid pro quo)—what the Talmud calls "fines" (qenasot)—to be inoperative not only in the Diaspora but, by implication, even in the land of Israel in the absence of Rabbis ordained by the Sanhedrin.[72] But what the actual relation of Babylonian halakhic authority to that of Palestinian halakhic authority was still remains unclear. After all, it was in Palestine that some remnant of the rabbinical authority originated by Moses was still extant.

Based on the scriptural source of much of Jewish civil law, it was assumed that cases calling for civil adjudication required three Rabbis ordained by the Sanhderin (or its equivalent) to serve as "expert judges" (mumhin).[73] Ordination (semikhah) was the procedure whereby the

---

[67] See B. Baba Kama 58b.

[68] See, e.g., B. Menahot 33a.

[69] See, e.g., B. Eruvin 11b; B. Avodah Zarah 72b. Cf. B. Eruvin 26a.

[70] See B. Baba Batra 65a; also, B. Kiddushin 70a; B. Hullin 124a. Because of all this, R. Nahman asserted his personal authority in civil matters. See B. Ketubot 94b; B. Sanhedrin 5a.

[71] B. Baba Kama 84b. See B. Gittin 88b.

[72] B. Sanhedrin 3a–b; B. Baba Kama 84b.

[73] B. Sanhedrin 2b–3b.

Sanhedrin and its rabbinical successors designated men who were to have authority in ruling in all areas of the law—but this procedure could only be performed in the land of Israel and these Rabbis could only exercise their full authority in the land of Israel.[74] Thus, when in the second century C.E. Rav was sent to Babylonia to exercise rabbinical functions, he was not given full ordination. Instead, he was given what amounted to a limited license to rule in certain ritual and civil matters.[75] Yet by the criteria of the land of Israel, he seems to be little more than an ordinary layman (*hedyot*).[76] Thus Rav, and those like him coming from Palestine to Babylonia, let alone native Babylonian Rabbis—none of whom could be fully ordained—would be unable to adjudicate many questions of civil law. If so, of what real use would their license be "to judge" (*yadin*) in civil cases? This question is answered by R. Joseph, a Babylonian Rabbi renowned for his traditional erudition: "We are exercising their agency [*avdinan shelihuteihu*]," namely, we Babylonian Rabbis are acting in lieu of the Palestinian Rabbis on their behalf.[77] Nevertheless, this answer is highly problematic. If the Babylonian Rabbis are literally the "agents" of the Palestinian Rabbis, who appointed them? Agency is not an autonomous function; the agent must be specifically appointed by the person whom he is representing. Yet we have no record that the Palestinian Rabbis ever appointed the Babylonian Rabbis to be *their* agents.[78] Quite the contrary, the Palestinian Rabbis seemed to be concerned about their Babylonian counterparts, who had greater political power.[79] Moreover, it is important to note that the assertion of Babylonian halakhic authority is made in the name of R. Nahman and R. Joseph, both of whom (unlike Rav) were born and bred in Babylonia and were not at all personally beholden to the Palestinian Rabbis.

In effect, the Babylonian Rabbis took for themselves whatever authority they needed to function in a Diaspora community as judges in civil and some criminal cases. Yet, as we have seen before, the Babylonian Rabbis were really the agents of the Exilarch, and the Exilarch was the agent of the Persian government. Without that governmental authority behind them, their decisions would have had no political force. In fact, the Talmud tells us of at least one occasion when a dispute in Jewish civil

[74] Ibid., 14a.

[75] Ibid., 5a–b.

[76] See B. Gittin 88b re Exod. 21:1 (alternate opinion).

[77] Ibid.

[78] See R. Joseph Karo, *Kesef Mishneh* on Maimonides, MT: Sanhedrin, 5.8, who questions whether the Babylonian Rabbis needed any authorization from anyone else to judge or whether all they needed was their own legal autonomy. See, also, R. Moses Schreiber, *Sheelot u-Teshuvot Hatam Sofer*: Orah Hayyim, no. 84.

[79] See B. Sanhedrin 5a re Gen. 49:10.

law was discussed by some Rabbis with the Persian monarch himself, King Shapur, and that he offered his own opinion as to which opinion he thought correct.[80] So, we might conclude that Babylonian civil jurisprudence was exercised by Jews for the sake of integrating Jewish civil procedures into the overall jurisprudence of the Persian Empire. If the Jewish authorities had insisted on total legal independence, fewer and fewer cases would have come their way because they would have been in no position to enforce their decisions in civil society. Nevertheless, they did not simply surrender all questions of civil and criminal law to the non-Jewish regime. Rather, they participated in the jurisprudence of that regime by not only adapting its law to their law, but also by enabling Jewish law to make its contribution to that general jurisprudence. In fact, the Talmud indicates that there were Babylonian officials who were even knowledgeable in Jewish ritual law and that they even showed their respect for its strictures when in the company of Jewish scholars.[81]

Along these lines, it is important to note that the most explicit statement of the principle "the law of the state is law" (*dina de-malkhuta dina*) (a principle we shall be analyzing shortly), formulated (and perhaps originally proposed) by Samuel, is reported by another Babylonian authority, Rabbah bar Nahmani (who lived a generation after Samuel's death), as having been told to him by Uqban bar Nehemiah, the Exilarch himself.[82] Thus it seems that the application of Persian law by Jews had the official warrant of the man appointed by the Persians to be the Jewish governor of the Babylonian Jews. To be sure, Rabbah certainly was not being informed of a principle he did not already know. Rather, the Exilarch seems to be informing him of the limited range of application of this principle. In other words, it was not just a matter of theory, but a matter of real legal practice. We shall return to consider this principle shortly.

The most striking difference in rabbinic attitudes toward gentile rulers of Jews can be seen in their differing attitudes toward the religion of the Roman rulers of Palestine in contrast to the religion of the Persian rulers of Babylonia. In the case of the Roman rulers of Palestine, most of the Rabbis saw their polytheism as working in tandem with their overall immorality.[83] But, as for what seems to have been the polytheism of the Persians, there is a strong attempt to explain it away, as it were. This meant, in effect, that Babylonian polytheism was seen as peripheral to the overall culture. What was taken to be essential to their culture was their

[80] B. Baba Metsia 119a and Rashi, s.v. "qameih Shvor Malka."
[81] See B. Avodah Zarah 30a and 76b.
[82] B. Baba Batra 55a.
[83] See, e.g., M. Avodah Zarah 2.1–4 and 3.1–6, texts that clearly deal with Roman practices in Palestine; also, Saul Lieberman, *Hellenism in Jewish Palestine*, 2nd ed. (New York: Jewish Theological Seminary of America, 1962), 115–38.

admirable system of social justice. And thus it was no accident that the Jews and Judaism flourished here. They did so because their communal and individual rights were systematically respected. The Talmud juxtaposes three rabbinic statements that indicate this great difference, a difference that had a profound effect on Jewish political theology.

> R. Eliezer said that any thought [*stam mahshevet*] of a gentile is idolatrous [*l'avodah zarah*]. . . . R. Nahman said, quoting Rabbah bar Aboah that there are no heretics [*minin*] among the gentiles. . . . R. Hiyya bar Abba said, quoting R. Yohanan, that gentiles outside the land of Israel are not idolators, but only [practicing] their ancestral custom [*minhag avoteihen*].[84]

The first statement is that of R. Eliezer ben Hyrkanus, who lived during the time of the destruction of the Temple and was still alive during Bar Kokhba's aborted revolution. His statement is typical, even though it seems his colleagues did not accept its full legal implications. Clearly, the culture of Roman Palestine was one with which faithful Jews could find little commonality, even on basic moral issues.

The statement of R. Nahman reflects a very different theological-political situation, however. This can be seen in his ingenious use of the term *min*, what I have called a "heretic." Literally, the term means a "sectarian," namely, a Jew who willingly adopts and proclaims heterodox religious views that are considered idolatrous or dangerously close to idolatry.[85] In many ways, such a heretic, who has separated him- or herself from normative rabbinic teaching, is treated as if he or she were a gentile.[86] The key to the application of this term is the fact that such a heretic is conscious of what he or she affirms or denies, and that this affirmation or denial is voluntary. Thus, saying that there are no such gentile heretics outside the land of Israel—here, Babylonia—means that Persian-Babylonian polytheism, of most Babylonians anyway, is taken to be a matter of cultural habit, but one lacking in any true religious conviction. They are unlike Jewish heretics, who actually believe what they say and what they do. This is why the Talmud connects his statement with the statement of R. Yohanan bar Nappaha, the most important Palestinian Jewish authority of the third century C.E. From both sides of the border between Roman Palestine and Persian Babylonia, there is Jewish agreement of what differentiates the two respective cultures, and how Jews must relate to each of them differently.

Whether these Rabbis in fact believed that their Babylonian contemporaries were really monotheists at heart is hard to tell. However, they surely

---

[84] B. Hullin 13a–b.
[85] See, e.g., M. Megillah 4.9.
[86] See B. Avodah Zarah 26b.

had in mind that Noahide law, which pertains to all gentiles, requires gentiles *religiously* to not practice idolatry and to not blaspheme God.[87] Blasphemy means not cursing the God of Israel, that is, not wishing in public that God be dead.[88] But the Babylonians, especially their Persian rulers, by their overall respect for Jewish religious practice (which they left alone) and their involvement with Jewish social practice, would hardly have been guilty of the type of blasphemy that the Romans used to torment the Jews.[89] As for idolatry, whereas Jews were expected to have both general monotheistic intent and specific monotheistic practices, gentiles were only expected to have general monotheistic intent. In fact, this difference goes back to Scripture, when the Aramean general Naaman adopted Israelite monotheism. But when he asked the prophet Elisha whether "the Lord would surely forgive your servant" (2 Kings 5:18) for having to participate in official idolatrous rites back home in Aram, the prophet assured him his request was already granted, sending him off with the words, "go in peace" (5:19).

Clearly, the Babylonians were not "secularists" in the modern sense of that term. They certainly had transcendent concerns. Nevertheless, because of their morally impressive *secularity*, the Rabbis concluded that they couldn't really be polytheists in their hearts. Nevertheless, the Rabbis did not carefully inquire into the exact character of their religious practices as they did with the Romans. So, whereas Roman idolatry was considered essentially linked with Roman injustice, Babylonian idolatry was seen as an unintended relic of a culture that must really be monotheistic in principle, whether the Babylonians were fully aware of this or not. Furthermore, unlike in the days of Nebuchadnezzer described in the book of Daniel, the Persian rulers of Babylonia did not deify the state in the person of its king.[90] As such, they kept the secular realm separate from the sacred. Whatever actually constituted their positive relationship with God, minimally it seemed to be consistent with standards of justice that the Rabbis surely believed were instituted by God. After all, it was R. Yohanan bar Nappaha who refused to consider the Babylonians idolators, and who taught that the first of the Noahide laws is the mandate for every human community to establish a just legal system to engage in adjudication according to the due process of law.[91] In other words, this is the foundation of Jewish-gentile relations. It is primarily political and only secondarily theological.

[87] See B.Sanhedrin 56b re Gen. 2:16.

[88] See M. Sanhedrin 7.5; B. Sanhedrin 56a; also, B. Megillah 24b re Isa. 8:17; Novak, *The Image of the Non-Jew in Judaism*, 85–106.

[89] See, e.g., B. Gittin 56b. Cf. 1 Sam. 17:43–45.

[90] See 93–94 above.

[91] B. Sanhedrin 56b re Gen. 2:16 and 18:19.

Concluding that this was indeed the case in Babylonia was enough to ensure that there was and could be a solid political-legal relation between Babylonian Jews and Babylonian gentiles.

Samuel's Principle

The principle "the law of the state is law" (*dina de-malkhuta dina*) was first enunciated by the Babylonian authority Mar Samuel of Nehardea, whom we have already encountered in this chapter, and who lived approximately between 165 and 257 C.E. Literally, the words used in the formulation of this principle mean "the law of the kingdom [*malkhuta*] is law." Nevertheless, I prefer to translate them as "the law of the state is law" because, whereas every state known to the Jews in talmudic, geonic, and early medieval times was a monarchy of some sort or another, the idea that Jews can live in good faith under regimes not governed by halakhah should not be restricted to monarchies. The are more options than, on the one hand, a halakhic theocracy—which, at present, can only be an unrealizable ideal for those Jews who desire it—and, on the other hand, a monarchy, of which there are hardly any left in the contemporary world, and those that are left are regimes under which no sane Jew would care to live. (By "monarchy" I mean an absolute monarchy, not the type of modern constitutional monarchy in which I as a Canadian live most democratically.) We shall deal with the question of monarchy or kingship in the next chapter when the medieval rationales for Samuel's legal principle will be discussed. But one should take "kingdom" to designate what *was normally* the case in talmudic times. Yet that *need not be the only* form of polity to which Jews *could* relate in good faith at some later time. As the Talmud says: "The Rabbis spoke in the present tense [*be-hoveh*]," meaning we need to abstract the principles the Rabbis were employing from the particular historical circumstances to which they were originally applied.[92]

The definition and application of this principle has one of the widest ranges of any juridical principle presented in the Talmud.[93] But since this definition and application have been an ongoing process, both halakhically and theologically, we must now look at it at the point of its historical origins and then trace its development. Only then can we intelligently bring it into modernity for both halakhic and theological purposes.

[92] M. Shabbat 6.6.

[93] For historical background, see J. Neusner, *A History of the Jews in Babylonia* 2 (Leiden: E. J. Brill, 1967), 69, 95, 134–44.

We do not know the exact historical circumstances in which Samuel formulated the principle "the law of the state is law," other than it was applied to the new Sassanid dynasty in Persia, whose rise to power seemed to have been beneficial for the Babylonian Jews. We also do not have any type of justification for this principle from the mouth of Samuel himself. Normally, in talmudic discourse, such justification would either base the new principle on an even more general older principle, or it would base it on the interpretation of a scriptural passage. Actual justification of Samuel's principle along these lines had to wait for the speculations of medieval talmudists.[94]

In the five places where Samuel's dictum is quoted in the Babylonian Talmud, the principle it states is simply assumed.[95] The contexts in which it is assumed all concern real-estate ownership and taxation. The two are related inasmuch as both involve the notion that in principle the state owns all the land in its domain, and that private property is an entitlement from the state.[96] As such, all matters of title to real estate are contingent upon the law of the state. Thus the state has the right to seize property, that is, rescind its entitlement. The right of the state to tax the inhabitants of the territory it rules is a partial exercise of that right. The right of the state to seize the property of those who do not pay their taxes is a complete exercise of that right. And the state has the right to transfer property from one "owner" to another or to the public domain.[97]

The validity of the exercise of this collective right depends on its being exercised through an objective system of law that treats all those subject to it fairly. Such a system, which we would now characterize as functioning through *the due process of law*, is to be distinguished from the type of appropriation of property that operates unfairly, one that allows government officials to arbitrarily engage in robbing private property with impunity. Another difference, which we shall see better when we deal with the later justifications of this principle, is whether the right of taxation is one that those being taxed have consented to. Once again, we shall see the difference between the government under which the Jews had to live in Roman Palestine and the government the Jews seem to have wanted to live under in Babylonia.

[94] See 124–32 below.

[95] B. Nedarim 28a; B. Gittin 10b; B. Baba Kama 113a; B. Baba Batra 54b and 55a. The magisterial study of this principle and its historical development is S. Shilo, *Dina de-Malkhuta Dina* (Jerusalem: Jerusalem Academic Press, 1974). I am very much indebted to this study for my analysis of Samuel's principle and my reflection on its deeper meaning.

[96] See B. Yevamot 89b re Ezra 10:8 and Josh. 19:51; B. Baba Kama 80b–81b; B. Baba Batra 99b–100a.

[97] See B. Baba Batra 8b and Tos., s.v. "akafeih."

In four of the five places this principle is quoted in the Talmud, the concern is about the legitimacy of Jews applying Persian law in their own civil dealings. In this sense, the principle is a generalization of several aspects of Jewish involvement in the Persian political-legal system. So, for example, the Mishnah rules that Jews should avoid any dealings with monies collected by "tax collectors" (ha-moksin).[98] The assumption here is that these tax collectors, who were actually tax farmers working under contract to the Roman conquerors of the land of Israel, are gangsters. As such, any monies they have in their possession have the taint of stolen property. But aren't their activities state sanctioned? They are not merely private robbers (listim).[99] So, doesn't the ruling of the Mishnah contradict the principle "the law of the state is law"? (Or, since the ruling of the Mishnah is earlier than the enunciation of Samuel's principle, how can Samuel seemingly contradict the Mishnah?) The Babylonian Talmud proposes two answers to this contradiction.[100]

The first, given in the name of Samuel, is that the Mishnah is dealing with taxes that are not collected according to any publically established, impartial criterion but, instead, are what the tax collector could seize according to his own whim and ability to victimize people who had no recourse to the true justice of the due process of law. The Mishnah is taken to be dealing with a situation where there is no prior limitation (qitsvah). The implication is, of course, that such tax collection is conducted according to the due process of law, with it prior limitations on what may and may not be done, as distinct from state-sanctioned gangsterism. Thus the monies collected by tax collectors (who seem to be state officials as opposed to criminals working under contract to the state) do not have the taint of stolen property.

The second answer, given in the name of the Palestinian authority R. Yannai, is that the Mishnah is dealing with someone having no government authorization at all.[101] (How he is different from a private robber is hard to tell; perhaps he is someone who turned over some of the money he collected to the government, even though the government had not in any way appointed this "freelancer" to do so initially or even subsequently.) The implication here is, of course, that with government authorization, irrespective of the methods of collection, the monies collected by such a person would not have the taint of stolen property. After all, being taxes (mekes), the government would get its share of the money somehow or other. Thus R. Yannai's answer seems to be resigned to the fact that

[98] M. Nedarim 3.4.
[99] Cf. Yevamot 25b.
[100] B. Nedarim 28a.
[101] Ibid.

even the inept and often arbitrary Roman rule of Palestine, with its frequently incoherent practices, was better than the total anarchy that would have replaced it if it had not been respected. Like an earlier Palestinian opinion that without the Roman peace (*pax Romana*), "a man would swallow up his neighbor," R. Yannai's answer seems to be a Jewish version of the principle "harsh law is better than no law" (*dura lex sed lex*).[102]

The difference between the regime under which R. Yannai had to live and the one under which Samuel seems to have wanted to live is that R. Yannai was living under an imperial system that by its very conquest of the land of Israel was essentially criminal. It was a regime that engaged local criminals to enforce its specific robbery of Jewish property by sanctioning their tax collecting as a form of laissez-faire enterprise, unencumbered by objective, impartial criteria in fact. Samuel, conversely, was living under a regime that had not robbed his people of their liberty, and it was a regime that practiced the due process of law. Hence its tax collectors were government officials answerable to these objective, impartial criteria. As such, Jews could participate in this regime, even as tax collectors among their own people, in good faith. Samuel and his fellow Babylonian Jews did not have to grudgingly settle for a regime only a little better than anarchy, as did R. Yannai and his fellow Palestinian Jews.

So far, we see Jews acting as the local representatives of the Persian government in good faith. That is, Jews applying Persian law to fellow Jews on behalf of the Persian government. How seriously the Jews took this role, even in the period after the editing of the Babylonian Talmud in fifth century C.E., is seen in the way post-talmudic Babylonian Jewish authorities (*geonim*) dealt with the communal status of Jewish tax collectors.

The Mishnah had declared that the practice of certain occupations, such as professional gambling, disqualifies those who practice them from functioning as witnesses in legal proceedings.[103] The veracity one needs to assume about any witness cannot be assumed in the case of those who choose these disreputable occupations as their profession.[104] This exclusion was clearly a matter of public condemnation designed to deter Jews from choosing such professions altogether. Those who do choose them are, in effect, made into second-class citizens.[105]

Tax collectors (*moksin*) are not explicitly mentioned in the Mishnah's list of those excluded from functioning as witnesses, but a tradition is recorded in the Babylonian Talmud that adds them to this list along with those simply called "collectors" (*gaba'in*).[106] In the ensuing inquiry as to

---

[102] M. Avot 3.2.
[103] M. Sanhedrin 3.3.
[104] B. Sanhedrin 24b–26b.
[105] Ibid., 26b.
[106] Ibid., 25b–26a.

the reason for this traditional addition, it is unclear whether "tax collectors" or only "collectors" or both are being discussed. The reason given
is that "they" were originally acceptable as reputable citizens because they
only collected what had been initially stipulated for them to collect (*m'ai
de-qayyets lehu*), namely, by the government. When they took more for
themselves than what had been initially stipulated for them to take by
law, they were disqualified, treated, in effect, as outlaws because of what
the Rabbis took to be a character defect in them.[107]

A geonic version of this text (which seems to have beeen written after
the editing of the Babylonian Talmud) distinguishes between "tax collectors" and "collectors" without, however, disputing that both are rightly
disqualified from functioning as witnesses. "Collectors" are those who
take more for themselves than has been stipulated by the law. "Tax collectors," though, are those who in assessing their fellow Jews, for what seems
to be a graduated income tax, are more lenient with the wealthy (who, it
would seem, have bribed them to be so) than they are with the poor, thus,
in effect, robbing the latter and unjustly enriching their wealthy "friends"
with tax "discounts."[108] Moreover, unlike the actual Talmud text of which
this is an interpretation, the geonic version states that originally these men
were acting according to the principle "the law of the state is law." That
is, they were originally exercising their official responsibilities in good
faith. When they violated the rights of those they were appointed to respect, they forfeited their right to full communal status in the Jewish community. Conversely, it is most unlikely that the principle "the law of the
state is law" would have been applied in Roman Palestine, much less ever
be formulated there.

So far we have seen that the principle "the law of the state is law" is
used in the Talmud more as an explanation of certain practices that were
already the case among the Jews of Babylonia than as an actual constructive principle in the development of the law itself. However, in one place
there is at least a suggestion of something more, that is, the potential
for something more. Thus the Mishnah states: "All official documents
[*shtarot*] deposited in gentile courts [*b'ark'aot*], even though their signa-
tories are gentiles, are valid [*kesherim*], except for bills of divorce and the
manumission of slaves."[109] In and of itself, what this might mean is that
the gentile courts are better able to take care of civil documents than
are the Jewish courts.[110] Nevertheless, the Babylonian Talmud seems to
overexplain the situation dealt with in the Mishnah by invoking the prin-

[107] Ibid., 25b and Tos., s.v. "stam."
[108] Taubes, *Otsar ha-Geonim*: Sanhedrin, pp. 207–209.
[109] M. Gittin 1.5.
[110] See 102–3 above.

ciple "the law of the state is law."[111] The Talmud then goes on to explain why the gentile courts may not be used for bills of divorce and manumission: they involve specifically religious matters for Jews, in which the law of the gentiles has no province.[112]

This Babylonian explanation does not simply apply to the use of gentile secretarial services; it strongly suggests that the gentile courts could be places where Jews can bring their cases for justice. Why? Because it can be assumed that the gentile courts, at least in Babylonia, operate according to the Noahide standard of "law" (*dinim*), which can be understood today as the due process of law.[113] The difference between this invocation of Samuel's principle, and the four invocations of it, is that in these latter places we see how Jews applied non-Jewish legal procedures among themselves, whereas in this place, the Jews bring their own cases to the gentiles. To be sure, Jews could prefer to decide their own cases among themselves by traditional Jewish criteria. Nevertheless, there are cases in which the Jewish courts are either unable or unwilling to effect justice. As such, the choice for Jews would be gentile justice or no justice at all. Thus, Maimonides, writing in the twelfth century, attempts to resolve the contradiction between this sort of use of "the law of the state is law" (probably written in the fifth century C.E.) and the prohibition of using gentile courts (uttered in the first century C.E. by R. Tarfon), which we analyzed earlier in this chapter, as follows:

> Whoever involves gentile judges in law cases [*kol ha-dan*] and and in their courts, even when their laws are similar to Jewish laws is, therefore, wicked [*rasha*], and it is as if he has ridiculed and blasphemed and acted arrogantly against the Torah of Moses our Master. . . . But, if the gentiles are in power and one's fellow litigant is obstinate [*alam*], and one cannot get one's due from him through Jewish judges, let one [nonetheless] sue him first before Jewish judges. If he does not want to come, let one get an authorization [*notel reshut*] from the [Jewish] court and rescue [*u-matsil*] his interest from his fellow litigant through gentile judges.[114]

Here Maimonides still requires initial authorization from a Jewish court. But what if this is impossible? What if the Jewish court does not even have enough political power to give such authorization or some kind of legal judgment for the gentile court to enforce? In answer to this question, the Spanish Jewish jurist, exegete, and theologian Nahmanides (d. 1270)

---

[111] B. Gittin 10b.
[112] Ibid.
[113] Ibid., 9b and Rashi, s.v. "huts."
[114] MT: Sanhedrin, 26.7. Cf. *Teshuvot ha-Rambam* 1, ed. J. Blau (Jerusalem: Miqitsei Nirdamim, 1960), no. 27, pp. 39–40 and n. 1 thereon; 2, no. 408, pp. 685–86.

ruled that in a case where a Jewish court is too frightened by a Jewish criminal to even write a document authorizing restoration of misappropriated property, the Jewish victim of this person may go directly to the gentile court for justice.[115] Nahmanides' main talmudic source for this ruling is found in the principle "one may take the law into his own hands" (*dina le-nafsheih*) when not doing so would leave him with "considerable loss" (*pseida*).[116] Here, of course, one is not literally "taking the law into his own hands," which suggests some sort of vigilante action; rather, one is taking the case (*dina*) out of the powerless hands of the Jewish court into the powerful hands of the gentile court—that is, when the gentile court's power is structured by and for true standards of justice.

Here, though, we are still dealing with a situation where the Jewish court has judicial authority de jure, but lacks sufficient police power de facto. Nevertheless, when a Jewish court does not even have judicial authority de jure, let alone de facto police power, it would seem one is all the more justified in going directly to a non-Jewish court for justice, even in a suit with a fellow Jew who will only bow to the authority and power of a court authorized and empowered by the state.

Secularity and Secularism

The talmudic principle "the law of the state is law" is the linchpin of the argument being made in this book. But because of its contemporary importance, we need to immediately detach it from any inference that it is a form of Jewish secularism. This requires a more philosophical reflection about what should and should not be inferred from it.

In modern times one could expand this principle in a way that requires the acceptance of secularism, but is contrary to the covenantal foundation of Judaism.[117] This would uproot Samuel's great principle from the theological-political system in which it emerged and traditionally functioned. Conversely, one could narrow the range of this principle as much as possible so as to severely limit the value of secularity for Judaism, setting the two realms at loggerheads. To avoid these two extremes, we must once again clearly differentiate between *secularity*, which is consistent with *the*

---

[115] *Teshuvot ha-Ramban*, ed. C. B. Chavel (Jerusalem: Mosad ha-Rav Kook, 1975), no. 63, p. 96. See, also, B. M. Lewin, *Otsar ha-Geonim*: Gittin 88b (Jerusalem: Mosad ha-Rav Kook, 1941), p. 210; *Hagahot Maimoniyot* on Maimonides, MT: Sanhedrin, 26.7; R. Asher (Rosh): Baba Kama, 8.17 re B. Baba Kama 92b; R. Moses of Coucy, *Sefer Mitsvot Gadol*, pos. no. 107 re Y. Sanhedrin 1.1/18a.

[116] B. Baba Kama 27b. Cf. B. Baba Batra 34b and Rashbam, s.v. "ve'im amru."

[117] See D. Biale, *Power and Powerlessness in Jewish History* (New York: Schocken, 1986), 103–06.

covenant between God and the Jewish people, and *secularism*, which is inconsistent with, indeed antagonistic to, that master covenant. The philosophical reiteration of this differentiation will be a short detour from our more historical look at "the law of the state is law" but, nonetheless, it might be helpful in preventing us from getting bogged down in the many textual and historical details we must carefully examine.

The principle "the law of the state is law" is a legitimate authorization of limited secularity for Jews; it is not an illegitimate surrender to unlimited secularism. Throughout this book, I differentiate between Jewishly legitimate secularity and illegitimate (Jewishly speaking, at least) secularism. The confusion of the two, even by nonsecuralists, must be overcome in the interest of a vibrant, contemporary Jewish political theology.[118]

Throughout this book, *secularism* is defined as the idea that human beings can and should constitute their corporate life only with reference to their capacity for social construction. *Secularity*, though, is simply the realm of interhuman, multicultural interaction that does not look to any unique community with its singular historical revelation and special tradition as the exclusive source of social legitimization. For the participating cultures in a truly secular regime, their ultimate communal legitimization comes from the founding revelations of their own communities, which have been transmitted and developed by their respective traditions. Basic moral principles that come out of these respective traditions can then be coordinated into universal principles through philosophical reasoning.[119]

Since Socrates, we have known that the best way to do this kind of philosophical reasoning is to engage others who hold traditional ideas different from our own. We do this as a moral task because we want to live with these others in peace, justice, and mutual understanding.[120] This is done when we reason that no tradition can claim the moral allegiance of its adherents as rational human beings without prior affirmation of what we have come to see as universal moral norms. The historical overlapping of these norms among various cultural traditions shows that they are not the imperial projections of any one cultural tradition onto all the others, as philosophical and psychological relativists would like us to believe.

First, these norms must be understood and accepted in the context of each tradition in which they are originally found. This is the theological task. Second, they must be constituted by and through inter-cultural dialogue. This is the philosophical task. Third, one must discover normative overlappings among the various traditional moralities. This is the histori-

---

[118] See 26–27 above.
[119] See Novak, *Natural Law in Judaism*, 16–26, 188–91.
[120] See Plato, *Crito*, 46D.

cal task. Fourth, there is the political task, which is to show how at least some of these universal moral norms can have concrete authority in a multicultural society. And I am convinced that Babylonia during most of the talmudic period was, in fact, such a multicultural society. It seems to have been a place where the contributing traditions and their respective theologies were respected for their ultimacy in the lives of their adherents, where philosophical dialogue was possible on political and legal questions, and where a common law and politics were possible and often real.[121]

Secularism is often explicitly atheistic, always implicitly so. But secularity does not require atheism; in fact, it functions more coherently without the atheism most modern secularists have demanded as the condition of its rational acceptability. Secularity functions best when the sacred limits the profane and the profane is not reducible to the sacred. Atheists, though, by collapsing the sacred into the profane and thus, inevitably, transferring the ultimacy of the sacred to the profane, cannot affirm the very difference that a cogent secularity seems to presuppose. The principle "the law of the state is law" is a Jewish recognition of the validity of secularity for Jews. How wide ranging that principle is meant to be has been a debate among traditional Jewish thinkers. Nevertheless, it is unwarranted speculation about the essence of this principle to ground it in secularist premises, even though, as we shall see in subsequent chapters, this was what was done by such modern thinkers as Baruch Spinoza and Moses Mendelssohn.[122]

Secularity can best be constituted by persons who look for their beginning and end in what is beyond their own constructive capacities, and who can recognize a similar quest in people who are not members of their own community, who do not accept the authority of their own revelation, who are not parts of their own tradition. (This might very well include secularist Jews as well.) From the recognition of this general quest, even before it is answered by any historical revelation, certain universal norms can be rationally expressed. In any multicultural social environment, such rational norms are best fulfilled through a secular realm that does not privilege any one tradition over another, yet does not present itself as a unilateral substitution for all traditions. Furthermore, this secular realm is more than simply the operation of an arbitrary consensus. Rather, it is the operation of rational commitments about which common agreement through persuasion is possible and desirable.

---

[121] To be sure, there are times when the Rabbis mention religious persecution at the hands of the Persians (see, e.g., B. Gittin 16b–17a); however, such persecution seems to have been on the whole restricted to the acts of certain Zoroastrian fanatics. See B. Kiddushin 72a.

[122] See chapter 6.

The great task for modern Jewish political theology is to accept human-made secularity with its necessary limitations, to see its positive value for normative Judaism, and to resist any reduction of Judaism to secularist premises. A proper understanding of the principle "the law of the state is law," in both its origins and development, is an important part of the theological-political task for contemporary Jewish thinkers. This principle is the most explicit Jewish construction of secularity. It seems that this construction is done by means of a social contract. This involves a legitimate secondary autonomy, which as we saw in the previous chapter is more than a choice between existing options, but less than the type of autonomy that makes itself a god. It is best to call it "voluntariness" as a contract is voluntary: making new options, but making them in response to old needs. This is certainly the case with a social contract. In contemporary terms, this might be seen as the principled overlapping of *secularities*. But it is not based on either a prior secularism or a projected secularism. Neither the Jews nor the gentiles can be seen to have come to any consensus that this interhuman social construction should be either the beginning or the end of authentic human community.

In the next chapter we shall examine how medieval Jewish theologians reflected on the foundations and further applications of Samuel's principle.

Chapter Five

Kingship and Secularity

Royal Law

In medieval Jewish speculation about the reason for the principle "the law of the state is law," we see the most explicit presentation of the idea of the Jewish social contract. This comes out most clearly and effectively in the justification supplied for Samuel's principle by the twelfth-century French exegete R. Samuel ben Meir (Rashbam). In his comment on the most detailed discussion of Samuel's principle in the Talmud, Rashbam writes with precise theoretical insight:

> All real estate and produce taxes, all royal judicial procedures [*mishpatei mela-khim*] that they [the kings] regularly [*regeelim*] employ [*le-hanhig*] in their kingdoms, they are law [*dina hu*]. That is because all the members of the kingdom willingly [*mi-rtsonam*] accept upon themselves the laws of the king [*huqqei ha-melekh*] and his judgments. Therefore, it is complete law [*din gamur hu*].[1]

So, we see that the king's right to make laws and administer them is derived from the governed. The governed willingly, meaning autonomously, contract with their ruler. They accept his rule because he is able to govern them more wisely and more effectively than they are able to govern themselves. In the case of the Jews, for whom Rashbam is of course theorizing, this means that they acknowledge that the foreign monarch, under whom they happen to be living, is governing them in a way they have negotiated with him in good faith.[2]

Although notions of some sort of social contract between the king and his people were already being discussed in Europe at the time of Rashbam, the real relationship then between kings and their subjects did not resemble the type of contractual relationship from which the idea of a social contract is derived and developed.[3] So, even though in principle Rashbam

---

[1] B. Baba Batra 54b, s.v. "ve-ha'amar Shmuel."

[2] For the complicated political status of Jews in medieval Europe, see S. W. Baron, *A Social and Religious History of the Jews* 11 (New York: Columbia University Press, 1967), 4–33.

[3] See J. W. Gough, *The Social Contract*, 2nd ed. (Oxford: Clarendon Press, 1957), 2–48.

seems to be talking about a social contract between a king and *all* his subjects, what Rashbam is saying in fact only pertains to the relationship between a king and his Jewish subjects at the time Rashbam is writing. What the actual agreement between the Babylonian Jews and their Persians rulers was in the days of the Talmud, about which Rashbam is ostensibly commenting, is not totally clear. It does, however, suggest some sort of social contract, perhaps like that of a separate state within a larger confederation (*imperium in imperio*). Rashbam, though, is projecting from his own experience of kingship in relation to the Jewish community onto the text of the Talmud. This is the only kind of kingship with which he was personally familiar. That is also the way one reads a normative text, which the Talmud surely was for Rashbam, as distinct from a mere historical datum. Nevertheless, he was certainly aware from his reading of the Talmud that the political situation of the Babylonian Jews was much better than the political situation of European Jews in his own time, the time of the First Crusade.

Actually, unlike the king's other subjects, the Jews were not really his "subjects" at all, even though they were certainly not yet meant to be his equals as is the case in a true social contract between the government and the governed. The Jews were more like guests or resident aliens in someone else's land. On the other hand, though, with the exception of the clergy, who were subjects of the church and its canon law, all the other Christians in the kingdom were the king's subjects. The king was their liege lord. This was the reality of the medieval feudal system. But the Jews could not—indeed, did not want to—be parts of a corporate body that required this kind of Christian identity of all its subjects. Also, despite widespread Jewish suffering in medieval France and the Rhineland, especially during the First Crusade, the fact is that political status as a *foreign* Jew was much better than that of a *native* serf.[4] (And, as for the clergy, at least in the case of the local priests, monks, and nuns, the Jews had more intellectual advantages.)

The king was a Christian ruler governing Christian subjects in temporal matters. The bishops were Christian rulers governing Christian subjects in eternal matters. The separation of church and state was only functional, not substantial.[5] The church was the branch of "Christendom" (that is, Christian polity) that dealt with sacred matters, with what was involved in such *sacraments* as baptism, the Eucharist (the central feature

[4] Even though the Jews were called *servi camerae*, their status was one of an immediate communal relationship with the sovereign, one that was often contracted. See Baron, *A Social and Religious History of the Jews* 9:135–92.

[5] See H. J. Berman, *Law and Revolution* (Cambridge, Mass.: Harvard University Press, 1983), 273–94.

of Christian worship), marriage, and holy orders (the clerical professions). The state was the branch of Christendom that dealt with secular
matters such as civil and criminal law, war and peace. (Of course, these
realms were not hermetically sealed off from each other, as seen from the
famous church-state conflicts in the Middle Ages.) As such, Jews were not
part of Christendom in either the sphere of the church or the sphere of
the state. Each sphere of Christendom had to deal with Jews living in its
midst as members of a foreign nation. This is why the arrangements between Christendom and Jews were made with Jewish communities (*qehillot*). Most often, the sphere of Christendom with which medieval Jews
dealt was the state. In fact, it seems for the most part, Jews were able to
negotiate a better political arrangement with state officials than they were
able to do with church officials.[6] This was no doubt the case inasmuch as
the theological rivalries between Judaism and Christianity largely involved sacred matters that were the business of the church rather than
civil matters that were the business of the state. In Muslim regimes, on
the other hand, the civil status of the Jews was much less a matter of
negotiation since the Jews there already had a definite status as second-
class citizens (*dhimi*) according to Islamic law (*shar'iah*).[7]

Everyone, with the exception of church officials (and their church institutions) and the Jews (for very different reasons to be sure), was the king's
serf. Just as property cannot very well contract with its owner, so serfs
could not have a real contractual relationship with their liege lord. This
being the case, the Jewish contractual relationship with medieval Christian monarchs can be seen as presaging how a social contract might characterize a society in which no one is any longer the subject of the sovereign
because everyone is now an equal participant in sovereignty, that is, the
autonomy of the civil order. Loosening this model from the idea of kingship—that is, the idea of kingship as an interminable relationship between
the sovereign and his people—goes a long way in enhancing its relevance
for the situation of Jews (and members of other traditional communities)
in a constitutional democracy, and even for the situation of Jews in the
currently secular State of Israel.

The questions that need to be kept in mind when looking at the ramifications of this early theoretical presentation of a Jewish social contract
are: (1) Is the system of the king's law the laws that the king himself has
made, or is it a system of law already in place that the king administers?

[6] See Yitzhak Baer, *A History of the Jews in Christian Spain* 1, trans. L. Schoffman (Philadelphia: Jewish Publication Society of America, 1978), 138–85.
[7] See *Islam* 2, ed. Bernard Lewis (New York: Harper and Row, 1974), 215–35.

(2) Do those who are partners in this social contract with the king simply submit themselves to a system of law totally formulated by their contract "partner," or can the king's *partners* actually participate in the formulation of the law under which they and the king must live? (3) Does this social contract admit of termination for cause? That is, can these people exit the social contract because of noncompliance with the terms of the contract by the king? Or, can these people even participate in a movement to remove the king from office for breach of contract with his people if he refuses to abdicate?

We see beginnings of answers to these questions in the way Nahmanides (Ramban) picked up on Rashbam's basic theory of contractual kingship in the thirteenth century. (Nahmanides was the first Spanish-Jewish or "Sephardic" scholar to incorporate in his writing the work of Franco-German or "Ashkenazic" scholars like Rashbam and his grandfather Rashi.) After his specific discussion of some of the finer points of actual legal practice in Rashbam's comments on the principle "the law of the state [that is, "the kingdom"] is law," Nahmanides elaborates Rashbam's more theoretical point:

> When we say "the law of the kingdom is law," we mean specifically those laws recognized [*yedu'in*] by the king throughout his kingdom, matters which he and all the other kings before him have employed [*hinhigu*]. And they are written in the royal chronicles and codes [*u-ve-huqqei ha-melakhim*]. . . . We infer this from the wording of "the law of the kingdom [*dina de-malkhuta*] is law," not "the law of the king [*dina de-malka*] is law." So, it means the law recognized by all the kings. And even in the case of the holy kings of Israel, royal law is recognized as in the Scripture written by Samuel the prophet, about which the Rabbis said that whatever is mentioned in the section about the king [*be-farshat ha-melekh*], a king is permitted [by the Law] to do [*muttar bo*].[8]

The combined implications of what might be termed "the Rashbam-Ramban theory" are staggering when spelled out, especially for Jewish social contract theory. Like any such explication, though, one cannot claim for many of his or her inferences now being made that they *were* the conscious intent of the authors of the original statements from which they are being inferred. One can only hope to show that his or her speculations do not distort the original insights upon which they are based by leading to conclusions the original authors could not have possibly ever accepted. This is how discourse within a living tradition develops. Moreover, since

---

[8] *Hiddushei ha-Ramban*: B. Baba Batra 55a. "The law of the king" of which he speaks is initially discussed on B. Sanhedrin 20b.

we are dealing with a matter of speculation rather than of actual experience, the insights presented are less precise than would be reflection on a matter for which there are real cases calling for coherent adjudication.

By connecting the law-of-the-state principle to the institution of kingship, even as it functioned in ancient Israel, Nahmanides has located an inner Jewish necessity for the formulation of this principle.[9] That is, this principle is not just a pragmatic accommodation of Jews to a foreign regime that happens to be fair and friendly to the Jews living in it and under it politically. Rather, the essential secularity of this principle is rooted in the ancient institution of kingship, one that was considerably adjusted to conform to, even enhance, the essential covenantal existence of the people of Israel in biblical times when it was introduced, and that was the subject of considerable speculation in rabbinic times long after it had ceased to operate among the Jewish people. We now need to consider the basic questions the institution of kingship raises for Jewish self-understanding.

The Torah seems to present kingship as an option for the people of Israel.

When you enter the land which the Lord your God gives you and you take possession of it and dwell therein and you then say, "I shall place a king over myself like all the nations who surround me," do place [*som tasim*] a king over yourselves whom the Lord your God will choose. . . . And when the king is seated on his royal throne, he shall then write a copy of this Torah [*mishneh ha-torah ha-z'ot*] from a scroll [taken] from before the levitical priests. It shall be with him and he shall read it all the days of his life . . . so that his heart not swerve from the commandment [*ha-mitsvah*] neither to the right nor the left, so that he may lengthen the days of his reign, he and his sons in the midst of Israel. (Deuteronomy 17:14–15, 18–20)

[9] Interestingly enough, Nahmanides' most important disciple, R. Solomon ibn Adret (Rashba), whose views on Judaism and secularity we will examine later in this chapter, argues that *dina de-malkhuta dina* does not apply to Jewish kings. The reason he gives, quoting *Tosafot* in the name of a R. Eliezer (although not found in our text of the *Bavli*), is that "all Israel are partners [*shuttafin*] in the land of Israel" (*Hiddushei ha-Rashba*: B. Nedarim 28a; see R. Nissim Gerondi, *Ran* thereon, s.v. "be-mokes"; R. Menahem ha-Meiri, *Bet ha-Behirah* thereon, ed. A. Liss, p. 118). A Jewish king is thus the servant of the people who own the land in common, whereas a gentile king rules over people living in *his* land. For Ibn Adret, then, Rashbam's idea of the social contract pertains to a gentile king not a Jewish one. In the case of a Jewish king, the social contract has much more mutuality built into it, and hence is much more akin to more modern notions of social contract that we will examine in the following chapters. In the case of a gentile king, the rule of the king is prior to the people's rather passive acceptance of it. A gentile king's social contract with his subjects along these lines anticipates Hobbes's view of the social contract. See Thomas Hobbes, *Leviathan*, chap. 18, ed. M. Oakeshott (New York: Collier Books, 1962), pp. 134–35.

Here we seem to have a model of a constitutional monarch, one who rules the people according to the revealed law of God, a law (*torah*) whose accurate text is the preserve of the national sanctuary and its priests.[10] The Talmud infers from these verses in Deuteronomy a mandate to the people to appoint a king as soon as they enter the land of Israel.[11]

Nevertheless, the tradition faced the following exegetical problem: Since the Torah has already prescribed monarchy, a monarchy subject to its revealed law, why then was the prophet Samuel, long afterward, so upset when the people of Israel ask for a king? Why is Samuel so upset when his prophetic endorsement of the election of a king is demanded? Wasn't their request a request for his prophetic confirmation not only of a right the Torah has entitled them to exercise but, even more, his confirmation of their exercise of a duty mandated by the Torah? In the attempt to solve this exegetical problem, some important political insights emerge. This is because the Rabbis are talking about how a text from the past speaks to perennial political questions.[12]

The Talmud attempts to solve this problem by noting that the request for a king is mentioned twice in succession, but that the two requests are not identical. The request, "give us [*tenah lanu*] a king to judge us" (1 Samuel 8:6) is seen as coming only from "the elders" (*ha-zeqenim*).[13] It is a valid request since it is presumed that the learned elders are asking for the king to administer Torah law, a law in whose administration they already play a major role.[14] On the other hand, the request "appoint for us [*simah lanu*] a king to judge us, [as is the case] with all the [other] nations" (8:5), is seen as coming from "unlearned persons" (*ammei ha'arets*) whose motives are corrupt.[15] Their corrupt motives seem to be their desire to be like the other nations. And what distinguishes these other nations from Israel? Is it not that the other nations, unlike Israel, are *not* governed by the law of the Torah. In other words, whereas the elders, who themselves already administer the law of the Torah, are satis-

[10] See 2 Chron. 17:7–9; *Sifre*: Devarim, no. 160; T. Sanhedrin 4.7; Y. Sanhedrin 2.6/20c.

[11] B. Sanhedrin 20b.

[12] For a review of various classical Jewish views of kingship, see D. Polish, *Give Us a King* (Hoboken, N.J.: KTAV, 1989).

[13] B. Sanhedrin 20b.

[14] Thus in the Torah's prescription of the administration of justice in Deut. 17:8–20, the authority of the elders is mentioned before that of the king. For rabbinic views of the precedence of the elders (qua Torah scholars, see *Sifra*: Qedoshim re Lev. 19:32, ed. Weiss, 91a and B. Kiddushin 32b re Num. 11:16 and Prov. 8:22), see, e.g., T. Horayot 2.8; Y. Horayot 3.5/48b; B. Horayot 13a.

[15] B. Sanhedrin 20b.

fied with that law and only request a more powerful royal administrator
to lead them in their work, those who are not involved in that administration of the law, in effect, want a new law to govern the nation more successfully. For the Rabbis, it would seem, there was to be a compromise
between these two opposing positions. The king was to be allowed to
supplement the law of the Torah, especially in areas pertaining to public
policy, but this new law of the king was not to be regarded as a replace-
ment for the law of the Torah. It was to function parallel to it. The king
was still to be bound by the Torah's more general norms and to act on
their behalf.[16]

It is important to point out that the difference here is not what Scripture
usually emphasizes as differentiating Israel from the other nations—that
the nations are all idolaters and that Israel alone worships the One God.
If this were the case, it would be difficult to understand why in this scriptural account God is willing to compromise with the people over something that everywhere else in Scripture is beyond compromise.[17] Yet God
accepts the fact that "they have rejected [ma'asu] My rule over them" (1
Samuel 8:7). Why? Because this means God's law will no longer be the
sole norm in all the affairs of state. God is willing to co-rule with a human
king in the mundane affairs of state in a way that God would not share
his ultimate sovereignty, which is the subject of worship, with any other
god. The Lord God of Israel is not to be made first among equals (*primus
inter pares*) in any pantheon, yet he is willing to share political authority
with kings. Indeed, this goes back to the opening of Genesis where God
shares his dominion of the earth with humans created in his image (Genesis 1:26).

The question is just how God's preeminence in this political situation
is maintained. One early rabbinic source interprets the words "do place a
king over yourselves who the Lord your God will choose" (Deuteronomy
17:15) to mean "through a prophet" (*al pi nav'i*).[18] Apparently following
this source, the eleventh-century commentator R. Abraham ibn Ezra insists that the king must be appointed by God acting through a prophet or
the *Urim ve-Tumim* oracle, but not by popular election.[19] However, an-

[16] See Maimonides, MT: Melakhim, 4.10. Cf. ibid.: Malveh ve-Loveh, 2.4; Sanhedrin, 24.10.

[17] To my knowledge, only one of the Rabbis of the talmudic period attributed idolatrous motives to the popular demand for a king. See *Sifre*: Devarim, no. 156, p. 208 (the view of R. Nehorai).

[18] Ibid., no. 157, p. 208. See B. Sukkah 27b.

[19] *Commentary on the Torah*: Deut. 17:15. There Ibn Ezra calls the command to appoint a king a "permission" (*reshut*). However, this does not seem to mean an option the people can take or leave, for if that were the case, his emphasis on divine selection as distinct from popular election would not make sense in the overall context. Therefore, it seems better to

other early rabbinic source does not mention a prophet at all, but only requires the Sanhedrin to appoint a king.[20] And, if one sees the Sanhedrin as a legislative body needing popular approval of its acts—perhaps even reflecting popular opinion as is so often the case with representative assemblies—this view is consistent with Scripture's account of how Israel got a king in the first place. The king is not appointed *until* the people ask for a king and approve the appointment of Saul, the king the prophet Samuel has presented to them (1 Samuel 10:24). Furthermore, the first king of Israel had to be reconfirmed by the people shortly after his initial appointment (1 Samuel 11:14–15), especially after he had proved himself a successful military leader, which was the main reason the people originally demanded the appointment of a king. Indeed, one late medieval commentator suggests that not even prophetic confirmation of the Sanhedrin's appointment of a king, let alone prophetic presentation of a king to the people initially, is required.[21] As we shall see, most halakhic discussions of kingship emphasize its human initiation.

This latter view is consistent with the scriptural account of the historical origins of kingship in Israel, where, it seems, the prophet is forced to accept the people's demand for a king and can only try to select a king for them whom they will find favorable. In other words, God confirms the people's election (almost in the sense of *vox populi vox Dei*). And in so doing, the prophet sets down the conditions of what seems to be a social contract between the people and their king. The prophet's role here is not that of legislator as much as of mediator in the negotiation of a social contract between the king and *his* people and the people and *their* king. Thus Samuel's answer to the people's demand is: Yes, you may have a king, but this is what kingship will entail: "[Y]ou will become his servants" (1 Samuel 8:17). In other words, the king will have the right—and the power with which you entitled him to have this right—to use your lives and your property as he sees fit.

---

interpret *reshut* here to mean a divine warrant, without which one might assume kingship to be an attempt to *replace* divine authority altogether. See ibid.: Exod. 21:19 re B. Baba Kama 85a; also, D. Novak, *The Theology of Nahmanides Systematically Presented* (Atlanta, Ga.: Scholars Press, 1992), 84–85. Furthermore, in the Talmud (B. Eruvin 45a re 1 Sam. 23:22 and Rashi, s.v. "harei"; B. Yoma 73a re 1 Sam. 30:8), the *Urim ve-Tumim* oracle is only acknowledged as a guide regarding the strategic choices the king has to make when waging war, but it is not used in the selection of a king.

[20] T. Sanhedrin 3.4.

[21] R. Abraham de Boten, *Lehem Mishneh* on Maimonides, MT: Melakhim, 1.3. Although Maimonides himself states here: "A king is not initially appointed except by decree [*al pi*]of the court of seventy elders [the Great Sanhedrin] and by prophetic decree [*al pi nav'i*]," in ibid.: Sanhedrin, 5.1, he does not mention a prophetic decree. This suggests Maimonides did not see a prophetic decree as a sine qua non for the appointment of a king, but only something desirable (cf. ibid.: Melakhim, 1.8 re 1 Kings 11:35).

In the Talmud's discussion of this answer, one Rabbi sees it as a means of frightening the people.[22] The implication here is that maybe the people will realize that kingship will entail a considerable loss of individual and familial liberty, and maybe the people will have a change of heart and cease their royal quest. But this, of course, brings one back to the basic problem of what is wrong with the people requesting what the Torah seems to have required them to request. So another Rabbi says that the prophet is telling the people what the king's rights will be.[23] In this interpretation, the message is not meant to dissuade the people. Rather, the message is to inform them of what is actually involved in the *institution* of kingship they are seeking. Thus, we have the rudiments of a social contract between the king and the people. The people now have enough information about the conditions of kingship to be able to rationally deliberate about whether to become subjects of the king. Thus the first opinion, which predicts what the king *will* do, is a preview de facto. The second opinion, which prescribes what the king *shall* do, is a preview de jure.

Royal Justice

The actual initiation of *kingship* as a political reality, over and above the appointment of a *king* mandated by the Torah, brought with it the idea that the king is allowed to take considerable liberties with the civil rights of the people, rights that are codified in the Torah. One could see this as the king's entitlement to act extraordinarily in extraordinary circumstances, like his right to impose martial law from time to time. But it could also imply that the prophet Samuel's institution of kingship not only makes the king the administrator of the law of the Torah, but also entitles him to devise a parallel legal system for the sake of the common good of his realm. This is also the implication of Nahmanides' comparison of the law of the (gentile) kingdom (*dina de-malkhuta*) with the law of "the holy kings of Israel," especially his insistence that *malkhuta* means a *system* of royally administered and developed law, but not the de novo decrees of an individual king (*malka*).[24] Therefore, just as the gentile kings rule according to a system of royal law that they have the right to develop and apply, so the kings of Israel have a right to rule from within a legal system they have inherited and to apply it.[25]

[22] B. Sanhedrin 20b.

[23] Ibid.

[24] *Hiddushei ha-Ramban*: B. Baba Batra 55a.

[25] Nevertheless, Nahmanides does not follow Rashbam's view that kingship is rooted in a social contract with the people. Instead, in his *Commentary on the Torah*: Deut. 17:14–15 (a work written at the end of his life, long after his novellae on the Talmud), Nahmanides

According to Rashbam, the system of royal law is an entitlement to the king coming from those who are to live under the political rule of the king. For Rashbam too, it would seem that this royal entitlement is not simply the right to make ad hoc rulings in unusual cases, a sort of martial law. Rather, it is a regular form of distributive justice and not an intermittent form of rectification of unusual political crises.[26] Even though Nahmanides is silent on the question of a social contract between the king and his subjects, Rashbam, who inspired some of his thoughts on the question of kingship, is quite explicit on this as the foundation of royal law. And whereas Rashbam is silent on the question of whether this recognition of royal law also applies to Jewish kings, Nahmanides is quite explicit about it. This is why I have called the combination of their respective insights the "Rashbam-Ramban theory." It is a theory that synthesizes their respective insights, even though neither of them could have totally accepted it.

To be a strong precedent for the idea of a social contract, we need to discover in the idea of the law-making king (1) whether the king is elected by his subjects; (2) whether the king himself judges subjects; (3) whether the king is judged by his subjects; (4) whether the king can be removed from office by his subjects. Positive answers to these questions would go a long way to bringing us to the point where we can constitute a viable idea of a Jewish social contract and use it to suggest how the current theological-political situation of the Jews might be understood through it and even directed by it.

However, as already noted, we will have to develop this idea from out of rather sparse and scattered sources. Furthermore, I suspect that rabbinic discussion of these questions was also quite guarded since Jews were usually living under rulers who would be highly suspicious of forceful positive answers to these questions. Such answers would be a threat to the royal power many of them considered a right they received directly from God to rule *over* their people unencumbered by anything except, maybe, the church. These Christian rulers may have had some sort of contractual relationship with the Jewish communities living within their

---

follows Ibn Ezra's view of kingship as initiated by divine selection (see n. 19 above). He opines that the people are required to request a king *from* the Sanhedrin, presumably whose members are divinely inspired or who themselves rely on a prophet or an oracle. He thus emphasizes that all kingship, whether Jewish or gentile, is by divine right (re Dan. 4:29). Therefore, his earlier thoughts on kingship are more germane to the idea of a social contract than are his later thoughts on the subject.

[26] See Aristotle, *Nicomachean Ethics*, 5.2/1130b30–1131a30. Distributive justice is more concerned with what we now call public policy; rectifying justice is more concerned with the type of ordinary adjudication most likely to be conducted by the courts according to the usual statutory law and legal precedents.

domain, but this did not involve the kind of equality implied in positive answers to the above questions. As for their own gentile subjects, there wasn't much of a hint of this type of equality. Thus the Jewish authors had to write with caution, frequently looking over their shoulders for the Christian censor ready to declare Jewish writing subversive of the established order, religious or secular.

As for the appointment of the king, the commandment "do place a king over yourself" (Deuteronomy 17:15) is considered a positive commandment that the community is obligated to fulfill. It is a commandment "to appoint a king for themselves" (le-ha'ameed lahem).[27] The question is, who is meant by "themselves"? Since the preceding section in Deuteronomy deals with the authority of the Supreme Court (bet din ha-gadol), what later became known as the Sanhedrin (literally, the body that "sits togther"—synhedrein—to adjudicate and legislate), it would seem that this august body had the privilege and obligation to appoint a king. But this begs the question, inasmuch as we need to know how one was appointed to the Sanhedrin. The usual rabbinic answer is that new members of the Sanhedrin were appointed by those who were members when there was a vacancy due to either the death or removal from office of one of their colleagues.[28] But this assumes there was an unbroken chain of tradition in the Sanhedrin from Moses to at least the Rabbis of the second century C.E. This chain of tradition was taken to be the transmission of the living, speaking, personal repositories of the Torah: the verbal or "Oral" Torah (torah she-b'al peh).[29] Nevertheless, the Talmud also admits that there were times when the Sanhedrin was under the control of the Sadducees, which means there were times when the chain of Oral, Mosaic tradition, at least in the Sanhedrin, was broken, since the Sadducees did not accept the authority of the tradition.[30]

When pharisaic-rabbinic authority was restored, as it seems to have been after the destruction of the Second Temple in 70 C.E. (with the quick demise of the largely priestly, pro-Roman Sadducees) in the rabbinic court of Yavneh, it is likely that this restoration was due to popular pressure for the appointment of popular (perhaps even "populist") religious and political officials.[31] Thus even at the time when the Sanhedrin did function, there may have been popular pressures as to who would be accepted to serve an apprenticeship designed to prepare him for eventual member-

[27] Sifre: Devarim, no. 156, p. 208; B. Sanhedrin 20b. See Maimonides, Sefer ha-Mitsvot, pos. no. 173.

[28] M. Sanhedrin 4.4.

[29] M. Avot 1.1. See Maimonides, MT: Sanhedrin, 1.3.

[30] See M. Sanhedrin 7.2; B. Sanhedrin 52b; also, S. B. Hoenig, The Great Sanhedrin (Philadelphia: Dropsie College, 1953), 57–58.

[31] See B. Berakhot 27b–28a.

ship in the Sanhedrin (or its near equivalent). Along these lines, the Talmud indicates that the theological-political triumph of the School of Hillel over its rivals, the School of Shammai, occurred because the former employed more persuasive and less coercive tactics in public policy discussions than did the latter.[32] Also, there are suggestions in the Talmud that in civil matters, the people preferred judges of their own choice rather than those appointed for them by higher rabbinic authorities.[33]

The best example of how the Rabbis saw royal power as coming from the people can be found in a discussion over the meaning of the crime of "rebelling against royal authority" (mored be-malkhut). Interestingly enough, the scriptural verse brought in to shed light on the source of this prohibition (violation of which would be a crime) does not pertain to the first literal kings of Israel, David and Saul but, rather, to Joshua, the successor of Moses, who also played a kingly role. (This may have been a way of lessening the appearance that actual monarchy had been introduced only in the time of the prophet Samuel.) The verse cited is: "Any man who rebels [yamreh] against what you say [et pikha], who does not listen to your words, to everything you command him, he shall die" (Joshua 1:18).[34] Most important, the speakers in this text are the tribal leaders of Israel (no doubt representing their respective constituencies in what might be considered a parliamentary role) who, just before passing over the Jordan into the Promised Land, tell Joshua: "[E]verything you have commanded us we shall do; and wherever you send us we shall go" (1:16).[35]

Then, however, the Talmud asks whether this death sentence applies to one who refused a royal order to violate Torah law. The answer is no; Torah law may not be overturned by any royal decree since the verse just cited ends with the words "only be strong and of good courage!" The word "only" [raq] in rabbinic hermeneutics is meant to make what it introduces in a scriptural verse an exception to what has just preceded it.[36] (Also, the Talmud may have had in mind Moses' earlier charge to Joshua: "Be strong and of good courage" [Deuteronomy 31:7].) The king is to be obeyed in his own specified political turf, but not on the more general moral issues that are the subject of the Torah's law of interhuman relations. This is the business of the Rabbis, especially those serving in the Sanhedrin. And as for religious questions involving the positive rela-

---

[32] See B. Eruvin 13b. Cf. Y. Shabbat 1.4/3c; also, Saul Lieberman, Ha-Yerushalmi Kifshuto 1 (New York: Jewish Theological Seminary of America, 1995), 38.

[33] B. Sanhedrin 23a; Y. Sanhedrin 3.1/21a. See R. Joseph ibn Habib, Nimuqei Yosef on Alfasi: Sanhedrin, chap. 3, ed. Vilna, 3b re M. Avot 1.1 and B. Sanhedrin 7b re Exod. 20:23–21:1.

[34] B. Sanhedrin 49a.

[35] Cf. B. Kiddushin 43a for a more absolutist view of royal authority.

[36] See, e.g., Y. Berakhot 9.5/14b.

tionship between God and humans specified by the Torah's law, here the king has no voice at all. This is the business of the priests who run the Temple. Kings are not to become priests and priests are not to become kings.[37] Indeed, there has always been some sort of distinction between religious (or "cultic") and secular authority.

In commenting on this talmudic text (specifically in Maimonides' codification of it), the late fifteenth-century Egyptian-Jewish exegete and jurist R. David ibn Zimra (Radbaz) notes that this text deals with someone "who rules [ha-molekh] by decree [al pi] of a prophet or whom all Israel have agreed upon [hiskimu alav]. But, if he is only one man who rules over Israel by force [be-hazaqah], the people of Israel are not obligated to listen to him, and whoever disobeys [ha-mamreh] his orders is not considered to be a rebel against royal authority [mored be-malkhut]."[38] Whether prophetic appointment is a sine qua non or not for kingship to be reestablished is a matter of debate, as we have already seen. But it would seem that popular approval—even if not by a formal plebiscite (although one need not rule that out in principle)—is most definitely a sine qua non.

Along these lines, the author of a widely read medieval treatise on the 613 commandments of the Pentateuch raises the question of how the commandment "do place a king over yourselves" (Deuteronomy 17:15) can be considered a commandment for all generations (le-dorot), which was Maimonides' criterion for what is to be taken as one of the perpetual commandments of the Written Torah.[39] Wasn't the prophetic appointment of King David and his progeny presented in Scripture meant to be the one and only time the king qua royal dynasty was *ever* to be appointed? Hasn't this commandment *already* been fulfilled once and for all? The answer this author proposes is, "if there be cause so that we need him [she-nitstarekh lo]."[40] One can infer from this oblique answer that the people or their representatives could appoint a king (should the political opportunity present itself) when no member of the Davidic dynasty could be identified (which itself would seem to require prophetic verification).[41] Or, even if one could find a suitable, verified member of the Davidic dynasty, the people could appoint him king even when there is no prophet

---

[37] See 2 Chron. 26:16–21; Y. Sotah 8.3/22c; Y. Horayot 3.2/47c. Cf. B. Kiddushin 66a.

[38] *Radbaz* on Maimonides, MT: Melakhim, 3.8. Ibn Zimra might have had in mind the rabbinic idea that popular Jewish acceptance of a practice has a quasi-prophetic authority (see Y. Pesahim 6.1/33a; B. Pesahim 66b). Also, the "agreement of all Israel" might well mean a definite majority (see B. Avodah Zarah 36a; Maimonides, *Commentray on the Mishnah*: Kiddushin 1.7).

[39] See Maimonides, *Sefer ha-Mitsvot*: intro., no. 3.

[40] *Sefer ha-Hinukh*, no. 497.

[41] See T. Horayot 2.8; Y. Horayot 3.5/48b; B. Horayot 13b.

around to confirm his appointment. Since there has been such a long hiatus between the present and the reign of the last Davidic king, Jehoiachin (2 Kings 25:27–30), in the sixth century B.C.E., the reappointment even of someone who has been ascertained to be of Davidic stock would, for all intents and purposes, be the appointment of a king de novo.

Nevertheless, the question remains: Doesn't the king violate the law of the Torah by being able to execute persons whom the Torah does not allow to be executed? The answer to this question is that the king has the power to adjust, even introduce, criminal penalties for the sake of what he considers the common good, which is what is in the best political interest of the state he personifies. For the same reason, the king has the right to levy taxes. And it is suggested from what we have seen above about royal law, that the king does this not on an ad hoc basis but, rather, from within a system of authorized law and administration functioning parallel to the law of the Torah. This is what the people have elected the king to do. But this alone is what the texts from the books of Joshua and Samuel add to Deuteronomy's mandate to appoint a king. Therefore, when it comes to the personal conduct of the king, he may not exempt himself from the law of the Torah.

This is clearly scriptural teaching. It comes out in the famous admonition of King David by the prophet Nathan for his sin of adultery with Bathsheba and his sin of inciting the death of her husband Uriah the Hittite (2 Samuel 12:1–10), and the admonition of King Ahab and his wife, Queen Jezebel, by the prophet Elijah for stealing the vineyard of Naboth and arranging for Naboth's unjustified execution (1 Kings 21:17–26).[42] Although the king has considerable power to set public policy, even by standards that are secular and not religious (that is, not specified by revealed law), in the end he is still answerable to the law of the Torah. The question is: Who may judge the king when he seriously violates the law of the Torah? That is, who may punish the king for his crimes? From the scriptural accounts of Nathan's condemnation of King David, and Elijah's condemnation of King Ahab and Queen Jezebel, it would seem that the condemnation of the king comes from God through a prophet, but the actual punishment is left to God alone. Nevertheless, we shall now see how some Rabbis might be suggesting something more than this total deference to God in the area of the judgment of the king.

The Mishnah states that "the king neither judges [lo dan] nor is he to be judged [lo daneen]."[43] The criterion of judgment here is clearly the law of the Torah. Can the king ever adjudicate according to Torah law?

---

[42] See D. Novak, *Covenantal Rights* (Princeton, N.J.: Princeton University Press, 2000), 205–209.

[43] M. Sanhedrin 2.2; also, M. Horayot 2.5.

According to the Babylonian Talmud, the Mishnah is speaking about "the kings of Israel," but as for "the kings of Judah," they judge and are judged.[44] The historical question is: Who are "the kings of Israel"? (As for "the kings of Judah," they are clearly the kings of the Davidic dynasty.) The quickest answer is that they are the kings of the Northern Kingdom of Israel, the kingdom that broke off from the Davidic, Judean dynasty after the death of King Solomon (1 Kings 12:20–21). However, in the light of the example given in the Talmud of the criminal behavior of the Maccabean king Alexander Janaeus, it is more likely that the Rabbis meant to distinguish these kings from the true kings of the Davidic dynasty. The Hasmonean kings were considered usurpers of Davidic royal privilege and Roman stooges. Conversely, there has always been an ambivalence about the kings of the Northern Kingdom of Israel since, on the one hand, they had some prophetic appointment but, on the other, they participated in a cult that was clearly set up to oppose the official Sanctuary in Jerusalem (1 Kings 12:25–33).[45] About the Maccabean kings, there was no such ambivalence. They were illegitimate and proved it by their actions, which served neither God nor the Jewish people.

When it came to the Davidic kings there was also no such ambivalence, but for the opposite reason. They were the kings God clearly intended to rule Israel. Indeed, when it came to the Davidic dynasty, there was a rabbinic tendency to romanticize King David when reflecting on the sovereign past the Jews had long ago lost, and to idealize him in messianic speculations about the eschatological future.[46] Even some of the obvious sins of King David, recorded in Scripture with prophetic condemnation, tend to have been whitewashed by some of the Rabbis.[47] But the original Maccabean kings, certainly by the time of Herod in the first century B.C.E., were regarded as tyrants who had abused their imperial power over the Jews. Moreover, unlike even the kings of the Northern Kingdom, these Maccabean kings and their descendents—with whom the Rabbis had more recent experience—ruled with no prophetic mandate at all. And finally and most importantly, these kings had long ago sold out Jewish sovereignty (to be exact, quasi-sovereignty) to the Roman conquerors of the land of Israel.[48]

The assumption that "the king neither judges nor is he judged" in speaking about the Maccabean kings is based on the story brought in

---

[44] B. Sanhedrin 19a.

[45] See T. Horayot 2.2; Y. Horayot 3.2/47c:10; also, Maimonides, MT: Melakhim, 1.8 re 1 Kings 22:10.

[46] See, e.g., B. Moed Qatan 16b re 2 Sam. 233:8; B. Pesahim 119b re Ps. 116:13.

[47] See, e.g., B. Kiddushin 43a re 2 Sam. 11:11.

[48] See Josephus, *Jewish Antiquities*, 14.29ff., B. Sotah 49b, and parallels. The Rabbis emphasized the miracle of the oil for one day burning for eight days rather than the Maccabean military victory in 165 B.C.E. See B. Shabbat 21b. Indeed, there is no "Tractate Hanukkah" in the Mishnah.

the Talmud's discussion of this principle. It is about the servant of King Alexander Janaeus (although it may actually have been about King Herod) who killed someone by the king's order.[49] The king is summoned to appear before the Sanhedrin, but when he actually confronts the members of the Sanhedrin, they are intimidated by him into silence. At this point, Simeon ben Shetah, who had the courage to charge the king with the crime of royally mandated murder, calls upon God to punish his colleagues for their cowardice. The story closes with the angel Gabriel coming to "grind them [the colleagues] into the ground."[50]

The moral of this story is that it is too dangerous for the Sanhedrin to dare judge a king operating with Roman imperial authority, especially for what seems to have been a crime of state. As for the ordinary judicial proceedings of the court, it is unlikely that any king would want to bother himself with such details. He has to save his royal stature and authority for more important matters. But such was not to be the case with the true kings of Israel, that is, in the rabbinic speculation of what true Jewish kings shall do and will do *when* it is possible once again for them to rule. They were not to be above the law and its adjudication. Involvement in the operation of the law, whether as plaintiffs or as defendants, is not to be beneath their dignity. They can even be judged by ordinary judges. The kings appointed as agents of Roman imperial power in Judea were, for the Rabbis, "outlaws" because Jewish law could not touch them, and because involving them in a Jewish legal proceeding as defendants proved to be deadly for the Jews involved. The best the Jews could do was to try and keep them out of the Jewish judicial system altogether. And as was the case with so many examples of Roman rule in Palestine, the Rabbis used this one to point out what Jews should not do when they regain similar political power.

In the discussion of this principle in the Palestinian Talmud, it is assumed that the Mishnah is speaking about lawful Jewish kings. Neither the kings of Northern Israel nor the Maccabean kings are even considered. Yet based on scriptural evidence, written about a time when there really were Jewish kings (especially of the Davidic dynasty), the Mishnah's exclusion of the king from being a judge is questioned.[51] Didn't Scripture say about King David, the king par excellence, "And David was performing justice and righteousness [*mishpat u-tsedeqah*] for all his people" (2 Samuel 8:15)? We know of cases where King David issued legal opinions (1 Samuel 30:23–25; 2 Samuel 1:13–15). Indeed, the Babylonian Talmud sees judgment as a mandate from God to the Davidic kings, quoting a prophecy of Jeremiah: "To the royal house of Judah, Hear the word of the Lord. House of David thus says the Lord: Render justice [*mishpat*]

---

[49] B. Sanhedrin 19a. Cf. B. Kiddushin 43a re 2 Sam. 12:9.
[50] B. Sanhedrin 19b.
[51] Y. Sanhedrin 2.3/20a.

each morning, returning what has been robbed from the hand of the op-
pressor"' (Jeremiah 21:11).[52] Thus there seems to be agreement between
the two Talmuds that a true Jewish king may judge, and that his mandate
is to bring about basic justice in the world in a royal way. The question,
though, of just how the king may be a judge is discussed by some of the
commentators on the Babylonian Talmud.[53] Nevertheless, the question of
whether the king may be judged *by other human beings* is a great point
of difference between the two Talmuds.

The Palestinian Talmud agrees with the Mishnah about the king not
being judged by other human beings, who would be the members of the
Sanhedrin (undoubtedly, meeting in an extraordinary session). King David's words to God are quoted: "From before you shall my judgment
proceed" (Psalms 17:2). The implication here is that the judgment of the
king can *only* come *directly* from God.[54] Thus a later rabbinic text states:
"Our Rabbis teach us why they [the human court] may not judge him.
R. Jeremiah said [the verse from Psalms means] . . . so be it that no human
creature [*beriyah*] may judge the king except God."[55] To a great extent,
then, this line of Jewish thought about the role of kingship closely resem-
bles what in late medieval–early modern Christian thought came to be
known as the "divine right of kings."[56] In fact, the defenders of this doctrine (as well as its detractors) went straight to Scripture for their
prooftexts.[57]

Neither tradition, though, either that of the Palestinian Talmud or that
of the defenders of absolute monarchy in sixteenth-century England and
France, were reversions to the ancient Egyptian notion that the king is divine.[58] For both traditions, the king is clearly human, but a human so
closely related to God that he stands above the jurisdiction of any other
human being. The lesser cannot judge the greater. No one but God can
judge the king.[59] So, if the king, to cite the most egregious of all crimes, were
to proclaim his own divinity, the way some Roman emperors apotheosized
themselves during their own lifetimes, God would surely remove him from
office. Divine selection of the king does not make the king divine; it only

[52] B. Sanhedrin 19a.

[53] See B. Sanhedrin 18b, Tos., s.v. "ve-ha" (the view of Maharan); ibid. 19a, Tos., s.v.
"aval." Also, see R. Margaliot, *Margaliot ha-Yam*: Sanhedrin (Jerusalem: Mosad ha-Rav
Kook, 1977), 44a.

[54] Y. Sanhedrin 2.2/20a.

[55] *Devarim Rabbah* 5.7.

[56] See J. N. Figgis, *The Divine Right of Kings* (New York: Harper and Row, 1965),
8–53.

[57] See Jacques-Benique Bossuet, *Politics Drawn from the Very Words of Holy Scripture*,
trans. P. Riley (Cambridge: Cambridge University Press, 1990), 82–86, 263.

[58] Cf. J. Assmann, *Politische Theologie zwischen Ägypten und Israel* (Munich: Carl
Friedrich von Siemens Stiftung, 1992), 39–70; also, A. P. d'Éntreves, *The Notion of the
State* (Oxford: Clarendon Press, 1967), 182–90.

[59] See M. Horayot 3.3 re Lev. 4:22.

places the king beyond the power of any human jurisdiction.[60] As the Israeli scholar Moshe Halbertal astutely points out: "The moderate view that the king is not a god, although it allows for political authority, affords better protection against deification. . . . it allows room for human agents."[61]

The Babylonian Talmud, by presuming that the Mishnah's principle "the king neither judges nor is he judged" applies only to illegitimate Jewish kings, separates both of its clauses from what ought to apply to legitimate Jewish kings. Thus not only may the king judge, he may be judged. Indeed, the king must judge as he must be judged. That the king may be judged by his fellow Jews is explained by the Talmud rationally, that is, it gives a reason for the scriptural mandate we saw above for the Davidic kings to judge: "If they do not judge him, how can he judge them?"[62] To judge, then, presupposes that one has already had the experience of being judged. Philosophically, it could be said that a person is an object before becoming a subject; one speaks only after having been spoken to; language precedes thought; one has been grasped as an "other" before one can grasp an other one; one experiences a commandment (heteronomy) before one commands (autonomy). The Talmud then presents the reason this way, quoting the Palestinian authority R. Simeon ben Laqish: "Correct yourself [qashet atsmekha], and afterwards correct others."[63] Yet how can one "correct oneself"? Who is correcting whom? As Plato saw with great insight, we only rule ourselves when we have internalized a standard of judgment whose source is outside ourselves.[64] Hence, "correct yourself" is better translated as "be corrected," because of which you may then correct others. But what could the king be guilty of if not the breach of his contracted duty both to uphold the law of God and to serve the needs of the people?[65]

One would have hoped that the Talmud had developed this extraordinary insight, for which there is only an oblique scriptural connection.

---

[60] The most powerful statement of this idea in all literature is found in Shakespeare, *Richard II*, act 3, scene 3.

[61] "God's Kingship" in *The Jewish Political Tradition* 1, ed. M. Walzer, M. Lorberbaum, N. J. Zohar, Y. Lorberbaum (New Haven and London: Yale University Press, 2000), 132.

[62] B. Sanhedrin 19a re Jer. 21:12.

[63] Ibid., re Zeph. 2:1.

[64] *Republic*, 431A.

[65] For Jews until the twentieth century, this point was purely academic. However, in the history of kingship in England (where scriptural texts about kingship were regularly employed by both supporters and opponents of the monarchy), the question of whether the king is only under the judgment of God (*sub Deo*) or the judgment of God and the law (*sub Deo et lege*) was a matter of great practical political significance. Thus Sir Edward Coke, who led the opposition to the absolute power of the Stuart monarchy in the seventeenth century, quoting the thirteenth-century English jurist Henry de Bracton, bravely told his sovereign, King James I, that he was subject to the law *as humanly interpreted and enforced* "because the law makes the king" (*quia lex facit regem*). See E. W. Ives, "Social Change and the Law," *The English Revolution 1600–1660*, ed. E. W. Ives (London: Edward Arnold, 1968), 125; also, Gough, *The Social Contract*, 26.

Clearly the Palestinian Talmud's teaching that the king only judges others but is not judged by them has much more explicit scriptural evidence on its side. But, perhaps, the discussion in the Babylonian Talmud had to stop at this point because it was so speculative. Its profound political implications would have to wait for a time when Jews would have more political power than they did when the ancient Rabbis were engaged in such theoretical theology, whose practical potential had to wait for later times to even begin to become actualized in practice.

Nahmanides' theory about how the principle "the law of the state is law" applied also to "the holy kings of Israel" could be confined to reflection on the extra-halakhic prerogatives of the ancient Jewish kings and to speculation about the future, when Jewish kingship could be regained. This would require the literal translation "the law of the kingdom is law." However, we have seen that the choice of the word "kingdom" (*malkhuta*) could be seen as the usual, but not the necessary, definition of a nonhalakhic state and its systemic law. This is important to consider in order to answer two key questions: (1) Are the secular implications of this principle relevant for a situation where Jews have a degree of political autonomy short of actual kingship? (2) May Jews be participants in good faith in a political order that is republican rather than monarchial, which is much more likely to be a state that is more explicitly secular than monarchies have been? (In fact, republics have usually been antimonarchial in the sense that they most often have succeeded overthrown monarchies. As for the constitutional monarchies still extant, being governed by a parliament where the monarch "reigns" but does not rule, they are like republics for all intents and purposes.) To answer these questions, we need to look at the thoughts of three of the most profound Jewish political theologians who lived and worked in late medieval Christian Spain: R. Solomon ibn Adret (Rashba), who died in 1310 ; R. Nissim Gerondi (Ran), who died in 1380; and R. Isaac Abravanel, who died in 1508.

Ibn Adret's Halakhic Answer

R. Solomon ibn Adret was the most important disciple of Nahmanides. From his rabbinical seat in Barcelona, he had great political authority throughout the Jewish communities of northern (Christian) Spain. His legal and political opinions reflect a time when Jews had a good deal of political autonomy that was clearly the result of a social contract with the Christian monarchs. His opinions also reflect a time when, like in any contractual situation, there was considerable give-and-take. In one of his most famous opinions, which is more his rabbinical endorsement and justification of a public policy already in place than a specific legal ruling,

Ibn Adret shows the give-and-take involved in the Jewish community's relationship with the Castilian monarchy.[66] By making the standards of Jewish civil and even criminal jurisprudence consistent with the standards of contemporary non-Jewish jurisprudence, Jews were able to be participants in and not just supplicants before the legal system that was emerging at that time in northern Spain. And this was a legal system not directly beholden to Christian (canon) law—and certainly not to Jewish law (halakhah) or to Islamic law (*shar'iah*).[67] I call this law "non-Jewish" rather than "gentile" for this reason. This, of course, was only possible for Jews in good faith because they were convinced that the non-Jewish law they had adopted through participating in it was fundamentally just.

The most radical feature of the new Jewish jurisprudence in Christian Spain was that the Jews had the royal entitlement to execute criminals in their own community.[68] This entitlement, which may very well have been mandated by the government, created a serious halakhic problem for the Jewish community. First, halakhah requires that in order for capital punishment of Jews to take place, the following conditions must be met: (1) There must be two eyewitnesses to the crime (most often to the crime of murder). (2) These same eyewitnesses must have immediately warned (*hatra'ah*) the would-be criminal that what he or she is planning is prohibited by the Torah, and what the punishment for doing it will be. (3) This would-be criminal has to indicate to these same eyewitnesses that he or she is fully aware of this and still plans to commit the crime defiantly with full premeditation.[69] Needless to say, this would make any actual execution a near impossibility. (And, indeed, these rules may reflect Jewish unease with the whole institution of capital punishment, possibly due to Jewish disgust with the ease with which their Roman conquerors used capital punishment as a means of political terror.)[70] Furthermore, the Tal-

---

[66] *Sheelot u-Teshuvot ha-Rashba* 3, no. 393.

[67] See Baer, *A History of the Jews in Christian Spain* 1, 86–87. Some have also considered capital punishment as having been legally practiced by the Babylonian Jewish community in talmudic and geonic times. See R. Menahem ha-Meiri, *Bet ha-Behirah*: B. Sanhedrin 27a, ed. Sofer, p. 101. However, the fact that Ibn Adret, with his great mastery of the Talmud, did not cite this as a precedent for his own view makes Meiri's interpretation doubtful. Cf. H. Z. Taubes, *Otsar ha-Geonim*: B. Sanhedrin 27a (Jerusalem: Mosad ha-Rav Kook, 1966), pp. 220–22.

[68] Baer, *A History of the Jews in Christian Spain* 1, p. 315. See , also, Fritz (Yitzhak) Baer, *Die Juden in Christlichen Spanien* 1 (Berlin; Akademie des Wissenschaft des Judentums, 1929), 1039–40.

[69] See T. Sanhedrin 11.1; B. Sanhedrin 40b–41a; M. Makkot 1.7 re Deut. 17:6; also, D. Novak, *The Image of the Non-Jew in Judaism* (New York and Toronto: Edwin Mellen Press, 1983), 173–79.

[70] See, e.g., M. Makkot 1.10; also, D. Novak, *Jewish Social Ethics* (New York: Oxford University Press, 1992), 174–78.

mud says that forty years before the destruction of the Second Temple in 70 C.E., the Romans took away from the Jews the power to execute their own criminals.[71]

Despite this overall halakhic problem, the Jews of Christian Spain did, nevertheless, practice capital punishment, and they did so according to what seem to have been the same standards employed by the non-Jewish state. Moreover, these Jews did not seem to be troubled by this unusual practice, that is, a practice unusual among Jews for the previous thirteen hundred years. So when R. Asher ben Yehiel (Rosh, d. 1328), a prominent German authority who came to Spain to become the Chief Rabbi of Toledo (with Ibn Adret's endorsement), he was shocked to discover that capital punishment was being administered there and elsewhere by Jewish officials to other Jews in northern Spain.[72] These Spanish Jews were doing what no other Jews he had ever heard of were doing. Didn't such a practice require a Sanhedrin? And, besides, they were executing criminals according to standards far less strict than those the Sanhedrin was believed to have employed when it was functioning in the land of Israel.

When R. Asher questions his new community about all this, they answer, "It is the king's decree" (*hormana de-malka*).[73] This choice of language is significant because it is the term, which we saw in the preceding chapter, that was used in the Talmud by a Jewish official of the Roman government to justify his punishment of Jewish criminals who had violated Roman rules.[74] In the Talmud, though, when this answer is given, Elijah the prophet is reported to have told this Jewish-Roman official that this answer is unacceptable and that he should leave Roman Palestine altogether rather than participate in the judicial activities of such an inherently unjust, illegitimate regime. It is most significant that R. Asher, who might well have rephrased the answer of the secular Spanish-Jewish officials in talmudic language, does not repeat Elijah's retort. Despite the well-known dangers of arguments from silence, I still infer from R. Asher's silence that he could not compare the Christian polity, in which he was now living as Chief Rabbi, with the Roman regime in ancient Palestine. In northern Spain at that time, the Jews were not living as a conquered people. Moreover, they had a social contract with the state. As such, they could live there in good faith, and if pressed, they would have to find halakhic justification for what they were already doing in conjunction with the non-Jewish state.

---

[71] B. Sanhedrin 41a; also, B. Berakhot 58a. Cf. John 18:31.
[72] *Teshuvot ha-Rosh*, 17.8.
[73] Ibid.
[74] See 105–6 above.

Ibn Adret gives the following justification for the practice that shocked R. Asher:

> I think it proper [*ro'eh ani*] that if the witnesses are considered trustworthy by the adjudicators [*ha-berurim*], the adjudicators are permitted [*resha'im*] to exact monetary fines [*qenas*] or physical punishments [*onesh ha-guf*] according to what seems proper to them. And this upholds society [*ha'olam*]. If we were to base everything on the laws collected in the Torah and we only punished in assaults [*havalot*] and other such matters as the Torah stipulates, society would be destroyed [*nimtsa ha'olam harev*].[75]

The "adjudicators" mentioned here are Spanish Jewish officials who had authority from the state to judge civil and even criminal Jewish cases. Ibn Adret gives their office halakhic legitimacy.[76]

Ibn Adret, who in other more theological issues is rightly considered to have been an arch-conservative, explicates a truly radical idea here. The idea goes back to the institution of monarchy in ancient Israel, but Ibn Adret gives it an unambiguous formulation it did not have before, even in the theory of his teacher Nahmanides. That is, the law of the Torah is necessary and indispensable, yet it is insufficient politically—at least in an unredeemed world. In certain areas, then, the law of the Torah must allow for a secular system of law and government. Thus his main prooftext from the Talmud for this section of his responsum is: "R. Yohanan said that Jerusalem was only destroyed because . . . they based their judgments [*deeneihem*] on the law of the Torah, but they did not go beyond the letter of the law [*lifneem me-shurat ha-din*]."[77] Now in the other places in the Talmud where the principle "going beyond the letter of the law" is applied, it denotes the occasional reliance on equity rather than on literal statute to decide a case when reliance on literal statute would lead to great injustice.[78] It is invoked in cases where, in effect, the end of civil jurisprudence—which is saving the innocent from injustice being done to them—trumps the legal means, which if carried out literally would result in harming the innocent. But Ibn Adret is saying more than this. He is using this theological reflection on why Jewish society broke down at the time of the destruction of the Second Temple in 70 C.E. to justify the existence of a parallel *system* of law to that of the Torah and not just an ad hoc invocation of equity. He is talking about a body of rules and a

[75] *Sheelot u-Teshuvot ha-Rashba* 3, no. 393.

[76] See S. M. Passamaneck, "The *Berure Averot* and the Administration of Justice in XIII and XIV Century Spain," *Jewish Law Association Studies* 4, ed. B. S. Jackson (Atlanta, Ga.: Scholars Press, 1990), 135–46.

[77] B. Baba Metsia 30b.

[78] See, e.g., ibid., 83b re Prov. 2:20.

body of officials to enforce them, not just a selection of exceptions to Torah law effected by Rabbis.

In amassing talmudic sources to justify secular Jewish jurisprudence in northern Spain, Ibn Adret cites the general fact that the Babylonian Rabbis already in the second century C.E. instituted penalties (qenasot) for crimes that were not stipulated either by the Torah or by previous rabbinic tradition[79]—although he connects this with an earlier Palestinian source that justifies extraordinary penalties in cases when this was "required by the hour," meaning ad hoc measures designed to curb flagrant lawlessness.[80] Yet the fact is that the penalties instituted in Babylonia were clearly meant to be a more permanent legal institution.[81] In this way it is like the law of the state (dina de-malkhuta), which can make claims on Jews because it is systemic and not random (even though, as in any legal system, the innovation of ad hoc measures provides for legal emergencies).[82] These new institutions were required precisely because, as we saw earlier, many of the penalties stipulated by the Torah were taken to be operative only in the land of Israel, and only to be administered by Rabbis who had been ordained by the great Sanhedrin (bet din ha-gadol).[83] Without the introduction of other penalties, in what amounted to the institution of a distinct penal system, Ibn Adret states that the more lawless elements of the community would act without the fear that readily-applied punishment engenders. The result of such legal restraint for lack of a traditional warrant would be near anarchy.

I suspect that Ibn Adret still wants to think of even these new Babylonian penalties together with clearly ad hoc measures because he is somewhat uneasy with the implication that Torah law needs a supplementary, parallel system of law.[84] However, aren't these new measures examples of rabbinic legislation that, even if not strictly ad hoc, are still temporally conditioned by the fact that they are subject to repeal (in principle if not always in fact), a point noted earlier?[85] As such, the difference between an ad hoc ruling (hora'at sha'ah) and a rabbinic institution is still one of degree rather than of kind. It is unlike the difference in kind between both ad hoc rulings and rabbinic institutions on the one hand and the stipulations of the Written Torah on the other. Torah commandments

[79] B. Baba Kama 27b.
[80] B. Sanhedrin 46a. See Maimonides, MT: Sanhedrin, 24.4.
[81] See B. Baba Kama 27b and Tos., s.v. "qenasa" re ibid., 84b.
[82] See, e.g., B. Kiddushin 73b–74a.
[83] See 88 above.
[84] For his concerns that dine de-malkhuta totally supplant Jewish civil and criminal law, see Sheelot u-Teshuvot ha-Rashba 2, no. 134 and 6, no. 254; also, Novak, The Image of the Non-Jew in Judaism, 81, n. 76.
[85] See 87–88 above.

(*mitsvot d'oraita*) alone admit of no human repeal.[86] Nevertheless, Ibn Adret did not seem to want to consider the fact that rabbinic legislation (*mitsvot de-rabbanan*), as distinct from rabbinic legal exegesis of Scripture, is just about as radical an idea as royal law. Both systems of law are able to be truly innovative. Ibn Adret's conservatism seems to have kept him away from making any such comparison.

In conclusion, Ibn Adret gives a general reason for everything he has specified before: "Under any circumstance, the adjudicators [*ha-berurim*] need to be deliberate in these matters and to act after seeking counsel [*hamlakhah*], and that their intention should be for the sake of God."[87] This last clause is more than a pious flourish. It indicates that even in their secular activities, the official actions of Jewish political and legal authorities should be on behalf of God, the ultimate if not always direct source of all law and justice. The "constructive rectification of the state" (*tiqqun ha-medinah*) must be placed in this ultimate context. It is a secularity that does not look to any kind of secularism for either its origin or its end.

Gerondi's Theological Answer

R. Nissim Gerondi, who lived two generations after R. Solomon ibn Adret, was very much part of the northern-Spanish Jewish culture in which Ibn Adret had so much power and influence. Despite the fact that Gerondi had no qualms about differing with Ibn Adret on specific questions of interpretation, he continued Ibn Adret's political theology, a political theology influenced by Ibn Adret's great teacher Nahmanides. Indeed, he continued this political theology with greater philosophical candor and rigor.

In what might well be his most significant theological-political discourse, Gerondi begins by emphasizing the need for justice in society and then distinguishing between two types of justice: one, "true justice per se" (*mishpat tsedeq amitti b'atsmo*); and, two, "the commandment of the king" (*mitsvat ha-melekh*). Then he explicitly says what we have been seeing to be implicit in the reflections and speculations of his predecessors: "Political order [*siddur ha-medini*] would be incomplete with this [true justice per se] alone, so God had to complete its improvement [*tiqquno*] with the commandment of the king."[88] In other words, the health of what in early modern terms would have been called the "body politic" re-

[86] See B. Kiddushin 29a re Num. 15:23.

[87] *Sheelot u-Teshuvot ha-Rashba* 33, n. 393.

[88] *Derashot ha-Ran*, no. 11, ed. L. A. Feldman (Jerusalem: Institute Shalem, 1973), p. 190.

quired, as it were, for God to allow the institution of royal law. And like
rabbinic law, with which we have seen some essential commonalities,
royal law is not the right to make ad hoc emergency rulings nor is it
expressed in the perpetual laws of the Torah.[89] Rather, it is a body of law
that the law of God has *authorized in general*, leaving its specifics to
human invention. Of course, like the need for rabbinic law, the need for
royal law exists because the law of the Torah—which for Gerondi embod-
ies true justice per se—is in the circumstances of this evil and unredeemed
world insufficient. That is, it is not politically efficient enough. He then
repeats in his own wording Adret's point about the anarchy that would
ensue were the Jews to only employ Torah law in the ordering of their
polity.[90]

Following this essential distinction between divine law and human law,
Gerondi makes the startling point that the essential difference between
Torah law and "the laws of the other nations" (*nimusei ummot ha'olam*)
is that the latter are solely concerned with political order whereas the
former are designed to bring "the divine effusion" (*ha-shefa ha'elohi*) to
inhere among the Jewish people.[91] Furthermore, he designates the law of
the other nations as "rational" (*min heqesh ha-sekhel*) whereas Torah law
is supernatural in both its source and its effect. Here he means the part
of Torah law that deals with the direct relationship between God and the
Jews, those practices that would be instantly recognized as unique features of Jewish religion (*ha-huqqim*). But even the Torah's civil and criminal law, although having some things in common with the rational law of
the nations, nonetheless, has more in common with the often mysterious
religious law of the Torah. This is why the Sanhedrin met in the Temple
precincts, so as to bask in the divine Presence who dwells in the Temple.
In fact, Gerondi goes so far to say that some of the laws of the nations
are indeed more rational than some of the Torah's civil and criminal laws
(*mishpatei ha-torah*), yet this is no defect because the king will complete
(*mashlimo*) what the Torah seems to have left incomplete.[92]

It is only when the people want the secular law of the king to be primary
rather than a supplement to the divine law of the Torah that their desire

---

[89] See 85–88 above.

[90] In his insightful study of medieval Jewish political theology, *Politics and the Limits
of Law* (Stanford, Calif.: Stanford University Press, 2001), Menachem Lorberbaum sees
Gerondi's political theory as "secularizing" (124). He then speculates that "his model here
is the relationship of the *kahal* to the rabbinical establishment, the actual modus vivendi
of rabbinical and civil leadership in the Catalonian *kahal*. The *kahal* has political and
legal autonomy, but the rabbis are the arbiters of claims pertaining to justice and religion"
(146–47).

[91] *Derashot ha-Ran*, no. 11, pp. 190–91.

[92] Ibid., p. 192.

for a king is sinful. This, according to Gerondi, was the sin of the people of Israel when they demanded a king from the prophet Samuel. Therefore, even though the king is permitted to make various specific changes in his own law from what the Torah mandates in the treatment of human beings, he is to be ever mindful of his subordination to the more general norms of the Torah even in this area where he has the most power and authority. This, for Gerondi, is the significance of the commandment to him that "he write for himself a copy of this Torah, which shall be with him and the he read it all the days of his life, in order for him to learn to fear the Lord his God by keeping all the words of this Torah" (Deuteronomy 17:18–19). Thus, even when executing a murderer without the Torah's requirement of two eyewitnesses and forewarning (*hatra'ah*), the king should not do this to demonstrate his political and extra legal power but rather to enhance the more general norm "you shall not murder" (Exodus 20:13; Deuteronomy 5:17).[93]

The king is answerable to God and he is answerable to the people. The king is answerable to God because he is still a Jew living under God's covenant with Israel, a covenant whose constitution is the Torah. Gerondi considers this at the heart of the Torah's warning to the king "that his heart not be exalted [*le-viltti room*] over his brethren, that he not swerve from the commandment right or left" (Deuteronomy 17:20). The king must remember that he, like every one of his fellow Jews, is under the law of God; indeed, the ultimate purpose of his election to the royal office is to enhance that law.[94]

Quoting from an unpublished work of R. Jonah Gerondi, R. Nissim Gerondi argues that the king is answerable to the people because kingship has been given to him *by* the people for the sake of their immediate political needs. His power is *from* the people who want him (*she-yirtsu he-hamon*) to have it in order to better serve them. Moreover, since the people are the direct source of his power, they can also remove it from him if they so choose.[95] It seems that the choice to remove the king from office would be because of his failure to serve the people effectively. This often is due to the king's exaltation of himself at the expense of the people.

Gerondi's mention that the king's appointment *and his continuation in office* depend on the will of the people is reminiscent of Rashbam, who, it will be recalled, was an important influence on Nahmanides, in whose school of thought one can certainly place Gerondi. However, Gerondi brings us closer to the idea of a Jewish social contract by his mention of

[93] Ibid., p. 203.
[94] Ibid., p. 194.
[95] Ibid., p. 202. He also quotes B. Horayot 10a-b re 1 Kings 12:7, where God tells King Solomon, "you shall be a servant [*eved*] to this people."

the fact that what the people can give the king they can also take away from him. Like a contract, then, this relationship between people and king has conditions, which if violated could terminate the contract. Like a contract, this relationship is conditional and terminable. It is, therefore, unlike a covenant, especially unlike *the* covenant between God and Israel. This is why, it seems, upon mentioning this as being the essence of Jewish kingship, he immediately contrasts it with God's kingship *over* Israel, where Scripture calls God "the honorable king" (*melekh ha-kavod*— Psalms 24:7–10), that is, the king to whom honor inherently *belongs* as opposed to the human king to whom honor is only *granted* on condition.[96]

Abravanel's Philosophical Answer

With R. Isaac Abravanel, often called by his aristocratic Spanish name, "Don Isaac Abravanel," we see the end of the tradition of Jewish political theology in Christian Spain. This is because Abravanel directly experienced the end of Jewish life in Spain with the expulsion of 1492. And even though Sephardic culture has survived the expulsion to this day, its political expression could not continue since the political situation of the Jews of Spain could not be retrieved but only remembered. Abravanel concludes an intellectual tradition that began with Nahmanides two centuries earlier in the thirteenth century, and that owes some of its inspiration to Rashbam's views of kingship in the twelfth century. Abravanel, then, is the direct beneficiary of those great thinkers who went before him and so influenced him. Yet he also had a distinct advantage over them: he had direct experience of statecraft in what was then the most powerful nation in Europe.[97]

His experience was not just confined to inner Jewish politics or even to the politics of Jewish-Christian relations, both of which were still somewhat marginal political spheres compared to his role as a leading minister in the government of King Ferdinand and Queen Isabella. Moreover, after the expulsion of the Jews from Spain in 1492, Abravanel held a high ministerial position in Portugal, that is, until the expulsion of the Jews from that country in 1497. Finally, during the last years of his life, until his death in 1508, he held an important position in the government of the Venetian Republic. Thus Abravanel was able to add all of his experience as an international statesman to his great learning in both Jewish and non-Jewish sources. This makes his insights about kingship, the kingship

---

[96] Ibid., p. 202.

[97] See B. Netanyahu, *Don Isaac Abravanel*, 5th rev. ed. (Ithaca, N.Y.: Cornell University Press, 1998).

many Jews hoped would return to them, of especial interest. They have much to offer our reflections about the type of secularity that can emerge from the proper constitution of the Jewish social contract. We see him at his theological-political best when dealing with the institution of kingship in his commentaries on the appropriate sections in Deuteronomy and 1 Samuel that deal with the mandate for a king and the actual appointment of one.[98]

In addition to his greater political sophistication, Abravanel was much better read in non-Jewish sources than his predecessors (at least as evidenced when comparing his writings with theirs). Thus, in dealing with Jewish kingship, he discusses with easy familiarity the views of Greek philosophers and Christian theologians along with the appropriate passages from Scripture, Talmud, and Midrash, and the works of earlier Jewish thinkers. Because of this, his treatment of the question of kingship, which has important implications for Jewish social contract theory, is more comprehensive than any we have seen so far. It encompasses scriptural exegesis, political acumen, halakhic analysis, theological critique, and philosophical insight. And whereas the earlier theologians tried to present some form of social contract along with reflections on the value of the institution of kingship for Jews, Abravanel is explicitly antimonarchial, so in this sense he differs explicitly from his theological predecessors who were promonarchial. Nevertheless, by so doing, he is able to suggest a better way of dealing with the idea of a social contract than by way of kingship.

As an exegete, Abravanel reads the scriptural mandate for kingship as a casuistic rather than apodictic statement. The usual way of understanding the mandate in Deuteronomy 17:14–15 is apodictic, that is: "*When* you enter the land . . . *then* take possession of it, *then* say [*v'amarta*] I shall place a king over myself . . . *then* do place [*som tasim*] a king over yourself whom the Lord your God will choose."[99] Since the people have already been commanded to enter the land of Israel and possess it (Numbers 33:53), the opening word (*ki*) presents a temporal condition of four sequentially mandated acts: (1) to enter the land; (2) and to take possession of it; (3) and to appoint a king; (4) to obtain God's selection of who is to be your king. Following the logic of this interpretation of the Deuteronomic mandate, one can only presume that the criticism of the people's request for a king by Samuel (1 Samuel 8:6) is Samuel's perception that the motives of the people are for the appointment of an absolute monarch who will usurp the kingship of God. But Abravanel reads the logic of the mandate quite differently, namely, "When you enter the land

---

[98] See his *Commentary on the Former Prophets*: 2 Sam. 12:9.
[99] See 128–30 above.

. . . and you then take possession of it, *if* you say [*v'amarta*] I shall place a king over myself, *then* do place [*som tasim*] over yourself whom the Lord your God will choose [who will be] from the midst of your brothers, [so] you may not set over yourself a foreign man [*ish nokhri*] who is not your brother."[100]

Abravanel's main point is that there is no mandate (*mitsvah*) whatsoever to appoint a king. The general appointment of the king is up to the people (*me'atsmekhem*). So, *if* the people want a king, *then* they must appoint a king *by* seeking specific divine approval (presumably through a prophet as was the case with Saul and David, who were selected by Samuel), and that approval cannot be for anyone but a native-born Jew. But there is no mandate for the people to want a king at all; it is only that if they want a king, this is the way they must go about it. They could just as easily not want a king with impunity. Abravanel's reading of the verses from Deuteronomy this way is, no doubt, the result of his thorough misgivings about monarchy.

Politically, Abravanel points out how much better governed are the Italian city-states like Venice, Florence, and Genoa—which were republics—than are the contemporary monarchies. Having personally served two monarchs, the kings of Spain and Portugal, and then having served the Venetian Republic, it is hard to argue with Abravanel's wisdom in these matters. It is the result of the extensive political experience of a very wise and worldly man. Then, more philosophically, Abravanel cites the rationality of the rabbinic principle about legal disputes "When there is one and many [*yahid ve-rabbim*], the law is according to the many."[101] Presumably, the "many" of a republican majority (which may not be strictly democratic but more oligarchical) are appointed by popular approval, or are at least closer to popular influence than a king would be in his frequently royal isolation from the people. Moreover, as distinct from monarchy, they need neither divine presentation of themselves to the people for their confirmation nor even the people's presentation of them to God for God's confirmation.

On halakhic grounds, Abravanel points out that the usual argument for the need for kingship is flawed because of its assertion that the king must be given extraordinary legal powers, especially in the area of criminal punishment, for the sake of maintaining public order. This view presupposes that the ordinary halakhic system is insufficient to this necessary political task. But Abravanel is quick to point out that halakhah itself gives the Sanhedrin the extraordinary political authority that most of his predecessors (including R. Nissim Gerondi) thought could only devolve

---

[100] *Commentary on the Torah*: Deut. 17:14–15.
[101] B. Berakhot 9a and parallels. See, also, M. Eduyot 5.7.

upon a king.[102] This fits in well with Abravanel's republican politics inasmuch as the Sanhedrin functioned as a representative body whose policies depended on the opinion of the majority of its members who, presumably, had been persuaded by good arguments to either adjudicate or legislate the way they did. As we saw earlier, this characteristic of rabbinic public policy making, because of its conditionality and repealability, has significant contractual aspects about it.[103] A king, on the other hand, seems to have been able to simply rule from the throne as he saw fit, independent of whether he had been persuaded by anyone else or not.

Also, on halakhic grounds, Abravanel compares the people's desire for a king, which the Torah enables them to fulfill by appointing one, to the surprising Deuteronomic institution of the "war bride" (*yefat to'ar*). Here the Torah (Deuteronomy 21:10–14) permits a Jewish soldier to take a gentile woman captured in war back home to be his wife. But there are conditions. He must treat her with wifely respect, and allow her to mourn her dead parents (who, presumably, were killed in the war in which this Jewish soldier served in the victorious army). Only then may this soldier continue to live with this woman as his wife. And, if he doesn't want to continue living with her, he must then release her as a free woman (presumably with a divorce settlement) rather than sell her into slavery. She may only be his lawful wife, not his slave and not his whore. The Rabbis add that the woman must convert to Judaism to remain with this man.[104] As would be the case in any other conversion, this captive woman cannot be converted to Judaism against her will.[105] Therefore, this marriage requires mutual consent, both sexual and religious, on the part of both parties.

Nevertheless, the Rabbis also seem quite troubled about the moral implications of this "permission" (*reshut*). Isn't it, at least initially, a matter of legalized rape? Their answer is: "The Torah is only speaking because of the bad inclination [*keneged yetser ha-ra*]."[106] For the Rabbis, the "bad inclination" almost always refers to unrestrained libido.[107] In other words, the Torah is only making the best of an inherently bad situation. Under the great anxieties of battle, men are going to capture women and have sexual relations with them. The Torah, then, says in effect: "*If* you do that, *then* this is how it must be done." However, there is no mandate for men to do this in the first place. It is what men usually do, not what they

---

[102] *Commentary on the Torah*: Deut. 17:14–15 and 17:8, no. 5 re B. Sanhedrin 46a.

[103] See 81–90 above.

[104] See *Sifre*: Devarim, no. 213 re Jer. 2:27; B. Yevamot 47b.

[105] See B. Ketubot 11a and Rashi, s.v. "yeholin limhot"; also, R. Mordecai ben Hillel Ashkenazi, *Mordecai*: Yevamot, no. 40 in the name of R. Eliezer ben R. Joel ha-Levi (Ravyah).

[106] B. Kiddushin 21b–22a.

[107] See ibid., 30b.

are commanded to do by God. The implication here is that men would be better advised to try to resist what for most of them is, alas, an irresistible temptation. The comparison to the desire for kingship is striking. Furthermore, whether he was fully aware of it or not, by this comparison Abravanel is also making a suggestive point about the erotic attachment between a people and their king.

Abravanel's theological critique of kingship is withering. First, he points out that the majority of the kings of both Judah and Northern Israel were moral and religious disasters. He even contrasts them with the "judges" (*shoftim*) who led the people before the official beginning of kingship in Israel, and who were on a higher moral and religious level. And the tragedy of Jewish kingship is, for him, no accident. The reason for this—although Abravanel does not make this logical connection explicit, it fits into his over view of kingship—is that the relationship between the king and the people is covenantal! That is, the king is selected by God, and the people only confirm the king whom God has sent them via a prophet. As such, there are no conditions (*einena be-ten'ai*) in this relationship because it is covenantal. As such, the people are stuck with the divinely appointed king; they cannot remove him from office no matter how bad he is. There is no contract here, or even the semblance of one.

The main point we can infer from Abravanel's theological critique of monarchy is that the covenant with the king often interferes with the people's covenant with God. This is because of the mystique of kingship itself, its profoundly religious connotations. The king is inevitably presented as God's regent on earth, at times even God's counterpart on earth. Therefore, it would seem, a republican state is theologically preferable to any monarchy—that is, any monarchy where the king is above the public judgment of his fellow human beings, and where his judgment by God is essentially private: between him and God alone. Kings have a way of competing with God.[108]

It is fascinating that Abravanel tells us that he made these points about what amounts to the "divine right of kings" in a discourse (*be-drush*) he delivered "before kings with their sages." Presumably he was speaking before either Spanish or Portuguese royalty. "Their sages" (*hakhmeihem*) were likely their governmental ministers, but they could have also included Catholic theologians who were involved in political matters at the highest level of state. Obviously, he was telling *them* exactly what *they* wanted to hear. This discourse was, no doubt, given by royal invitation. Christian kings were often told that their kingship should be modeled

---

[108] See Abravanel, *Commentary on the Former Prophets*: Judg. 8:23, viz., where Gideon refuses to become king of Israel because only God can be the true king.

upon scriptural kingship. Since that model is only found in their "Old Testament," it is likely that a discourse on the subject by a Jewish scholar of Scripture like Abravanel, who was also such an important statesman, would attract their keen interest.

Whether or not there were any other Jews present when this discourse was actually spoken by Abravanel is hard to tell. Nevertheless, what is important for posterity is that Abravanel repeats his main theological argument in his commentary on Scripture, and here he is writing in Hebrew, making arguments to his fellow Jews. When seen in the full context of all his thoughts on the subject of kingship, one can surmise that his main theological point made earlier to gentile royalty was meant to have an opposite effect on his Jewish readers. (At one point before in his comments on Deuteronomy 17:14–15, he says that kingship may be necessary for the gentiles, but it is not so for the Jews, who are under the direct rule of God.) What appeals to the gentiles about kingship should repel the Jews. So, it would seem that kingship is best kept on the eschatological horizon, only to be restored by and with an apocalyptic Messiah. In the meantime, the Jews are advised to seek a better form of government than kingship. Thus it is his republicanism, argued for exegetically, halakhically, politically, philosophically, and theologically—it is this republicanism that has tremendous potential for the development of Jewish social contract theory.

In concluding this part of our inquiry, though, there is one advantage to the views of the admirers of kingship over the antimonarchial views of Abravanel: They are better able to conceive of a system of law and public policy that does not require religious authorization on specific points, but only requires general religious authorization and general conformity with the law of God revealed in the Torah. This gives Jewish secularity, or even Jewish participation in a multicultural secularity, enough independence to function without clericalism or "theocratic" politics. But Abravanel, by assuming that the Sanhedrin (or its equivalent) can function with both religious conservatism and secular innovation, made a category error that today's theocratic politics (in such places as Iran) boldly illustrates. "Theocrats" like ideological "secularists" fundamentally confuse the sacred (*qodesh*) and the profane (*hol*). Secularists end up making the profane holy; theocrats end up making the holy profane. So, what Jewish social contract theory requires, I think, is the secular independence seen in rabbinic speculation about *kingship*, but without an actual monarch. That type of beneficial secularity is far better off without the political rule of either monarchs or clerics.

Abravanel brings us to the portals of modernity, especially to the theological-political question of modernity, a question that is still very much with all of us, and certainly still with all the Jews. Unfortunately, he could not bring us to this place by any direct route. The Jews, especially, were thrown into modernity without adequate preparation, certainly without adequate political preparation. (Although maybe this can be said about everybody.) As such, Jews today can only attempt to partially retrieve the profound insights of Abravanel and all his predecessors and recontextualize them within a truly critical political theology.

Chapter Six

Modern Secularity

The Dawn of Modernity

Abravanel's enthusiasm for republican government, within his overall treatment of Jewish ideas of polity, added another important dimension to Jewish social contract theory that had been developing within Jewish communal existence in Christian Spain from the thirteenth to the fifteenth century. To be sure, the Jewish political relationship with a Christian polity in Spain, which was the historical context of Sephardic political theology from Nahmanides to Abravanel, ended with the expulsion of the Jews in 1492. (With the expulsion of the last Muslims in Spain along with the Jews, the type of multicultural society in which a social contract can truly operate ended in Spain.) Nevertheless, the Sephardic refugees of that expulsion were involved in a remarkably similar relationship with another Christian polity, this time Protestant rather than Catholic, and in the Netherlands rather in Iberia, a century or so after the expulsion from Spain in 1492 and from Portugal in 1497. This next relationship was one between the Jews, as a separate nation with considerable internal autonomy and authority, and the larger Dutch Christian host nation. And in fact, this relationship continued until the Netherlands became enough of a modern secular society to offer the Jews, indeed require them to become individual citizens of the state like everyone else.[1]

It would have been interesting, perhaps historically significant, if a theologian of Abravanel's ability had emerged in that community, who could have worked out the further implications of the essentially contractual relationship of the Jewish community with the larger host nation that, until the beginning of the end of a respected Jewish existence in Christian Spain (around 1391), had been the epitome of how well Jewish communal life could generally operate within an officially Christian polity. However, this did not happen. Perhaps this was so since, by the seventeenth century, the status of Christendom and that of the Jews in the world were beginning to change radically. The modern secular nation-state was already on

---

[1] See *Encyclopedia Judaica*, 12:980–82.

the horizon. As such, the whole theological-political question would have to be radically rethought.

Traditional Jewish thinkers, even those of the sophistication of the Amsterdam rabbis of the seventeenth century, did not seem up to the task of developing a Jewish political theology adequate to the changing circumstances of Western Europe in general and of the Jews specifically. The theoretical resources of the Jewish tradition on the question of the theological-political possibilities for the Jews, with the gradual loss of their political autonomy and inner-communal authority, required a more radical retrieval of these theoretical resources than these rabbis could supply. But in all fairness to them, the practical task of reintegrating Jewish converts to Catholicism back into Judaism, plus the practical task of keeping Jews out of trouble with the new and friendly Dutch Protestant hosts, rightly took all of their time and efforts. They had enough to do in the present without engaging in what might lie on the future horizon of western Europe and the theological-political condition of the Jews therein. In fact, most important, they were quite satisfied with the contemporary status quo in the Netherlands as it pertained to their Jewish community.[2]

Baruch Spinoza: Covenant as Social Contract

Ironically, the great political theologian who emerged out of this Sephardic community was Baruch Spinoza (d. 1677), a man whose relationship with the Jewish people and with Judaism is so problematic that it is still being debated today. Whether Spinoza should be considered a Jewish thinker has been a subject of ongoing debate for centuries.

Spinoza could be considered a Jewish thinker inasmuch as he was not only born a Jew, but was also quite well educated in the classical Jewish sources. Despite his banishment from the Amsterdam Jewish community, he did not seem to have joined any other religious community; yet he did not join any other Jewish community either. Even Spinoza's departure from his own Jewish community was his own free choice. His excommunication (*herem*) was thus an afterthought. Nevertheless, Spinoza did remain interested in Judaism, and it is significant that at the time of his death he was working on a book about biblical Hebrew.[3] Finally, excommunication does not mean one has been expelled from the Jewish people itself. One can always return to a normative Jewish community as long

---

[2] See S. M. Nadler, *Spinoza* (Cambridge: Cambridge University Press, 1999), 1–26.
[3] See ibid., 324–26.

as one is willing to live according to Jewish law.[4] As far as Judaism is concerned, it can be said that Spinoza is still in limbo.

Spinoza's method of departing from Judaism was unprecedented. Indeed, one could read his *Tractatus Theologico-Politicus* as a subtle justification of that departure. Moreover, it can be considered the first explicit discussion of social contract by a modern Jewish thinker. Even if Spinoza is not deemed a Jewish thinker, he was still someone concerned with Judaism and the situation of the Jews. What we shall see is that Spinoza uses social contract theory to argue his way out of Judaism; hence it is central to the emendation of his personal theological-political dilemma. To be sure, one should not reduce Spinoza's philosophy to autobiography. His life influenced his thought no doubt; it did not cause it, however. Any true philosopher, like Spinoza, speaks in the first-person existentially if not always grammatically, yet that first-person speech, by intending truth for himself and all others like him, is paradigmatic, not solipsistic. Spinoza did this in the most radical way by arguing that Judaism, according to its own covenantal criteria, had ceased to exist, and by hinting that he and his Jewish contemporaries finally had a rational alternative to their theological-political marginality.[5] Thus he is a Jewish thinker and a non-Jewish thinker: Jewish in so far as he could speak of the Jewish tradition from personal experience; non-Jewish because he saw no future for that tradition.[6] Perhaps it might be best to characterize Spinoza as a "post-Jewish" thinker.

His radical redefinition of Judaism, especially what at least had been *his* Judaism, was both theological and political. And since Judaism is a twofold covenant, vertically with God and horizontally among the Jewish people themselves, the two components of his radical redefinition of that dual covenant are correlated by him at every significant point in his treatment of Judaism. Theologically, Spinoza inverted what might be the central doctrine of Judaism: the divine election of Israel. Formerly, it was always taught that God had chosen the Jews. Spinoza asserted that, in fact, it was the Jews who chose God.[7] Closely correlated to this theological inversion is Spinoza's political assumption that the covenant between

---

[4] See D. Novak, *The Election of Israel* (Cambridge: Cambridge University Press, 1995), 189–99.

[5] See *Tractatus Theologico-Politicus* (hereafter "TTP"), preface, trans. S. Shirley (Leiden: E. J. Brill, 1992), p. 54. See, also, S. B. Smith, *Spinoza, Liberalism, and the Question of Jewish Identity* (New Haven, Conn.: Yale University Press, 1997), 16.

[6] See Novak, *The Election of Israel*, 22–29; also, "Spinoza and the Doctrine of the Election of Israel," *Studia Spinozana* 13, ed. S. Nadler, M. Walther, E. Yakira (Würzburg: Königshausen und Neumann, 2002), 81–98.

[7] TTP, chap. 16/p. 247. See ibid., chap. 17/p. 255.

God and Israel is in essence a social contract. The correlation is centered
on the status of God as the sovereign of the Jewish people.

According to Scripture and Jewish tradition, God chose the Jews for
an unconditional, interminable covenantal relationship. But according to
Spinoza, the Jews chose God to be their sovereign at Mount Sinai through
Moses. The condition of the election of God by the Jews is that God
maintain their political independence sufficiently enough that the Jews
need not be under the direct rule of anyone else. Being conditional hence
terminable, though, this covenant is a humanly initiated social contract
rather than an unending divine covenantal promise as taught by Scripture
and Jewish tradition. For this reason, Spinoza saw the loss of Jewish political independence at the time of the destruction of the First Temple in 586
B.C.E. and the ensuing Babylonian exile as, in effect, the end of the covenant qua social contract.[8] God cannot remain the sovereign of the Jews if
God has not enabled the Jews to retain sufficient political independence
to make God's sovereignty over them a political reality. Thus Spinoza
places great emphasis on the fact that Scripture seems to teach that the
sovereignty the Jews located in God during the days of their political independence had already been overcome by the time they pledged their loyalty to the king of Babylonia (and, by implication, to every other ruler
under whose political rule they have had to live thereafter).

Actually, one can put Spinoza's self-justification of his own departure
from Judaism into the following syllogism: The covenantal relationship
between God and the Jewish people called "Judaism" has ended with the
loss of Jewish political independence (major premise). I, Baruch Spinoza,
am born into the Jewish people (minor premise). Therefore, Judaism no
longer has any claim upon me (conclusion)—or on any other Jew. The
leaders of his Jewish community, whether they knew his arguments or
not, responded to him by rejecting him with great anger.[9] But later Jewish
thinkers had to respond to his arguments, because his radical redefinition
of Judaism is so astute.

Since Spinoza certainly recognizes that humans are social beings by
virtue of their natural need for the cooperation of others in developing
their own life thrust (*connatus*), and since the Jews are part of humanity,
the Jews need a social alternative to their by now politically dead covenant.[10] And that new social alternative would have to be politically superior to what the Jews had already lost. It is clear that Spinoza did not
consider "Christendom" (that is, Christian polity)—which had been proposed to the Jews since the time of Constantine as the solution to their

[8] Ibid., chap. 17/pp. 255–56; chap. 19/p. 282.
[9] See Nadler, *Spinoza*, 116–54.
[10] See *Tractatus Politicus*, 1.3; 2.15–16, trans. S. Shirley (Indianapolis, Ind.: Hackett,
2000), pp. 34, 43–44; also, *Ethics*, IV, P35, scholium, trans. E. Curley, *Spinoza Collected
Works* 1 (Princeton, N.J.: Princeton University Press, 1985), p. 564.

theological-political marginality—a sufficient political solution. Despite his seeming preference for Christianity over Judaism in the *Tractatus Theologico-Politicus*, careful reading of his book shows that Christianity is only a theological way station in the movement into a truly introspective philosophy. But Christianity as a historical religion has no original political teaching of its own. Accordingly, it offers no real political alternative to the lost Jewish polity of biblical times. And even though Spinoza regards Judaism as passé, the memory of the biblical Jewish polity still has much to teach those who desire to establish a new secular polity worthy of human loyalty given freely.[11]

Following this point, it is important to note that Spinoza's notion of the covenant as a terminable and thus conditional social contract is not the same argument for the termination of God's covenant with the Jews as had been presented by Christian supersessionism. For Christian supersessionists, the covenant with Israel is a social contract, but one initiated *by* God *to* Israel, not vice versa. As such, it is conditional hence terminable. And, the terminating condition is not what God has failed to do for Israel but, rather, what Israel has failed to do for God. It is Jewish sinfulness rather than divine inaction resulting in Jewish political impotence that terminates the covenant with the Jews for the Christian supersessionists. Of course, their view of the termination of the "old" covenant with the Jews enabled them to argue that it has now been replaced by the "new" covenant with the church. The church for them is the "new Israel." As such, in their view, not only should the Jews disappear as a people, they should disappear as Jews by becoming Christians.[12]

It seems that Spinoza did not invoke this type of supersessionist social contract thinking, because there is no evidence that he wanted the Jews to become Christians. Rather, it seems he wanted the Jews—and the Christians along with them—to become something more radical. What he wanted, it seems, was for the members of both covenantal communities

---

[11] TTP, preface/p.54; chap. 18/pp. 272–79.

[12] Not all Christians are or have ever been supersessionists. A persistent strand of Christian theology has argued that God's covenant with the Jewish people, precisely because it is a covenant and not a contract, is interminable. The issues these nonsupersessionist Christians have with the Jews are: (1) as gentile followers of Jesus of Nazareth (for them, the Christ), they are also part of God's covenant with Israel, indeed the superior part, which is something the Jews deny; (2) they, not the Jews, understand the true intent of the covenant (which, for them, is Christ). It is important to note that the Christian readers of the *Tractatus Theologico-Politcus* were Dutch Calvinists. And Calvin himself explicitly asserted that the covenant with the Jewish people had not been broken because God does not break his promises. See *Institutes of the Christian Religion*, 4.16.14–15 re Romans 11:16 and 29, trans. F. L. Battles (Philadelphia: Westminster Press, 1960), 2:1336–38. So, it would seem that Spinoza's equation of the covenant with a social contract, which is conditional and terminable, makes him more of a supersessionist than his Dutch Calvinist readers were. For an important contemporary Christian nonsupersessionist theology, see R. K. Soulen, *The God of Israel and Christian Theology* (Minneapolis, Minn.: Fortress Press, 1996).

to become citizens of a new secular state, and for this new secular state to supply them with all the civic religion they would need politically.[13] For this reason, the Jews had nothing to gain politically by becoming Christians. Thus the secular state he envisioned had nothing to learn from Christianity, much less should it become one more Christian state in Christendom.

Spinoza's radical redefinition of Judaism is not nihilistic since he wants the theological-political situation of the ancient Jewish covenant described in Scripture to be the model for the new secular type state he envisions. In other words, he wants ancient Judaism's form but not its content to be transposed into something radically new. The secular state along with its new civic religion is to be a new Judaism, but one that no longer needs the Jewish people at all. For him, then, there is to still be a "remnant of Jacob in the midst of the nations" (Micah 5:6), but as an idea rather than as an actual physical presence in the world.[14]

In order to be neither Jewish nor Christian nor atheistic, this radical new theological-political realm needs its own religious dimension, which seems to be some sort of religion of a very liberal Protestant kind, if not a kind of unitarianism. As for the true philosophical religion, one that transcends the political needs of society, this is within the purview of individual philosophers who dwell *in* the polity but are not truly *of* it.[15] Yet neither of these religions, whether the civic or the philosophical, is a covenantal religion. Philosophical religion is a natural theology, rooted in nature not in historical revelation. It is certainly not Judaism. Civic religion is politically determined. It functions in a polity that has been founded in a social contract. This social contract, though, is one that has been initiated by human individuals for the fulfillment of their individual needs. It is not initiated by God nor can it be so conceived. Thus it is only natural in the sense that it is initiated and maintained for the sake of the enhancement of the individual human drive to live and physically flourish in the world.[16] Not being communal, this civic religion is not covenantal. It is only part of the social contract between a human individual (but not a Jew or a Christian) and his or her society, a contract that recognizes no historical antecedents. As such, it could not be Judaism.

Philosophical religion too, which is for the sake of the God of nature (*Deus sive Natura*), is not communal, hence it is not covenantal. For Spi-

---

[13] See Smith, *Spinoza, Liberalism, and the Question of Jewish Identity*, 119.

[14] See ibid., 114–17.

[15] TTP, chap. 20/p. 291. See *Tractatus Politicus*, 1.1/p. 33. That this philosophical religion of Spinoza truly intends God, albeit not literally the God of the Bible, is well argued by Richard Mason, *The God of Spinoza* (Cambridge: Cambridge University Press, 1997), 169–70.

[16] See TTP, chap. 17/p. 267.

noza, humans do not truly relate to God in their communal being, but only as natural beings. Since human communities are, in fact, societies invented by individuals for the fulfillment of their individual physical needs, human societies themselves are not natural. Only individuals are natural entities, hence only individuals can relate to God for the satisfaction of their intellectual needs. Humans invent societies. Societies do not give birth to humans. In Spinoza's terms, human society seems more attuned to the divine attribute of extension; human philosophy seems more akin to the divine attribute of thought.[17]

Contrary to both Spinoza's civic religion and his philosophical religion, a covenantal religion (that is, one based on a historical revelation) functions as the substantial life of a primary community, one that gives its members a sense of their place in the cosmos, their role in the ontological scheme of the universe. Certainly, for Judaism, that scheme is historical. That history is the ongoing story of God's dealing with Israel (what some have called *Heilsgeschichte*, "salvific history"). But for Spinoza, history is a purely inter-human, ephemeral affair, hence civic religion is of no cosmic significance. Only an individual's philosophical relation to God is of cosmic significance. Nevertheless, since the cosmos is eternal, for Spinoza, the temporality that is the essence of history is not a factor in the individual's relation to this timeless, cosmic God.[18] Thus, being atemporal, the God of Spinoza cannot very well have a historical relationship with anyone.

The only hope Spinoza seems to see for Judaism and the Jewish people in this new world is brought out in a famous, enigmatic passage in his *Tractatus Theologico-Politicus*. There Spinoza writes, en passant as it were, one striking sentence: "Indeed, were it not that the fundamental principles of their religion discourage manliness [*effoeminarent*], I would not hesitate to believe that they will one day—given the opportunity— such is the mutability of human affairs—establish once more their independent state [*imperium*], and that God will again [*de novo*] choose them."[19] Much has been made of this passage. Indeed, some have seen it as the forerunner of modern political Zionism.[20] But taken in the context of Spinoza's political theory, one can infer from it that Spinoza saw the possibility of the reinstitution of the ancient Jewish covenant. Since, for him, that covenant was in fact a social contract, initiated *by* the Jews *to* God to be operative *in* their own land, all that is required is that the Jews

---

[17] See *Ethics* 2, P1 and P2.

[18] See Novak, *The Election of Israel*, 115–38; 23–26.

[19] TTP, chap. 3/p. 100 = Latin text in *Opera* 2, ed. J. van Vloten and J.P.N. Land (The Hague: M. Nijhoff, 1914), p. 133.

[20] See Novak, *The Election of Israel*, 44–49.

regain their own land of Israel. (In Spinoza's days, that was a mere wish, but by the early twentieth century, when Spinoza became a hero for some Zionists, that mere wish became a definite possibility, then a reasonable probability, and, finally, a definite reality.)

However, the problem facing the Jews seems, in his view anyway, to be twofold: one, the Jews have no realistic expectation that they will be able to return to their old land; two, the postbiblical Jewish religion has clearly made the Jews politically passive. This is what has made the Jews "un-manly" (literally, effeminate), the word used in a political not a sexual sense. As such, even if the Jews could regain their old land, it is doubtful they would be politically assertive enough to be able to reinstitute the covenant qua social contract by themselves. This is due to the largely apocalyptic character of traditional Jewish messianism, which has long been teaching the Jews to patiently wait for God to redeem them. This redemption will not come because of their own efforts but, almost, despite them.[21] Furthermore, since Spinoza clearly thought that in ancient times the Jews chose God rather than God choosing the Jews, his statement that "God will again choose them" must be taken figuratively. That is, just as in ancient times the Jews projected their choice of God onto God, turning it into God's choice of them, so this could happen again. But of course, for Spinoza, this second divine election of Israel cannot be taken literally any more than the first election of Israel can be taken literally. In truth, God cannot make choices at all because time is not an attribute of God and all choices are made in time.[22]

Nevertheless, being so hypothetical, Spinoza's discussion of the con-tractual reconstitution of the Jewish people had nothing practical to offer Jews standing at the portals of secular modernity. And as we have seen, his more practically relevant theory of the social contract was not a con-tract Jews qua Jews could enter, and certainly not one they could enter with a justification from the Jewish tradition. The only practical conclu-sion for Jews that could be drawn in Spinoza's time from his social con-tract theory is that they assimilate into the liberal, secular state that he seemed to have thought could be realized in the Netherlands.[23]

Moses Mendelssohn: Judaism as a Religious Denomination

Spinoza's radical redefinition of the ancient covenant, which turned it into a social contract, had a profound effect on the Jews who came after him, even on those Jews who, unlike Spinoza, chose to remain within Judaism and the Jewish community. The most prominent of these was the philoso-

[21] See 95–100 above.
[22] See Novak, *The Election of Israel*, 23–26.
[23] See Smith, *Spinoza, Liberalism, and the Question of Jewish Identity*, 202–205.

pher and scriptural exegete Moses Mendelssohn (d. 1786). Unlike Spinoza, though, whose social contract theory was quite hypothetical, especially as it applied to the Jews, Mendelssohn developed a social contract theory that had direct application to the political situation of the Jews of his own time in Prussia. These Jews were anxiously engaged in a struggle to gain full citizenship in the secular nation-state that was emerging there, a struggle that only culminated after Germany became fully united under largely Prussian rule in 1871.[24]

Mendelssohn's great work in political theory was entitled *Jerusalem: Or on Religious Power and Judaism*. This work was written for both gentiles and Jews. To the gentiles, Mendelssohn wanted to argue that the Jews could become full citizens in the new secular nation-state because they were fully prepared to leave behind the corporate claims of the Jewish communities (*qehillot*) on individual Jews.[25] In other words, the Jewish community would and could voluntarily give up their theological-political power (*Macht*).[26] To the Jews, Mendelssohn wanted to argue that they could become full citizens of this new secular nation-state in good Jewish faith because Judaism, as he conceived it (hence "and Judaism" in the title of his book), lent itself to becoming one religious denomination among several in this (or any) secular nation-state.

The best way to understand Mendelssohn's theory of the social contract, especially as it pertains to the place of the Jews in the new secular politics of modernity, is to see how he relates three terms and their referents. These terms are "nature," "state," and "religion."

Concerning nature he writes:

> If men are not bound by nature to any duty [*Pflicht*], they do not even have a duty to keep their contracts [*Verträge*]. If there is in the state of nature, no binding obligation [*Verbindlichkeit*] other than that based on fear and powerlessness, contracts will remain valid only as long as they are supported by fear and powerlessness.[27]

Here Mendelssohn is explicitly arguing against Hobbes, who had asserted that humans enter a social contract with their rulers because the state of nature, which was their chaotic prepolitical situation, not only afforded

[24] See Alexander Altmann, *Moses Mendelssohn* (University, Ala.: University of Alabama Press, 1973), 421–74.

[25] For insightful discussion of this radical change in the corporate status of the Jews, see Jacob Katz, *Tradition and Crisis* (New York: Schocken, 1971).

[26] For a general look at the essential problem for Jews in making the case for their communal inclusion in a secular society, see S. L. Stone, "The Jewish Tradition and Civil Society," *Alternative Conceptions of Civil Society*, eds. S. Chambers and W. Kymlicka (Princeton, N.J.: Princeton University Press, 2002), 131–70.

[27] *Jerusalem*, trans. A. Arkush (Hanover, N.H.: University Press of New England, 1983), 36–37. The German text (hereafter "German") is taken from *Moses Mendelssohns Gesammelte Schriften: Jubiläumausgabe* 8, ed. A. Altmann (Stuttgart: Friedrich Fromann, 1983), 106.

them no protection from criminals, but also provided them with no moral norms to prevent them from becoming criminals themselves.[28] Not wanting either to be the victims of criminal violence or to become violent criminal themselves, humans enter into a contractual agreement (*Vorabredung*) with the state to live peaceful, law-abiding lives.[29]

However, the problem is: How can one make one's contractual commitment to enter into civil society and its polity if the place whence one comes—the state of nature (*Stande der Natur*)—does not provide one with any moral norms?[30] How can one be expected to keep one's agreements if one has made them in a situation where there is not even the moral principle that contracts be kept (*pacta sunt servanda*)? Therefore, Mendelssohn, explicitly following Locke rather than Hobbes, insists that there is enough morality in the prepolitical situation of human beings to enable them to contract a civil society and polity with the moral integrity they have already derived from nature. This is because civil society is meant to enhance already natural human sociality, not to create human sociality de novo.[31] Nature, specifically human nature, makes demands upon us (duties) even before we make contractual claims on the society with which we have entered into a social contract.[32] In fact, because we already have these moral norms in hand so to speak, we are able to make moral claims on the state. Natural duties, then, precede civil rights; indeed, natural duties make civil rights possible.

But if humans came to the state with nothing moral in hand, then the only claims possible would be those the state could make upon them. Therefore, the prior, natural morality humans have in their prepolitical (but not presocial) situation is also their protection against an absolutist state, which is the type of state Hobbes argued for (he was in fact arguing for the Stuart monarchy in Britain) and that repelled those who knew how morally destructive such a state could actually be.

We can now see how nature and the state are correlated, that is, how one moves from the natural human situation of prepolitical sociality to the situation of the morally constituted state. That movement, which does not leave natural morality behind, is effected by the social contract. We

[28] In his commentary on Arkush's translation of *Jerusalem*, on pp. 156–57, Alexander Altmann shows that Mendelssohn oversimplified Hobbes's actual position.

[29] *Jerusalem*, 37 = German, 106.

[30] The term "state of nature" is an English translation of the Latin *status naturalis*. Although accurate, it is nonetheless confusing since "state" could easily be confused with "state" as used for a polity (*civitas*) as in *der Staat*. Hence the German *der Stande der Natur*, used by Mendelssohn, meaning "the natural condition," is much less confusing.

[31] See John Locke, *Second Treatise of Civil Government*, chap. 2.

[32] *Jerusalem*, 37–38. See J. W. Gough, *The Social Contract*, 2nd ed. (Oxford: Clarendon Press, 1957), 193–203.

now need to see how Mendelssohn views religion, and how Judaism fits into that overall view. What is the relation of religion to nature and to the state?

Mendelssohn calls religion, which for him is the relations of humans to God, by the name "the church" (*die Kirche*).[33] As a professing Jew, he does not mean that this term refers only to the Christian religion. Instead, he uses it in its political rather than theological sense. In the same way, even traditional Jews today have little problem speaking of "church-state relations" when they specifically mean Judaism's relation to the secular state.[34] "The church" is thus a synonym for "religion." Nevertheless, by using the term "church," Mendelssohn is actually altering its meaning for both Jews and Christians. For Jews, being a "church" within a larger secular state means that the historical Jewish community, as the repository of the Jewish tradition, can no longer make communal claims on the Jews who profess it. For Christians, being a "religion" (that is, *a* church rather than *the* church) within a larger secular state means the state can and should no longer look to any one religion, especially still dominant Christianity, for its legitimacy. The implication here is that the Christian church, which until Mendelssohn's time had claimed to be the ultimate source of political legitimacy for any state in Europe, would have to become just *a* religion among several others. Indeed, now all religions within the state are to be *for* the state rather than *from* the state or *by* the state. And the state is not to be *from* the church or *by* the church—any church. Thus the state is to be religiously neutral and religion is to be politically neutral. Now their relation is to be mutually respectful rather than hierarchal. On this point, Mendelssohn writes: "The only aid [*Beystand*] religion can render the state consists in *teaching and consoling*; that is, in imparting to the citizens, through its divine doctrines [*göttliche Lehren*], such convictions as are conducive to the public weal [*gemeinnützige Gesinungen*]."[35]

It would seem that for Mendelssohn, there is a natural religion as well as a natural morality. And just as one is not bound to natural morality by contract, so one is not bound to natural religion by contract. Thus, after speaking of "a social contract" (*gesellschaftliche Vertrag*), Mendelssohn writes:

> Not so the church! It is founded on the relationship [*Verhältnisse*] between God and man. God is not a being who needs [*bedarf*] our benevolence, requires our assistance, or claims any of our rights [*unsern Rechten*] for his own use, or

[33] See ibid., 41 = German, 111.

[34] See 218 below.

[35] *Jerusalem*, 45 = German, 114. Mendelssohn's German rendition of the Latin *bonum commune* is *das gemeine Beste* (ibid.).

whose rights can ever clash or be confused with ours. These erroneous notions must have resulted from the . . . inconvenient division of duties into those toward [*gegen*] God and those toward man. The parallel has been drawn too far.[36]

Now, for Mendelssohn, all rights and duties are correlated. Furthermore, he holds that rights are claims based on needs. As such, we have a duty to help our neighbor since our neighbor has a rightful claim upon our help, and this is *because* our neighbor *needs* our benevolence. He or she confronts us with a need and thus obliges our dutiful response. All legitimate duties are responses to the claims made through legitimate rights. The state too has needs, namely, obedience of its authority by its citizens. But since God has no needs because of his omnipotence, God cannot, need not, make any real claims upon us. God does not really make any direct claims upon us because he has no need to do so. Therefore, natural religion consists of our love of God (rather than God's love of us), which is our free response to God's benevolence as our creator and sustainer in nature or as our benefactor in history.[37] It is not a matter of natural duty, much less a matter of contract. It is only a matter of more general acknowledgment and gratitude. From nature we know all we have to know about God's omnipotence and selfless beneficence to humans. From history, as we shall soon see, Mendelssohn asserts that we learn more vivid illustrations of that omnipotence and benevolence.

Our natural love of God leads to our benevolence toward other creatures. "We ought, from love of God, to love ourselves in a rational manner, to love his creatures; just as we are bound, from a rational love of ourselves, to love our fellow men."[38] Now certainly, Mendelssohn is not equating love of God with self-love. Rather, it seems, our love of God leads to our love of his creatures, the first of whom are ourselves. Then, we extend that self-love to love of our fellow humans. Moreover, the state is best equipped to deliver human benevolence from one to the other. Therefore, even though our love of God cannot be mandated by the state since God has no claims upon the state, the citizens of the state can still be served when the state draws upon the religious motivation to neighborly love. Although the state has to frequently "compel [*zwingen*] actions beneficial to the public," it is better served when it draws upon the more voluntary religious commitments of its citizens.[39] So, Mendelssohn writes:

And it is here that religion should come to the aid of the state, and the church should become a pillar of civil felicity. It is the business of the church to convince

[36] Ibid., 57 = German, 126. Hence *dessen Rechten* (ibid.), when referring to God, must be taken figuratively not literally.

[37] Ibid., 46; 47; 58–59; 58.

[38] Ibid.

[39] Ibid., 72 = German, 140.

people, in the most emphatic manner, of the truth of noble principles and convictions; to show them that duties toward men are also [*auch*] duties toward God . . . that serving the state is true service of God [*ein wahrer Gottesdienst*].[40]

It would seem, then, that any religion the state is to tolerate must be able to justify itself to the state by making the state an end to which that religion (or any religion) is to be a means.

Religious Pluralism in a Secular State

So far, though, Mendelssohn has only shown that some sort of natural, prepolitical ur-religion need be recognized by the state. Indeed, Mendelssohn is convinced that "eternal religious truths" are basically available through the proper human exercise of natural reason.[41] So far, then, Mendelssohn has not shown why either Judaism or Christianity is needed by such a secular state, for this state is able to resist the temptation of deifying itself due to its recognition of the natural knowledge and love of God. This state does not seem to need either Judaism or Christianity to avoid official atheism or, what Hobbes meant by calling the state "this mortal god."[42] Moreover, whereas one transfers many of one's natural rights to the state via the social contract, one cannot transfer any of one's natural rights to know the truth about God and to love God because of it, since these rights are "inalienable" (*unveräusserlich*).[43] Indeed, "the members of society [*Gesellschaft*] could not have granted [*einräumen*] that right to them [the church or the state] by any contract whatsoever."[44]

Nevertheless, although the natural knowledge and love of God are readily available through the proper exercise of universal human reason, the historical dimension of human existence seems to require that these eternal truths be taught through various human cultures. Indeed, for Mendelsssohn, the level of rationality achieved by any nation (which seems to be at a level less comprehensive than that of the state) is the sign of how culturally elevated it has become.[45] And culture is transmitted through rituals and authoritative commandments that intend the eternal truths of the ur-religion of nature. History becomes the "verification" (*bewahrt*) of these eternal truths.[46] The practice of historical religions like Judaism is

---

[40] Ibid., 43 = German, 112.
[41] Ibid., 89–90.
[42] *Leviathan*, chap. 17, ed. M. Oakeshott (New York: Collier Books, 1962), p. 132.
[43] *Jerusalem*, 70 = German, 138.
[44] Ibid., 62 = German, 130.
[45] Ibid., 42–43.
[46] Ibid., 98 = German, 165.

the active verification of these truths—when this practice is motivated by proper rational intention. Mendelssohn emphasizes this when he points out that Judaism does not really make any dogmatic demands on its adherents. Indeed, Judaism (or any historical religious culture for that matter) does not have to do so, since whatever doctrines are believable anyway have already been learned by persuasion through universal reason. Actually commanding assent to such doctrines by making them dogmas would only call their truth value into question.

Mendelssohn's Jewish readers who were still practicing any religion were still practicing traditional Judaism (Reform Judaism would not appear for almost another half century; Conservative Judaism even later). As such, they probably would not have appreciated how undogmatic Judaism could possibly become. But Mendelssohn's Christian readers, many of whom were already practicing decidedly untraditional forms of Christianity, could readily appreciate the subtle, Protestant, voluntaristic point Mendelssohn seems to be making here. Religion is not just a matter of free choice like natural morality, where one can either fulfill the duties it obliges or defy them. Rather, religion is a matter of free will, which is what one is persuaded—not commanded—to do. It is what one would command oneself because it is good in and of itself. Thus true religion gently persuades its adherents that the worship of God is good in and of itself because God's power and God's beneficence attract our free assent.[47]

The state is to tolerate religion because the state can only enforce duties to those who need them performed on their behalf. The state cannot enforce duties to God, who does not need anything performed on his behalf. Therefore, the state must tolerate religion since a citizen's relation to God is none of the state's business. The state must leave religion alone, that is, any religious community that does not act as a state within a state (*imperium in imperio*) by imposing and enforcing its own duties on its own members. This is the reason Mendelssohn argues that the Jewish community must give up its traditional internal discipline of excommunication (*herem*), since by exercising that right it is imposing duties upon its members that too closely resemble what is the sole governing business of the state.[48] On the more positive side, the state should actually encourage religion when religion sees its main function in the world to be to inspire people to serve the state and obey its laws out of inner conviction, thus giving them what Mendelssohn calls "a more exalted [*erhabenere*] sanction."[49]

[47] Ibid., 43; 118–19.
[48] Ibid., 77–80; 72–74.
[49] Ibid., 58 = German, 127.

Mendelssohn had kept Judaism (and every other historical religion) out of the social contract between the state and its citizens. Religion is something that is essentially private, and it can be shown that privacy is what the polity (*respublica*) allows as a subtraction (*privatio*) from its domain—why?—because it is not of enough political importance for the polity to bother itself about it. This is quite different, however, from the much more Jewish argument that the secular state should not interfere with the practice of any religion because, at least as regards historical religions like Judaism and Christianity (and Islam), one's religion is one's prior attachment to a primary community with a transcendent warrant.[50] If anything, one's religion is more public than one's citizenship, not less so. As such, a person's religious community is beyond the authority of the state for two reasons: one, it precedes the state in time; two, it deals with a dimension that is above the domain of merely inter-human politics. Thus a religious community like Judaism has both an ontological and a historical prior claim upon its members. Accordingly, in the more Jewish idea of the social contract I am trying to present in this book, the Jewish community must learn how to support the state, and to demand respect not just tolerance from the state.

From a perspective coming out of the Jewish tradition, it could be said that Mendelssohn ceded too much to the state. Moreover, he was dealing with a state that recognized no real prior limits to its domain, but only its own self-limitation in private areas like religion. There alone was it willing—intermittently—to stay out of the way of what individual citizens do among themselves in their own allotted time and space. Only a stronger idea of social contract could recognize rights prior *to* the state to be greater than subsequent entitlements *from* the state. Accordingly, it would be capable of better limiting the power of the state. But this idea could be more cogently argued in Locke's England after the true establishment of a limited constitutional monarchy in 1688 than it could in Mendelssohn's Prussia of 1783 (the year of the publication of *Jerusalem*).

So far, Mendelssohn has only shown that some sort of highly voluntary religion could function legitimately in the state he sees founded in a social contract. But he still has to persuade his readers that there should not simply be one official religion in such a state (as Spinoza had argued), and that it should not replace a historical religion like Judaism for the Jews, and a more traditional Christianity for Christians. Moreover, as a traditional Jew himself, he has to persuade his Jewish readers that they should remain loyal to traditional Judaism in this Prussian state, a state to which

---

[50] See 8–9 above.

they must be prepared to give their full political allegiance in return for the rights of full citizenship.

Mendelssohn's argument against one official religion is stated as an address to the Christian majority in Prussia, the same people he wants to support Jewish appeals for the rights of full citizenship.

> Brothers! If you care for true piety, let us not feign agreement where diversity is evidently the plan and purpose of Providence. . . . For the sake of your felicity and ours, do not use your powerful authority to transform some *eternal truth*, without which civil felicity can exist, into a *law* [*Gesetz*], some religious opinion, which is a matter of indifference to the state, into an *ordinance of the land*![51]

Here Mendelssohn is making a powerful argument for the civic validity of what we would call today "religious pluralism." Yet this is only one of four possibilities for the relation of state and religion.

One, the state could continue with one official religion, which would be, of course, Christianity (in Prussia this would be Lutheranism). But this would severely compromise the secular character of the state, even if minority religions were tolerated (as Jews sometimes were in officially Christian polities). The state could not, then, claim to be based on a social contract between humans qua humans. Two, the state could institute its own new religion (Spinoza's option, as we have seen). But in that event the state would have to inevitably formulate some dogmas (however minimal) of this new religion, and these dogmas would claim their validity from the fact that the state prescribed them. But we have seen that this is not the civic task of the state. The state is not in the truth business, and Mendelssohn rightly saw that religion is very much about truth.[52] Three, the state could be officially atheistic. But that could lead to either a repression of the legitimate religious needs of its citizens, or to a sublimation of those needs into the state setting itself up as a rival god to the old God the people had previously worshiped.[53] (Twentieth-century Fascism, Nazism, and Communism have shown with unprecedented horror how that happens.) Fourth and finally, the state could recognize or respect the various ways its citizens deal with their religious needs and respect all the religions that enable humans to do so, that is, all religions that make a positive contribution to public morality as the state proclaims it and enforces it. This would only exclude religions that disturb public peace. For Mendelssohn, it seems, only this pluralistic approach prevents the state from either

---

[51] *Jerusalem*, 138 = German, 203.

[52] Ibid., 90.

[53] Mendelssohn wanted very much to steer a middle course between atheism and "fanaticism." See ibid., 63, 136.

dictating one particular traditional religion, or dictating its own invented religion, or turning civic obedience into a religion itself (which is what many saw as the intention of Hobbes's idea of the state).

Traditional Judaism Continued in the Secular State

Mendelssohn has argued for the civic need of a plurality of religions, but so far he has only shown how religions that are voluntary associations of like-minded believers fit his definition of religion.[54] Yet Mendelssohn needs to argue for the place of Judaism in this civic scheme, specifically his own traditional Judaism, which happens to have been the only form of Judaism available in his lifetime. After all, Mendelssohn was a Jew fully observant of the commandments of the Torah and Jewish tradition, and he clearly expected his fellow Jews to remain as faithful to traditional Jewish practice as he did. He therefore needs to argue for the continued validity of traditional Judaism, but isn't traditional Judaism very much a system of duties that are both taught and enforced in a highly structured communal context? No one could possibly confuse this Judaism with the liberal Protestant or Unitarian-like Deism of Mendelssohn's gentile friends and supporters. Indeed, Mendelssohn, in what have become the best known lines in *Jerusalem*, asserts: "Judaism boasts of no *exclusive* revelation of eternal truths that are indispensable to salvation, of no revealed religion in the sense in which that term is usually understood. Revealed *religion* is one thing, revealed *legislation* [*geoffenbarte Gesetzgebung*], another."[55] Nothing remotely like the religion of law Mendelssohn is here asserting could be confused with the type of voluntary, individualistic religion he seems to have been arguing for earlier in the book.

Any perceptive reader of *Jerusalem* would have to ask the following question: Isn't "legislation" law-giving (its literal meaning in German), and doesn't a system of law present duties to those under its authority?[56] Yet as we have seen, Mendelssohn only recognizes duties between humans, some of which are enforced by the state in its legislation and adjudicated by the state's courts when disputes arise about how that legislation is to be applied. Even if the specific duties Judaism presents to its adherents do not conflict with the specific duties enforced or invented by the state, doesn't the very claim of the traditional Jewish community, as a lawful society, to impose duties on its adherents—who are also citizens

[54] Ibid., 135–36.

[55] Ibid., 97 = German, 164.

[56] For Mendelssohn, religious authority in essence is only exemplary of the morality religion is supposed to help the state teach its citizens. See ibid., 43.

of the state—in principle conflict with their duties of citizenship? Isn't the traditional Jewish community, even without the police power it had enjoyed under the *ancien régime* when it was a separate corporate entity, in political conflict with a state that claims to be the sole enforcer and adjudicator of duty?

One could simply leave these questions unanswered and conclude that Mendelssohn has made a cogent argument for why the secular state should tolerate a plurality of religions, especially Judaism, which theretofore had been the least tolerated religion in Europe. But one could also conclude, based on the premises of his theological-political theory, that he has not yet made a cogent argument for why Jews should remain faithful to the traditional Jewish commandments as taught and enforced in the traditional Jewish community.[57] He has not accounted for the fundamentally communal context in which all of these commandments must be kept. And even if Mendelssohn could show that Jewish communal order did not end with the loss of Jewish national sovereignty, as Spinoza had argued, he does not seem able to tell us why that communal order ought to be continued by Jews who have become citizens of a modern, secular nation-state. Furthermore, if this is the case, Mendelssohn has provided no way for Jews who live in such states to make their communal claims upon the state, the first of which is that their membership in their religious community takes priority over their citizenship in the state. This means the state is not entitled to determine the actions that define one's life: like marriage, parenting, worship, and preparation for death. Hasn't Mendelssohn confused religion with philosophy since he seems to want to reduce religion, which is originally so communal, into an individual, philosophical preference like being a Platonist or an Aristotelian? Isn't the communal character of a religion like Judaism a necessary condition for Judaism to be a system of commandments? Isn't Judaism the religion of communal praxis par excellence?

As we shall presently see, despite his philosophical acumen, great Jewish learning, and undoubted loyalty to Judaism and the Jewish people, Mendelssohn's argument for the continuity of Judaism as a moral imperative is quite convoluted. This suggests how difficult it was for him to make a straightforward argument for Jewish loyalty to the Jews as distinct from his easier task of making an argument for Jewish enfranchisement to the gentiles. But let us now see how Mendelssohn's argument might be reconstructed, even if in the end it is not true.

---

[57] See ibid., 128 = German, 194, where Mendelssohn calls the covenanted community a *Gemeine* (in later German, *Gemeinde* or "congregation"), which is distinct from the state which he calls a *Gesellschaft* (see ibid., 57 = German, 126). The difference between the two forms of society is that membership in a *Gesellschaft* is by voluntary contract; membership

Judaism can be conceived as a system of duties, but those duties are to be distinguished from the political duties required by the state. Mendelssohn is explicit that "to every right, therefore, there corresponds [*entspricht*] a duty."[58] But in his view, one has to understand the covenantal claims of God in the Torah as essentially different from the rights exercised by the state in its law-giving. Thus one could say that the rights of the state upon its citizens, which they have accepted in the social contract, are "perfect rights" that, according to Mendelssohn, pertain when "all the conditions under which the predicate belong to the subject are invested in the holder of the right."[59] This means that the holder of this kind of right has a full claim on those under its authority, and those to whom this right is addressed are duty bound to respond to it without deciding whether they want to take such a right upon themselves or how much of it they want to take upon themselves. This set of normative relations comprises "compulsory rights and compulsory duties [*Zwangpflichten*]."[60] The free yet unconditional acceptance of the social contract by the citizens of the state binds them to the authority of the state without question. Hopefully, that authority is truly concerned with the common good of all the citizens and not just with its own perpetuation and expansion.

This is the relation of the state and its citizens: The state needs to command its citizens and the citizens need to obey the state's commands, both for the sake of the common good. As distinct from natural morality, which is internal, these public rights and duties are "external," that is, they are enforceable by the police power of the state.[61] Nevertheless, Mendelssohn notes: "Blessed [*Heil*] be the state which succeeds in governing the nation by education itself; that is, by infusing it with such morals and convictions [*Gesinnungen*] as will of themselves tend to produce actions conducive to the common weal [*gemeinnützigen*], and need not be constantly urged on by the spur [*Sporn*] of the law."[62] In other words, the chief service of religion and of general culture (which in Mendelssohn's time were so closely connected) in and for the secular state is to enable the people to internalize as much as possible their civic duties, thus diminishing the need for too much police action. Too much overt expression of state authority inevitably suggests that people are prisoners in their own society rather than free persons who have created the society by freely coming together in a social contract.

---

in a *Gemeinde* is by involuntary election: by birth for native-born Jews; by being accepted into the community for converts to Judaism. Also, see 23–24 above.

[58] Ibid., 46 = German, 115.

[59] Ibid.

[60] Ibid., 47 = German, 115.

[61] Ibid.

[62] Ibid., 41 = German, 110–11.

But there are also "imperfect" rights and their corresponding duties. They are not compulsory. Rather, these duties are "duties of conscience" (*Gewissenpflichten*), which means they are more voluntary than perfect duties are.[63] Unlike those who are "impelled" (*getrieben*) by the state to perform actions, those who are only "induced" (*veranlasset*) to perform imperfect duties by religion have the option at least to decide just how they want to fulfill their duty.[64] But this of course means that, contrary to perfect duties, these duties are not responses to perfect rights. Accordingly, God does not command the way the state commands. Unlike the state, it would seem that God merely offers his commands as requests (*Bitten*) to which human conscience can determine how it wants to comply.[65] For Mendelssohn, God does not command like the state because unlike the state God has no needs.[66] Being already perfect, God has no need to exercise perfect rights at all. As such, "Omission of compulsory duties is an offense, an injustice; omission of duties of conscience, however, is merely unfairness [*Unbilligkeit*]."[67]

Furthermore, unlike Spinoza, Mendelssohn does not deem the covenant between God and Israel a social contract. The social contract can only be made by persons who come to it with their natural rights. But rights presuppose needs. Because God is beyond all need, he is beyond all rights and thus beyond all contracts made for the sake of the enhancement of rights. The people have a need for political well-being, but, it would seem, the state soon became capable of satisfying this need. As for needs of humans not satisfied by the state, Mendelssohn would probably argue that they are satisfied by God as the author of nature rather than by any covenantal agreement between God and humans. Yet Mendelssohn characterizes the covenant as follows:

> [It is] [l]aws, precepts, commandments and rules of life, which were to be peculiar [*eigen*] to this nation and through the observance of which it should arrive at national felicity as well as personal felicity [*Glückseligkeit*] for each of its individual members [*Glied*]. The lawgiver was God, that is to say, God not in his relation as Creator and Preserver of the universe, but God as Patron and Friend by covenant [*Bundesfreund*] of their ancestors, as Liberator . . . they were imposed [*auferlegt*] upon the nation and all their descendants as an unalterable duty and obligation [*Schuldigkeit*].[68]

---

[63] Ibid., 47 = German, 115.
[64] Ibid., 119 = German, 184.
[65] Ibid., 47 = German, 115.
[66] Ibid., 57.
[67] Ibid., 47 = German, 15.
[68] Ibid., 127 = German, 192–93.

However, doesn't Mendelssohn seem to place obedience to God on a stronger normative plane than obedience to the imperfect duties of conscience, about which he says: "The concept of *duties toward God* [is] a mere half truth"?[69] But doesn't the covenant seem even more compulsory than the social contract? Mendelssohn, though, has an answer to that objection, and his answer is historical.

Mendelssohn argues that when the covenant, what he calls "the original constitution" (*ursprünglichen Verfassung*), was instituted at Sinai, "state and religion were not conjoined, but *one*, not connected, but identical. Man's relation to society and his relation to God coincided and could never come into conflict."[70] As such, there was not "the least division or plurality in either the political or the metaphysical sense. . . . everything down to the least was part of the *divine service*."[71] At this level, the divinely governed state did not have to exercise any perfect rights inasmuch as God, "this monarch," does not "have any needs. He demands nothing from the nation but what serves its own welfare and what advances the felicity of the state. . . . The community [*Gemeine*] was a community of God."[72] Nevertheless, this happy state of affairs soon began to break down.

> [T]he Mosaic constitution did not persist long in its erstwhile purity. . . . the edifice developed a fissure which widened more and more until the parts broke asunder completely. The nation asked for a visible king as its ruler, a king of flesh and blood, perhaps because the priesthood had already begun to abuse the authority which it had among the people, or perhaps because the splendor of a neighboring royal household dazzled the eyes. . . . Now the constitution was undermined, the unity of interests abolished. State and religion were no longer the same, and a collision of duties was no longer impossible.[73]

At this point, Mendelssohn is dealing with the theme of the need of the Jewish people for secular authority in their early history, which is the theme discussed in the previous chapter. Being the traditional scholar (*talmid hakham*) he surely was, Mendelssohn was no doubt familiar with the major scriptural, talmudic, and medieval sources of the idea of covenant previously analyzed in this book. Furthermore, he was answering Spinoza's charge mentioned above, namely, that when the people had to transfer their political allegiance to a foreign monarch, they thereby lost their covenantal status altogether. Why? Because the theological and the politi-

[69] Ibid., 123.
[70] Ibid., 128 = German, 193.
[71] Ibid.
[72] Ibid. = German, 193.
[73] Ibid., 132.

cal either function in tandem or dissolve altogether. In one sentence, here is his answer to Spinoza: "The state was under foreign dominion [*Botmäs-sigkeit*], and received its orders from foreign gods, as it were, while the native [*einheimische*] religion still survived, retaining a part of its influ-ence on civil life."[74] This has been the theological-political situation of the Jews at least since the days of the Roman Empire.

Unlike Spinoza, though, Mendelssohn does not consider this theologi-cal-political dualism a weakness but, rather, a strength. Of course, it does make for a divided way of life, yet bearing the inevitable tension enables one to not be taken in by the illusion of cultural isolation offered by reli-gious obscurantists or the illusion of the merger of state and religion of-fered by assimilationists. Hence Mendelssohn advises his Jewish (and, by implication, his Christian) contemporaries: "Adapt yourselves to the mor-als [*Sitten*] and the constitution [*Verfassung*] of the land to which you have been removed, but hold fast to the religion of your fathers. Bear both burdens as well as you can."[75] Thus Spinoza, the secular assimila-tionist, seems to have been much more hopeful about the ability of the secular state to provide a unified way of life for its citizens than Mendels-sohn was. But Mendelssohn's expectations seem to have been more sober, and, indeed, subsequent history shows that he was more prescient.

Whereas Spinoza had assumed the Jewish community could not func-tion authoritatively without full national sovereignty, Mendelssohn thought the Jewish community could not function authoritatively without the police power it had in premodern societies. But this had to change once Jews, as individuals, became citizens of a new secular nation-state. Mendelssohn differed from Spinoza in thinking that Judaism could still make cogent claims on individual Jews as a *religion* in the modern sense of the term, that is, as a nonauthoritative voluntary commitment made by humans to God. But it is not *from* God as in revelation. Mendelssohn pins those claims on loyalty to the law-abiding Jewish past, which has always been loyalty to God-given law (*torah min ha-shamayim*).

Mendelssohn's Problematic Legacy for Judaism

The great problem with Mendelssohn's formulation of social contract theory for Jews is that it does not give the covenant primacy either theo-logically or politically. As such, from a perspective rooted in the Jewish tradition, Mendelssohn's theory is inadequate. It is also philosophically flawed. Indeed, both the theory itself and the dubious forms of Jewish

---

[74] Ibid., 133 = German, 197.
[75] Ibid., 133 = German, 198.

identity it seems to have inspired are inadequate to Judaism and flawed in their reasoning. Mendelssohn, well meaning to be sure, nonetheless did not prepare Jewish political theology well enough for the challenges that have come from Jewish participation in secular nation-states, especially for Jewish participation in modern constitutional democracies. The results of this have been quite bad for the development of a stronger Jewish social contract theory.

First, the theory itself. Even by his own conceptualizations of rights, duties, and social contracts, Mendelssohn has misinterpreted the covenant. When it comes to rights, even by Mendelssohn's own conceptuality, it could be cogently said that God does have *perfect* rights. This is because Mendelssohn is wrong in assuming God has no needs (*Bedürfnisse*).[76] For Mendelssohn, all needs are due to a lack in the one who needs, hence ascribing needs to God would presume that God is less than perfect, that God has some need or other that *needs* to be filled by what is not God. And this means that what God would need is prior to God in the same way that the woman I need to marry has to *already* exist in order for me to need her. Thus a God who has primordial needs does not absolutely transcend what is not God. Such a God would be coequal with the world. To ascribe need to God is to radically compromise divine perfection. Nevertheless, though, this assumes that all needs are prior to their subject and none subsequent. But it is only the needs of creatures that are prior. That is, we are needy by nature. We do not invent our needs. We can only discover our *needs*, express them in *desire*, then *learn* whom that desire intends. Only thereafter can we intelligently *choose* how we shall direct that needy desire, and finally *hope* that our desire shall be truly *fulfilled*. But Scripture quotes God saying: "My plans [*mahshavotai*] are not your plans; my ways are not your ways. . . . as the heavens are higher than the earth, so are my ways higher than your ways and so are my plans are higher than your plans" (Isaiah 55:8–9).[77]

Based on the evidence of Scripture, it is incorrect to say that God created the world, or that God created Israel by electing it in the covenant, *because* of some prior need. Nevertheless, one can still say that once God has created the world, God *subsequently wills a need* for the conscious and freely chosen cooperation of human creatures in the covenantal real-

---

[76] Ibid., 128 = German, 194.

[77] The Hebrew *mahshavah* is usually translated as "thought." However, it does not mean thought as contemplation, which is rendered in biblical Hebrew as *higayon* (see, e.g., Ps. 19:15), but, rather, it means "deliberation," i.e., planning/willing to do something. See, e.g., Exod.31:5. It is practical not theoretical reasoning. It would seem that even God, as creator, engages in practical reasoning since we can only imagine him thinking about what to make or how to respond to what he has made. See D. Novak, *Natural Law in Judaism* (Cambridge: Cambridge University Press, 1998), 113–20.

ization of creation. There is no prior necessity in God's need; instead, God is now *concerned* for his creation, which is expressed through his covenantal desire to be with his elected partner Israel (*am segulah*) whom God "desires" (*hashaq*) in order to "keep the covenant" (Deuteronomy 7:7, 9).[78] God elects Israel to need it for the sake of their mutual relationship. Unlike us humans, God's needs are the result of God's willing to be concerned and designating what he needs in order to substantiate that concern. God's needs are projected into the world; they do not intend a world already there before him. Conversely, we human creatures have no choice about our needs; our needs precede our will. Our concern with what is not us, with the other that transcends us, is inescapable. Our needs define us.[79] Our only choices are how to fulfill our needs, and how to order our needs when they conflict with one another. But we do not have the freedom to not need anyone at all. This is because we did not create others; rather, we have been planted in their midst.

In our human situation in the world, our needs are expressed in our desires. Our desires then require knowledge to ascertain whether what we need is real or only a phantom. If real, then our desire can be attained; if a phantom, though, our desire is an existential waste. Indeed, this is the case when humans think they can create a real other rather than be discovered by others and then discover them. Only after desire has been linked to knowledge can we intelligently choose the means to the end: the fulfillment of our desire.[80] Conversely, God's will leads to God's knowledge of what he has created. Then God's concern for those he has created expresses itself in his desire for the response of the covenanted partners he has elected.[81] (As for hope, since God alone knows the end of cosmic history, he has no need for hope; only we need God to be the ultimate end of our hope.)[82]

Rooted in a scripturally based theology, we can now say that God has needs, and that these needs are covenantal (*tsorkhei gavoah*).[83] Given this, God has perfect rights by Mendelssohn's own definition of perfect rights. And since all rights have correlative duties, the perfect covenantal rights of God fully intend the perfect covenantal duties of Israel, God's junior partner in the covenant. These perfect covenantal duties are much stronger than Mendelssohn's "duties of conscience," with their highly

[78] See Exod. 19:5–6.
[79] See D. Novak, *Natural Law in Judaism* (Cambridge: Cambridge University Press, 1998), 172–73.
[80] See Aristotle, *Nicomachean Ethics*, 3.3–4/1112a20–1113a24.
[81] See D. Novak, *Covenantal Rights* (Princeton, N.J.: Princeton University Press, 2000), 62–63.
[82] See Jer. 37:16; B. Berakhot 34b re Isa.64:3.
[83] See Nahmanides, *Commentary on the Torah*: Exod. 30:46.

voluntaristic implications. The covenantal rights, which these perfect duties presuppose, are expressed in the commandments (*mitsvot*) of the Torah, which are the perpetual claims God makes upon his people.

God's claims upon his people are twofold: They are awesome claims and benevolent claims. In God's awesome claims, he expresses his need to rule over his people as their sovereign. To this type of claim, the people must respond awesomely, with fear (*yir'ah*). This fear is not so much fear of what God will do *to* them if they disobey him as it is fear of the commanding presence of God who is so overwhelming. On the other hand, in God's benevolent claims, God shows the people how he has enabled them to fulfill their need for God to be their true benefactor. To this type of claim, the people must respond accordingly, with love (*ahavah*). It is not so much love of what God will do *for* them as it is love of what God does for them now by actively including them in the covenant. Furthermore, some have seen the observance of the negative commandments ("thou shalt nots") as motivated by the restraining fear of God, whereas the practice of the positive commandments is motivated by the effusive love of God.[84] This dialectic of the fear of God (*yir'at ha-shem*) and the love of God (*ahavat ha-shem*) is one of the great recurring themes of Jewish theology throughout the ages.

This comes out in the opening words of the Decalogue: "I am the Lord your God who brought you out of the land of Egypt, out of the house of slavery" (Exodus 20:2; Deuteronomy 5:6). It is a statement that calls both for awe and for love on the part of Israel (the "you" here). Israel is always to be *awesomely* mindful of God's power, which overcame the power of Pharaoh, the world's most powerful ruler (hence the designation of God as "awful" in older English).[85] Israel is also to be *lovingly* mindful of God's beneficence toward them, constantly shown in the giving of the Torah, the very purpose for which God took Israel out from Egyptian slavery—and by extension, liberated Israel from slavery to any other creature, no matter how powerful.[86] Further, this is more than simple gratitude for past favors. Yet for Mendelssohn, it would seem, the keeping of the commandments of the Torah is a matter of gratitude for what God did as "[p]atron and Friend by covenant of their ancestors [*Vorfahren*]."[87] Unlike the Rabbis, who constantly emphasize how God *is* the lawgiver, Mendelssohn states that "[t]he lawgiver *was* God [*die Gesetzgeber war Gott*]," and that "[t]hese laws were *revealed* [*wurden geoffenbart*]."[88] The

---

[84] See Y. Berakhot 9.5/14b; Nahmanides, *Commentary on the Torah*: Exod. 20:8.

[85] See *Mekhilta*: Yitro re Deut. 7:8, ed. Horovitz-Rabin, p. 222.

[86] See ibid., p. 219.

[87] *Jerusalem*, 127 = German, 193.

[88] Ibid. Cf. *Sifre*: Devarim, no. 33 re Deut. 6:6, ed. Finkelstein, p. 59; B. Berakhot 63b re Deut. 27:9.

use of the past tense here is certainly not careless on the part of a writer as careful as Moses Mendelssohn. Moreover, as we shall soon see, gratitude for the past can quickly degenerate into a merely nostalgic Judaism.

Not only are God's rights perfect, they are more perfect than those exercised by the state. Unlike the rights of the state, the rights of God are not mediated by any contract with those to whom they are addressed, who are the children of Israel in the covenant. Unlike contracted rights, God's covenantal claims are unconditional.[89] Instead, God's covenantal rights are akin to the natural obligations (*Verbindlichkeit*) that the social contract presupposes.[90] The social contract is "a compact [*Pactum*] into which [one] has voluntarily [*gutwillig*] entered."[91] But the natural obligations that the social contract presupposes are not voluntary, that is, they are not dependent on even the voluntary acceptance of them in general by the people, let alone on the specific acceptance of any or all of them one by one or together.[92] And it is only those under such natural obligation who, for Mendelssohn, would be in any position to make a cogent commitment to a social contract.

Mendelssohn's underestimation of the political priority of the covenant stems from a mistake in his general theory of the social contract, especially as he applies it to his understanding of Judaism. The mistake is as follows: Mendelssohn assumes, largely following Locke, that one goes from the state of nature to civil society. One's basic social rights and duties are already known in the state of nature, but one needs civil society for their fulfillment.[93] One moves from the state of nature to civil society via the social contract. But for a prominent strand of the Jewish tradition, one actually goes from the state of nature—that is, the state of natural sociality—on to God's covenant with Israel and its concrete life mandated by the Torah. The structure and content of natural, pre-Sinaitic sociality is the morality of what the Rabbis call "Noahide law," that is, the essential prohibitions of idolatry, murder, incest, robbery, and the like.[94] It is necessary for human community, but not sufficient for its deep cultural existence. That cultural depth comes from the Mosaic Torah and the tradition it continually spawns. Earlier natural sociality is presupposed by this Torah and its tradition and it is not overcome by the new special revelation at Sinai. Instead, this pre-Sinaitic morality functions as a regulator of unethical excesses that might emerge in the interpretation of the revealed

[89] See 30–33 above.
[90] *Jerusalem*, 36 = German, 106.
[91] Ibid., 37 = German, 106.
[92] Ibid., 48–49.
[93] Ibid., 56.
[94] See B. Sanhedrin 56a—b; also, D. Novak, *The Image of the Non-Jew in Judaism* (New York and Toronto: Edwin Mellen Press, 1983).

commandments.[95] And it is a general guide for its new legislation in the absence of a specific source for dealing with unprecedented ethical problems.[96] It is also a general guide for Jewish-gentile interaction, even the interaction of a social contract.

It is only after the Jewish people have been sufficiently socialized within the covenantal community, a community vitally concerned with human origins prior to nature and human destiny beyond the natural world, that Jews can participate in a social contract, either among themselves or with non-Jews, in good faith. Natural morality per se is an abstraction since no one actually lives under it in this world. It functions as a formal guide, not an existential origin. Natural morality does not itself, however, constitute any real community in the world. It cannot provide real communal priority for those living under the rule of any human regime. This is why it cannot really limit the extension of state power, which is the greatest power humans have ever devised for themselves. Natural morality can only suggest certain internal restraints within the powerful existence of the state itself. But only a real historical covenant, concretely affirming its past, present, and future, provides its members enough wherewithal to participate in a social contract without being totally enveloped by the state that any social contract has created.

Any Jew who has not been fully socialized in *the* covenant enters a social contract—even with his or her fellow Jews—naked and vulnerable to whatever use or misuse those in political power hold in store.[97] Therefore, contrary to Mendelssohn's convoluted notion of the covenant, only a covenantal life that sufficiently intends its present and future as well as its past is both adequate to the evidence of Scripture and Jewish tradition and sufficient to enable Jews to honestly participate in and benefit from any social contract. Without such a life, though, any Jew—even one as learned and observant as Moses Mendelssohn—is not yet ready for an active rather than passive existence in a modern secular society. This even includes participation in a society that pays serious attention to the idea of the social contract in its political self-understanding.

Mendelssohn's theory of Judaism is inadequate to the Jewish tradition because it renders it subordinate to a non-Jewish universe, and because it provides an insufficient basis for the traditional Jewish practice that was lived by Mendelssohn himself within that essentially non-Jewish universe.[98] Subsequent Jewish history, especially in Germany (and I mean

[95] See Aharon Lichtenstein, "Does Jewish Tradition Recognize an Ethic Independent of Halakha?" *Modern Jewish Ethics*, ed. M. Fox (Columbus Ohio: Ohio State University Press, 1975), 62–67.

[96] See Novak, *Natural Law in Judaism*, 68–69.

[97] See 25–29 above.

[98] See Shmuel Trigano, *La demeure oubliee*, rev. ed. (Paris: Gallimard, 1994), 287–306.

nineteenth-century Germany, long before the Holocaust), indicates how myopic Mendelssohn's vision of the Jewish future really was.

As we have seen, Mendelssohn has a general view of natural religion, which is a universal awareness of God that transcends any particular historical tradition. For Mendelssohn, all historical religions are attempts to "command actions only as tokens [*Zeichen*] of convictions," thus all their "laws refer to, or are based upon eternal truths of reason, or remind us of them, and rouse us to ponder [*Nachdenken*] them."[99] As a historical religion, Judaism is basically ancient not modern. It is "piety" in the sense of its original meaning in the Latin *pietas*, namely, loyalty to one's ancestors. It looks backward not forward.[100] In Mendelssohn's time, loyalty to ancestral Judaism could only be expressed in traditional, halakhic Judaism since this was the only Judaism available then. But soon after Mendelssohn's death, liberal Judaism, first Reform and then Conservative, appeared, offering modern Jews religious alternatives to the strictly halakhic Judaism of the past. As such, modern Jews could still remain—or think they remained—loyal to the Jewish tradition without having to be under its normative yoke either in practice or in faith.

Reform Judaism, in its early stage when heavily influenced by notions of historical progress, emphasized the universalism of natural theology as something that Judaism was striving toward. But because of Kant's seeming destruction of the metaphysics that concentrated natural theology on the creativity of God in the larger world, Reform Jewish thinkers emphasized God as the source of the moral law developed by rationally autonomous human nature.[101] Kant's influence on liberal Jewish theology was direct and pervasive.

Moral law is, by Kantian definition, that which is universalizable.[102] In fact, in post-Kantian Jewish-Christian polemics in the nineteenth and early twentieth centuries, some bolder Jewish thinkers argued that contrary to prevailing Christian (especially Protestant) anti-Jewish prejudice, Jewish morality was more universalizable than Christian morality.[103] As such, they implied that Judaism not Christianity would better serve the religious purposes of the enlightened citizens of a secular nation-state like Germany. Following this kind of strident universalism, Reform Judaism

---

[99] *Jerusalem*, 73, 99 = German, 140, 166.

[100] See 9–10, n. 17 above.

[101] See Leo Baeck, *The Essence of Judaism*, trans. V. Grubenwieser and L. Pearl (London: Macmillan, 1936), 59–72.

[102] See *Groundwork of the Metaphysic of Morals*, trans. H. J. Paton (New York: Harper and Row, 1964), 88–92.

[103] See Leo Baeck, "Romantic Religion," *Judaism and Christianity*, trans. W. Kaufmann (Philadelphia: Jewish Publication Society of America, 1958), 240–56.

took a highly eclectic stance as regards the particular religious practices and doctrines of the Jewish tradition. In fact, it was often hard-pressed to offer any cogent retort to the Ethical Culture movement, founded by a former Reform rabbi, Felix Adler (d. 1933), which asserted that a truly universalizable ethics needed no religion at all, certainly not Judaism.[104] But even when it could still argue for some Jewish specificity, Reform Judaism, by its very endurance, applied Ockham's Razor to Mendelssohn's theological assumptions. That is, it showed that Mendelssohn required the acceptance, both in theory and in practice, of more premises than are necessary for the survival of a recognizably Jewish religion. Judaism, for the subsequent reformers, could survive much more minimally.

Until very recently, Conservative Judaism seemed to be a marriage of convenience between moderate Reform Jews who wanted to preserve more of the Jewish tradition than most other Reform Jews did, and moderate Orthodox Jews who wanted less cultural isolation than many Orthodox Jews did. By generally avoiding the hard doctrinal questions of the truth of revelation and the authority of halakhah, Conservative Judaism, in the middle of the twentieth century anyway, was able to function much like political parties in America did at that time—on the most politically pragmatic level possible, bringing together disparate elements in a loose coalition. (All this changed by the last third or so of the twentieth century when American Conservative Judaism adopted an egalitarian ideology indistinguishable from that of Reform.) When Conservative Judaism at that earlier time had to say something about what it affirmed, it adopted a slogan like "tradition and change," which could never propose any consistent criteria for determining when tradition was to be maintained and when it was to change.[105] Of course, this only showed that Conservative Jews had no coherent affirmation of the governing authority of halakhah as normative Judaism. Even more basic than this, the general Conservative avoidance of the question of the verbal revelation of the Torah removed any theological challenges to this basically laissez-faire Judaism.

Whereas early Reform Judaism bought into Mendelssohn's more universal notion of religion per se, Conservative Judaism until quite recently bought into Mendelssohn's more antiquarian notion of Judaism. Judaism is an appreciation of the Jewish past—that is, as long as it doesn't inhibit whatever a group of Jews think is their successful entry into the future. Along these lines, Conservative Jewish thinkers liked to speak of "our

[104] See B. Kraut, *From Reform Judaism to Ethical Culture* (Cincinnati: Hebrew Union College Press, 1976).

[105] See *Tradition and Change*, ed. M. Waxman (New York: Burning Bush Press, 1970).

tradition," forgetting of course that *tradition* is a *traditio*, a handing-down and ongoing explication of concrete revelation of the God who says "no" as absolutely as he says "yes."[106]

With the general disillusionment of contemporary Jews with liberal universalism, primarily because of its seeming inability to prevent the Holocaust and its growing support of the political isolation of the State of Israel as a Jewish state, the antiquarian side of Mendelssohn's Judaism has gained new influence on non-Orthodox Jews. To be sure, though, his view of Judaism has been mediated by many intervening uses of it, since very few contemporary Jews, even when well educated Jewishly, have read Mendelssohn firsthand. Furthermore, without the balance of Mendelssohn's natural theology or something logically akin to it, this type of antiquarian Judaism degenerates into nostalgia, even kitsch. Mendelssohn's theology is not strong enough in its Judaism to get contemporary Jews either out of assimilationism as a likely historical result of unchecked universalism or out of mere ethnicity as a likely historical result of unchecked antiquarianism. But to be fair to Mendelssohn, his philosophical theology is intellectually cogent enough to not be immediately blamed for the excesses that have been influenced by it. They would have most likely happened even without Mendelssohn.

Whereas the insights and theories of Jewish thinkers from the talmudic Rabbis to Abravanel can be retrieved for the formulation of a contemporary Jewish social contract theory—which is how Jews can intelligently enter a social contract with non-Jews (and perhaps among themselves too) in good faith—alas, such is not the case with Mendelssohn. So the reason I have devoted almost an entire chapter in this book to his political theology is because of its great influence (even if frequently mediated) on the way modern Jews have religiously negotiated modernity, especially their participation in the modern secular state. Mendelssohn is the first unambivalently Jewish thinker in modernity to deal with the idea of the social contract and then apply it to his understanding of Jews and Judaism. For this he deserves direct attention in our present reflections on the Jewish social contract. Indeed, he deserves far more attention than what might be given to later Jewish thinkers who thought along his lines, but with far less philosophical gravitas. As the Rabbis put it so nicely: "To the words of the master or the words of the disciple, to whose words do we listen?"[107]

---

[106] For a critique of Conservative Judaism, when this author was still part of its community, see D. Novak, "Toward a Conservative Theology," *The Seminary at 100*, eds. N. B. Cardin and D. W. Silverman (New York: Rabbinical Assembly, 1987), 315–26.

[107] B. Kiddushin 42b and parallels.

Nevertheless, all this having been said, Jews need to overcome Mendelssohn rather than retrieve him. He simply does not give Jews enough wherewithal to enter a social contract and still return home to Jewish community (understood in the deepest ontological sense) fully intact. Mendelssohn's universalism did not enable Jews to have enough Judaism left after entering the social contract to be able to transcend mundane politics. This could only be done by an understanding of what membership in a deeper covenantal community, with its very different past, present, and future, means. And Mendelssohn's antiquarianism, by virtue of its being constituted as an exception to the universal political order, did not enable Judaism to be an active participant *in* the political order but rather in being a case of special, sectarian pleading *from* the political order. Judaism needs more than the tolerance of the secular state. A fully cogent commitment to *the* covenant, both theologically and politically, alone enables Jews to be active participants in a social contract rather than passive recipients of either the secular state's totalizing enclosure or its patronizing disinterest. Yet one cannot retrieve this Jewish political tradition without carefully working one's way through Mendelssohn's philosophy, and the even more formidable task of working through the assumptions of Spinoza's philosophy (both theoretical and practical) that were accepted (consciously or unconsciously) by modern Jewish thinkers from Mendelssohn to Hermann Cohen.[108] At the end of the day, Mendelssohn is a much better Enlightenment philosopher than he is a Jewish theologian. But this shows that one cannot simply develop a philosophy outside of Judaism and then use it to theoretically explain Judaism adequately, or use it to propose practical solutions to current Jewish political problems. Nevertheless, Jews are still very much living with Mendelssohn's political legacy.

---

[108] See Novak, *The Election of Israel*, 50–54.

Chapter Seven

The Social Contract and Jewish-Christian Relations

The New Jewish-Christian Situation

From a fuller perspective in the Jewish tradition, we have seen the theological inadequacies of Mendelssohn's formulation of the idea of social contract, especially in its relation to the whole Jewish tradition. As for its philosophical inadequacies, we must also understand that the political situation of both the Jews and his own society at that time did not encourage the development of a richer social contract theory, certainly not by Jews. As for the political situation of the Jews at that time, they were still at a decided disadvantage when compared to their Christian countrymen. The Jews were still trying to attain full citizenship in the state, but they had not yet achieved it. Indeed, German Jews would not achieve it until almost a century after Mendelssohn's death in 1786 and, even then, they still lacked the political power and cultural self-confidence to exercise this citizenship fully. Moreover, the Jews had powerful opponents to their bid for full citizenship.[1] These opponents were for the most part traditional Christians who still saw civil society and the more secular state as part of "Christendom." At best, in their view, the Jews must remain in the category of second-class foreigners.

The only allies Jews had were very liberal Protestants (like Mendelssohn's great friend, the playwright Gotthold Ephraim Lessing). However, unlike the more traditional Christians who still had a communal-covenantal type of religion, the liberal friends of the Jews were, in large measure, in revolt against that traditional, communal-covenantal Christianity and in favor of a much more individualistic type of religion. As such, Jews like Mendelssohn, who very much wanted and needed the aid of these liberal Protestants in the Jewish struggle for full political enfranchisement, could not very well emphasize the strong communal-covenantal theology of Judaism and its philosophical implications.

Indeed, at that time it was only the Christian enemies of the Jews who had a strong covenantal theology. But being supersessionists who thought

---

[1] See Alexander Altmann, *Moses Mendelssohn* (University: University of Alabama Press, 1973), 461–74.

Jews were no longer part of God's covenant with Israel, their covenantal theology hardly had a theological place for the Jews. And, since they saw the need for an explicit theological warrant even for the secular state, their theological exclusion of the Jews easily translated into a stance advocating the political exclusion of the Jews.

In order for the development of an authentically Jewish social contract theory to be historically relevant, there would have to be a marked change in the theological-political situation of the Jews and of the wider non-Jewish societies in which they not only happen to be living but, even more important, where they want to be living. I would like to propose in this chapter that such a radical change in the theological-political situation of the Jews and of the wider non-Jewish societies in which they live has begun to take place in such historically English societies as Britain, the United States, and Canada. To me, this is no accident considering the role covenantal theology played in English efforts to separate the religious communal (or "ecclesial") realm from the political realm without, however, succumbing to the secularist attempt to totally privatize religion by making it nothing more than an individual option.[2]

It is now time to bring Jewish covenantal theology into what could be a truly multicultural conversation about the social contract. But when bringing their ideas into the public square, Jews should understand that before they can speak to strangers in civil society, especially an English-language civil society, they must talk with their closer cultural neighbors, with whom they have more in common, with whom they speak more of the same language. Only with Christians can Jews speak in a biblically based language. Now that many Christians are willing to live on equal political footing with their Jewish neighbors, and this certainly includes the arena of ideas, Jews need to speak with those who are nearer to them before venturing into an arena with those who are farther from them. For Jews to attempt an end-run around Christians in their desire to be included in civil society and its discourse, which has long been the case and still is the case with many liberal Jews, means that Jews have to cede more to secularism than would be the case when Jews make common theological-political cause with Christians to whom they have to cede much less. And, of course, I mean with those Christians who do not make conversion to Christianity the precondition of their making common theological-political cause with Jews. Working with these Christians be-

---

[2] Along these lines, especially among the English and then the American Puritans, see J. D. Eusden, *Puritans, Lawyers, and Politics in Seventeenth Century England* (New Haven, Conn.: Yale University Press, 1958), 121–25; Perry Miller, *Errand Into Wilderness* (Cambridge, Mass.: Harvard University Press, 1956), 60–68; John Witte, Jr., "Blest Be the Ties That Bind: Covenant and Community in Puritan Thought," *Emory Law Journal* 36 (1987), 549–97.

fore working with secularists makes Jews much less naive and less philosophically vulnerable in public discourse.

Of course, no one except a prophet could have predicted the radical
change in the relationship between Jews and Christians since Western civilization narrowly escaped physical and moral annihilation in the Second
World War. Having narrowly escaped physical annihilation, Jews have
had to look at the world surrounding them anew. There some Jews have
discovered Christians facing them on the immediate horizon in a new and
favorable way. Having narrowly escaped moral annihilation, Christians
have had to look at the surrounding world anew. There some Christians
have discovered Jews on the immediate horizon in a new and favorable
way. This new and mutual discovery can be located on three levels.

First, mutual discovery has occurred on the theological level.[3] Through
sound historical scholarship, more Christians than ever before have
learned how close Christianity has always been to its Judaic roots. The
current Christian retrieval of Christianity's true origins has not only
looked to the Hebrew Bible but also to the Second Temple Judaism out of
which Judaism until this very day has been continually emerging. This is
why Judaism can no longer be dismissed as historical relic, a mere proto-
Christianity. Through the same type of scholarship, Jews have discovered
that Christianity is not a one-time deviation from Judaism. Rather, it has
been developing in a trajectory continually parallel to that of Judaism.
Jews need to see how much Christianity has had to be similar to Judaism
in order to continually differ from it. From this, some Jews have learned
that they can discuss the Torah with Christians in a way they cannot discuss it with any other gentiles. Thus Jews and Christians today have found
a way to talk with each other that is mutually affirming and no longer
either offensive or defensive as was the case in the theological disputations
of the Middle Ages and in the ideological polemics of earlier modernity.

Second, mutual discovery has occurred on the political level. Until quite
recently, however, the political relationship of Jews and Christians in modernity had been almost totally hostile and suspicious. Jews had been
seen by many Christians as in the vanguard of the atheistic trajectory of
modernity. Truth be told, some of the most prominent atheistic theorists
have been Jews, and some of the most effective public atheism has been
promoted by certain Jewish organizations.[4] By "public" or de facto atheism, I mean public policies that advocate "don't ask, don't tell" when

---

[3] For the most serious discussion of these theological issues, see *Christianity in Jewish
Terms*, eds. T. Frymer-Kensky, D. Novak, P. W. Ochs, M. S. Signer (Boulder, Colo.: Westview
Press, 2000).

[4] See 218–20 below.

it comes to mentioning the name of God or the "G" word in political discourse—even when used by a religiously observant Jew, Senator Joseph Lieberman, a candidate for the office of vice president of the United States in 2000. Because of this sad fact, all Jews have been seen by many Christians as leading the attempt to keep religion—whether their own or that of the vast majority who affirm some form of Christianity—out of the public square, especially in North America. Indeed, many Christians have assumed that Judaism itself is identical with the modern progressive ideal that requires the public square to include only those "naked" Christians who have divested themselves of anything Christian at all, at most keeping Christianity strictly private, in the closet as it were. What most Christians do not realize, however, is that the public atheism of some prominent Jews, individually or collectively, has been even more injurious to Judaism in our society than it has been to Christianity, inasmuch as naked Jews are still more vulnerable to public disappearance than naked Christians are.[5] Without God and the Torah, what else do Jews have to maintain their true identity in the world?

Christians, on the other hand, have been seen by many Jews as those who resist the ideal of modern progress precisely because it promises political and cultural equality to the Jews. To be sure, there are Christians who still long for the premodern world they think they once controlled, a control that inevitably made Jews political outsiders and cultural pariahs. Nevertheless, many Christians now realize that the notion that Christianity per se actually controlled premodern, European or American, civil society has been in many ways a romantic fantasy about a past that cannot be retrieved. Moreover, many Christians have come to the conclusion that even when such religious control of civil society did in fact obtain, it was as disastrous for Christian witness of the Kingdom of God as it was for justice in civil society. Thus the American Catholic political theologian George Weigel, when speaking of the political theory and practice of Pope John Paul II, forcefully stated, "the 'Constantinian arrangement' has been quietly buried."[6] In other words, the idea that the secular state requires an official religion, and that the official religion must be Christianity (the Roman Catholic Church in particular), which began in the fourth century with the Christianization of the Roman Empire by Emperor Constantine, has been set aside in favor of a more truly democratic idea of polity. Indeed, more and more Christians now do not regard modern political secularity as something to be overcome but, rather, as another new challenge

[5] See Richard John Neuhaus, *The Naked Public Square* (Grand Rapids, Mich.: Eerdmans, 1984), 261.
[6] "Papacy and Power," *First Things*, no. 110 (2001), 20.

to Christian survival and witness in a still unredeemed world. Hopefully, more and more Jews will appreciate this development in Christian thought and action.

Fewer Jews now than in the not so distant past still eagerly embrace secular modernity in the guise of various secularist ideologies. That embrace too was a romantic fantasy about an ideal, utopian future. But fewer Jews today see an earthly Messiah in modern political secularity. So, what we see instead is a more sober and less enthusiastic relation to the modern secular political situation—neither overly negative nor overly positive—by both Christians and Jews. Many more Jews and Christians want the public square to be pluralistic, which is neither partisan nor naked. Theoretically, at least, this has led to the discovery of some important new political commonalities between Christians and Jews. These commonalities should not only be noted, but encouraged. The political playing field between the two communities is more even than it has ever been and encourages some new thinking in the area of political theology, especially by Jews for whom such an even political playing field is a novelty. (The absence now of an even political playing field between Jews and Muslims—and between Christians and Muslims—prevents Muslims from being part of these public discussions as they are now constituted. Please God, this will change sometime for the sake of true multiculturalism in Western societies where Islam has only recently arrived.)

Because of these political developments, we are at a point in history, certainly in North America, when Jews and Christians can recognize each other first as the closest neighbor rather than as the most threatening enemy. It is only very recently that some Jews and some Christians have recognized that they are neighbors, possibly even friends, and not enemies, in this world. The power of contemporary secularism, with its enmity against religion, has forced this mutual recognition on both sides of the Jewish-Christian religious divide.[7] There is nothing like a new common enemy to force people out of old isolations. Those who still affirm "the earth is the Lord's" (Psalms 24:1) are becoming more and more aware of becoming "strangers on earth" (Psalms 119:19).

So far, we have seen the changed theological situation and changed political situation in the ongoing Jewish-Christian encounter. Both are in their infancy and so they seem to provide Jews and Christians with more material for fruitful thought among themselves and for discourse with each other into the future. Yet each has its shortcomings, indeed, to such an extent that I wonder whether the most important aspect of our new relationship is strictly theological *or* strictly political.

---

[7] See D. Novak, *Jewish-Christian Dialogue* (New York: Oxford University Press, 1989), 3–14.

The shortcoming of purely theological discourse between Jews and Christians, even when informed by sound historical scholarship, is that in the end it has to conclude that the difference between the two communities is greater than all their commonalities. The great difference, of course, is about Jesus. Truth be told, it is precisely when both Jews and Christians eschew the kind of rhetoric that assumes the other can be argued into one's own faith position—be that argument exegetical, historical, or philosophical—that the difference actually becomes more pronounced. Eschewing polemical confrontations in theology means that Jews and Christians can live better together *in spite* of their overriding theological difference. But, after all is said in theological dialogue between members of the two communities, and no matter how philosophical it becomes, theology is still the conceptualization of the language of revelation and the liturgy it entails; yet the central institutions of worship, respectively, exclude each other necessarily. Jews cannot and should not receive communion in any church; Christians cannot and should not be called to the public reading of the Torah in any synagogue. This divide outweighs even the most sincere experiences of dialogical intimacy.

The shortcoming of purely political discourse between Jews and Christians, even when informed by sound political theory, is that it seems to be largely built upon the accurate perception of a common enemy. For a long time we have been up against the militant secularism that permeates so much of the culture and now has great political power. By "secularism" I mean the ideological matrix that regards human-made law as not only necessary for modern life—a point that Jews and Christians who have not retreated to sectarian enclaves can readily accept—but as sufficient for human fulfillment as well. It is the modern embrace of the view of the ancient sophists that "man is the measure of all things."[8]

This belief in secularism is an ideal inasmuch as most secularists today see too much religion still operating in the public square. Hence it is much more than the acceptance of the fact of modern *secularity*. All modern secularity really requires is that our public norms and the arguments one makes for them must not invoke the authority of Jewish or Christian— or any historical—revelation, even if these public norms are consistent with one's communal revelation and the authoritative teachings one's tradition has derived from that revelation. Thus Jews and Christians can only make public arguments for the moral positions they advocate that are based on ideas of the general human condition rather than on the singular experience of God speaking directly to one's traditional community. But it is ideological secularism, not the affirmation of secularity per

---

[8] This was the motto of the ancient Greek sophist Protagoras, quoted by Plato, *Theaetetus*, 152A, 178B; *Cratylus*, 386A. Cf. *Laws*, 716C.

se, that largely defines the culture of the universities, the media, the foundations, the courts, that is, the most powerful elite culture in our society. It is what inspires them all. It is very much their moral engine. This culture, which is often quite self-consciously the heir of the Enlightenment, regards both Judaism and Christianity as impediments in its quest for radical egalitarianism, which is as old as the temptation of Adam and Eve by the serpent that they too can become "like God" (Genesis 3:5) and, therefore, replace God altogether. Jews and Christians can live in peace with secularity; they cannot live in peace with secularism as an ideal commanding its own realization in history, however.

Furthermore, recent terrible atrocities, especially those committed against the United States of America, and against both Jews and Christians all over the world, have presented to Jews and Christians a very real enemy in the fact of a type of militant Islam—now called "Islamism" to distinguish it from more irenic types of Islam. This enemy despises Judaism and Christianity, not only because Jews and Christians enable their adherents to religiously resist acceptance of Islam, but also because most Jews and Christians today, even most of the traditionalists among them, have accepted political secularity in the form of modern democracy, and economic secularity in the form of capitalism. How ironic it is, though, that only Judaism and Christianity can provide sufficient inspiration to defend true secularity against this new ideological assault.

Jews and Christians can, of course, find much commonality in their struggle against their common enemies—both ideological and even military—yet commonality on these fronts could easily become one more ephemeral political alliance within modern political secularity itself. Enemies, after all, come and go, even as Jews and Christians believe they themselves will remain until the end of history. Current political anxiety often propels people into desperate political ventures, where they blindly embrace or are embraced by political ideologies that need no justification from Judaism or Christianity, even when these ideologies are not explicitly hostile to either tradition. When this happens, it is often impossible to discern just who is using whom. Jews and Christians should be wary of having Judaism or Christianity or even the commonality between them—what is best called "biblical religion"—become the religious frosting on somebody else's ideological cake. If opposition to a shared enemy is all that unites Jews and Christians politically, they risk slipping into all the usual political paranoia—that is, the *need* for a common enemy. Because of this inevitability, Jews and Christians must discover a mutuality that is more positive and enduring, one that does not need a common enemy.

For me, that commonality must come out of concern with what Baruch Spinoza rightly called—even if he wrongly answered it—*the theological-political* question. This is the third level of mutual discovery by Jews and

Christians. It is especially fruitful for Jews when thinking of how they can participate in a socially contracted society in good faith, which is what I mean by the term "the Jewish social contract." In retrieving the sources in the Jewish tradition that pertain to this question, Jews can also discover some striking similarities in Christian political theology. This similarity, of course, is no accident inasmuch as both traditions root themselves in the same book: the Hebrew Bible, which is Scripture for both communities.[9]

Political Theology

The theological-political question is not primarily the theological question of how Jews or Christians affirm God among themselves, nor is it primarily the political question of how they navigate in the various wars they have to fight. Instead, it is the question of how faithful Jews and faithful Christians can enter into civil society and survive there intact, let alone flourish, without, however, either conquering civil society or being conquered by it. It is the question of how Jews and Christians, both of whom worship the Lord God of Israel, and both of whom derive their law from this God's Torah (however differently), can join modern civil societies—which we have seen are inherently secular—and actively "seek the peace of the city" (Jeremiah 29:7) with religious integrity.[10] And it is the question of whether Jews and Christians need each other for that entrance into civil society in order to "exit it whole" as the Talmud once put it about another dangerous yet tempting place.[11]

The important thing to remember here is that Jews and Christians participate in various societies. But Jews and Christians are only parts of one singular community, respectively. The one is always prior to the many. A person's community is always prior to his or her political associations. There is a fundamental difference between being a *participant in* something and being a *part of* something.[12] Many Jews and Christians are theologically and politically confused because they do not understand this essential difference and the priority of being a part-of over being a participant-in. Faithful Jews and faithful Christians, each in their own way, are members of but one community respectively—a true "body politic"— founded and sustained by God. As citizens of modern nation-states, though, they are all cofounders of their own civil societies and institutions, along with those who are neither Jews nor Christians.

---

[9] See Novak, *Jewish-Christian Dialogue*, 64–66.
[10] See B. Berakhot 58a re 1 Chron. 29:11.
[11] B. Hagigah 14b. See T. Hagigah 2.4 re Cant. 1:4.
[12] See 7–9 above.

Jews are part of the Jewish people, and this is their most primary identity. Christians are part of the church—the body of Christ—and this is their most primary identity. Only subsequently do Jews and Christians participate in various associations, and they can only participate in these in good faith when they justify the participation by references to the ends for which their own communities live and thrive. Furthermore, unlike the totalitarian regimes that regard those under their political control as *dispensable* and *disposable* parts, the Jewish people and the church see themselves as covenanted communities elected by God, both collectively and individually. Since God's election creates an everlasting covenant with all the members of his people, every member of the covenanted community is *indispensable* and *nondisposable*—at least in this world. All members of the community are elected communally and individually. All are promised ultimate redemption with the community—if they remain faithful with it to their God. Covenantal election, either by birth or conversion, means that one can never be fully excluded from the people of God—at least in this world.[13] The most that can happen here is that some individuals must be subjected at times to communal disapproval, even social isolation, in order to enable them to repent and return to the fold. But this is never permanent expulsion. The promise of reacceptance makes repentance possible and desirable. This explains why one can be loyal to one's primary communities in a way that one can never be loyal to any other human association of the world, even to the best of humanly constructed societies.

For these reasons, Jews and Christians can never regard any civil society, even those of the nation-states where they have thrived, like the United States and Canada, as a comprehensive whole in which they are integral parts. No matter how much one loves one's current political associations, no matter how patriotic one might rightly become because one's state truly promotes God's law of universal justice, no matter how much one might be willing to even risk one's life for the continued liberty of one's own society, no Jew and no Christian should ever regard any other human group in which he or she participates to be the chosen people. For Jews and Christians, only Israel is chosen, however "Israel" is defined in their respective communities. To my knowledge, no historical community other than the Jewish people and the Christian church has ever claimed to be communally elected by God. So I do not see how any Jew can say he or she is practicing Judaism, or how any Christian can say he or she is practicing Christianity, and nonetheless think themselves parts of something larger, more inclusive, and thus more important than the people of

---

[13] See B. Sanhedrin 44a re Josh. 7:11; also, D. Novak, *The Election of Israel* (Cambridge: Cambridge University Press, 1995), 189–99.

God. This is the case with any worldly society, no matter how beneficent it is, no matter how just, no matter how noble.

To be a Jew, essentially and not just accidentally, is to regard the Jewish people as one's sole primal community. Election by the unique God requires total and unconditional loyalty to but one people. All other social bonds are partial, however long-standing, however just, however lovable. No human society in which Jews participate can ask them to subordinate their membership in God's people to that other society's ultimacy. A person can have multiple temporal locations in this world, but he or she can only be part of one body forever. Whatever other societies a Jew is connected to, he or she is only a *participant therein, never a part thereof.*

Neither Judaism nor Christianity can look to some society or other for its primary orientation in the world. This theological-political fact provides more commonality between Jews and Christians than any theological fact or any political fact taken separately. This is because Judaism and Christianity are religions that originate in God's election, are constituted by God's covenant, and anticipate God's redemption. Thus, when Thomas More was willing to suffer death as a martyr at the hands of Henry VIII because he insisted on being "the king's good servant, but God's first," he did not mean that his service to God was that of the individual man Thomas More. Rather, he meant that his service to God was that of Thomas More the Catholic, who is a part of the Catholic church's connection to God.[14] To confound the priority of the church to the state, as More judged King Henry to be doing, would be to substitute a humanly ordained society for the divinely ordained "congregation of the Lord" (1 Chronicles 28:8). But God's people and human authority can only coexist when the latter considers itself conditional, not absolute. As the Talmud puts it about abuses of human authority becoming absolute, "to whom do we listen, to the words of the master or to the words of the pupil?"[15]

This great difference, this great ordering of the priorities of Jews and Christians, was brought home to me several years ago by an eloquent Christian lady at a conference on the city held at the University of Toronto. This lady was born and raised in Barbados. Her ancestors were brought there as slaves from Africa. She had originally come to Canada as a domestic servant, and then became a high school teacher in Toronto. At this conference, one of the main speakers was an African American political activist, and the main thrust of his remarks was that our primary definition of who we are as persons is racial. Thus the speaker insisted

---

[14] See Peter Ackroyd, *The Life of Thomas More* (London: Vintage, 1999), 394; also, J. Monti, *The King's Good Servant but God's First* (San Francisco: Ignatius Press, 1997), 405–51.

[15] B. Kiddushin 42b and parallels.

that everyone present accept the supposition that our stake in civil society is to further the racial agenda of our particular race. Following these remarks, the lady stood up and with consummate dignity said something like the following to him—and to us:

> Sir, I must differ with you. Of course, I am black, and being black I have suffered the persecution and discrimination that has been the lot of most blacks in a largely white society. Nevertheless, I will not allow you to define me as a person by your criterion of blackness. I am a Christian first and foremost. I am a black *Christian* like I am a Canadian *Christian*. Both "black" and "Canadian" modify the name "Christian," not vice-versa. What I ask of society is the freedom to be a good Christian and that society enable all people to be treated with just respect.

So much for the new secularist trinity of race, gender, class!

Following this statement there was a moment of stunned silence, during which I was quite jealous that this great soul wasn't a Jew speaking for me as a Jew. But in my heart of hearts, I think she was speaking for me as a Jew, whether she intended to or not. What she was saying is that who we are, and how we navigate in the world, does not come from definitions like race, where others tell us who we are, which in the end only means we are not like them.[16] The lady was saying that our persecutors must not define who is our primary community. Rather, Jews and Christians are defined by God's relationship with them, by their election into the covenant, and how they either accept or reject that covenantal election. In hearing this authentically Christian voice, I heard an echo of the voice of Jonah, who when asked who his god was, finally had to admit, "I am a Hebrew and I fear the Lord, God of the heavens" (Jonah 1:9). Only after this admission could he go to the pagan city of Nineveh and have anything at all to say there. And to his utter surprise, the pagans there actually listened to his message and turned away from their evil path.

I have related this moving story because it illustrates two important points about the theological-political situation Jews and Christians find themselves in at present. Moreover, it indicates how the first point is something Christians can learn from Jews, and the second point is something Jews can learn from Christians.

What Christians can learn from Jews, something epitomized by this story, is that to be a Christian, which is to be one of the two peoples in the world who claim to be covenanted by the Lord God of Israel, is also to be but one of many peoples in the as yet unredeemed world. Even though Christians believe—as do Jews about the Jewish people—that the church is in the vanguard of the Kingdom of God on earth, the Kingdom

---

[16] See 15–17 above.

of God on earth will not be brought any nearer by assuming that the Church can or should claim authority over others in the world as it is presently constituted politically. The task of any people of God is to survive in the world, and to work in the world so that the political order be one in which their survival is not only possible but is positively facilitated. This not only means working for a political order where religious liberty is the most important right that civil society is obligated to uphold but, also, a political order where enhancing the dignity of human life in its various forms is the raison d'être of the society, especially the state created by that society. Indeed, the protection of religious liberty, which is the political right to respond to or turn away from the God who elects us, is the epitome of human dignity by which all other rights are grounded.

In theological terms it means that humans are in the image of God, and that they are capable of a relationship with God.[17] In political terms it means that civil society must only be seen as subsequent in authority to this supreme relationship. Civil society must respect the prior human freedom of any of its participants to either accept or reject any historical revelation that purports to realize the relationship between God and humans in the world. And, revelation is *in the world, not of it*.[18] This recognition that humans are not ultimately beholden to the political orders of the world, that they do not even own their souls, is a Jewish point best appreciated by black Christians, who have suffered great persecution and see their redemption as Christians coming from God, not from any human power. This is why black Christians more than most other Christians have so identified with the initiation of God's redemption of his people Israel in the Exodus from Egypt.

What Jews can learn from Christians, something epitomized by this story, is that Judaism is a religion. Now, unfortunately, many Jews and many Christians have been deluded by Jewish secularists to think that Judaism—or "Jewishness"—is not a religion essentially because even non-religious Jews are considered part of the Jewish people. Therefore, it is argued that Jews are an "ethnic group" for whom Jewish religion is an arbitrary form of identification. But this is false. Even nonreligious Jews, even atheistic Jews, are part of the Jewish people *because being a Jew is being elected by God*. This is fundamentally different from either selecting one's own society or the mere accident of birth. It is God who makes a Jew a Jew; it is not a human choice, either one's own or that of one's ancestors or that of one's enemies.[19] Election is a fundamentally religious

[17] See D. Novak, *Natural Law in Judaism* (Cambridge: Cambridge University Press, 1998), 167–73.

[18] This is why Jewish tradition affirms that the Torah is *from* God, but is now *in* the world. See M. Sanhedrin 10.1; B. Baba Metsia 59b re Deut. 30:12 and parallels.

[19] See Novak, *The Election of Israel*, 1–21.

fact initiated by God not man. Those who repudiate their obligation to keep the commandments of the Torah—that is, Judaism—may have left Judaism in practice, but they are still part of Judaism by their very existence. They are "absent without leave"; yet they may not be court-martialed. Of course, Jews hope and pray that these errant sons and daughters who have strayed from the covenantal home will return, but neither their souls nor the souls of the Jews who have never left the covenantal home would be well served if faithful Jews attempted to coerce those who have left back into the fold. Such efforts at human coercion have failed, do fail, and will continue to fail. More than guilt is needed to bring these errant Jews back.

For most Jews, their election begins at birth. And even for those Jews who were not born Jews, their conversion to Judaism—their election in being "born again"—is not in essence their own decision.[20] Their own decision to become part of the Jewish people only means that the community must not force conversion on anyone. Instead, converts must feel that compulsion to convert as originally coming from God alone. Their free consent is a necessary but not sufficient condition of their being identified as Jews. And if baptism is indelible, and if most Christians are baptized as infants, then most Christians become Christians like most Jews become Jews.[21] Even if being baptized as a Christian is being "born again," and even if it is performed for an adult—*birth* is the most involuntary human event possible. (Indeed, the same term "born again" appears in Greek in the New Testament and in Hebrew in the Talmud.)[22] So it is only a modern, voluntaristic view of the covenant as some sort of social contract that supposes that being a Jew or being a Christian is an individual option to be initiated or terminated by human will.

Of course, some Jewish secularists have conceived of Jewish identity along racial, even racist lines. In the end, though, this means that it is the persecutors of the Jews who define who they are. But election into the covenant is not to be taken as a matter of blind fate, as an accident of birth, something that often seems to have a fatal end. If Jewish identity is conceived along racial lines, then to be a Jew at this time only means to be someone who escaped Hitler's genocide. But victimhood is not election. Racial victimhood, in the end, can only be cursed. Election, conversely, is a blessing even if it means being more vulnerable than others in the world.

---

[20] See 23–25 above.

[21] Re the indelibility of baptism for most Christians, see *Catechism of the Catholic Church* (London: Geoffrey Chapman, 1994), 288; also, *Companion to the Catechism of the Catholic Church* (San Francisco: Ignatius Press, 1994), 471.

[22] See 1 Peter 1:3; also John 3:3. Cf. B. Yevamot 22a and parallels.

For these reasons, everything that is associated with Jewish ethnicity, including Jewish attachment to the land of Israel and support of the Jewish state therein, is only cogent when defined in essentially religious categories. This should be the Jewish sense of self-identity, to themselves, to Christians, and to the various secular polities in which they now live. Neither racist definitions of a Jew, which require no free acceptance or rejection of one's fate, nor voluntaristic definitions of a Jew, which are based on the illusion of self-creation, can represent a coherent picture of who is a Jew. Being a Jew is neither fatal nor autonomous. It is only covenantal. Christians who truly appreciate the covenantal character of Christianity are in the best position to understand who Jews essentially are because they understand who they themselves are.

Beyond Liberalism and Conservatism

Because some modern nation-states have demanded the total subordination of everyone under their domain, and the horrendous historical results of these demands, a number of politically thoughtful people in North America and Europe have re-embraced the idea of the social contract, in its liberal, Lockean form, as an antidote to this totalitarianism. The fact that Jews and Christians have been particular victims of these modern totalitarian regimes makes the idea of the social contract appealing to them too. Like any contract, the social contract between citizens in a society to constitute themselves into a polity is conditional and therefore limited. Like any contract, the social contract does not create its parties but, rather, its parties create it or project it out of their own prior interests and for their own subsequent purposes. The parties to the social contract transcend it by having a communal past before it has been established, a communal life outside the present domain of the social contract, and a communal future in a time after there is any need left for a social contract. All of us come from somewhere else; all of us can live our lives most deeply if not yet completely somewhere else other than in civil society; all of us can hope to return in the end whence we came. But where is this "somewhere else"?

Those secularists who think that the democratic polity is their true home often become quite antidemocratic precisely because they cannot exercise the very limitation of the polity that is the hallmark of a democracy, which is limited government. Having "nowhere else" beyond the polity in the past, present, and future, they inevitably identify with the polity and take it to be the ultimate expression of their own particular interests. As such, they cannot coherently limit the power of the state and the civil society it structures. They can only hope to capture that power in order to make the state their own. That inevitably leads them to attempt to socially and politically marginalize all those who do not accept the ultimacy of the secular state and the predominance of secularists therein. Moreover, unlike even the philosophers of Plato's republic, these doctrinaire secularists do not strive for vision of a transpolitical good, one beyond all human procedures.[23] For them, what you see now is all you ever get. No wonder they are so impatient with Jews and Christians, who have such metapolitical, let alone metaphysical commitments. It is only when secularism becomes overtly ideological that it starts to take on metaphysical airs. Marxism is the most obvious example of this.

Secularists, whether self-identified or not, can be either liberals or conservatives. Despite all their so-called differences, most of those who now call themselves liberals and most of those who now call themselves conservatives accept the idea of the social contract and its corollary of the moral necessity of a limited state. They only differ on *what* should limit the power of the state. This involves their differing locations of the "somewhere else" whence persons come to civil society and where they wish to return. Moreover, most contemporary liberals and conservatives accept the most basic liberal idea that individual persons are self-possessed. The specific difference between them seems to be that contemporary conservatives emphasize the self-possession of their material property, whereas contemporary liberals emphasize the self-possession of their bodies. As the Talmud once noted, some people prefer their property over their bodies; other people prefer their bodies over their property.[24] (But the Talmud assumes that we are to love God more than either our property or our bodies.) Both liberals and conservatives today seem to want to be able to look forward to long weekends away from their political world, when and where they can enjoy either their property or their bodies. This is far different from working toward the Sabbath, though.

Because the idea of the self-possession of one's own body is used by most liberals to justify such biblically prohibited practices as abortion, euthanasia, and homosexual marriage, many thoughtful Christians and Jews have been gravitating in a more conservative political direction of late. The conservative—or, perhaps, "libertarian"—idea of the self-possession of one's material property is less likely to be used as a warrant for many biblically prohibited practices than is the case with the current liberal idea of bodily self-possession. Only when it comes to indifference to or rejection of biblically mandated concern for the poor do some conservatives seem to be religiously objectionable. Furthermore, whereas most liberals today seem to explicitly derive their morality from their secular

[23] See *Republic*, 485A–486A.
[24] B. Berakhot 61b re Deut. 6:5.

political commitments, more conservatives seem to explicitly derive their morality from prepolitical commitments to religions like Judaism and Christianity. Assuming this explicit derivation to be motivated by authentic conviction, it is understandable why Jewish and Christian ideas of human nature and community, which are most often identical, seem to have more influence on conservatives than they do on liberals today.

Nevertheless, Jews and Christians, as distinct from either liberals or conservatives today, come to the social contract not as individuals but as fully communal beings. The covenant characterizes a divinely chartered human community that, although not perfect itself, testifies to the perfect Kingdom of God. As such, Jews and Christians can make the promises any contract presupposes because they are already bound by the covenantal promise of God, the initial part of which has already been fulfilled. Each in their own way, Jews and Christians live in a transcendent dimension as they respectively understand it, however weak it now appears. They are only utilizing the secular world, however strong it now appears. They should not look to this world for their salvation, now or ever. They should, nonetheless though, contribute to the well-being of the secular world when its goals are truly pragmatic and not utopian. But those who look to this world for their salvation are inevitably disappointed and become dangerous cynics. Humans can only contribute to the temporal successes, the finite justice, of this world. They cannot save this world from the mortality that is the lot of every human enterprise, since humans themselves are but mortal creatures.

This is precisely how Jews in medieval Europe were able, at least at times, to live with integrity in Christians polities. It was because the Christian monarchs with whom they could contract did not require the ultimate existential commitment of the Jews. In other words, they offered the Jews and their own people a secular modus vivendi. But when the ultimate existential commitment of the Jews was required by Christian monarchs like Ferdinand and Isabella of Spain in 1492 in their demand for conversion or expulsion, faithful Jews had to leave Spain because the social contract had been broken. In this case, the Christian monarchs had overstepped their secular authority over the Jews. After the expulsion from Spain, Jews could never again trust any essentially Christian polity again.[25]

The Jewish social contract with Christian Spain was the epitome of the Jewish social contract theretofore. Its failure led Jews to look forward to a time when they could make a social contract in truly secular space. This is why most Jews saw the French Revolution, with its dismantling of a

---

[25] See Yithak Baer, *A History of the Jews in Christian Spain* 2, trans. L. Levensohn and H. Halkin (Philadelphia: Jewish Publication Society of America, 1978), 424–56.

Christian *ancien régime*, as liberation, even though it also brought in its wake the dissolution of the autonomy of the traditional Jewish communities (*qehillot*). Unfortunately, this modern enthusiasm led to an embrace of various forms of ideological secularism, as we saw in the previous chapter, rather than a philosophy of human nature and classical Jewish theology. None of these modern Jewish secularisms, though, enabled Jews to develop a truly Jewish idea of the social contract. In order to do that, Jews have to radically reassess their views of Christians, especially the still Christian majority in North America.

Jews and Christians must be wary of any social contract that has a beginning but no final limit. Being a human device, such a contract can only be a rival to the covenant made by God with his people, which also has a beginning but no final limit. Hence any contract Jews and Christians enter must be both humanly initiated and humanly terminable. Only then can the covenant truly transcend this political arrangement. Civil society must be a challenge, not a pseudomessianic temptation. Fortunately for Jews and Christians, the type of democratic polity that has emerged in the West does not in principle require the absolute commitment required by God and his covenanted community. Only secularist totalitarianisms have attempted to replace the covenant with their own absolute claims on the existential commitments of those under their control. This is why Jews and Christians have such a stake in the success of democratic polity. And indeed, because their entrance into the social contract comes out of their covenantal commitments, Jews and Christians can have a far greater personal attachment to their social contract with a democratic polity like the United States and Canada than they can have to any private contract negotiated between merely individual parties.

The entrance of Jews and Christians into the social contract as communal beings already socialized elsewhere means that they bring along to civil society their forms of human community, which need to be officially recognized by civil society both for their sake and civil society's sake. Jews and Christians also bring these forms of human community to civil society for the benefit of all its citizens, even for those of other religions, even for those who are secularists. These two purposes function in tandem. It is in the best communal interest of Jews and Christians to live in societies that affirm in law and public policy what Jews and Christians consider universally just. Only in such a political order can Jews and Christians live their own communal life in a way that does not make them, in effect, outlaws. In other words, they can only live willingly, and not just necessarily, in a society whose normative structure allows them to be present in the world wearing their own communal garb as well as wearing the garb they think all people need for protection in public. Moreover, the forms of human community they bring to civil society, like marriage, are so socially beneficial that most of us would not object to their being appropriated even by those members of civil society who do not want to have any religious affiliation at all. Indeed, the desire of Jews and Christians should be to give more to civil society than they take from it. This is a good deal more than what is usually meant by merely "political" strategy these days. Finally what Jews and Christians bring to civil society is an idea of trust adequate to its importance for the social contract.

The Question of Trust

For those who see the idea of social contract at the core of the constitution of a truly democratic society, the question of trust is of paramount importance. A contract involves trust among the parties to it. Without trust, it is unlikely any contract could even be initiated much less endure. Explicit trust, especially, is needed for a social contract, where the parties to the contract are unfamiliar with one another. Here they cannot assume the implicit trust more often found in private contracts, where the parties are often personally familiar with one another, in fact, sometimes even members of the same intimate community. (In such intimate communities many contracts are unwritten, even unstated at times.)[26] In a social contract, one cannot say to the others, I trust you because I have had long experience living with you, because this assumes a long tradition of association. But the social contract begins with strangers coming together for the first time, as it were. A social contract establishes a society de novo. Thus a social contract requires explicit transcommunal trust.

The paramount importance of trust is brought out quite well by Charles Fried, a prominent American legal theorist, in his book on the foundations of contract law. He writes:

> When my confidence in your assistance derives from my conviction that you will do what is right (not just what is prudent), then I trust you, and trust becomes a powerful tool for working our mutual wills in the world. So remarkable a tool is trust that in the end we pursue it for its own sake; we prefer doing things cooperatively when we might have relied on fear or interest or worked alone.[27]

That is a great insight, one designed to turn our thinking away from making contracts of any kind simply the instruments of our selfish, individualistic projects. And so Professor Fried implies that contracts must be seen as

---

[26] See B. Baba Batra 175b; B. Shevuot 41b.
[27] *Contract as Promise* (Cambridge, Mass.: Harvard University Press, 1981), 8.

a specific manifestation of a deeper mode of interpersonal relationship.[28] Could our attraction to contracts perhaps be seen as a sign of a deeper covenantal desire on our part? Nevertheless, Professor Fried does not ask the obvious question: How is trust initiated and maintained in any contract, especially in a social contract? Is this trust essential prior to the contract or only subsequent to it? Does trust among the parties to the social contract enable the social contract to be initiated and endure by itself, or does trust have to be mandated and enforced for the parties to the social contract after its initiation? But Professor Fried does speak of "what is right" and "not just what is prudent" (or what might be called "pragmatic" in the vulgar sense of that term). Does he mean that those entering contracts have to have a prior idea of what is right and hold that idea in common? Can they not simply decide what is right be negotiated in the contract itself? Finally, these questions lead to the most basic questions of all: Why should I trust someone else, especially when that person is unfamiliar to me now? Indeed, isn't a social contract made with such unfamiliar others? Why should I trust them at all? How can I trust them at all? Do I need to know something about these others I am being asked to trust, or is trust a "leap of faith" into an unknown, an arbitrary agreement to agree, as it were?

At this point in our inquiry, it might be useful to look at a classic rabbinic text that deals with the question of trust between Jews and gentiles, and then examine how this text was interpreted in the Middle Ages in the context of Jewish-Christian relations. Since I am advocating that Jews and Christians enter a social contract similarly, and that they enter it after some agreement among themselves, it is important to see how Jews and Christians can be conceived of as entering a contract with each other. To be sure, the contract discussed here is a private one; nonetheless, as we have seen, the idea of a social contract is modeled on the reality of private contracts. Therefore, we can draw strong analogies from this rabbinic discussion of trust in partnerships for present Jewish thinking about the idea of the social contract in the context of a constitutional democracy, and with whom such a social contract can be entered, in good faith on both sides.

The Talmud expounds the scriptural verse "You shall not mention the name of other gods; it shall not be heard in your mouth" (Exodus 23:13) as follows:

> One should not enable [*yigrom*] others to take a vow in its name or uphold one in its name. This supports the view of the father of Samuel, since the father of Samuel said that it is forbidden [*asur*] for one to enter a partnership [*shuttfut*]

---

[28] See B. A. Misztal, *Trust in Modern Societies* (Cambridge: Polity Press, 1998), 9–24.

with a gentile since he [the gentile] might have to take an oath [*shevu'ah*] and he will swear it [invoking] his god. But the Torah says: "it [the name of the other god] shall not be heard in your mouth."[29]

Of course, the scriptural verse itself is addressed to Jews. They are the ones who are forbidden to invoke the name of any other god. The verse itself does not mention gentiles at all, only "other gods," who are assumed to be what the gentiles worship and what the Jews must avoid worshiping, even avoiding the invocation of their names. Nevertheless, it seems that the father of Samuel understands the words "it shall not be heard in your mouth" (*lo yisham'a al pikha*) to mean: *Your entrance into a contract might cause the name of another god to be invoked by a gentile.* But this could mean that a Jew may not directly require a gentile to take an oath in the name of his or her god, which, indeed, is a point made in an earlier rabbinic text.[30] Such an oath would normally be required when one of the parties is suspected of breach of contract. But the father of Samuel is going further than this in his interpretation of the verse. He is asserting that since it is likely that in the course of a partnership one of the partners might have to take an oath (for example, that he did not misappropriate partnership funds), and that a gentile partner will no doubt swear in the name of his god, one should not even enter a partnership with a gentile initially lest one *indirectly* cause him to swear in the name of his god.[31] This might happen even if the Jew never directly requires the gentile to take an oath in the name of that gentile's god.

Rabbenu Jacob Tam, the most important rabbinical authority in northern France in the twelfth century, offers a radical reinterpretation of the opinion of the father of Samuel reported in the Talmud[32] that has profound implications for the whole question of trust between Jews and Christians and their similar, perhaps joint, participation in a social contract.

First, Rabbenu Tam rules that a Jew may accept an oath taken by a gentile in the name of his god in a case when not doing so would result in monetary loss for the Jew.[33] This is a recognition of the fact that Jews would court economic disaster if they could not enter into commercial

---

[29] B. Sanhedrin 63b.

[30] *Mekhilta*: Mishpatim, ed. Horovitz-Rabin, p, 332. See M. M. Kasher, *Torah Shelemah*: Exod. 23:13, n. 182.

[31] The Hebrew term I have translated as "enable" is *gorem*, which technically denotes remote causality, e.g., when one indirectly harms another human being. Even indirectly causing someone else to sin is considered harmful, hence prohibited (*asur*), yet one is not thereby culpable (*patur*). For the distinction between what is prohibited *ab initio* and what one is culpable for *post factum*, see B. Baba Batra 22b; B. Baba Kama 60a. Cf. B. Avodah Zarah 6b re Lev. 19:14.

[32] B. Sanhedrin 63b, Tos., s.v. "asur."

[33] See B. Avodah Zarah 6b; ibid., 2a, Tos., s.v. "asur."

contracts with the gentiles among whom they were living. Oaths are inevitably involved in such undertakings. But then Rabbenu Tam's discussion becomes more theological. He argues that the prohibition of entering a partnership with a gentile only applied in ancient times when all the gentiles were idolaters. However, in his time the Christians with whom Jews do business, which often means entering into a partnership with them, are not idolaters. Despite that in their oaths they either invoke the names of their saints (*qodashim shelahen*)—whom they do not assume to be divine—or even intend the name of Jesus, whom they do assume to be divine, they in fact mean (*daʿatam*) God as the Maker of heaven (*oseh shamayim*).[34] Thus, despite their invocation of various beings Jews would not consider divine, and even one whom these gentiles do consider divine, it is the ultimate meaning of gentile oath-taking that counts. God as "maker of heaven" is the minimal name for the creator God who, in rabbinic teaching, must be acknowledged by all human beings, both Jews and gentiles, albeit in different ways.[35]

Since, in rabbinic teaching, worship of other gods (*avodah zarah*) or "idolatry" is prohibited to all human beings, a Jew needs to know the god to whom the gentile is ultimately swearing an oath.[36] No one would take an oath in the name of a god he or she does not worship.[37] So, if it can be shown, ultimately if not immediately, that Jews and Christians are worshiping the same God, then there is no problem in a Jew's entering a partnership with a Christian, even ab initio. That it is the same God in whose name the oath is taken outweighs the fact that Jews and Christians will formulate their respective oaths (and their respective liturgies) quite differently. Thus moral commonality does not entail religious unanimity.

Several subsequent halakhic authorities draw this implication from Rabbenu Tam's political-legal theology as he expressed it in his reinterpretation of the original talmudic opinion about partnership with gentiles.[38]

---

[34] In *Tosfot ha-Rosh*: B. Sanhedrin 63b, published in *Sanhedrei Gedolah* 3, ed. B. Lipkin (Jerusalem: Makhon Harry Fischel, 1970), p. 190, Rabbenu Tam's opinion is presented as follows: "[E]ven though they intend Jesus of Nazareth . . . they mean the Maker of heaven and earth." It is difficult to ascertain whether these are the *ipsima verba* of Rabbenu Tam or only a paraphrase of them. See, also, *Hagahot Maimoniyot* on Maimonides, MT: Avodah Zarah, 5.10.

[35] See Jonah 1:9; *Sifre*: Devarim, no. 313 re Deut. 32:10.; *Beresheet Rabbah* 59.8 re Gen. 24:7; also, Rashi, *Commentary on the Torah*: Gen. 24:7.

[36] For the prohibition of gentile idolatry, see T. Avodah Zarah 8.4; B. Sanhedrin 56b.

[37] See Maimonides, MT: Avodah Zarah, 5.10; Shuttfin, 5.10.

[38] For general agreement with Rabbenu Tam's stance toward Christians, see R. Mordecai ben Hillel Ashkenazi, *Mordecai*: Avodah Zarah, no. 809 in the name of R. Eliezer ben Joel Halevi (Ravyah). For those medieval authorities who interpret Rabbenu Tam's opinion to mean one is even permitted ab initio to enter a partnership with a Christian, see R. Joseph Karo, *Bet Yosef* on Tur: Hoshen Mishpat, 182, s.v. "asur." For those medieval authorities,

In fact, it might be an additional attraction to a Jew entering into a contract with a Christian to know that, in the event of the type of doubt that requires one to take an oath, this gentile is answerable to the same God as is his or her Jewish partner.[39] The deeper issue that emerges from this rabbinic text and its medieval reinterpretation, which is certainly germane to discussion of Jewish and Christian involvement in a social contract, concerns the question of how one's theology is related to one's being a suitable object of someone else's trust.

This question is taken up by the fourteenth-century Provençal authority R. Menahem ha-Meiri, who, in his comments on the same talmudic text Rabbenu Tam reinterpreted, basically agrees with that reinterpretation, recognizing as it does the different status of Christians in the post-talmudic period.[40] This is consistent with Meiri's views about his own Christian contemporaries (and Muslim contemporaries, about whom Rabbenu Tam did not seem to have an opinion). In one place, he refers to "the nations who are bound [gedurot] by the ways of religion and law [dattot ve-nimusim]."[41] In another place, he refers to these "nations," meaning Christians and Muslims, as "being bound by the ways of religion and who renounce polytheism [elohut]."[42] The key to this development, as it were, of Rabbenu Tam's view of Christians, is the connection Meiri makes between belief in the creator God and belief in a normative universe. In fact, the word dat means both "law" and "religion," which is based on the assumption that all law is essentially divine law, either directly or indirectly.[43]

In the teaching of Scripture, the creator God takes responsibility for his creation. That is, he not only makes the universe, he makes the universe his own cosmos by governing it justly and beneficently. Humans are unique, being able to desire the beneficence of divine justice, to apprehend some of its more general features, to rationally formulate it, and to put it into practice. As Job said: "In Your love you granted me life; Your command [pequdatekha] kept me alive" (Job 10:11).[44] This is what many

---

though, who interpret Rabbenu Tam's opinion to only mean acceptance *post factum* of a Jew's partnership with a gentile, see R. Asher, *Rosh*: Sanhedrin, 7.3; *Teshuvot ha-Rosh*, 18.11; *Tur*: Hoshen Mishpat, 182.

[39] See 35 above.

[40] *Bet ha-Behirah*: Sanhedrin 63b, ed. A. Sofer (Jerusalem: n.p., 1965), p. 239.

[41] *Bet ha-Behirah*: Baba Kama 38a, ed. P. Schlesinger (Jerusalem: n.p., 1967), p. 122.

[42] *Bet ha-Behirah*: Avodah Zarah 20a, ed. A. Sofer (Jerusalem: Qedem, 1964), p. 46.

[43] See *Bet ha-Behirah*: Avot, intro., ed. B. Z. Prag (Jerusalem: Makhon ha-Talmud ha-Yisraeli ha-Shalem, 1964), p. 16; also, A. Kohut, *Aruch Completum*, 3:169; D. Novak, *The Image of the Non-Jew in Judaism* (New York and Toronto: Edwin Mellen Press, 1983), 351–56; *Jewish-Christian Dialogue*, 42–56.

[44] Trans. Robert Gordis, *The Book of God and Man* (Chicago: University of Chicago Press, 1965), 250. If Job was a gentile, which is what the preponderance of Jewish commen-

Jews and Christians have seen as stemming from human reflection on our universal nature and the claims it makes upon us. This general revelation also precedes the fuller revelation that comes in the histories of the particular faith communities.[45] Whereas each faith community cannot judge the veracity of what could be called the special revelations of other faith communities, each one can, nonetheless, recognize the presence of this general revelation in other faith communities, and even among people who do not affirm any special revelation at all. (In the Middle Ages, such people would be called "the philosophers.") Anyone who affirms this general revelation of the divine law of the universe is worthy of respect for affirming a non-negotiable morality. Such would not be the case, of course, if all law is taken to be merely human invention. Why can't one human being nullify or change what another human being has ordered? It seems that humans will only unconditionally obey a god. For Jews, Christians, and Muslims, only the one creator God is God; anyone else is only a fellow creature. "I am the first and I am the last, and there is no god other than me" (Isaiah 44:6). To make any fellow creature a god is to commit idolatry. All other "gods" are only human projections. "Our God is in the heavens beyond, doing whatever he wants; their idols are only silver and gold, the work of human hands" (Psalms 115:3–4). Though the idols represent powers that are natural, hence not human creations, their depiction in humanly made images is what makes them "divine" in the eyes of their worshipers.

The commands of fellow creatures—and the only fellow creatures who are capable of commanding us are our fellow human creatures—are only valid either when they are derived from divine law or when they are enacted in order to enhance divine law. Minimally, no human commands should ever be allowed to contradict divine law.

We can now see how belief in the one creator God and the idea of a universal law, surely binding on all humans, come together. And this is why idolatry is for Judaism, Christianity, and Islam, the primal sin.[46] Idolatry is the most basic denial of the truth that only one God has created us and it is only that one God whom all humans are to obey unconditionally. Thus Maimonides sees the prohibition of idolatry rooted in the scrip-

---

tary assumes (see ibid., 225 re B. Baba Batra 15b, etc.), and he lived before the Sinaitic revelation, then this reference to God's "command" (*pequdah*) can only mean a general divine law for all humankind. For *pequdah* as "commandment," see, e.g., Ps. 19:9; 119:34. Cf. ibid. 119:73.

[45] That precedence of general to singular revelation is logical (as a presupposition), chronological (as a prelude), but not one of ontological priority. God's direct, more concrete word is always more important and authoritative than his indirect, more abstract word. See Novak, *Natural Law in Judaism*, 142–48.

[46] See, e.g., B. Kiddushin 40a and parallels; Maimonides, MT: Avodah Zarah, 2.4.

tural command: "From falsehood [*mi-dvar sheqer*] remove yourself" (Exodus 23:7).[47] And from this, one can see why one is to totally avoid any involvement in the oath of an idolater, however indirect that involvement might be. It is not just that idolatry is proscribed, so that involvement in an oath with an idolater would be like "aiding a transgressor" in violating a specific commandment.[48] It is also that, to be involved in idolatry is to be involved in the most fundamental of all lies. Therefore, it is not just that an idolater is to be avoided, it is that an idolater cannot be trusted. Even when idolaters tell the truth, even when they keep their promises, this is accidental to their ultimate commitment, which is the lie of all lies.

Distinguishing between the idolater and the worshiper of the one true God enables a faithful Jew to get an answer to these questions from any gentile with whom he or she is publicly related: Why should I believe your commitment to do what you have promised me? Why should I accept you as my partner in society? Why should I trust you?

It seems that I as a faithful Jew have good reason to trust you as a gentile enough to become associated with you in a social contract if you affirm an unchanging law, which is not of your own making nor the making—and therefore the unmaking—of any other human being or of any other group of human beings. As such, *I have good reason to believe that you will not change your word to me because you have based your word to me on a word made by God, which God has promised never to withdraw or change.* Your promise made to me and my promise made to you, upon which the social contract is truly founded, must be part of that larger, more lasting, commitment. Since humans are mortal and thus subject to the greatest of all changes, which is death, their commitment has to be to an immortal word, one not subject to death, the change of all changes. "The grass withers and the flower fades, but the word of our God endures forever" (Isaiah 40:8). For biblical believers, like Jews and Christians, God's faithfulness (*emunah*) to creation, which makes creation endure and intelligibly cohere (*emet*), is to be imitated by human fidelity to the agreements made among themselves.[49] Such agreements like the social contract are not only made *among* humans; they are made *before* God.[50] This is what gives them cosmic significance. This is why God's judgment is invoked should the agreement made before him be willingly broken. "Loyalty (*hesed*) and truth meet; justice and peace kiss. Truth shall sprout form the earth, and justice will look down from heaven" (Psalms 85:11–12).

---

[47] *Commentary on the Mishnah*: Avodah Zarah, 4.7, ed. Kafih, p. 238.
[48] See B. Avodah Zarah 55b.
[49] See Novak, *The Election of Israel*, 126–29.
[50] See 48 above.

So faithful Jews and Christians can trust one another to keep their word by virtue of their respective commitments to a law not of their own making. So if either party breaks his or her word, he or she can be held up to the law upon which the oath was taken, and to the God who gave that law. That God will surely judge those who violate his law and their agreements modeled on that law. Thus there are good reasons for mutual trust at entering into partnerships, both private and public, with each other. (It is only when we accept the same special revelation, however, that we become part of the same primal community.) Moreover, when one affirms the special, historical revelation to one's faith community, one has behind oneself much covenantal experience. This is what makes contractual relationships truly cogent for Jews (and I think for Christians too). Indeed, one can keep one's promises because one believes God is keeping his promises. Covenanted communities are founded on divine promises. Having experienced covenantal faithfulness, one has a real basis for keeping one's commitments to others. One models one's fidelity to others on God's faithfulness to creation and to God's covenanted community.[51] When a covenant member deceives any other human, he or she is perverting God's faithfulness by deceitful use of the covenantal reputation.[52] Minimally this divine faithfulness is evident in the close availability of elementary divine moral law, coming from God's covenant with creation, to every rational, truth-seeking human being. Only liars and hypocrites have removed themselves from the governance of this law.

Jews, Christians, Atheists, and Secularists

Does this mean, then, that Jews and Christians can only enter a social contract with those who, like them, have already affirmed the creator God in good faith (the original sense of *bona fides*)? In other words, can an atheist be trusted? Can Jews or Christians enter into a social contract with atheists and still maintain their religious integrity? This is an important question for Jews and Christians since they have to interact in civil society today with far more atheists than overt idolaters (although the adherents of certain distinctly modern ideologies might qualify for having a god other than the one true creator God). Indeed, this question is constantly thrown up to religious people by those who are quick to point out that

---

[51] For the connection between faithfulness and justice, see Jer. 5:1; Prov. 12:17. For the connection between God's covenant with creation and God's covenant with Israel, see Isa. 54:9–10.

[52] See T. Sotah 7.3; T. Baba Kama 7.8–8; *Mekhilta*: Mishpatim re Exod. 22:3, pp. 294–95; B. Hullin 94a; Maimonides, MT: Deot, 2.6 re Prov. 12:19 and Ps. 51:2.

there are virtuous atheists who are trustworthy, and religious scoundrels who are not. Furthermore, a negative answer to this question, too hastily given, puts religious people in the position of having to affirm a religious test for citizenship in a democracy. But isn't this as undemocratic as the type of doctrinaire secularism that would outlaw religion incrementally step by step?

The answer to the question hinges on what one means by "atheism." The classic rabbinic answer was to define an atheist as one who followed the Hellenistic philosopher Epicurus (hence such people are called in rabbinic Hebrew *apiqorsim*).[53] Epicurus did not deny the possibility that there are gods in the sense of there being superhuman causal powers. After all, this is not logically impossible. What Epicurus denied was that even if these gods exist somewhere, they are not concerned with human affairs on earth, and that they have no desire to rule humans, and that they do not care to judge human affairs.[54] The gods, for him, have no public authority. The Rabbis said that for such a person, "there is no law and there is no judge" (*leyt din ve-leyt dayyan*).[55]

Certainly, in private, there are such persons who have no god. For example, the type of princes for whom Machiavelli wrote are those who see fulfillment of their desires for power as their primary motivation.[56] But it is a mistake, I think, for religious people to quickly conclude that such egoists or libertines have a god too in what they desire. Since these people identify with their desires, there is not enough transcendence here to warrant calling the objects of their desires gods. Because our desires do not manifest themselves to us in lawlike fashion, that is as *nomos*, it is a mistake to render our unencumbered fulfillment of them "autonomy."

The gods come into the picture when persons seek public approval of their own desires. Thus "the morally debased person (*naval*) who says in his heart 'there is no god' [*ein elohim*]" (Psalms 53:2) only says this in private.[57] In public this same person must acknowledge that he or she is under the judgment of some godlike power, and it is to this law that he

[53] See M. Sanhedrin 10.1; Maimonides, MT: Teshuvah, 3.8; *Guide of the Perplexed*, 3.17 re Jer. 5:12. For the need to answer the charges made by *apiqorsim* against Judaism, see M. Avot 2.14.

[54] See Epicurus, *Fragments*, nos. 57–58, trans. C. Bailey, *The Stoic and Epicurean Philosophers*, ed. W. J. Oates (New York: Random House, 1940), 50; also, Cicero, *De Finibus*, 1.18.

[55] See Vayiqra Rabbah 28.1; Qohelet Rabbati 1.4 re Eccl. 1:3; *Targum Jonathan ben Uzziel*: Gen. 4:8.

[56] See *The Prince*, chap. 8.

[57] The usual English translation (as in the King James version) is: "The fool saith in his heart, there is no God." This is based on the Vulgate: *Dicit insipiens in corde sua non est Deus*. But the Hebrew *naval* denotes willful moral vice, not intellectual error (*in-sapiens*). See, e.g., 1 Sam. 25:25.

or she can be held accountable by other persons. If not, why would any strangers want to become involved with someone who is answerable to no one? What would prevent such an unaccountable person from doing whatever he or she wants to do to me now, thinking he or she is answerable to no one in the end?

In public everyone at some point must invoke some godlike authority, because at some point everyone has to speak normatively. At some point, one has to affirm an authority beyond which there is no appeal. Even if there is no personal god here, there is a godlike command.[58] One cannot participate in any public activity and expect even minimal ad hoc trust without eventually having to acknowledge some higher law. The best example of this is speech itself, which requires laws of grammar in order to be intelligible, laws that no one speaker of a language could arbitrarily make alone.[59] Thus through grammar a speaker of a language is commanded how to speak correctly. And just as a speaker desirous of promoting his or her interests or point of view requires the prior guarantee of grammar to get the point across to other speakers of that language, so any person participating in society requires the prior guarantee of law in order to be able to justify the fulfillment of his or her desires with other persons in society peacefully (shalom).[60] Our desires, as distinct from our purely physical appetites, are for the company of other persons already there with us in the world. Desire, then, is always essentially political; appetite is more physical. Interpersonal desire is governed by moral law as physical appetite is governed by biology. In both cases, what governs has a priority over what is governed. In this sense, the rule is transcendent.

Once there is a transcendent law to govern all our human desires, there is a god of some sort or other. It seems that we could only unconditionally obey what is generically superior to ourselves in both power and intelligence. Thus, for example, once a Jew discovers that his or her parents are generically similar to him- or herself (most often discovered in adolescence), that the parents are fallible and mortal like their children, the parents have already been divested of the godlike status they had when their children were infants. Only now is one required to honor and respect one's parents because of the commandment of the everlasting God, who is different in kind both from children and parents and who thus has prior claims on both.[61]

---

[58] See Immanuel Kant, *Critique of Pure Reason*, B847. See, also, D. Novak, "Law: Religious or Secular?" *Virginia Law Review* 86 (2000), 576–81.

[59] See Ludwig Wittgenstein, *Tractatus Logico-Philosophicus*, trans. D. F. Pears and B. F. McGuiness (London: Routledge and Kegan Paul, 1961), 5.4731, 5.552, 5.6–62, 6.13, 6.3, 6.373.

[60] See M. Avot 3.2, where one is to pray to God, the ultimate authority, for the lawful authority of the state in preventing violence by its police power.

[61] See *Sifra*: Qedoshim re Lev. 19:3, ed. Weiss, p. 87a; B. Yevamot 5b re Lev. 19:3 and Tos., s.v. "kulkhem."

The public question, then, is not a god or no-god, but *whose god*. To be sure, someone whose public god is not the one creator God, but some human institution like the state and its law elevated to divine status (as was done in the most impressive philosophical way by Hobbes), might be someone with whom I, as a faithful, law-abiding Jew, can share private friendship and public space.[62] In terms of private friendship, there is enough intellectual commonality between me and my atheistic friends and colleagues that we can largely bracket discussion of the God question. Neither they nor I are interested in converting the other to our own onto-logical point of view. And we have had enough personal experience with each other to trust each other's character. As for sharing public space with atheists, I can do this simply because the social contract in a democracy may not mandate that a citizen have *some* religion any more than it may mandate that all the citizens have the *same* religion, or even that the state officially establish *one* religion. Any such religious mandates from the state would have the state acting in *loco Dei* instead of allowing the reli-gious (or areligious) commitments of its citizens to transcend its authority by freely seeking their salvation elsewhere.[63] Any such mandates would make the ultimate commitments of its citizens dependent on the warrant or approval of the state.

The state can acknowledge the one creator God, as is the case in the United States, with the invocation of God in its founding document, the Declaration of Independence, and as is the case in Canada with the invo-cation of God in the first sentence of the Charter of Rights and Responsi-bilities. And it can do so without the official establishment of any religion or religions. There are two reasons for this acknowledgment. One, it is assumed that the majority of the citizens of United States and Canada believe in this God. Thus not to mention him at all would be tantamount to allowing the state to be atheistic, that is, to deny the existence of God. To refuse this acknowledgment would be, in effect, to repudiate the reli-gious past of all the cultures who have sustained the state. One cannot pretend that religious claims are being made de novo, and that previously no one ever heard of God. As such, the burden of proof is on atheistic denial not theistic affirmation (even though atheistic secularists are trying to reverse the burden of proof, making theists like Jews and Christians justify public beliefs that have heretofore been taken for granted). Hence, not to mention God, considering the history of Western civilization, is tantamount to denying a God who, even for most atheists, once was there.[64] To do this would allow the wishes of a small atheistic minority to

---

[62] For the godlike status of the state, for Hobbes, see *Leviathan*, chap. 18, ed. M. Oakeshott (New York: Collier Books, 1962), p. 32.

[63] See *Esther Rabbah* 8.6 re Est. 4:14.

[64] See Friedrich Nietzsche, *Thus Spake Zarathustra*, prologue: 2–3, trans. T. Common, *The Philosophy of Nietzsche* (New York: Random House, 1954), pp. 4–8; also, M. J. Buck-

trump the existential commitments of the vast majority of citizens, who see the highest moral authority in their lives to be the commandments of God. As for agnosticism, one cannot be neutral, certainly not in public, on the God question. At some crucial point, there will be a need to invoke a nonrepealable, final authority. Someone has to have the final word in disputes of great social significance. The second reason for public acknowledgment of the transcendent God is that it prevents the state from ever presenting itself as godlike. Indeed, such godlike self-presentations have occurred quite vividly in those modern states that have been officially or even unofficially atheistic, without God either de jure or de facto.

So even though for democratic reasons I as a faithful Jew can enter the social contract with atheists in good faith, this is because they are neither the majority of the citizens of my country nor are they in positions of power strong enough—yet—to make the society thoroughly atheistic. A thoroughly atheistic society is one in which public recognition of the moral sovereignty of the creator God is outlawed, and where the religious beliefs and practices of the citizens are relegated to an ever narrower private sphere. Moreover, inevitably, the elimination of the creator God in public makes room for the establishment of some other god, one subject to greater human control. Society, like nature, abhors a vacuum.[65]

What this means is that even though one cannot publicly require some or any religion on the part of the citizens, there are powerful arguments both historical and philosophical, for why it is most unlikely that constitutional democracies like ours, with the limited government that essentially characterizes them, could have been either initiated or maintained by people who had no God, or a god less than the one creator God of heaven and earth. This being the case, it is difficult to see how a Jewish social contract that, as we have seen, is a social contract into which Jews as Jews can enter in good faith, could be initiated or maintained in the West, except where one can assume that the vast majority of one's fellow citizens, in one way or another, worship the same God as Jews do. This is why I can trust them, even when I do not know most of them personally. They have an ascertainable cosmic address quite similar to my own.

The Jewish social contract will be in serious trouble if an atheistic elite in the United States or Canada is able to dictate the further elimination of religio-moral commitment from the public square. Should this happen, faithful Jews and faithful Christians will have to seriously consider whether the social contract they or their ancestors entered has not by now been broken. In that case, the options of Jews and Christians will be

---

ley, *At the Origins of Modern Atheism* (New Haven, Conn.: Yale University Press, 1987), 28–30.

    [65] See Aristotle, *Physics*, 4.7/214a20–30.

fourfold: One, they could mount a concerted political effort to restore the country to its founding principles, which have clearly recognized the sovereignty of God and the liberty to worship that God to be a right truly prior to the state and not a revocable entitlement from the state. Two, they could withdraw from public life and become sectarian enclaves like the Amish or the Hasidim. Three, they could seriously consider emigration to a more receptive society. The fourth option would be armed revolution, which as far as I am concerned, is never justified in any society in which one is not being held prisoner.[66]

It seems to me that the task of Jews and Christians today in both the United States and Canada is to work together to be better able to limit the power of the state—and any powerful elite that sees the state as its own—for the sake of themselves, for the sake of the adherents of other religions, and even for the sake of adherents of no religion. If, as I have been arguing, atheism can only be cogent when private, a state that acknowledges the truly transcendent God is much more likely to respect privacy than a state that worships its own immanent power and sees its domain as pervasive. It is ironic, but I think nonetheless true, that Jews and Christians are more likely to defend the private rights of atheists to be atheists than doctrinaire secularists are likely to protect the rights of Jews and Christians. It is likely that doctrinaire secularists will inevitably require public and private acceptance of their ideological gods by all citizens, those having a religion, those having no religion, and even those who have no religion and do not want one.

For all these reasons, I see my task as a Jewish participant in a social contract both in the United States and in Canada (having dual citizenship) to retrieve the Jewish covenantal tradition that made it possible for Jews to enter contracts both private and social. Hopefully, my retrieval of this tradition in this book designed for a more general readership will benefit others struggling with theological-political issues similar to mine.

[66] See Plato, *Crito*, 51D.

Chapter Eight

The Jewish Social Contract in Secular Public Policy

Jews, Judaism, and Public Policy

The idea of the Jewish social contract, as it has been formulated from within the Jewish tradition, has important public policy implications, especially for North American Jews living in the United States or Canada, countries in which the idea of a social contract in general has played an important role in political discourse. Hence the idea of the Jewish social contract can be readily intelligible here.

Before proposing a Jewish public policy stand on any specific issue like religion-state relations (often called "church-state" relations), one should have some clear understanding of why Jews as Jews should propose any public policy at all in a non-Jewish, secular society like the United States or Canada.[1] By "public policy proposal," I mean what a particular group, like the Jews, proposes for the larger secular society in which it is a full and active participant. By a "secular society," I mean a society that does not look to any singular revelation of God in history as its founding event, thus allowing members of any or no religious tradition to be equal participants in its founding.

Without serious consideration of this question, a "Jewish" stand on any public policy issue is likely to be ineffective insofar as its justification has not been sufficiently put forth. Without such justification, the initial reaction of the society at large, to whom such a Jewish public stand on any specific issue, like church-state relations, is addressed, is likely to be: "Who are the Jews to be telling *us* what *they* think *we* should do?" Indeed, lack of a clear understanding has prevented some Christian groups (who have far more experience than the Jews in taking such stands on public policy issues) from being as politically persuasive as they could be. Jews, who are relative newcomers to the proposal of public policy issues in a secular society (other than for their own immediate self-interest in combating anti-Semitism and promoting the security of the State of Israel), should take

---

[1] For the use of the term "church" to connote any religious community in a secular setting, see 167 above.

appropriate heed. In other words, Jews should do their philosophical homework on this general political question, and their theological homework on it as a Jewish question, before they enter into political discourse.

Before addressing the political question of church-state relations, however, one must move beyond two opposite positions held by many in the contemporary Jewish world outside of the State of Israel (where the question seems essentially different from this general political question in the Diaspora). These two extremes essentially preclude the possibility of advocating policies that are both Jewish and public. The first such extreme might be termed "liberal," the second "sectarian."

The liberal stand has been one that the major secular Jewish organizations have long taken. Basing their arguments on the public duty to protect the private realm of individual citizens, these organizations, for the most part, have only taken public stands on issues in which society seems to be infringing on the privacy rights of individual citizens by making religious demands on them. It is important to recognize that this stand assumes Jewish religious demands on society are inherently undemocratic because they are religious, hence the exercise of religion must only be the assertion of a privacy right that society has the duty to keep strictly private.[2]

Seeing the traditional American concern for the separation of church and state as based on this classical liberal respect for individual privacy, these Jews have argued that there should be no religiously based advocacy of any issue of public policy inasmuch as religion, a private matter, has no right to make any public claims at all. Its only legitimate claim is to let its adherents conduct their own religious affairs among themselves in protected seclusion. (Due to considerable historical differences, church-state relations on a number of points, especially on questions of public education, have to be judged differently in Canada than in the United States.) At most, the "Jewish" character of such advocacy has been based on the fact that even in democracies like the United States, it has been the experience of many Jews to find themselves in public situations where members

---

[2] The most distinguished and successful proponent of the strict separationist argument was the constitutional lawyer the late Leo Pfeffer, who was for many years counsel for the American Jewish Congress. Pfeffer argued some of the most famous church-state cases before the U.S. Supreme Court. Aside from his legal briefs, Pfeffer's political views are found in his *Church, State, and Freedom*, rev. ed. (Boston: Beacon Press, 1967). There on p. 3 he writes: "Americans . . . today generally take it for granted that their religion is a private matter of no concern to the men elected or appointed to run their government." He then continues: "To the primitive savage, all of life may be said to be religious." Later on p. 238 he notes that mention of God in official statements of the United States are "ceremonial verbalizations [that] could frequently not be avoided . . . [but] of themselves they are of no practical importance." See, also, his *God, Caesar, and the Constitution* (Boston: Beacon Press, 1975). For a more recent presentation of this argument, from a historian, see Naomi W. Cohen, *Jews in Christian America* (New York: Oxford University Press, 1992).

of a Christian majority have exercised social pressure on Jews to participate in publicly endorsed Christian religious practices (like prayers in
schools), either actively or passively. Accordingly, on an issue like church-
state relations, whose public advocacy is usually made in what seems to
be religious terms, the liberal stand turns out to be quite consistent: Religion is a strictly private affair, both for the Jews and for everyone else.

The "Jewish" character of this type of advocacy turns out to be that
Jews are seen as the most visible victims of political or social pressures
placed by a majority on a minority to have, in effect, their religious privacy invaded. But, surely, Jews are not the only victims of the refusal of
a majority to recognize the privacy rights of a religious minority. In fact,
certainly in North America, other minority religious groups have suffered
far more public persecution than the Jews. This point often makes com-
parisons between modern European Jewish history and modern North
American Jewish history rather spurious. Such forms of public persecution as pogroms and forced conversions are not part of the Jewish experience in North America, whereas they have been part of the experience of
such groups as Mormons, Quakers, and Roman Catholics. Despite this
historical fact, the liberal Jewish stance portrays Jews as if Jews are the
most vulnerable religious minority in the history of North America,
which, in fact, they are not and have never been.

In a political, or more specifically a legal context (the courts being the
place where this type of Jewish advocacy has usually been conducted, and
where it has won some significant legal victories), I see this liberal stance
as "assimilationist" because it does not allow Jews to speak in the public
square as Jews sui generis, but completely assimilates them into a larger
class of anonymous private citizens.[3] In a social context, it is equally assimilationist because it assimilates Jews into a larger class of "victims of
public persecution" (which usually turns out to be, at most, social rather
than strictly political or legal pressure to conform). Since this approach
to public policy has ruled out a truly distinct Jewish voice from speaking
in public ab initio, it would consider "Jewish public policy" a political
oxymoron. By its principles, what is "Jewish" must be kept private, and
what is "public" kept "nonsectarian."[4]

Furthermore, it is important to bear in mind that this type of liberal
advocacy, which wants religious claims to be kept *out of* the public

---

[3] This type of political liberalism, which bases itself on the primary individualism of the
right to privacy, has been the subject of much philosophical critique of late by a number of
thinkers generally considered "communitarian." See, e.g., Alasdair MacIntyre, *After Virtue*
(Notre Dame, Ind.: University of Notre Dame Press, 1984); Charles Taylor, "The Politics
of Recognition," *Philosophical Arguments* (Cambridge, Mass.: Harvard University Press,
1995), 225–56.

[4] In marked opposition to the whole approach of Pfeffer et al., among some younger
American Jewish thinkers, see *American Jews and the Separationist Faith*, ed. D. G. Dalin
(Washington, D.C.: Ethics and Public Policy Center, 1993).

square, is essentially different from that which wants racial or ethnic barriers to participation *in* the public square abolished. Based on this difference, one should applaud the efforts of some secular Jewish organizations to eliminate racial segregation, and the reverse racial segregation of affirmative-action-type quotas, from all spheres of public life. But it is too bad that these same organizations do not see the similarity between efforts to keep religions *and* racial or ethnic minorities out of the public square. Such exclusionary efforts, based on prejudice against particular races or ethnic groups, are as unjustified as the opposite attempts to privilege one religion or one racial/ethnic group. The true task of such political advocacy should be to promote the social inclusion of all and the social privilege of none.[5]

The sectarian stand, conversely, is one that has characterized much of the public policy advocacy of the Orthodox Jewish communities in North America. Unlike the liberal, assimilationist stand, which basically claims for Jews the right to maximal participation in public life in a way totally separate from their private Jewish claims, the sectarian stand has been one that argues for maximal Jewish separation from public life and its claims. Whereas the liberals want a place in the public square for Jews who are unencumbered by their Judaism, the sectarians want an increasing number of exemptions for Jews from the public square altogether. Indeed, they want their exceptionalism to be the basis of their claims on the public for maximal practice of their own, seemingly peculiar, privacy. It would seem they want religiously observant Jews to be tolerated in our society as we tolerate such arcane "sects" as the Amish. Thus, whereas the liberals want Jews to be in the public square as much as possible in anonymous garb, the sectarians want to wear their distinctive garb (both literally and figuratively) as much as possible in their own protected enclaves. And, whereas liberals usually invoke the language of universalism ("everyone ought to be enabled to do X"), sectarians usually invoke the language of the conscientious objector ("we alone ought to be enabled to do Y").[6]

The best example of the difference between these two seemingly opposite Jewish stands on public policy questions per se is that of public funding for parochial or religious day schools. The liberals, whose greatest

[5] For a critique of the strict separationist view by a Christian social theorist whose views have gained increasing influence on more socially conservative Jews, see Richard John Neuhaus, *The Naked Public Square* (Grand Rapids, Mich.: Eerdmans, 1984). For the most recent critique of the inability of liberal thinkers to recognize a true place for religiously based participation in a democracy, see J. Judd Owen, *Religion and the Demise of Liberal Rationalism* (Chicago: University of Chicago Press, 2001).

[6] Some of the most important Orthodox arguments have been made by the constitutional lawyer Nathan Lewin. For some of his briefs and related materials, see J. D. Sarna and D. G. Dalin, *Religion and State in the American Jewish Experience* (Notre Dame, Ind.: University of Notre Dame Press, 1997), 271–81.

battles (and many victories) have been over issues of religious practices in the public schools, have been opposed to public funding for parochial schools (like current proposals for school vouchers) because it violates the strict separation of church and state (to which they hold with a dogmatic literalism). No public support of any religious institution, no matter how pluralistic, can be tolerated without opening the door for the religious takeover of civil society by the most dominant religious community in that society—in their view. As such, only state-run schools can be truly neutral. The sectarians, conversely, argue in favor of public funding for parochial schools as not only a negative right (that is, a right not to have the state dictate where one's children are to be educated, as long as the parochial school fulfills minimal, state mandated, educational criteria), but also as a positive entitlement.

The theory behind this sectarian approach to the education of children is twofold. One, there is the economic argument, which appeals to the common good. It is argued that it is cheaper for the state to provide a voucher for parents to send their children to schools that are legally private (since only part of their funding comes from the state) than it is for the state to provide full education to all children for free. Two, and far more significant, there is the real political argument. It is argued that the virtual monopoly of public schools in the area of the mandatory education of children has led to an undemocratic overextension of the power of the state in the social life of its citizens, especially in the area of moral education.

There is no doubt that the Orthodox approach to public policy questions is faithful to the normative Jewish tradition, yet it does not seem to be able to cogently advocate public policy for the secular society in which Jews are fully enfranchised citizens. In other words, it still seems to assume that Jews are political outsiders who can only engage in special pleading. Nevertheless, it seems that while the liberal or assimilationist approach ignores the specific strictures of the normative Jewish tradition, it does cogently recognize the full political enfranchisement of the Jews in North American societies. It recognizes quite well the fact that in these societies Jews are not the external objects of a foreign polity (as they were in premodern times), but very much active subjects within the political process of these societies. This being the case, I would like to suggest here a possible Jewish public policy on the religion-state question. It is hoped that this suggestion will incorporate Orthodox fidelity to the Torah and the Jewish normative tradition (especially as defined by halakhah), and that it will incorporate liberal Jewish interest in the larger public realm that we Jews necessarily and happily actively participate in. The background in Jewish social contract thinking we have been exploring in the previous chapters should indicate that even the Orthodox, who are steeped in the Jewish tradition, have not yet discovered or even accessed the riches Jewish tradition holds for preparing Jews to negotiate the social contract in a secular, democratic society from a position of true theological and historical strength.

Criteria for Jewish Public Policy

The vast majority of Jews in the world today would agree that the best place for Jewish life to survive, and flourish, is in a democracy.[7] This is why almost all Jews who can choose where they want to live have chosen to live in democracies like the United States and Canada. Even most of the increasing number of Jews who have chosen to live in the State of Israel have chosen to live there primarily because it is a democracy. And even those religious Jews who have chosen to live in the land of Israel because it has a unique sanctity for Jews do not regard Israel's democracy as a reason to prevent them from living there. And even those religious Jews who want the State of Israel to become a state fully governed by halakhah would only want that transition to come about through democratic means, namely, through the choice of the vast majority of Jews in Israel (and probably in the whole Diaspora as well). In other words, very few religious Jews would want a religious state imposed on the rest of the Jews through an antidemocratic coup d'état. (This is why the followers of the late, explicitly antidemocratic Meir Kahane are a fringe group even in Jewish religious circles, almost as much as those *haredi* or ultra-Orthodox groups who refuse to recognize the national sovereignty of the State of Israel de jure and sometimes even de facto as well.) Therefore, it is quite certain that contemporary Jews want to be full participants in any democracy in which they live, be it in Israel or the Diaspora, and that they want to be more than simply tolerated guests as they had been in almost all premodern, non-Jewish societies. This means they not only want to follow somebody else's public policy proposals, but that they want to propose some of their own. Specifically, what can Jews propose to the secular, democratic society at large concerning religion-state relations that it is possible for that society to accept with democratic integrity?

There should be three criteria to guide any Jewish public policy proposal: (1) the Torah and Jewish tradition; (2) Jewish communal interest; (3) the common good of the larger society in which we participate. Furthermore, the invocation of these three criteria should be internally consistent, that is, there should be no contradiction between an argument from

---

[7] See D. Novak, *Covenantal Rights* (Princeton, N.J.: Princeton University Press, 2000), 29–31, 204–205.

Torah and tradition, an argument from Jewish communal interest, and an argument from concern for the common good of a secular society. So, when there is any public policy issue calling for a Jewish position to be taken, the following questions should be asked: (1) What should a traditional Jewish position be on this issue on this issue of public policy? (2) How should this position be argued to Jews themselves? (3) How should this position be argued to others?

As for a first criterion for a Jewish public policy position, it is only when it is grounded in the Torah and Jewish tradition that it has any Jewish authenticity.[8] Happily, in Western democracies like the United States and Canada, the right of religious freedom is not simply an entitlement from the state. It is recognized by most to be a positive right prior to the power of state, which the state is duty bound to respect—to confirm rather than initiate. This means one not only has the right to worship as one pleases (which usually means the right to affiliate with the worshiping community of one's choice), but also such humanly received rights as the right to base one's moral actions (that is, actions that pertain to interhuman affairs) on what one's religious tradition accepts as the will of God. Only a religious affiliation, as opposed to mere ethnic or racial identity, comes with its own morality built in. For most people in North America (but probably not in Europe anymore), their religious outlook and their moral outlook are inextricably intertwined. Therefore, the right of the free exercise of one's religion is prior to the state's duty to protect it. But in order for Jews to properly exercise our religious morality in public, we must understand what it demands of us first, that is, what it requires us to do ("thou shalt") and what it requires us not to do ("thou shalt not").

The fact that a group of Jews, even a large group of Jews, can and do advocate policies that are contrary to the Torah and Jewish tradition, even if these claims are only made on fellow Jews, does not make these policies *Jewish* in a coherent way. Thus, for example, there is a publicly identifiable group of Jews who have adopted Christianity, yet who still consider themselves Jews and believe their Christianity to be a form of Judaism. They usually designate themselves "Messianic Jews." Yet, why has there been unanimous rejection of their "Jewish" claims by the entire Jewish community? The only cogent answer is because the Jewish tradition has unambiguously taught that Christianity is no longer a part of Judaism, and that any Jew who practices Christianity has betrayed the Torah and Jewish tradition in a radical way—even though as individuals they are

---

[8] The most famous enunciation of this principle was made by the the ninth-century Jewish theologian Saadiah Gaon in his *The Book of Beliefs and Opinions*, 3.7, trans. S. Rosenblatt (New Haven: Yale University Press, 1948), p. 158: "Furthermore, our nation of the children of Israel is a nation only by virtue of its laws."

still regarded by religious Jews as part of the Jewish people because Jewish identity is irrevocable (and this is by religious, not racial, criteria).[9] This is the most extreme example, but the general principle behind it has wider application.

Let me cite another less extreme example of this point about the centrality of the Torah and tradition in presenting "a"—not *the*—Jewish view on any question of public policy. About twenty years or so ago, several Jewish scholars, myself included, were invited by a major Jewish organization to write essays on four or five general social and political issues from "a Jewish point of view." When the papers were completed, we were to meet with a committee charged with editing and publishing them under the imprimatur of this prestigious organization. Of the papers written, only one provoked any real controversy, the one on the question of abortion, a topic about which the author is an acknowledged expert. Even though this scholar recognized that Jewish tradition permits, sometimes even mandates, an abortion when the fetus presents a threat to the life or health of the mother, he honestly admitted that there is no right to abortion sanctioned by the normative tradition. As such, the debate among traditional legal authorities is not about whether there is a right to abortion; rather, there is only debate about the extent of the range of threats to the mother that can justify an abortion as a dispensation from a general prohibition. (The author of the paper himself recognized a wider range of such threats to the mother than do many—but not all—traditional halakhic authorities.)[10] This is why abortion has always been extremely rare among traditional Jews. In other words, no matter how many such threats one designates, the assumption is that abortion itself is prohibited, and that the burden of proof is on the mother and her advocates to show why there should be dispensation from this prohibition. It is a situation in which the burden of proof is on the accuser, that is, the mother who is accusing her fetus of being a direct threat to her life or her health.[11]

When this paper on abortion was presented to the committee for editing and final approval, the vigorous controversy began. One member of the committee, a professor of social work at a prominent American university,

[9] See D. Novak, *The Election of Israel* (Cambridge: Cambridge University Press, 1995), 189–99.

[10] For the range of traditional Jewish opinions on abortion, all of which recognize specific cases where abortion is mandated, and none of which recognizes any general right to abortion, see David M. Feldman, *Birth Control in Jewish Law* (New York: New York University Press, 1968), 251–94.

[11] The main rabbinic sources are M. Ohalot 7.6; *B.* Sanhedrin 72b; Maimonides, MT: Rotseah, 1.9. Also, see D. Novak, *Law and Theology in Judaism* 1 (New York: KTAV, 1974), 114–24; *Covenantal Rights*, 28–31. For the rabbinic principle of the burden of proof being on the accuser, see B. Baba Kama 46a—b.

protested that the paper did not reflect her opinions or those of her Jewish colleagues and friends. At this point, I entered the debate. I reminded the objector that the papers were not sociological surveys of what various American Jews think about the issues researched. Rather, they were about what the traditional Jewish sources say about these issues. Sometimes there is great debate within the sources themselves on a given issue, as, for example, that of capital punishment: Some are in favor; others are opposed (at least de facto).[12] However, despite the "pro-choice" opinions of the objector and her colleagues and friends, there is no such debate about elective abortion in the Jewish tradition. The only debate is about the extent of the legitimate exceptions to the prohibition of abortion.[13] So I suggested to her that she write a counterpaper to the one she so opposed, and show what is truly *Jewish* about her opinion other than the obviously "Jewish" name of its author. Indeed, it would have been interesting if she had accepted my challenge, but to my knowledge no such counterpaper was written. One could say that such a paper was not written because it could not have been written as "a Jewish point of view" with any real cogency. Accordingly, primary attention should be paid to the question of what Judaism requires of Jews among themselves. Only then can Jews go out into the world to tell the world what is required of them too. This, of course, is less than what Jewish tradition requires of Jews themselves.

Now there are, of course, great debates among Jews as to what exactly constitutes Torah and tradition, what makes them authoritative, and how they are to be applied to current situations where moral judgment on the part of the Jews is called for. Unfortunately, for contemporary Jews, there is not the type of consensus that pertained when the Jews accepted the Torah at Mount Sinai in Moses' version of it. Nor is there the type of consensus that pertained when the Jews accepted Ezra's designation of the correct text of the Written Torah.[14] Nor is there the same type of consensus that pertained when the Jews accepted the Babylonian Talmud as the authoritative interpretation, application, and elaboration of the Written Torah.[15] Nor is there the same type of consensus that pertained when the Jews accepted the *Shulhan Arukh* of R. Joseph Karo to be the most authoritative code of Jewish law. Nor is there the type of consensus that pertained, quite recently, when almost all Jews everywhere accepted the "Law of Return" (*hoq ha-shevut*), which asserted the right of any Jew anywhere to return to the land of Israel and receive Israeli citizenship

---

[12] See D. Novak, *Jewish Social Ethics* (New York: Oxford University Press, 1992), 174–80.

[13] See B. Sanhedrin 57b re Gen. 9:6; ibid., 59a and Tos., s.v. "leika."

[14] See 78–80 above.

[15] See B. Sanhedrin 24a and Tos., s.v. "belulah."

immediately. Nevertheless, anyone who speaks in the name of Judaism must be required by both his or her fellow Jews, and by non-Jews if he or she is addressing them in the name of Judaism or even "Jewishness," to demonstrate how what they are saying is not the latest figment of their own imagination. In other words, *Judaism* is a public language that has rules of usage that any speaker of it has inherited not invented.[16] As such these rules must be employed in order for one's Jewish speech to be intelligible—*and* credible.

The first question any Jew should ask him- or herself is not "what does the Jewish religion say about X?" but, rather, "what does *our* holy Torah require *us* to do in situation X?" In other words, "what does *my* God and the God of *my* Jewish ancestors demand of *me* here and now?"[17] The former question could be asked by anyone; the latter, however, could only be asked by a Jew. There can be and there always have been disputes about just *what* is commanded in any specific situation, but there can be no dispute among traditional Jews *that* the Torah does require something be done in any significant human situation; that is, no one in the tradition denies that God spoke to the Jews forever in the commandments of the Torah, commandments that pertain to everything human.[18] Without this sense of divine commandment (*mitsvah*), I do not see how any public proposal can claim to be coherently—that is, traditionally—Jewish. Any Jew who cannot speak in the first person about Judaism cannot speak for Judaism.

Getting back to the question of public funding for religious primary and secondary schools, it is clear that the Torah commands Jews to educate their children in the Torah and Jewish tradition, as well as in ways that enable Jewish children to be productive members of society.[19] Originally it is located in the commandment "you shall teach them [the teachings of the Torah] to your sons" (Deuteronomy 11:19). This original commandment, however, only refers to a one-on-one father-son relationship, which we today would see as informal education or "home schooling" (which, by the way, some parents are demanding that the state recognize as their right).[20] Nevertheless, in most cases, formal education begins when a father delegates a teacher or teachers in a school to fulfill this pedagogical obligation for him.[21] It is understood that most fathers are

---

[16] See Ludwig Wittgenstein, *Philosophical Investigations*, 2nd ed., trans. G.E.M. Anscombe (New York: Macmillan, 1958), 1.18.

[17] This is best expressed in the talmudic principle "greater is one who is commanded and practices than is one who is not commanded and practices" (B. Kiddushin 31a and parallels).

[18] See M. Avot 5.22.

[19] See M. Kiddushin 1.11; B. Kiddushin 29a; also, M. Kiddushin 4.13.

[20] T. Kiddushin 1.8; B. Kiddushin 29b re Deut. 11:19.

[21] Maimonides, MT: Talmud Torah, 1.3.

unable to teach their sons on a regular basis due to either intellectual or emotional or financial impediments. Furthermore, the community must provide schools for those whose fathers cannot pay for their education, or who have no fathers at all.[22] And although the question of formal education required for girls has a long history of discussion in Jewish tradition, the overwhelming consensus today, even in the most traditional circles, is that the obligation to provide primary and secondary education for Jewish girls is practically the same as that for Jewish boys.[23] Most important for our argument here, there is precedent for Jews receiving support for Jewish welfare institutions like schools from non-Jewish sources.[24] In our day, in fact, an even stronger case can be made for actively accepting state aid for Jewish schools since the state is an institution in which Jews participate as equals with non-Jews. In other words, it is possible for Jews to claim such aid as a justified entitlement, perhaps even as part of their prior right to religious liberty, rather than as merely arbitrary charity. But in order to make this claim intelligently, one needs to be aware of the contractual relation between Jews and any secular democratic polity.

As for Jewish communal interest, it is clear that Jewish day schools have contributed much to the Jewish community by educating a more learned and more religiously committed Jewish constituency in North America.

With these two considerations examined, we now must examine the question of Jewish advocacy based on considerations of the common good. This is the question of what Jewish tradition considers required of non-Jews as well as Jews. Accordingly, three questions must be asked: (1) Does Judaism recognize any universal moral norms? (2) If so, how are the gentiles to know in general what the moral norms are? (3) Are Jews obligated to advocate what Judaism considers universal moral norms, and, if so, how?

Unfortunately, as we have seen above, most liberals have totally separated religious advocacy (making it private) and moral advocacy (making it public). Thus, for them, the above questions are meaningless insofar as they presuppose a public presence for a religiously based political morality. So we must turn to orthodox or traditional Jews (whatever their official denominational affiliation) for such answers. We must address our questions to those Jews who follow in the traditional paths, who still look to Scripture and Talmud and the Codes for moral authority, that is, for governance and not just arbitrarily accepted guidance—authority that

---

[22] B. Baba Batra 21a.
[23] See D. Novak, *Law and Theology in Judaism* 2 (New York: KTAV, 1976), 54.
[24] B. Baba Batra 8a and Tos., s.v. "yetiv"; Maimonides, MT: Melakhim, 10.10.

has both a mandate and a veto. It is a sad fact that traditional Jews have lost a common Jewish moral language with those Jews who have strayed from the traditional paths, especially those who have done so with conscious conviction. Traditional Jews can only speak to liberal Jews on general moral issues, alas, as they would speak to morally earnest gentiles. Only on political questions, where one can locate a factor of even secular Jewish self-interest, can traditional Jews sometimes still speak to liberal Jews as Jews.

Jewish Suspicions of General Morality

Before directly dealing with the common good of a multicultural, secular society, we must consider why many Jews, especially many traditional Jews, have lately shied away from such universal involvement.

After the Holocaust, and after the 1967 Six Day War, many Jews are now uncomfortable with talk of a general morality encompassing them along with all others. It is felt that affirming any universal moral criterion is a recipe for obsequiousness and assimilation. This is in large part due to a historical reading of two failed Jewish universalisms in modern times.

One, there is the universalism of pre-Hitler German Jewry (and of their American cousins of German-Jewish origin), who were convinced they could justify the presence of Jews and Judaism in a larger society that seemed to be constituted by universal criteria of justice for all persons. Of course, we all know now that Germany rejected any such universalism beginning in 1933, adopting instead a racist, xenophobic ideology, and that the Jews were its chief victims. In retrospect, then, these German Jews (and, similarly, the French Jews whose devotion to France and the ideals of the French Revolution were betrayed by the Vichy government) are considered to have been dangerous and self-deluded, having assumed a universalism that was not there and had never been there. Perhaps, this type of thinking concludes, Jews would have been better off if they had looked out more for their own particular interests and those of the rest of the Jews instead of looking out for the whole world, as it were.[25]

Two, there is the failed universalism of the Jewish communists, who were convinced that the "Jewish Question" would be solved by the type of egalitarian society the Soviet Union claimed to be building for itself and for the entire world. The fact that this so-called egalitarian project led to one of the worst forms of despotism the world had ever known, and that this communist despotism regarded Jewish participation an ob-

[25] See Gershom Scholem, "Jews and Germans," *Commentary*, 42.5 (1966), 31–38; also, Novak, *Jewish Social Ethics*, 242, n. 42.

stacle to be overcome by any means, led most Jews (even former Jewish communists) to conclude that the universalism of the Jewish communists (whether Stalinists or Trotskyites) was a program for Jews to willingly cooperate in their own cultural and political destruction and, in many cases, their physical destruction as well.

Even if these two universalisms, one liberal and the other socialist, had not turned out to be so anti-Jewish in both theory and practice, there is still, on the one hand, the problem of submitting Jewish public policy positions to judgment by criteria that are not based on Jewish tradition and that regard Jewish communal interest as dispensable. But on the other hand, without the acknowledgment of some kind of general morality, how can Jews possibly participate in a society with non-Jews and be taken seriously as equal participants in that society? Moreover, one cannot say that this is only a problem for Diaspora Jews since it is also a problem for Jews in the State of Israel. How can Israel make a moral case in the increasingly international, global society, and how can Israel justify its rule of non-Jews living in its country, except by an appeal to some sort of universal morality?

The Unavoidability of General Morality

The solution to the above problem, which some have called the "universal-particular" tension in Judaism, is not solved by simply seeing some sort of back and forth or "dialectic" between the two poles. This approach is inadequate because it cannot tell us exactly when the particular trumps the universal and when the universal trumps the particular.[26] Rather, one should see Jewish ascent to universal moral standards as different from ascent to totalizing standards that attempt to include all human relationships within their orbit. Such a morality is not all-inclusive, and certainly not ultimate in its demands. Therefore, to agree to certain universal criteria in making a moral case in a multicultural, pluralistic context does not mean that these criteria are sufficient to govern all aspects of human life, nor does it mean that these criteria even govern the deepest aspects of human life. This universal morality only governs a finite universe: the world of a multicultural society, which essentially differs from the infinite universe of a monocultural society that attempts to rule every aspect of its members' lives. An example from recent American history illustrates this point.

In the United States, one could well say that the most important moral debate the members of society have engaged in for the last fifty years

[26] See D. Novak, *Jewish-Christian Dialogue* (New York: Oxford University Press, 1989), 129–38.

or so is the debate over civil rights, specifically the struggle to end civil disabilities based on race. With the defeat of Nazi racism in World War II quite fresh in most minds, especially in the minds of many Jews, it became increasingly evident that the promise of the Declaration of Independence that "all men are created equal" was being seriously violated in the public treatment of racial minorities, especially those who are now called "African Americans." In fact, one could see *the* debate of twentieth-century America as a continuation of *the* debate of nineteenth-century America: the debate over slavery.

Many Jews were in the forefront of the struggle for civil rights. But was their involvement solely based on universal criteria to the exclusion of what the Torah and tradition and Jewish communal interest would warrant, or was their involvement based on Torah and tradition and Jewish communal interest *with which universal moral criteria are consistent*? In other words, are one's general moral commitments arrived at by circumventing the perspective of Judaism and the Jewish people, or are one's general moral commitments seen as emerging from these two perspectives so that they must be consistent with these two perspectives? This latter approach was best advocated, in both word and deed, by my late revered teacher, Abraham Joshua Heschel (d. 1972). Accordingly, I followed his precept and example and marched in Washington in 1964 on behalf of the passage of the Civil Rights Act, with a *kippah* (skullcap) on my head. And I did so with many fellow Jews and with many gentiles (mostly Christians), whose presence in this civil struggle did not preclude wearing their own distinctive religious garb with all its significance, both literal and symbolic. Certainly Jews could sympathize with the civil disabilities suffered by many black Americans. Hence the civil rights struggle could be seen as a matter of concern for the Jewish community, and indeed it was, to the great credit of the Jewish community.

Here there was no conflict between universal morality, Jewish tradition, and Jewish communal self-interest. There is only a conflict when Jews become "universalists" in the sense of advocating a totalizing and doctrinaire criterion of *egalitarianism*, even elevating it to a level of ultimate concern. When this happens, though, the separation necessary for the specific life of Jews and Judaism in such areas as marriage and worship is deeply (and perhaps fatally) compromised. In and of itself, Jewish involvement in the civil rights struggle has been consistent with the Torah and Tradition and with Jewish communal self-interest. Thus this involvement has been consistent with the Torah's teaching that there be one standard of interhuman justice (*mishpat ehad*) in civil society.[27]

We can now return to the question of how Jews can advocate criteria of universal morality in good faith.

[27] See Novak, *Natural Law in Judaism*, 76–82.

Many orthodox Jews would answer that just as God commanded a specific morality to the Jews, so God commanded a more universal morality to the gentiles. And just as God's law to the Jews is written in the Torah and the Rabbinic writings, so is God's law to the gentiles written there. Therefore, in order for the gentiles to know their moral obligations, they have to ask the Jews, which means they have to submit to the moral authority of Judaism.[28] Now, in and of itself, this position is not morally offensive since it is not the type of imperialism that would make slaves out of outsiders, slavery occurring when a politically or even culturally dominant group makes more stringent rules for outsiders it controls than for insiders who control them. But Judaism has more stringent rules for Jews than it does for any gentiles who come under Jewish authority.[29]

Nevertheless, this approach is irrational and undemocratic because it does not answer the obvious question: Why would non-Jews want to come under the moral authority of Jews enforcing Jewish law? (Even in the State of Israel, non-Jews are only living under the *secular* political authority of the Jews, but in religious matters—including marital and most familial matters—they are under the authority of their own *religious* communities. Thus they are not living under Jewish religious authority there.) Why would non-Jews want to live under Jewish religio-moral authority in a second-class status when they could just as easily fully convert to Judaism and thus attain first-class Jewish status? It would seem to require what could be well described as de facto conversion to a particular historical revelation—Judaism—by accepting its moral authority.

Unfortunately, though, this is what is implied much of the time when orthodox Jews advocate "the Jewish position" on any major issue of public morality. This has been especially so in the burgeoning field of biomedical ethics, where there seems to be keen interest in what Judaism and other religious traditions have to say about its fundamental moral questions (although where this general interest will ultimately lead is still quite murky). Moreover, other questions of public morality are being addressed to orthodox Jews, such as the religion-state question, that do not necessarily or even very often involve medical practices. Nevertheless, most of the answers proposed so far, if the experience of orthodox Jewish involvement in biomedical ethics is any guide, will turn out to be politically ineffective because of their philosophical inadequacy—that is, unless another type of moral argumentation is developed by orthodox Jews.

Fortunately, there is a more rationally inclined strand of the normative Jewish tradition that, if properly explicated, enables Jews to teach moral-

---

[28] For a possible source for this notion of a Jewish law for the gentiles, see Maimonides, MT: Melakhim, 10.11; also, D. Novak, *Jewish Social Ethics*, 189–95.

[29] See B. Sanhedrin 59a and parallels; also, B. Yevamot 22a.

ity to the world without, however, requiring conversion to Judaism either de jure (that is, literally requiring gentiles to become Jews for the sake of their moral integrity) or even de facto (that is, requiring gentiles to become the modern equivalents of the ancient "sojourners" or "resident aliens"— *gerei toshav*).[30] This centers around the key rabbinic category of the "Noahide laws," that is, the seven basic normative categories that have been seen as pertaining to all humankind in every time and place (all humankind being seen as the descendants of Noah, that is, those descendants of Adam and Eve, who did not pervert human nature and who thus deserved to survive the cataclysmic Flood). And in the rationalist strand of the Jewish tradition, it is assumed that these normative categories are known through what Maimonides, the greatest rationalist theologian in Judaism, called "rational inclination" (*mipnei hekhre ha-da'at*).[31] In other words, these norms are known through rational reflection on the ordinary, universal, moral experience of the justifiable claims all humans need to make one another and the recognition, therefore, of the unjustifiable claims humans make. Even Judaism presupposes the universal norms while simultaneously requiring more—but never less—of Jews.

Of these seven norms, four are most pertinent to modern moral discourse: (1) the prohibition of taking innocent human life (*shefikhut damim*); (2) the prohibition of sexual license (*gilui arayot*)—specifically the prohibition of incestuous, adulterous, homoerotic, and bestial acts; (3) the prohibition of robbery (*gezel*); (4) the prescription to any society to establish courts of law to enforce, as best it can, the other six categories of Noahide law (*dinim*).

Of the remaining three norms, (5) the prohibition of eating a limb torn from a living animal (*ever min he-hai*); (6) the prohibition of blasphemy (*qilelat ha-shem*); and (7) the prohibition of idolatry (*avodah zarah*), it seems hard to justify them in modern moral discourse. All we can say is that perhaps the prohibition of eating a limb torn from a living animal can be generalized into a rationally cogent prohibition of cruelty to sentient beings (what the Rabbis called "the pain of animals," *tsa'ar ba'alei hayyim*).[32] And perhaps, the prohibition of blasphemy can be generalized into a rationally cogent prohibition of "hate speech" against anyone's religion/god.[33] And perhaps, the prohibition of idolatry can be generalized into a rationally cogent prohibition of a type of modern pagan ideology, like Nazism, that advocates murder, robbery, and rape. Along these lines,

---

[30] See Nahmanides, *Commentary on the Torah*: Gen. 34:13; also, D. Novak, *The Image of the Non-Jew in Judaism* (New York and Toronto: Edwin Mellen Press, 1983), 53–56; *Jewish Social Ethics*, 195–201.

[31] MT: Melakhim, 8.11. See Novak, *The Image of the Non-Jew in Judaism*, 275–318.

[32] See B. Baba Metsia 32a re Deut. 22:4; B. Shabbat 128b.

[33] See Philo, *De Vita Mosis*, 2.205–206 re Exod. 22:28 (Septuagint version).

it should be noted that even though the Jewish tradition has always debated whether non-Jewish religions like Christianity and Islam are idolatrous, there has been a marked tendency in the tradition to respect other religiously based cultures whose general moral commitments are close enough to the Noahide norms Judaism takes to be universal.

Even though a Noahide-like morality can be learned through ordinary human reason, the historical fact is that it is usually learned as part of a richer, more specific religious tradition. Moreover, the sense of absolute obligation, which is so necessary for morality to be more than what is relatively useful to its subjects, is best inculcated when morality is learned as that which is the direct will of God to human beings and is transmitted by religious traditions based on revelation. For this reason, then, it would seem to be in the interest of universal morality that as many children in society receive the most explicitly moral education possible. Thus if education is about discovering truth intellectually, doesn't this process presuppose the moral norm to speak the truth and not lie? And it would seem that a moral education that presents moral norms as divine commandments is more effective than a secular moral education that cannot speak about God at all because it cannot speak about moral absolutes. But such a morally vacuous education has become more and more prevalent in public schools because of the lessening cultural consensus about morality in our secular society.

Nevertheless, those who have been educated in a historically "thick" religious morality can be easily taught that there are some norms within that morality that are so universal they do not need to be referred back to a particular revelation and its particular tradition. This affirmation of natural law is easier to make when it is presented as minimal in its demands than as some sort of as yet unrealized higher moral ideal.[34]

This does not mean I am suggesting that public education is not needed in a democratic society. Religious liberty requires that an exclusively secular education be provided for those who do not want a religiously based education for their children. It is similar to the fact that religious liberty requires that civil marriage ceremonies be provided for those who do not want religious marriage ceremonies. Nevertheless, I am suggesting, based on the Jewish obligation to encourage the gentiles to follow universal moral norms, that Jews can encourage state support of religious primary and secondary schools as the best places to foster this type of moral education.[35]

The question now is: How do we Jews translate this moral argument about the benefit of a state-supported religious education into a politically

---

[34] See Joseph Albo, *The Book of Principles*, 1.8. Cf. Thomas Aquinas, *Summa Theologiae*, 2/1, q. 99, a. 2.

[35] For Jewish support of gentile ethical/religious education, see Novak, *Jewish Social Ethics*, 230–32.

effective argument? Clearly, the range of morality is greater than the range of politics since society can only effectively enforce a part of morality.

The Political Argument for the Social Contract

Since no one can really claim to have no history, the current idea of social contract has to present it as a hypothetical construct. But since experience is a better foundation for practical reason than is hypothesis, would it not be more rational to look upon the social contract—better, social contracts—as real events in history made between people who have histories and do not want to forget them (that is, to be ignorant of them and their claims for continuity into the future)?[36] One can look at the acceptance of the Declaration of Independence in 1776, the ratification of the U.S. Constitution in 1788; or the acceptance of the Canadian Articles of Confederation in 1867, and the ratification of the Canadian constitution in 1982, as such events of social contract. The parties to these social contracts are not lone (autonomous) individuals but, rather, fully communal, socialized, historically situated persons. Canadians, with their idea of "founding peoples," have a clearer conceptualization of historical social contracts than do most Americans, even though most Canadians are still unclear whether "founding people" is an essentially religious—as in "French Catholics" and "English Protestants"—or an essentially racial/ethnic term—as in "Québecois" and "Anglos." Furthermore, the social contract is constantly renegotiated in every popular election of a government and in every debate on public policy in which moral principles are invoked.

Unlike the morality with which they entered the social contract, the sovereignty of the people who enter said contract is relative. That is, the people confer on the state its legitimacy, but their own existential legitimacy is conferred upon them by a law whose author they are not. When living according to their higher law in public, or when advocating some of its norms for the larger society by rational argument, religious citizens are exercising their religious liberty in the most politically significant way possible. The right to educate one's children, and the concomitant right of all others to educate theirs, comes from the prior realm *from which* we all entered *into* the social contract in a democratic society. Religious citizens can identify this prior realm in a real historical community rather than in an abstract "state of nature" or "original position."[37]

What a historical idea of social contract does is to confirm that the establishment of the secular state as the governing structure of civil society

[36] See D. Novak, *Natural Law in Judaism* (Cambridge: Cambridge University Press, 1998), 12–26.

[37] Cf. John Rawls, *A Theory of Justice* (Cambridge, Mass.: Harvard University Press, 1971), 122–50.

inherits more than it creates. Thus the state creates such institutions as the national currency, the military, official government institutions like the legislature, the judiciary, the administration, and the head of state. But what the state inherits from the overlapping histories of its contracting citizens is the fundamental law under which they live and that enables them to enter into any contract, public (social) or private with any real integrity. Thus, despite that the United States formally severed its political ties to Britain, it maintained its normative connection to English common law (which sees itself as rooted in the law of God). And our current understanding of civil marriage is very much part of that legacy.[38] Accordingly, in a very significant way, one can say that the state comes into existence to promote what its citizens have *already* accepted as moral law, not that the moral law is the creation of the state or even the social contract that created the state. It is only revolutions like the French Revolution of 1789, the German Revolution of 1933, and the Russian Revolution of 1917, that attempted to recreate the entire legal, social, and cultural order. And we all know too well the horrendous political, legal, social, and cultural results of these "godlike" attempts by new states—in the persons of their totalitarian rulers—to create totally new societies, indeed, totally new human beings.

One could well say that one of the primary reasons for the willingness of citizens of the United States and Canada to enter (affirm) or remain loyal to (confirm) the social contract of their respective societies is because these societies have in effect promised to preserve and enhance cultural institutions like heterosexual, procreative marriage, intergenerational families, and religious communal education, which the majority of the citizens of the state have *brought with them* into the new polity. (Thus it is significant that the United States, which refers to itself as a *novus ordo*, nonetheless does not regard its law as unprecedented.)

Since Jews, even by the admission of many friends and enemies, have as strong and coherent a tradition as can be found anywhere—especially as it pertains to moral education—it would seem that Jews, who are unambivalently committed to that tradition, ought to recognize the benefit to society as a whole by having the state not only tolerate the religious education of those children whose parents are committed to it, but should partially support it as well. This can be represented as a requirement of political advocacy for Jews in the larger secular society in which they live and where they are, happily, fully enfranchised as political equals alongside their fellow citizens.

---

[38] See John Witte, Jr., *From Sacrament to Contract* (Louisville, Ky.: Westminster John Knox Press, 1997).

Jewish Self-Interest and Political Alliances

It is an old Jewish question whether the Torah was given for the sake of the Jews or the Jews were chosen for the sake of the Torah.[39] However, there is actually a dialectic at work between these two positions. On the one hand, if the Torah was given for the sake of the Jews, then Jewish self-interest is itself Torah. If, on the other hand, the Jews were chosen for the Torah, then Jewish self-interest cannot identify itself with the Torah, but must justify itself by the Torah that transcends it. This also implies that the Torah was truly given for all humankind, and that the Jews are the only people so far to have accepted it fully.[40] I think one can correlate these two positions as follows: Since the Jews are the custodians of the Torah in this world, on any public policy question they should first ask themselves: Is this good or bad for the Jewish community? But since the Torah's intent begins but does not end with the Jews, they should ultimately ask themselves: Is this good or bad for humankind? The fact of the election of the Jews should persuade them that nothing that is bad for the Jewish people can be good for humankind. God did not condemn the rest of humankind when he chose the Jews for a special covenantal relationship. And the fact of Jewish custodianship of the Torah, ultimately for the sake of all humankind, should persuade Jews that nothing that is truly good for humankind can be bad for them.

Of course, this benefit has taken place within our *secular* society. Most Jews are happy to be living *within* secular society as first-class citizens rather than in a society *under* Christian or Muslim rule as resident-aliens. Nevertheless, Jews should be wary of current *secularism*, which is the view that society requires no transcendent justification for its existence and its moral authority. Whereas religious people can make a religiously based commitment to a secular society and not require it be made by everyone, doctrinaire *secularists* cannot accept any such religiously based commitment as valid for anyone. And although secularism is only one moral point of view among several in our society and culture, it often claims to be the only possible philosophical foundation for democracy, thus rejecting any view that bases itself on a transcendent justification to be hopelessly undemocratic, even antidemocratic.

Traditional Jews cannot, in good faith, make common cause with such secularists in our society, even though too many traditional Jews still do not understand this point very well. But Jews can make common cause

[39] See M. Makkot 3.16 re Isa. 42:21. Cf. B. Pesahim 68b re Jer. 32:25; also, Novak, *The Election of Israel*, 241–48.

[40] See *Sifre*: Devarim, no. 343; also, *Mekhilta*: Yitro, ed. Horovitz-Rabin, p. 205; also, T. Sotah 8.6.

with those traditional Christians (the chance of any common cause with Muslims at the present time is remote because of the Arab-Israeli conflict) whose immediate and long-range public interests are threatened by the type of militant secularism that opposes any public support of religious education.[41] (On the question of public funding of religious education, for significant historical reasons, the secularist threat is much more acute in the United States than it is in Canada, even though doctrinaire secularism is more powerful in Canada than in the United States.)

Jewish advocacy for such things as public support for religiously based education *for whichever community requires it* is very much a way Jews can exercise political responsibility in the secular order in which they now live. It is both an exercise of their religious right to continue their traditional way of life across generations, and it is their religious duty to support the common good of a society that truly facilitates their living a traditional Jewish way of life in its midst. Knowledge of the history, theology, philosophy, and rhetoric of Jewish social-contract thinking will surely help Jews advocate public policies that are good for all in the deepest sense. In this way, then, Jews have much to learn about the social contract from their own tradition, and much to teach members of other traditions, and even the secular world, about how to understand the moral and political power of the idea of the social contract for the true justification of democratic society.

---

[41] See chap. 7 above for the discussion of how the fairly recent new Jewish-Christian relationship can be employed by advocates of the Jewish social contract.

Bibliography

Classical Judaic Texts

Abraham ben David (Ravad). *Commentary on the Mishnah* in *Mishnayot*.
———. *Commentary on Sifra* in *Sifra*.
———. *Hasagot ha-Ravad* in Maimonides. *Mishneh Torah*.
Abravanel, Isaac. *Commentary on the Former Prophets*. Reprint. Jerusalem: Torah ve-Daat. 1956.
———. *Commentary on the Latter Prophets*. Reprint. Jerusalem: Torah ve-Daat. 1956.
———. *Commentary of the Torah*. Warsaw: Lebensohn. 1862.
Albo, Joseph. *Book of Principles*. 5 vols. Edited and translated by I. Husik. Philadelphia: Jewish Publication Society of America. 1929–30.
Alfasi, Isaac (Rif). *Digest of the Talmud* in *Babylonian Talmud*.
Apocrypha and Pseudepigrapha of the Old Testament. 2 vols. Edited by R. H. Charles. Oxford: Clarendon Press. 1913.
Asher ben Yehiel (Rosh). *Commentary on the Talmud* in *Babylonian Talmud*.
———. *Teshuvot ha-Rosh*. Zolkov: n.p. 1803.
Avot de-Rabbi Nathan. Edited by S. Schechter. Reprint. New York: Feldheim. 1967.
Babylonian Talmud (Bavli). 20 vols. Vilna; Romm. 1898.
Bemidbar Rabbah in *Midrash Rabbah*.
Beresheet Rabbah. 3 vols. Edited by A. Theodor and C. Albeck. Reprint. Jerusalem: Wahrmann. 1965.
Biblia Hebraica. 7th ed. Edited by R. Kittel. Stuttgart: Privileg. Württ. Bibelanstalt. 1951.
Boten, Abraham de. *Lehem Mishneh* in Maimonides. *Mishneh Torah*.
Devarim Rabbah in *Midrash Rabbah*.
Diqduqei Sofrim. 2 vols. Edited by R. Rabbinovicz. Reprint. New York: M. P. Press. 1976.
Eikhah Rabbati in *Midrash Rabbah*.
Esther Rabbah in *Midrash Rabbah*.
Gersonides (Ralbag). *Commentary on the Latter Prophets* in *Miqraot Gedolot*: Prophets and Writings.
Hagahot Maimoniyot in Maimonides. *Mishneh Torah*.
Halevi, David (Taz). *Turei Zahav* in *Shulhan Arukh*.
Halevi, Judah. *Kuzari*. Translated by Y. Even-Shmuel. Tel Aviv: Dvir. 1972.
(Rabbenu) Hananel. *Commentary on the Talmud* in *Babylonian Talmud*.
Heller, Yom Tov Lippmann. *Tosfot Yom Tov* in *Mishnayot*.
Holy Scriptures. 3 vols. English translation. Philadelphia: Jewish Publication Society of America. 1962–82.
Ibn Adret, Solomon. *Hiddushei ha-Rashba*. 3 vols. Jerusalem: n.p. 1963.

Ibn Adret, Solomon. *Sheelot u-Teshuvot ha-Rashba*. 5 vols. B'nai Brak: n.p. 1958.

Ibn Atar, Hayyim. *Or ha-Hayyim* in *Miqraot Gedolot*: Pentateuch.

Ibn Ezra, Abraham. *Commentary on the Torah*. 3 vols. Edited by A. Weiser. Jerusalem: Mosad ha-Rav Kook. 1977.

Ibn Habib, Joseph. *Nimuqei Yosef on Alfasi* in *Babylonian Talmud*.

Ibn Zimra, David. *Radbaz* in Maimonides. *Mishneh Torah*.

Isaac bar Sheshet Parfat. *Sheelot u-Teshuvot ha-Rivash*. Reprint. Jerusalem: n.p. 1975.

Ishbili, Yom Tov ben Abraham. *Hiddushei ha-Ritva*. 3 vols. Warsaw: n.p. 1902.

Isserles, Moses (Rema). *Notes on Shulhan Arukh* in *Shulhan Arukh*.

Jacob ben Asher, *Arbaah Turim*. 7 vols. Reprint. Jerusalem: Feldheim. 1969.

Jacob of Marvege. *Sheelot u-Teshuvot min ha-Shamayim*. Edited by R. Margaliot. Jerusalem: Mosad ha-Rav Kook. n.d.

Jacob Tam. *Kol Bo*. Edition Naples. B'nai Brak: n.p. 2002.

Joseph Bekhor Shor. *Commentary on the Torah*. Edited by Y. Nevo. Jerusalem: Mosad Ha-Rav Kook. 1994

Josephus. *Against Apion*. Translated by H. St. John Thackeray. Cambridge, Mass.: Harvard University Press. 1926.

———. *Jewish Antiquities*. 8 vols. English translation. Cambridge, Mass.: Harvard University Press. 1927–65.

Karo, Joseph. *Bet Yosef* in *Arbaah Turim*.

———. *Kesef Mishneh* in Maimonides, *Mishneh Torah*.

———. *Shulhan Arukh*. 7 vols. Lemberg: Balaban. 1873.

Kimhi, David. *Commentary on the Latter Prophets* in *Miqraot Gedolot: Prophets and Writings*.

Loewe, Judah. *Gevurot ha-Shem*. Cracow: n.p. 1582.

Maimonides. *Commentary on the Mishnah*. 3 vols. Translated by Y. Kafih. Jerusalem: Mosad ha-Rav Kook. 1964–67.

———. *Guide of the Perplexed*. Translated by S. Pines. Chicago: University of Chicago Press. 1963.

———. *Mishneh Torah*. 12 vols. Edited by S. Frankel. B'nai Brak: Shabse Frankel. 2001.

———. *Sefer ha-Mitsvot*. Edited by C. B. Chavel. Jerusalem: Mosad ha-Rav Kook. 1981.

———. *Teshuvot ha-Rambam*. 3 vols. Edited by J. Blau. Jerusalem: Miqitsei Nirdamim. 1960.

Margolis, Moses. *Pnei Mosheh* in *Palestinian Talmud* (ed. Pietrkov).

Masekhet Soferim. Reprint. Jerusalem: Sifre Ramot. 2000.

Megillat Taanit. Edition Amsterdam. Reprint. Jerusalem: n.p. 1997.

(ha-) Meiri, Menahem. *Bet ha-Behirah*: Avodah Zarah. Edited by A. Sofer. Jerusalem: Qedem. 1964.

———. *Bet ha-Behirah*: Avot. Edited by B. Z. Prag. Jerusalem: Makhon ha-Talmud ha-Yisraeli ha-Shalem. 1964.

———. *Bet ha-Behirah*: Baba Kama. Edited by K. Schlesinger. Jerusalem: n.p. 1967.

———. *Bet ha-Behirah*: Nedarim. Edited by A. Liss. Jerusalem: Makhon ha-Talmud ha-Yisraeli ha-Shalem. 1974.

————. *Bet ha-Behirah*: Sanhedrin. 2nd ed. Edited by A. Sofer. Jerusalem: n.p. 1965.

Mekhilta (de-Rabbi Ishmael). Edited by S. H. Horovitz and I. A. Rabin. Reprint. Jerusalem: Wahrmann. 1960.

Midrash Aggadah. Edited by S. Buber. Vienna: A. Fanto. 1894.

Midrash ha-Gadol: Beresheet. Edited by M. Margulies. Jerusalem: Mosad ha-Rav Kook. 1947.

Midrash Leqah Tov. 2 vols. Edited by S. Buber. Vilna: Romm. 1884.

Midrash Rabbah. 2 vols. Reprint. New York: E. Grossman. 1957.

Midrash Tanhuma. 2 vols. Edited by S. Buber. Reprint. Jerusalem: n.p. 1964.

Miqraot Gedolot: Pentateuch. 5 vols. Reprint. New York: Otsar ha-Sefarim. 1953.

Miqraot Gedolot: Prophets and Writings. 3 vols. Reprint. New York: Pardes. 1951.

Mishnah. 6 vols. Edited by C. Albeck. Tel Aviv: Mosad Bialik and Dvir. 1957.

Mishnayot. 12 vols. Reprint. New York: M. P. Press. 1969.

Mordecai ben Hillel Ashkenazi. *Mordecai* in *Babylonian Talmud*.

Moses of Coucy. *Sefer Mitsvot Gadol*. Reprint. Brooklyn: n.p. 1959.

Nahmanides. *Commentary on the Torah*. 2 vols. ed. C. B. Chavel. Jerusalem: Mosad ha-Rav Kook. 1959–63.

————. *Hiddushei ha-Ramban*. 2 vols. B'nai Brak: n. p. 1959.

————. *Kitvei Ramban*. 2 vols. Edited by C. B. Chavel. Jerusalem: Mosad ha-Rav Kook. 1963.

————. *Notes on Sefer ha-Mitsvot* in Maimonides. *Sefer ha-Mitsvot*.

————. *Teshuvot ha-Ramban*. Edited by C. B. Chavel. Jerusalem: Mosad ha-Rav Kook. 1975.

Nissim Gerondi (Ran). *Commentary on B. Nedarim* in *Babylonian Talmud*.

————. *Derashot ha-Ran*. Edited by L. A. Feldman. Jerusalem: Institute Shalem. 1973.

Palestinian Talmud (Yerushalmi). Edition Pietrkov. 7 vols. Reprint. Jerusalem: n.p. 1959.

————. Edition Venice. Reprint. New York: Yam ha-Talmud. 1948.

————. Ms. Leiden. Edited by Y. Sussmann. Jerusalem: Academy of the Hebrew Language. 2001.

Pesiqta Rabbati. Edited by M. Friedmann. Reprint. Jerusalem: n.p. 1963.

Philo. *De Vita Mosis*. Translated by F. H. Colson in *Philo*. vol.6. Cambridge, Mass.: Harvard University Press. 1935.

Pirqei de-Rabbi Eliezer. Reprint. Antwerp: Hotsaaat Sefarim Yam. n.d.

Rashi. *Commentary on the Former Prophets* in *Miqraot Gedolot*: Prophets and Writings.

————. *Commentary of the Latter Prophets* in *Miqraot Gedolot*: Prophets and Writings.

————. *Commentary on the Talmud* in *Babylonian Talmud*.

————. *Commentary on the Torah*. Edited by C. B. Chavel. Jerusalem: Mosad ha-Rav Kook.1982.

————. *Teshuvot Rashi*. Edited by I. Elfenbein. New York: n.p. 1943.

Saadiah Gaon. *The Book of Beliefs and Opinions*. Translated by S. Rosenblatt. New Haven, Conn.: Yale University Press. 1948.

Samson of Sens. *Tosfot Shants* in *Babylonian Talmud*.

Samuel ben Meir (Rashbam). *Commentary on the Talmud* in *Babylonian Talmud*.

Samuel ben Meir (Rashbam). *Commentary on the Torah*. Edited by A. Bromberg. Jerusalem: n.p. 1969.

Sanhedrei Gedoloah. 3 vols. Edited by B. Lipkin. Jerusalem: Makhon Harry Fischel. 1970.

Schreiber, Moses. *Sheelot u-Teshuvot Hatam Sofer*. 3 vols. Reprint. New York: E. Grossman. 1958.

Sefer ha-Hinukh. 2 vols. Reprint. New York: A. Y. Friedman. 1966.

Septuaginta. 6th ed. Edited by H. Rahlfs. Stuttgart: Privileg. Wurtt. Bibelanstalt. n.d.

Shemot Rabbah in *Midrash Rabbah*.

Shemot Rabbah. Edited by A. Shinan. Jerusalem: Dvir. 1984.

Shir ha-Shirim Rabbah in *Midrash Rabbah*.

Sifra. Edited by I. H. Weiss. Reprint. New York: Om. 1947.

Sifre: Devarim. Edited by Louis Finkelstein. New York: Jewish Theological Seminary of America. 1969.

Sirkes, Joel (Bah). *Bayit Hadash* in *Arbaah Turim*.

Tosafot in *Babylonian Talmud*.

Tosefta. Edited by S. Zuckermandl. Reprint. Jerusalem: Wahrmann. 1937.

Tosefta: Zeraim-Neziqin. 5 vols. Edited by Saul Lieberman. New York: Jewish Theological Seminary of America. 1955–88.

Vayiqra Rabbah. 3 vols. Edited by M. Margulies. Jerusalem: American Academy for Jewish Research. 1953–56.

Yalqut Shimoni. 2 vols. Reprint. New York: Pardes. 1944.

Yom Tov ben Abraham Ishbili, *Hiddushei ha-Ritva*. 3 vols. Reprint. New York: Otsar ha-Sefarim, 1961.

Zohar. 3 vols. Edited by R. Margaliot. Jerusalem: Mosad ha-Rav Kook. 1984.

Zundel, Enoch. *Ets Yosef* in *Midrash Rabbah*.

Modern Judaic Texts

Altmann, Alexander. *Moses Mendelssohn*. University, Ala.: University of Alabama Press. 1973.

American Jews and the Separationist Faith. Edited by D. G. Dalin. Washington, D.C.: Ethics and Public Center. 1993.

Atlas, Samuel. "Ha-ratson ha-Tsibburi be-Tehuqah ha-Talmudit." *Hebrew Union College Annual*. vol. 26. 1955.

Baeck, Leo. *The Essence of Judaism*. Translated by V. Grubenwiser and L. Pearl. London: Macmillan. 1936.

———. "Romantic Religion." *Judaism and Christianity*. Translated by W. Kaufmann. Philadelphia: Jewish Publication Society of America. 1958.

Baer, Yitzhak (Fritz). *Die Juden in Christlichen Spanien*. 2 vols. Berlin: Akademie des Wissenschaft des Judentums. 1929.

———. *A History of the Jews in Christian Spain*. 2 vols. Translated by L. Schoffman, L. Levensohn, H. Halkin. Philadelphia: Jewish Publication Society of America. 1978.

Baron, S. W. *A Social and Religious History of the Jews*. Rev. ed. 18 vols. New York: Columbia University Press. 1958–93.

Biale, D. *Power and Powerlessness in Jewish History.* New York: Schocken. 1986.

Buber, Martin. *Israel and Palestine.* Translated by S. Godman. London: East and West Library. 1952.

Christianity in Jewish Terms. Edited by T. Frymer-Kensky, D. Novak, P. W. Ochs, M. S. Signer. Boulder, Colo.: Westview Press. 2000.

Cohen, Hermann. *Religion of Reason out of the Sources of Judaism.* Translated by S. Kaplan. New York: Frederick Ungar. 1972.

Cohen, Naomi. *Jews in Christian America.* New York: Oxford University Press. 1992.

Elazar, D. J. *Covenant and Civil Society.* New Brunswick, N.J.: Transaction Publishers. 1998.

———. *Covenant and Polity in Biblical Israel.* New Brunswick, N.J.: Transaction Publishers. 1995.

Encyclopedia Judaica. 16 vols. 1972.

Entsyqlopedia Talmudit. 23 vols. 1955–98.

Etz Hayyim. New York: The Rabbinical Assembly and the United Synagogue of Conservative Judaism. 2001.

Federbush, S. *Mishpat ha-Melukhah be-Yisrael.* 2nd rev. ed. Jerusalem: Mosad ha-Rav Kook. 1973.

Feldman, D. M. *Birth Control in Jewish Law.* New York: New York University Press. 1968.

Gordis, Robert. *The Book of God and Man.* Chicago: University of Chicago Press. 1965.

Gulak, A. *Yesodei ha-Mishpat Ha'Ivri.* 2 vols. Tel Aviv: Dvir. 1967.

Halivni, David Weiss. *Peshat and Derash.* New York: Oxford University Press. 1991.

———. *Revelation Restored.* Boulder, Colo.: Westview Press. 1997.

Herzog, Isaac Halevi. *Sheelot u-Teshuvot be-Dinei Orah Hayyim.* Edited by S. Shapira. Jerusalem: Mosad ha-Rav Kook. 1989.

Hoenig, S. B. *The Great Sanhedrin.* Philadelphia: Dropsie College. 1953.

Kasher, M. M. *Torah Shelemah.* 11 vols. Jerusalem: Torah Shelemah Institute. 1992.

Katz, Jacob. *Tradition and Crisis.* New York: Schocken. 1971.

Kaufmann, Yehezkel. *The Religion of Israel.* Translated by M. Greenberg. Chicago: University of Chicago Press. 1960.

Kohut, A. *Aruch Completum.* 9 vols. Tel Aviv: Shiloh, n.d.

Kraut, B. *From Reform Judaism to Ethical Culture.* Cincinnati: Hebrew Union College Press. 1976.

Levy, B. B. *Fixing God's Torah.* New York: Oxford University Press. 2001.

Lewin, B. M. *Otsar ha-Geonim.* 13 vols. Jerusalem: Hebrew University and Mosad ha-Rav Kook. 1929–43.

Lichtenstein, Aharon. "Does Jewish Tradition Recognize an Ethic Independent of Halakha?" in *Modern Jewish Ethics.* Edited by M. Fox. Columbus, Ohio: Ohio State University Press. 1975.

Lieberman, Saul. *Tosefta Kifshuta.* 11 vols. New York: Jewish Theological Seminary of America. 1955–88.

———. *Ha-Yerushalmi Kifshuto.* vol. 1. New York: Jewish Theological Seminary of America. 1995.

Lipschuetz, Israel. *Comentary on the Mishnah (Tiferet Yisrael)* in *Mishnayot*.

Luzzatto, Samuel David (Shadal). *Commentary on the Torah*. Edited by P. Schlesinger. Tel Aviv: Dvir. 1965.

Margaliot, R. *Margaliot ha-Yam*: Sanhedrin. Jerusalem: Mosad ha-Rav Kook. 1977.

Mendelssohn, Moses. *Biur*: Beresheet. Vienna: Anton Schmid. 1818.

———. *Jerusalem* in *Moses Mendelssohns Gesammelte Schriften: Jubilaumausgabe*. vol. 8. Edited by Alexander Altmann. Stuttgart: Friedrich Fromann. 1983.

———. *Jerusalem*. Translated by A. Arkush. Annotated by Alexander Altmann. Hanover, N.H.: University Press of New England. 1983.

Meyer, Michael A. *Response to Modernity: A History of the Reform Movement in Judaism*. New York: Oxford University Press. 1988.

Netanyahu, B. *Don Isaaac Abravanel*. 5th rev. ed. Ithaca, N.Y.: Cornell University Press. 1998.

Neusner, Jacob. *A History of the Jews in Babylonia*. 2 vols. Leiden: E. J. Brill. 1967.

Novak, David. *Covenantal Rights*. Princeton, N.J.: Princeton University Press. 2000.

———. *The Election of Israel*. Cambridge: Cambridge University Press. 1995.

———. *Halakhah in a Theological Dimension*. Chico, Calif.: Scholars Press. 1985.

———. *The Image of the Non-Jew in Judaism*. New York and Toronto: Edwin Mellen Press. 1983.

———. *Jewish-Christian Dialogue*. New York: Oxford University Press. 1989.

———. "The Jewish Ethical Tradition and the Modern University," *Journal of Education*, no. 180. 1998.

———. "Jewish Marriage and Civil Law: A Two Way Street?" *George Washington Law Review* vol. 68. 2000.

———. *Jewish Social Ethics*. New York: Oxford University Press. 1992.

———. *Law and Theology in Judaism*. vol. 1. New York: KTAV. 1974.

———. *Law and Theology in Judaism*. vol. 2. New York: KTAV. 1976.

———. "Law: Religious or Secular?" *Virginia Law Review*. vol. 86. 2000.

———. *Natural Law in Judaism*. Cambridge: Cambridge University Press. 1998.

———. "Spinoza and the Doctrine of the Election of Israel." *Studia Spinozana*. vol. 13. Edited by S. Nadler, M. Walther, Y. Yakira. Wurzburg: Konighausen und Neumann. 2002.

———. *The Theology of Nahmanides Systematically Presented*. Atlanta, Ga.: Scholars Press. 1992.

———. "Toward a Conservative Theology" in *The Seminary at 100*. Edited by N. B. Cardin and D. W. Silverman. New York: Rabbinical Assembly. 1987.

———. "Toward a Jewish Public Policy in America," *Jews in the American Public Square*. Edited by A. Mittleman, J. D. Sarna, R. Licht. Lanham, Md.: Rowman and Littlefield. 2002.

———. "When Jews Are Christians." *First Things*. no. 17. 1991.

Passamaneck, S. M. "The *Berure Averot* and the Administration of Justice in XIII and XIV Century Spain." *Jewush Law Association Studies* 4. Atlanta, Ga.: Scholars Press. 1990.

Polish, D. *Give Us a King*. Hoboken, N.J.: KTAV. 1989.

Rabello, A. M. *The Jews in the Roman Empire*. Aldershot, U.K.: Ashgate. 2000.

Rosenzweig, Franz. *The Star of Redemption*. Translated by W. W. Hallo. New York: Holt, Rinehart, and Winston. 1970.

Sarna, J. D., and Dalin, D. G. *Religion and State in the American Jewish Experience*. Notre Dame, Ind.: University of Notre Dame Press. 1997.

Scholem, Gershom. "Jews and Germans." *Commentary*. vol. 42, no. 5. 1966.

Shilo, S. *Dina de-Malkhuta Dina*. Jerusalem: Jerusalem Academic Press. 1974.

Stone, S. L. "The Jewish Tradition and Civil Society," *Alternative Conceptions of Civil Society*. Edited by S. Chambers and W. Kymlicka. Princeton, N.J.: Princeton University Press. 2002.

Strauss, Leo. *Jewish Philosophy and the Crisis of Modernity*. Edited by K. H. Green. Albany, N.Y.: State University Press of New York. 1997.

Taubes, H. Z. *Otsar ha-Geonim*: Sanhedrin. Jerusalem: Mosad ha-Rav Kook. 1966.

Tradition and Change. Edited by M. Waxman. New York: Burning Busgh Press. 1970.

Trigano, Shmuel. *La demeure oubliée*. Rev. ed. Paris: Gallimard. 1994.

Urbach, E. E. *Hazal*. Jerusalem: Hebrew University/Magnes Press. 1971.

General Texts

Ackroyd, Peter. *The Life of Thomas More*. London: Vintage. 1999.

Aristotle. *Nicomachean Ethics*. Translated by H. Rackham. Cambridge, Mass.: Harvard University Press. 1926.

———. *Physics*. 2 vols. Translated by F. M. Cornford. Cambridge, Mass.: Harvard University Press. 1929.

———. *Politics*. Translated by H. Rackham. Cambridge, Mass: Harvard University Press. 1932.

Arndt, W. F., and Gingrich, F. W. *A Greek-English Lexicon of the New Testament*. 3 vols. Chicago: University of Chicago Press. 1957.

Assmann, J. *Politische Theologie Zwischen Äygten und Israel*. Munich: Carl Friedrich von Siemens Stuftung. 1992.

Barth, Karl. *Church Dogmatics* 2/2. English translation. Edinburgh: T. and T. Clark. 1957.

Berman, H. J. *Law and Revolution*. Cambridge, Mass.: Harvard University Press. 1983.

Bossuet, Jacques-Benique. *Politics Drawn from the Very Words of Holy Scripture*. Translated by P. Riley. Cambridge: Cambridge University Press. 1990.

Buckley, M. J. *At the Origins of Modern Atheism*. New Haven, Conn.: Yale University Press. 1987.

Burke, Edmund. *An Appeal from the New to the Old Whigs*. Edited by J. M. Robson. Indianapolis: Bobbs-Merrill. 962.

Calvin, John. *Institutes of the Christian Religion*. 2 vols. Translated by F. H. Battles. Philadelphia: Westminster Press. 1960.

Catechism of the Catholic Church. London: Geoffrey Chapman. 1994.

The Chosen People in an Almost Chosen Nation. Edited by Richard John Neuhaus. Grand Rapids, Mich.: Eerdmans. 2002.

Cicero. De *Finibus.* Translated by R. Woolf. Cambridge: Cambridge University
Press. 2001.

Companion to the Catechism of the Catholic Church. San Francisco: Ignatius
Press. 1997.

Daube, D. "The Peregrine Praetor." *Journal of Roman Studies.* vol. 41. 1951.

D'Éntreves, A. P. *The Notion of the State.* Oxford: Clarendon Press. 1967.

De Vaux, Roland. *The Early History of Israel.* Translated by D. Smith. Philadelphia: Westminster. 1978.

Duggan, M. W. *The Covenant Renewal in Ezra-Nehemiah.* Atlanta, Ga.: Society
of Biblical Literature. 2001.

Dworkin, Ronald. "The Original Position" in *Reading Rawls.* Edited by N. Daniels. Oxford: Blackwell. 1975.

————. *Taking Rights Seriously.* Cambridge, Mass.: Harvard University Press.
1978.

Epicurus. *Fragments.* Translated by S. Bailey in *The Stoic and Epicurean Philosophers.* Edited by W. J. Oates. New York: Random House. 1940.

Eusden, J. D. *Puritans, Lawyers, and Politics in Seventeenth Century England.*
New Haven, Conn.: Yale University Press. 1958.

Evans, J., and Ward, L. R. *The Social and Political Philosophy of Jacques Maritain.* New York: Charles Scribner's Sons. 1955.

Figgis, J. N. *The Divine Right of Kings.* New York: Harper and Row. 1965.

Fried, Charles. *Contract as Promise.* Cambridge University Press. 1981.

Goethe, Johann Wolfgang. *Faust.* Hamburg: Wegner Verlag. 1949.

Gough, J. W. *The Social Contract.* 2nd edition. Oxford: Clarendon Press. 1957.

Habermas, Jürgen. *Moral Consciousness and Communicative Action.* Translated
by C. Lenhardt and S. W. Nicholsen. Cambridge, Mass.: MIT Press. 1993.

Hegel, G.W.F. *Phenomenology of Spirit.* Translated by A. V. Miller. Oxford: Oxford University Press. 1977.

————. *Philosophy of Right.* Translated by T. M. Knox. Oxford: Clarendon Press.
1952.

Hobbes, Thomas. *Leviathan.* Edited by M. Oakeshott. New York: Collier Books.
1962.

Hume, David. *A Treatise of Human Nature.* Edited by L. A. Selby-Bigge. Oxford:
Clarendon Press. 1888.

Ives, E. W. "Social Change and the Law." *The English Revolution.* Edited by
E. W. Ives. London: Edward Arnold. 1968.

Jacques Maritain and the Jews. Edited by R. Royal. Notre Dame, Ind.: University
of Notre Dame Press. 1994.

Jenni, E., and Westermann, C. *Theological Lexicon of the Old Testament.* Translated by M. E. Biddle. Peabody, Mass.: Hendrickson Publishers. 1997.

Kant, Immanuel. *Critique of Pure Reason.* Translated by N. Kemp Smith. New
York: St. Martin's Press. 1929.

————. *Groundwork of the Metaphysic of Morals.* Translated by H. J. Paton.
New York: Harper and Row. 1964.

Kohlberg, Lawrence. "The Claim to Moral Adequacy of a Highest Stage of Moral Development." *Journal of Philosophy*. vol. 70. 1975.

Koppelman, Andrew. "Sexual and Religious Pluralism" in *Sexual Orientation and Human Rights in American Religious Discourse*. Edited by S. M. Olyan and M. C. Nussbaum. New York: Oxford University Press. 1998.

Kymlicka, Will. *Multicultural Citizenship*. Oxford: Clarendon Press. 1995.

Lampe, G.W.H. *A Patristic Greek Lexicon*. Oxford: Clarendon Press. 1961.

Lewis, Bernard. *Islam*. 2 vols. New York: Harper and Row. 1974.

Liddell, H. G., and Scott, R. *A Greek-English Lexicon*. Rev. ed. Oxford: Clarendon Press. 1996.

Locke, John. *Second Treatise of Civil Government*. Edited by G. B. Macpherson. Indianapolis, Ind.: Hackett. 1960.

MacIntyre, Aladair. *After Virtue*. Notre Dame, Ind.: University of Notre Dame Press. 1984.

Maritain, Jacques. *The Rights of Man and Natural Law*. Translated by D. C. Anson. San Francisco: Ignatius Press. 1986.

Mason, Richard. *The God of Spinoza*. Cambridge: Cambridge University Press. 1997.

McCarthy, D. J. *Treaty and Covenant*. Rome: Pontifical Biblical Institute. 1963.

Mendenhall, George. *Law and Covenant in the Ancient Near East*. Pittsburgh, Penn.: Presbyterian Board of Western Pennsylvania. 1955.

Miller, Perry. *Errand Into Wilderness*. Cambridge, Mass.: Harvard University Press. 1956.

Misztal, B. A. *Trust in Modern Societies*. Cambridge: Polity Press. 1998.

Monti, J. *The King's Good Servant but God's First*. San Francisco: Ignatius Press. 1997.

Nadler, S. M. *Spinoza*. Cambridge: Cambridge University Press. 1999.

Nagel, Thomas. *The View from Nowhere*. New York: Oxford University Press. 1986.

Neuhaus, Richard John. *The Naked Public Square*. Grand Rapids, Mich.: Eerdmans. 1984.

Niebuhr, Reinhold. *An Interpretation of Christian Ethics*. New York: Harper and Bros. 1935.

Nietzsche, Friedrich. *Thus Spake Zarathustra,*. Translated by T. Common in *The Philosophy of Nietzsche*. New York: Random House. 1954.

Novum Testamentum Graece. 24th ed. Edited by P. Nestle. Stuttgart: Privileg. Württ. Bibelanstalt. 1960.

Oxford English Dictionary. 20 vols. Oxford: Clarendon Press. 1989.

Owen, J. Judd. *Religion and the Demise of Liberal Rationalism*. Chicago: University of Chicago Press. 2001.

Pfeffer, Leo. *Church, State, and Freedom*. Rev. ed. Boston: Beacon Press. 1967.

———. *God, Caesar, and the Constitution*. Boston: Beacon Press. 1975.

Plato. *Cratylus*. Translated by H. N. Fowler. Cambridge, Mass.: Harvard University Press. 1926.

———. *Crito*. Translated by H. N. Fowler. Cambridge, Mass.: Cambridge University Press. 1914.

Plato. *Laws*. 2 vols. Translated by R. G. Bury. Cambridge, Mass.: Harvard University Press. 1926.

———. *Republic*. 2 vols. Translated by P. Shorey. Cambridge, Mass.: Harvard University Press. 1930.

———. *Theaetetus*. Translated by H. N. Fowler. Cambridge, Mass.: Harvard University Press. 1925.

Rawls, John. *A Theory of Justice*. Cambridge, Mass.: Harvard University Press. 1971.

Repolge, R. *Recovering the Social Contract*. Totowa, N.J.: Rowman and Littlefield. 1989.

Rorty, Richard. *Truth and Progress*. Cambridge: Cambridge University Press, 1998.

Rousseau, Jean Jacques. *The Social Contract*. Translated by W. Kendall. Chicago: Henry Regnery. 1954.

Sandel, M. J. *Liberalism and the Limits of Justice*. Cambridge: Cambridge University Press. 1982.

Sartre, Jean-Paul. *Anti-Semite and Jew*. Translated by G. J. Becker. New York: Schocken. 1972.

Shakespeare, William, *Richard II* in *Shakespeare: Complete Works*. Edited by J. Craig. London: Oxford University Press. 1905.

Sherwin-White, A. N. *Roman Society and Roman Law in the New Testament*. Oxford: Oxford University Press. 1963.

Smith, S. B. *Spinoza, Liberalism, and the Question of Jewish Identity*. New Haven, Conn.: Yale University Press. 1997.

Solomon, R. C. *A Passion for Justice*. Reading, Mass.: Addison-Wesley. 1990.

Soulen, R. K. *The God of Israel and Christian Theology*. Minneapolis, Minn.: Fortress Press. 1996.

Spinoza, Baruch. *Ethics* in *Spinoza: Collected Works*. 2 vols. Translated by E. Curley. Princeton, N.J.: Princeton University Press. 1985.

———. *Opera*. 2 vols. Edited by J. van Vloten and J.P.N. Land. The Hague: M. Nijhoff. 1914.

———. *Tractatus Politicus*. Translated by S. Shirley. Indianapolis, Ind.: Hackett. 2000.

———. *Tractatus Theologico-Politicus*. Translated by S. Shirley. Leiden: E. J. Brill. 1989.

Sumner, L. W. "Rawls on Civil Disobedience," *Canadian Journal of Philosophy*, supp. vol. 3. 1977.

Taylor, Charles. *Multiculturalism*. Princeton, N.J.: Princeton University Press. 1994.

———. *Philosophical Arguments*. Cambridge, Mass.: Harvard University Press. 1995.

Thomas Aquinas. *Summa Theologiae* in *Basic Writings of Saint Thomas Aquinas*. 2 vols. Edited and translated by A. C. Pegis. New York: Random House. 1945.

Tonnies, Ferdinand. *Community and Society*. Translated by C. P. Loomis. East Lansing: Michigan State University Press. 1957.

Vulgate. 3 vols. Rome: Officium Libri Catholici. 1955.

Walzer, Michael. *Spheres of Justice*. Oxford: Blackwell. 1983.

Weigel, George. "Papacy and Power." *First Things*. no. 110. 2001.

Witte, John, Jr. "Blest Be the Ties That Bind: Covenant and Community in Puritan Thought." *Emory Law Journal*. vol. 36. 1987.

———. *From Sacrament to Contract*. Louisville, Ky.: Westminster John Knox Press. 1997.

Wittgenstein, Ludwig. *Philosophical Investigations*. 2nd ed. Translated by. G.E.M. Anscombe. New York: Macmillan. 1958.

———. *Tractatus Logico-Philosophicus*. Translated by D. F. Pears and B. F. McGuiness. London: Routledge and Kegan Paul. 1961.

Index

Note: When "Rabbi" appears in parentheses after a proper name, it denotes a Sage mentioned in the Talmud and related rabbinic literature, who is called there either "Rabbi" or "Rav." When a Hebrew phrase appears in parentheses after a proper name, it denotes a more readily known abbreviation of the name of a post-talmudic rabbinic authority (often preceded by "R." for "Rabbi" in the notes) or the major literary work by which he is more readily known. When a Hebrew phrase appears in parentheses after a common name, it denotes the original Hebrew term of which the English term is a somewhat arbitrary translation.

NEW FORUM BOOKS

New Forum Books makes available to general readers outstanding original inter-disciplinary scholarship with a special focus on the juncture of culture, law, and politics. New Forum Books is guided by the conviction that law and politics not only reflect culture but help to shape it. Authors include leading political scientists, sociologists, legal scholars, philosophers, theologians, historians, and economists writing for nonspecialist readers and scholars across a range of fields. Looking at questions such as political equality, the concept of rights, the problem of virtue in liberal politics, crime and punishment, population, poverty, economic development, and the international legal and political order, New Forum Books seeks to explain—not explain away—the difficult issues we face today.

James Hitchcock, *The Supreme Court and Religion in American Life:*
Volume 1, The Odyssey of the Religion Clauses;
Volume 2, From "Higher Law" to "Sectarian Scruples"

Christopher Wolfe, ed., *That Eminent Tribunal:*
Judicial Supremacy and the Constitution

Patrick J. Deneen, *Democratic Faith*

David Novak, *The Jewish Social Contract:*
An Essay in Political Theology